Cath......... .... cum laude from Harvard in 2013, where she studied history and economics. In 2014, she received her MPhil in Modern European History from Christ's College, Cambridge, where she wrote her dissertation on the origins of modern counterintelligence practices and their implications on the debate surrounding the right to privacy. She is currently pursuing her JD at Harvard Law School.

'In 1945 an American president, his ambassador to the Soviet Union, and a British prime minister chose to make the trip to Yalta with their daughters in tow. Over the next weeks those "second mates" served as their fathers' eyes and ears, their tasters, confidantes, and chiefs of staff. They gate-kept and play-acted, eradicated bedbugs, held their vodka, and offered up toasts, as Stalin cunningly put it, "to the broad sunlight of victorious peace". In a rich, captivating narrative, Catherine Grace Katz gives us a wholly original Yalta, one seen from a different gender and generation'

Stacy Schiff, author of *Cleopatra* and *The Witches*

'Making superb use of unpublished diaries and letters, Katz demonstrates how illness, clandestine romance and fraying political relationships ran alongside the tortured negotiations that would shape the post-conflict world ... The women's keyhole perspective of these momentous negotiations humanises the Yalta summit as never before, shedding new insight on the minute-by-minute tensions of international diplomacy at a time when the future of millions depended on the outcome'

Spectator

'This book, however, is less the story of the three young women of the title, more of a close-focus look at the all-important conference, its political background and its aims and hopes for the coming peace: roughly summed up as collective security and self-determination for the liberated countries of Europe. Katz takes us through it, day by day. Katz, a Harvard scholar, is admirably impartial, showing us how unprepared Roosevelt was, refusing to be informed about European matters ... The research is impressive ... It is a riveting read and the detail is fascinating ... Oh, to have been a fly on the wall'

Anne de Courcy, *Daily Telegraph*

'Skilfully written and meticulously researched, it's an extraordinary work that reveals the human side underlying the politics ... *The Daughters of Yalta* is a thoroughly engrossing book, as acute about the contentious politics of the day as it is about the remarkable daughters who participated'

Wall Street Journal

'[In] Catherine Grace Katz's detailed behind-the-scenes account ... she skilfully marshals diaries, letters, oral histories, and memoirs to support her thesis that the pressures of wartime had warped normal familial bonds, so that the Western leaders' relationships with their daughters had become more like those between business partners than between parent and child. Loyalty and discretion were prized above all ... Packed with vivid personalities, jockeying aides, and insider observations about a pivotal moment in history'

New York Times Book Review

THE
DAUGHTERS
OF YALTA

★ ★ ★

*The Churchills,
Roosevelts and Harrimans:
A Story of Love and War*

★ ★ ★

CATHERINE GRACE KATZ

**WILLIAM
COLLINS**

William Collins
An imprint of HarperCollins*Publishers*
1 London Bridge Street
London SE1 9GF

WilliamCollinsBooks.com

HarperCollins*Publishers*
1st Floor, Watermarque Building, Ringsend Road
Dublin 4, Ireland

First published in Great Britain in 2020 by William Collins
This William Collins paperback edition published in 2021
1
Copyright © Catherine Grace Katz 2020

Book design by Martha Kennedy
Map by Mapping Specialists, Ltd.

Excerpts from *The Second World War, Volume VI: Triumph and Tragedy* by Winston S. Churchill reproduced with permission of Curtis Brown, London on behalf of The Estate of Winston S. Churchill. © The Estate of Winston S. Churchill

Excerpts from *A Love in Shadow* by John R. Boettiger. Copyright © 1978 by John R. Boettiger. Used by permission of John R. Boettiger. All rights reserved

The author is grateful to reprint material from The Churchill Archives Centre and The Kathleen Harriman Mortimer Papers by kind permission of Allen Packwood and David Mortimer, respectively

A catalogue record for this book is available from the British Library

ISBN 978-0-00-829975-0

Typeset in Kepler Std
Printed and Bound in the UK using 100% Renewable Electricity at CPI Group (UK) Ltd

MIX
Paper from
responsible sources
FSC™ C007454

FSC
www.fsc.org

For my family

Contents

PART III

'ALL THIS, AND MORE I HAVE WITH ME FOREVER.'

CRIMEA

to Simferopol ↗

YALTA

LIVADIA PALACE

KOREIZ VILLA

← to Sevastopol

VORONTSOV PALACE

Black Sea

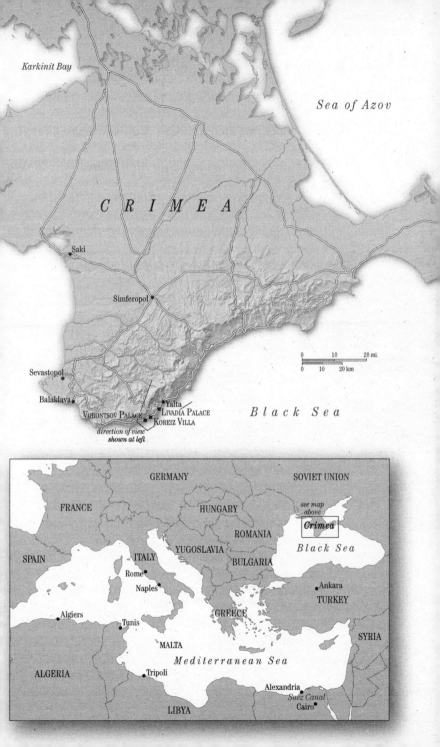

A List of Key Delegates at Yalta

This list serves to identify some of the individuals who feature prominently in this book. It contains only a small number of the hundreds present at the Yalta Conference. Note that some of these individuals had multiple titles. I have listed only those titles relevant to or easily recognisable based on their role in this story.

The American Delegates

- Franklin D. Roosevelt – *President of the United States*
- Anna Roosevelt – *Franklin Roosevelt's daughter and aide-de-camp; also known as Anna Roosevelt Boettiger*
- W. Averell Harriman – *American ambassador to the Soviet Union*
- Kathleen (Kathy) Harriman – *Averell Harriman's daughter*
- Major General Frederick Anderson – *Deputy commanding general, U.S. Strategic Air Forces, Europe*
- Charles Bohlen – *Assistant to the secretary of state, interpreter to Franklin Roosevelt*
- Lieutenant Commander Howard Bruenn – *Physician to Franklin Roosevelt, cardiologist*
- James Byrnes – *Director, Office of War Mobilization*
- Steve Early – *Press secretary*
- Edward Flynn – *Former chairman of the Democratic National Committee; Franklin Roosevelt's friend*
- Wilder Foote – *Assistant to the secretary of state*

- Alger Hiss – *Deputy director, Office of Special Political Affairs, Department of State*
- Harry Hopkins – *Special adviser to the president*
- Sergeant Robert Hopkins – *Harry Hopkins's son, a U.S. Army Signal Corps photographer*
- Admiral Ernest King – *Commander in chief, U.S. Fleet; chief of naval operations*
- Major General Laurence Kuter – *Assistant chief of staff for plans, U.S. Army Air Force, representing Henry 'Hap' Arnold, general of the army*
- Fleet Admiral William Leahy – *Chief of staff to the commander in chief (Franklin Roosevelt) of the U.S. Army and U.S. Navy*
- General George Marshall – *Chief of staff of the U.S. Army, general of the army*
- H. Freeman Matthews – *Director, Office of European Affairs, Department of State*
- Vice Admiral Ross T. McIntire – *Surgeon General, U.S. Navy; physician to Franklin Roosevelt*
- Eddie Page – *Second secretary and consul, American embassy, Moscow*
- Edward R. Stettinius – *Secretary of state*
- Major General Erwin 'Pa' Watson – *Military aide and secretary to Franklin Roosevelt; U.S. Army (Ret.)*

The British Delegates

- Winston Churchill – *Prime minister*
- Sarah Churchill – *Winston Churchill's daughter and aide-de-camp, section officer in the Women's Auxiliary Air Force; also known as Sarah Oliver*
- Field Marshal Sir Harold Alexander – *Supreme allied commander, Mediterranean theatre of operations*
- Major Arthur Birse – *Interpreter to Winston Churchill*
- Field Marshal Sir Alan Brooke – *Chief of the Imperial General Staff*

- Sir Alexander Cadogan – *Permanent undersecretary of state for foreign affairs*
- Sir Archibald Clark-Kerr – *British ambassador to the Soviet Union*
- Admiral of the Fleet Sir Andrew Cunningham – *First Sea Lord and chief of naval staff*
- Anthony Eden – *Foreign secretary*
- General Sir Hastings 'Pug' Ismay – *Chief of staff to Winston Churchill, deputy secretary to the War Cabinet*
- Lord Moran – *Physician to Winston Churchill*
- Marshal of the Royal Air Force Sir Charles 'Peter' Portal – *Chief of air staff*
- Commander Charles 'Tommy' Thompson – *Winston Churchill's aide-de-camp, Royal Navy*

The Soviet Delegates

- Joseph Stalin – *Marshal of the Soviet Union, general secretary of the Communist Party of the Soviet Union*
- General Aleksei Antonov – *First deputy chief of staff, Soviet army*
- Lavrentiy Beria – *People's commissar for internal affairs (NKVD)*
- Sergo Beria – *Lavrentiy Beria's son*
- Andrei Gromyko – *Soviet ambassador to the United States*
- Fedor Gusev – *Soviet ambassador to the United Kingdom*
- Marshal Sergei Khudyakov – *Deputy chief of the Soviet air staff*
- Fleet Admiral Nikolai Kuznetsov – *People's commissar of the Soviet navy*
- Ivan Maisky – *Deputy people's commissar for foreign affairs of the Soviet Union; former Soviet ambassador to the Court of St. James's (UK)*
- Vyacheslav Molotov – *People's commissar for foreign affairs*
- Vladimir Pavlov – *Interpreter to Joseph Stalin*
- Andrey Vyshinsky – *First deputy people's commissar for foreign affairs*

PART I

'She can handle them,
and that's why they're
going to take her.'

ONE

February 1, 1945

I n the winter of 1945, Livadia Palace, its once snow-white façade now covered in grime, stood empty on its perch above the Black Sea. The furniture and priceless art were long gone. Sinks, toilets and lamps had been ripped from their fittings and pulled from the walls. The Nazis had stolen everything, even the brass doorknobs.

Situated less than three miles down the coast from the resort town of Yalta, on the southern tip of the Crimean Peninsula, this palace had once been the summer home of the tsar and tsarina, Nicholas II and Alexandra. They had torn down the old Livadia Palace where Alexander III had died and replaced it with a new 116-room imperial retreat better suited to family life. The Mediterranean climate and black pebble beaches offered the tsar, tsarina, and their five children a respite from the humidity and opulence of Saint Petersburg. Palms and cypress trees filled the lush gardens surrounding the neo-Renaissance Italianate palace constructed from white Crimean stone. The tsar and his children bathed in the sea, played tennis, and rode horses over rocky trails while the tsarina sold her needlework at the bazaar, to raise funds for the local hospital. But amid the relative simplicity, there remained splendour. In the white ballroom, where French doors opened onto a courtyard, the tsar's eldest daughter, Grand Duchess Olga, celebrated her sixteenth birthday with a grand soiree. She swirled through the night in her pink gown, her hair swept high on her head for the first time, while her first jewels – a necklace made of thirty-two diamonds and pearls – sparkled in the chandeliers' light.

The tsar and his family visited Livadia only four times before they were murdered, in 1918, in a basement outside the city of Yekaterinburg. This brutality marked the end of the Romanov dynasty and imperial Russia. The Bolsheviks soon transformed the palace into a sanatorium for favoured Soviet workers needing rest, quiet, and treatment for tuberculosis. The comrades sterilised the gleaming white palace and removed or covered all signs of the Romanov family, just as they tore down monuments to royalty across Russia, replacing them with monuments to themselves. Then came the war, the second in a quarter century. In 1942, the Nazis overran the Crimea after a months-long onslaught of the nearby port city of Sevastopol, part of the grisly and ultimately ill-fated Operation Barbarossa, when the Nazis broke their non-aggression pact with the Soviets and charged east across the steppe. Only the tsar's summer palace would do for the Nazis' Crimean headquarters, so the invaders commandeered Livadia. In the spring of 1944, the Soviets finally reclaimed the Crimea and pushed the Nazis out, but not before the retreating enemy plundered Livadia Palace, taking everything they could carry.

It was here, in this despoiled palace in February 1945, that Kathleen Harriman, the glamorous, twenty-seven-year-old daughter of the fourth-richest man in America, now stood. Thousands of workers crowded the palace and the gardens, sawing, hammering, painting, fumigating, polishing and planting, not to mention installing much-needed plumbing. Cots had been set up for the conscripted labourers and the Romanian POWs the Soviets had brought in to clear the area of the wreckage the war had left behind, but there were still hardly enough places to sleep for everyone toiling away across the once imperial grounds.

Kathy and her father, W. Averell Harriman, the United States ambassador to the Soviet Union, had arrived several days earlier from Moscow, where they had lived for the past fifteen months. They had intended to fly, as they had little more than ten days to oversee final preparations for one of the most crucial conferences of the war, but bad weather had kept them grounded. In the end, their eight-hundred-mile journey by train had taken nearly three days as they crawled past the bombed-out villages and trampled countryside to which Kathy had grown accustomed over these past months. Every train station she saw was in ruins. 'The needless destruction is something appalling,' Kathy wrote to her childhood governess and friend, Elsie Marshall, nicknamed 'Mouche', back in New York. (Whether or not this observation would make it to Mouche was up to the censor.) To her older sister, Mary, she wrote, 'My God but this country has a job on its hands – just cleaning up.'

Though the war was by no means won, by late 1944, British and American forces had liberated Rome, Paris, Brussels and Athens from German and Italian occupation, while the Red Army marched westward across Poland and Romania. Notwithstanding the surprising and remarkably forceful counteroffensive of the Wehrmacht, Germany's combined fighting forces, in Belgium, France, and Luxembourg that December, which threatened to break through the western line in the bitterly cold Ardennes Forest, it was evident that the Allies had gained the upper hand. The war in the Pacific was far from over – American generals estimated it might last another eighteen months unless a secret, untested weapon could be finished in time, which might change everything. But the British prime minister, Winston Churchill; the President of the United States, Franklin Roosevelt; and the Soviet general secretary, Joseph Stalin, realised they had reached a critical juncture in Europe. As their armies raced to Berlin, the three leaders were facing complicated questions about the end of the war on the continent, questions they could resolve only face to face.

It was not the first time they had called such a meeting. In late November 1943, the 'Big Three', as they were known, had conferred in Tehran to lay the foundations for the long-awaited second front, which they launched just seven months later, on the beaches of Normandy. At the time, in an effort to appeal to Stalin, Roosevelt and Churchill had generously made the arduous journey to Tehran, a location significantly closer to Moscow than to London or Washington. Now it was only fair that Stalin should come to them. The western leaders proposed holding the conference in the Mediterranean, but Stalin claimed his health was too fragile to leave the Soviet Union. On the advice of his doctors, he refused to consider any location beyond his own country's borders. Churchill and especially Roosevelt believed they needed Soviet cooperation to guarantee victory in the Pacific and the success of Roosevelt's newly imagined organisation to secure world peace, as well as Stalin's long-term commitment to ensure political self-determination for recently liberated nations such as Poland. The two had more to lose in their vision of a democratic postwar world than did Stalin, whose Red Army unambiguously controlled Eastern Europe. Roosevelt quietly directed Averell Harriman to acquiesce to Stalin's request without much haggling – to confirm that he and Churchill would come to the Soviet Union before Churchill could raise any further objections.

The Black Sea coast was as far west as Stalin was willing to travel, and the string of resort towns along the southern coast of the Crimea, a stretch nicknamed the 'Romanov Route' for the number of residences that once belonged to the imperial family and their aristocratic friends, still held a certain allure among high-ranking comrades. Though the Soviets decried the corruption of the imperialist age, they apparently had no moral qualms about using these luxurious palaces themselves. After assessing various locations around the Black Sea, from Odessa to Batum, the Soviets and the Americans deemed Yalta and Livadia Palace the best of several options; the other choices were too damaged by war to accommodate large delegations or were less accessible by ship or plane. Harriman and the American embassy in Moscow begrudgingly agreed, even though, as Churchill underscored, the Black Sea was still littered with mines, making it impossible for the leaders to risk travelling to Yalta by ship – though some of their support staff would have to do so. By the New Year of 1945, it was decided: Roosevelt and Churchill would rendezvous on the island of Malta, sixty miles off the southern tip of Italy, and fly the remaining distance to the Crimea to meet Stalin at the former tsar's summer palace.

Though Livadia was an imperial residence, it was smaller than the 100,000-square-foot mansion in the Hudson River Valley where Kathy Harriman had grown up. It was also too small to house all three of the delegations, which seemed to swell exponentially with every passing day. Playing the genial, accommodating host, Stalin had graciously offered Livadia to President Roosevelt. As the largest palace of the several nearby, its ballroom was perfectly suited to hosting the formal meetings of the Big Three and their advisers, and, given that Roosevelt was paralysed from the waist down and confined to a wheelchair, Stalin thought the president would be most comfortable if he did not have to travel to the conference sessions each day. Meanwhile, Churchill and his party were to be accommodated at Vorontsov Palace, another Russian aristocrat's home the Soviets had nationalised, which was a thirty-minute drive down the road. Stalin opted for a slightly smaller estate nearby referred to as both the Koreiz Villa and Yusupov Palace, which was conveniently situated between the American and British residences. Vorontsov Palace and the Koreiz Villa were in a much better state of repair than was Livadia, though a certain uncomfortable aura surrounded Stalin's chosen abode. It had once belonged to the man who, according to rumor, had murdered Rasputin, the mystic (or charlatan, depending on one's perspective) and adviser to Tsarina Alexandra, whose unsavoury influence over the Romanovs had hastened their decline. Whether the inscrutable Stalin intended to send a message of some sort – of either intimidation or dark humour – in his selection of this particular villa, or if he simply found it to be the most comfortable, remained a mystery.

Once it was decided that the three leaders would gather at Yalta, the Soviets had just three weeks to turn the ransacked villas into a site fit for one of the largest and most important international summits in history. Lavrentiy Beria, the forbidding head of the Narodny komissariat vnutrennikh del – the dreaded NKVD, the Soviet Union's secret police – and the man Stalin could always rely on to execute his most unpleasant tasks, took charge of the preparations. This encompassed overseeing everything from structural repairs to the transport of provisions to the removal of any 'undesirable elements' from the surrounding area – including 835 supposed anti-Soviet individuals discovered over the course of the 74,000 security checks the NKVD had conducted within twenty kilometers of Yalta. Ambassador Harriman was to arrive approximately ten days before the conference to see that the improvements were up to American standards and to ensure that the logistical and protocol-related matters were in order, so that no problem, no matter how small, could hamper the progress of diplomacy.

In theory, Averell Harriman was responsible for the conference's final arrangements, but in reality, that was not exactly the case. Averell never passed up the chance to be at the centre of the day's action. In early 1941, isolationism still ran rampant in the United States and the nation remained neutral. Roosevelt had been eager to support the fight against the Nazis but could do so only while maintaining a position of neutrality. Thinking creatively, he discovered a loophole that accomplished his objectives, and the Lend-Lease programme was born: the United States would provide Britain and its allies with food, fuel, ships, aircraft, ammunition, and other war materiel that Britain would theoretically return after the war. When Roosevelt named Averell the Lend-Lease envoy in February 1941, he moved to London without a moment's hesitation to take up the post, despite the fact that the Blitz raged on. But after the United States entered the war, the action shifted east, and Averell was eager to follow it. Roosevelt offered him the position of ambassador to the Kremlin in the autumn of 1943, and he left London for Moscow without delay.

This time was no different. Three days after Averell and Kathy arrived in the Crimea, he flew off to Malta to meet Churchill and Roosevelt, eager to take part in any important pre-conference developments. Meanwhile, Averell left his daughter in Yalta to carry out the rest of the preparations at Livadia over the week that remained before the delegates arrived.

While surprising at first glance, it actually made perfect sense for Kathy to supervise this work. She spoke Russian; Averell did not. Realising that her father would never have time to master the language while also performing his ambassadorial duties in Moscow, Kathy had decided to learn Russian for both of them. As soon as they arrived in Moscow, where she was to serve as the official hostess of Spaso House, the residence of the American ambassador, Kathy hired a tutor. The small number of English-speaking Russian tutors in Moscow were already engaged, so she had to employ a French-speaking tutor and translate from Russian to French to English. Kathy practised her Russian at every opportunity, listening intently during productions at the renowned Bolshoi and Maly theatres and mumbling Russian phrases to herself as she walked down the street. Sometimes the locals gawked at her, but, as she told her sister, Mary, they tended to stare at her anyway because of her fur coat and silk stockings, scarce luxuries few in Moscow could afford. Her Russian was hardly perfect, but she spoke well enough to act as her father's interpreter at social gatherings. Now she took on the task of communicating with the Russian sentries, bureaucrats, and labourers in the melee at Livadia. Even if she struggled occasionally, she hoped the Russians would forgive her, just as she forgave them as they struggled to properly pronounce her name. The formal word for 'mister' in Russian was *Gospodin*, so the Russians addressed her as '*Gospodina [sic] Harriman*'. Many, however, found it impossible to pronounce the 'H' in Harriman, so 'Miss Harriman' came out sounding something like 'Gaspadeena Garriman', which reminded Kathy of the sound made by 'an old man clearing his throat early in the morning'.

It was not the first time Averell – always Averell or Ave, never Father or Daddy – had left Kathy to fend for herself in a remote place. During her four years at Bennington College in Vermont, Kathy spent her winter vacations at Sun Valley, Averell's ski resort in Idaho. It was the first of its kind in the United States. When Americans caught the ski craze following the 1932 Winter Olympics in Lake Placid, Averell realised that an enormous opportunity lay before him. As chairman of Union Pacific Railroad, he was looking to increase business on western railway lines. People needed a reason to go west, and a glamorous ski destination rivalling the Alpine resorts of Europe would be just the thing. A 'seaside ranch in the mountains', as it was billed, Sun Valley was an instant success – especially after Averell directed his engineers to invent and install the world's first chairlift. Sun Valley quickly became as much a home to Kathy as the Harrimans' city residence in Manhattan or their country estate, Arden House, in the Hudson River Valley. Kathy's parents had divorced when she was ten, and her mother, Kitty, had died of cancer when Kathy was just seventeen. Averell had remarried in 1930, to Cornelius Vanderbilt Whitney's ex-wife,

Marie Norton, and Marie naturally assumed the role of mistress of Arden. Though Kathy and her stepmother were on good terms and Arden House was surrounded by glorious grounds for riding and shooting, two of Kathy's most serious pursuits, Sun Valley was the place that truly connected Kathy with her father.

While Averell chased across the world, attending to his various endeavours, first in business, then increasingly in government, he left Kathy as his deputy for weeks at a time to assist with the day-to-day operations of the resort: assessing slope conditions, seeing to publicity, and looking after celebrity guests such as Ernest Hemingway, who soon called Sun Valley home. She even performed the occasional bit of reconnaissance on rival resorts, which had begun to spring up in the West. Though the family was remarkably wealthy, the Harrimans were not ostentatious and held something of a Spartan attitude. Kathy had attended the Foxcroft School, a boarding school in Virginia known for its fox hunts, its multi-day horseback expeditions to the Luray Caverns, and its requirement that its girls sleep on unheated outdoor porches every night, regardless of the weather. Embracing a life among the elements, at Sun Valley, Kathy quickly developed a passion for skiing. Before her father had chairlifts installed, she often made the five-hour trek up a mountainside – fashionably clad in a monogrammed jacket and cashmere sweater, her skis encased in sealskins – all for one run down the untouched Idaho powder. Her friends and family started calling her 'Puff' for the sound of her ragged breaths at high altitude, as, unyielding, she trudged higher and higher. But the precious weeks Kathy spent at Sun Valley meant so much more than athletic thrills. They served as a proving ground for a daughter determined to show herself worthy of standing at her father's side as an equal.

In many ways, helping to manage Sun Valley was the ideal preparation for the work Kathy now faced. But nothing could truly ready a person for the overwhelming amount of labour that had to be done before Roosevelt and his party arrived at Livadia Palace. Under Lavrentiy Beria's direction, the Soviets were frantically restocking the villas with whatever could be spared from Moscow's luxury hotels. More than fifteen hundred railcars, laden with building supplies, tools, furnishings, rugs, light bulbs, art, dishes, cookware and food, had heaved along on the thousand-mile journey to the Crimea. It seemed as if every moveable object within Moscow's renowned Hotel Metropol had been packed up and transported. Even the maids' uniforms for the conference were embroidered with the Metropol's distinctive 'M.' In addition to the obvious beds, tables and chairs, the more mundane items of daily life, such as coat hangers, shaving mirrors and ashtrays, had to be supplied. Kathy presumed some of these things were 'just being "requisitioned" out of homes' from the war-battered towns nearby.

There was also the problem of evicting the current residents, who had moved in when the Nazis moved out: bugs. The palace was infested with lice and bedbugs. As the motley team of Beria's NKVD forces, Red Army soldiers, local peasant labourers and the Romanian POWs scrambled to put everything in order, the U.S. Navy Medical Corps arrived to delouse the palace. They sprayed the furniture with a 10 per cent solution of DDT in kerosene and dusted all the linens with DDT powder, but even that draconian dose did not get rid of the bugs entirely. Kathy herself was all too well acquainted with Russian insects. On the train from Moscow to Yalta, something had bitten her near her eye. Her skin had swollen so badly that for a day or two she could barely see. International wartime diplomacy could be distinctly unglamorous, but Kathy remained unfazed.

It was because of her stalwart and unflappable nature that Kathy had become a fixture in her father's world. Thanks to her fifteen months in Moscow and the two prior years in London, where she had worked as a war reporter, Averell Harriman's attractive, opinionated daughter was well known to the military and civilian leadership of all three Allied nations gathering at Yalta. Her presence at Livadia Palace would come as no surprise to any of them, not even to Roosevelt. 'As this is her department, have arranged to take Kathleen along,' Averell had informed FDR by wire on January 17. 'I will leave her at Yalta to assist in the details of the arrangements there.' Roosevelt did not object.

It was ironic that this advance work in living arrangements and hospitality had become Kathy's domain. She had moved to London at the beginning of the war to work as a journalist – not, as she insisted multiple times, to be her father's housekeeper. In fact, one of the last things she had written to her sister, Mary, before moving to Moscow was 'I only hope there'll be no entertaining.' Kathy was woefully disappointed. Life in Moscow seemed to be one lavish caviar- and vodka-fuelled banquet after another. By now she knew to expect that supervising an enormous household staff and entertaining guests would be part of her work at Yalta, but over time she had come to realise that her role as her father's hostess and deputy was much more complex than simply organising parties and managing the house. Though never officially given a title, she was essentially serving as the Americans' protocol officer, a role often overlooked and underappreciated yet vital to international diplomacy. Overseeing protocol encompassed everything from observing and respecting the rituals and customs of foreign nations to making sure that the seating arrangements at a state dinner did not exacerbate petty grievances. Now it was up to Kathy to anticipate and eliminate all potential sources of cultural confusion, irritation, or distraction before the delegates arrived. Even something as seemingly innocuous as accidentally mistyping a deputy secretary's name on a place card could annoy that delegate, who would then take his irritation with him into the conference room. The follow-on effects could be damaging.

Important as the rituals of protocol were, Kathy was sometimes charmingly oblivious to them. Once, during a night out in London with her best friend, Pamela Churchill, the prime minister's daughter-in-law, she happened upon the king of Greece. Kathy greeted him with a simple American 'How do do!' Pam, by contrast, dropped to a deep curtsy. Kathy also was not inclined to defer to those who considered themselves her superiors. She had once caused a kerfuffle with Adele Astaire, the sister and former dance partner of the American movie star Fred Astaire, who had married Lord Charles Cavendish, after writing a rather sarcastic *Newsweek* article about Adele's contributions to the war effort. As a war reporter, Kathy had met and covered countless women who worked in factories, served as transport pilots, or nursed soldiers just behind the front lines. Adele's efforts as an 'amanuensis' – making improvements to the love letters soldiers sent home – could not compare (though Adele did make for good copy). In the article, Kathy observed that Adele 'still [wore] silly bows atop her graying hair'. *Newsweek* had also printed Adele's age – a generous forty-four – but Kathy could blame that on her editor. Unsurprisingly, Adele, a friend of Kathy's stepmother, had not taken kindly to this portrayal. When the former starlet next saw the younger woman at a restaurant in SoHo, she shrieked at her, calling Kathy a 'bitch to end all bitches' and threatened to 'break' her in London. Kathy was visibly amused, which made Adele all the more furious.

Now, much as Kathy might have liked to laugh at the Russian maître d'hôtel as he worked out the optimal arrangements of china and crystal place settings, she refrained from sharing her frank opinions. A war was raging; a diplomatic approach was essential. Among people who cared deeply about protocol, it was imperative that everything was done just right. It was a thankless job. If she executed everything correctly, no one would notice her work; if, however, she made a mistake, her father would take the blame for failing to make every provision for cross-cultural harmony. Helping the myriad challenging personalities in Roosevelt's entourage adapt to Russian customs would be difficult, even without the added complication of the trying physical environment. The Soviets had done their best to ensure the comfort of their guests, but nonetheless, the navy medical team had to warn the American contingent to lower expectations and encouraged 'a little good naturedness' from all parties.

As Kathy went from room to room at Livadia, inspecting the living arrangements, the ever-present NKVD officers in tow, she put her Russian-language skills to use. FDR's suite, once the tsar's private chambers, including his office and private dining room, was one of Kathy's chief concerns. The room now serving as the president's bedroom had an ambience of overbearing darkness. It was like a Pullman car carved from a heavy block of wood. The walls were panelled in mahogany; paintings in enormous gold-leaf frames lined the walls; orange-fringed silk lampshades abounded; plush green harem cushions were scattered across the floor. And in the middle was a massive wooden bed frame, an imposing style of furnishing the Soviets imagined that a visiting dignitary would desire. In pursuit of perfection, they had several times changed their minds about which Bokhara rug would best suit the room. Each change in opinion surfaced only *after* workers had moved the behemoth of a bed back into place.

But Kathy could be every bit as demanding and attentive to detail. When she found that painters in FDR's bathroom could not understand her Russian, she was undeterred. Catching their attention, Kathy pointed to the window and the sea beyond and then back at the walls. Back and forth, back and forth. The wall colour, she tried to explain yet again, had to match the colour of the water. Nearby, a plumber, who was supervising the repairs to the bathroom fixtures the Nazis had ripped from the wall, watched her. He did not seem amused. Perhaps this was because she had ordered the painters to change the colour at least six times already.

Kathy had more important issues to worry about than the slighted feelings of the plumbers and painters. A battalion-sized contingent of Cabinet members, State Department officials, and top-ranking military officers – not to mention the president of the United States – was about to arrive on the palace's doorstep. Bathrooms, or the lack thereof, were proving a particular nightmare, and Kathy did what she could to forestall ablution chaos. A mere nine toilets and four bathtubs were available to accommodate several hundred people, and only Roosevelt's suite had a private bath. Everyone else would either have to wait in line or use the latrines that had been hastily constructed in the garden. Even with the added nineteenth-century-style privies, thirty-five officers would be shaving in buckets beside their beds.

Rooming assignments also required strategic thinking. There were not enough private bedrooms in the palace to accommodate everyone whose credentials would have warranted the finest suites in New York's or London's most exclusive hotels. As it was, sixteen colonels would have to share one room as if in a barrack; junior officers would be stuffed in the eaves. The bedrooms on the first floor, nearest the president, Kathy reserved for his closest government advisers: his special adviser Harry Hopkins, Secretary of State Edward Stettinius, the Soviet expert and Russian interpreter Charles 'Chip' Bohlen, the director of the Office of War Mobilization and elder statesman James Byrnes, and Averell. Top-ranking military leaders she assigned to the second floor. As army chief of staff, General George Marshall outranked everyone. Kathy awarded him the tsar's imperial bedroom. Admiral

Ernest King, the second most senior officer in the U.S. Navy, would have to be satisfied with the tsarina's boudoir.

When Kathy could spare time, she fled to the outdoors. After a long Moscow winter, capped by the three days she and her father had spent inside a pest-ridden train en route to the Crimea, it was a relief to walk the sloping paths of the palace gardens, the cypress trees piercing the horizon, the snowcapped, craggy mountains looming in the background. The scenery reminded Kathy of Italy. Exploring the gardens was not the strenuous exercise she was used to, though the walkways naturally graded uphill. Still, the warm sun was welcome. During the previous, seemingly endless Russian winter, she had come down with a terrible bout of scurvy, which made her gums swell and bleed so dramatically, she thought her teeth would fall out.

These outdoor explorations provided insights and inspiration for an additional assignment Kathy had to complete before the guests arrived. Together with Eddie Page, one of the young Foreign Service officers at the embassy in Moscow, she was writing a pamphlet to assist the Americans with their brief immersion in local culture. As most of the American delegation had never set foot in the Crimea, nor in fact any other part of the Soviet Union, this pamphlet was meant to be a useful diplomatic instrument, full of information about the geography, history and significance of this unfamiliar part of the world. The task lacked the journalistic challenge of the hard-hitting reporting about developments on the fighting fronts that Kathy had begun to write for *Newsweek* just before Averell was called to Moscow, but at least it was something.

When Kathy first moved to London, she had no journalistic training beyond a general education in international affairs at Bennington College and experience assisting with public relations for Sun Valley. But journalism had been her ticket to London – and to Averell's world. It was only after her mother died that Kathy had truly come to know her father. Shortly after Kitty's death, Averell had written to his two daughters. In this letter, he told them that he had somewhat radical notions about parenting. He would never be able to replace their mother, as he simply was not the warm, affectionate type who showered his children with outward signs of love. He could, however, offer them something different.

After Averell's father, the self-made railway tycoon E. H. Harriman, died when Averell was seventeen, Averell's mother inherited the entirety of her husband's vast fortune. 'The Richest Woman in the World', as magazines dubbed her, became a formidable force in American philanthropy. Independence ran deep in the Harriman women. Averell's sister Mary Harriman Rumsey was a force in her own right. As a student, she became known for driving herself to Barnard College in a coach-and-four and for founding the Junior League, a national organisation inspired by the work of the settlement movement and the social reform leader Jane Addams. Mary Rumsey went on to become a key appointee in Roosevelt's National Recovery Administration, a New Deal organisation meant to stabilise business and employment opportunities after the tumult of the Great Depression. With such women as examples, Averell wanted his own daughters to be as independent as they desired – a rare sentiment among fathers of their class. In time, he hoped they would join him in his business affairs to whatever degree it suited them. If they could be patient with him and maintain an open mind, he was sure that, soon enough, they would become 'the finest & best of friends'. While Mary ultimately sought a more traditional life of marriage and family, Kathy eagerly took up Averell's offer.

When Averell wrote this letter, he could not have foreseen that in addition to working alongside him in Sun Valley, Kathy would spend four years at his side, navigating diplomacy in two European capitals embroiled in war. Averell's second wife, Marie, should have been the one to accompany him, but because of trouble with her eyesight she had elected to remain in New York. Averell encouraged Kathy to go in her place. To Averell, the idea of bringing his daughter to London was not some revolutionary concept. It was more like continuing a family tradition. When Averell was a boy, his father had insisted on taking the entire family – wife, sons and daughters – on his travels around the world. In 1899, when Averell was seven years old, the family embarked on the Harriman Expedition, a major exploration of the

Alaskan coast that Averell's father organised and sponsored, alongside America's pre-eminent scientists, artists, writers and photographers. Other summers, they drove across Europe in brand-new automobiles. Later, in 1905, in the wake of the Russo-Japanese War, Averell's father took the family to Japan, where he was looking to develop an around-the-world railway network.

Kathy was thrilled by Averell's invitation. Her childhood governess, Mouche, was English, and nearly every summer the Harriman girls had travelled to Britain or France. The experience had instilled in Kathy a natural kinship with Europeans and a sense of adventure. But at first, the American government refused to permit Kathy to join her father in London as she was not considered essential personnel. Averell contacted his friend Harry Hopkins, FDR's longtime colleague, adviser, and the person closest to the president. Hopkins secured a visa for Kathy to work in London as a war reporter, despite her lack of experience. Undaunted, Kathy wrote to Hopkins, 'Someone opens the door or passes the butter at the table – "thank you" is the polite result . . . But teaming that same "thank you" with the opportunity you've made possible for me just doesn't make sense . . . I'm extremely grateful & will continue being so for a hellova long time.' She flew from New York to Bermuda to Lisbon on a luxury 'flying boat', the *Dixie Clipper*, and arrived in London on May 16, 1941, less than a week after the worst air raid of the Blitz. More than five hundred Luftwaffe planes had bombarded London for nearly seven hours, leaving the historic chamber in the House of Commons a smouldering pile of char.

While in London, Kathy worked first for the International News Service and later for *Newsweek*, one of a number of businesses in which Averell had an ownership stake. But moving to the USSR with Averell meant resigning from *Newsweek* just as she was angling for a posting to cover the war in North Africa. 'I am thrilled at what you have done – and very proud. Don't worry about your future plans,' Ave assured her in a note. Once in Moscow, however, her journalistic endeavours had been largely limited to clipping and mimeographing articles to include in the daily embassy news bulletin, a task she compared to 'paper doll cutting'. Now, compiling this pamphlet on the Crimea, Kathy found that information about local history, both ancient and from the nineteenth century, was abundant. But she was having much more difficulty learning about the Crimea's more recent past. One afternoon, she decided to pay a call on an elderly local woman, Maria Chekhova, sister of the famed Russian playwright Anton Chekhov. Seeking relief from tuberculosis, Chekhov had moved to Yalta with his mother and sister in 1898, and it was there that he composed two of his most famous works, *The Three Sisters* and *The Cherry Orchard*. The writer had died in 1904, but his eighty-three-year-old sister still lived up the road from Livadia Palace, in his elegant white dacha, with views of the sea; somehow she had managed to save it from Nazi wrath. Kathy's visit to Miss Chekhova seemed to hold potential: who could have a better view of the past half-century of Russian history and culture? But though Miss Chekhova was 'charming, full of life and thrilled to be meeting some Americans', as Kathy wrote to Mouche, Kathy was 'having a hellova a time finding out about the pre-revolutionary history of this part of the coast, as the Soviets seem very reticent on the subject'. Chekhova also refused to tell Kathy anything 'about what happened during the year and a half of occupation'. As Kathy soon discovered, Maria Chekhova was hardly unique. At the palace, she found the same restraint. 'The natives who work around the place here at Livadia don't seem to know anything either,' she told her former governess.

When Kathy moved to Moscow in October 1943, people had warned her that daily life in Russia would be unlike anything she had ever known, compared to London in the immediate aftermath of the Blitz. 'I thought coming over here – starting to work for the Press and all that, would be the last time in my life that I'd be scared,' Kathy wrote to Mary just before leaving London. 'Now crashing London seems like chicken feed.' She had expected to find Moscow a city of ramshackle buildings made of wood and occupied by coarse, unsmiling people, but that was not the case. In some ways, Moscow looked much like any modern western city. American Lend-Lease trucks rumbled down wide boulevards, and streetcars were so completely crammed with people rushing around the city that they reminded Kathy of the trains returning to New York from New Haven after the Harvard-Yale game. But for all their hustling, Muscovites seemed to be in a perpetual rush to nowhere. All but the oldest citizens outpaced the young and athletic Kathy on the streets in their great hurry to join queues for food or drink, only to stand and wait in line for hours. Kathy might have asked them about these paradoxes, but she was not allowed to socialise with them. She was permitted to mingle only with the diplomatic community or the men in the American press corps, many of whom had Russian girlfriends who were 'out and out prostitutes'. Often, the only friend she had was her father. In a bustling city of millions, life was remarkably insular.

By 1945, the American people still knew very little about their eastern ally. There had been no diplomatic relations between Russia and the United States between 1917, when the Bolsheviks seized power, and 1933, when President Roosevelt finally recognised the Soviet Union. During that time, limited business or academic exchange occurred between the two countries; but even before the 1917 revolution, Russia held little interest for Americans. Few learned Russian as a foreign language. It was not until a professor at the University of Chicago adapted a French-Russian grammar book in the early twentieth century that a Russian-language textbook became available in America. By the time Kathy went to Moscow, there was still only one reliable English-Russian phrasebook for beginners: *Bondar's Simplified Russian Method*. Kathy had no idea such a thing existed, so she had to borrow a *Bondar* from a fellow American diplomat when she arrived.

Learning the language was only the first barrier to overcome when attempting to understand the Soviet Union. Kathy found the Soviet citizens with whom she had incidental contact in Moscow or on the ski slopes of the Lenin Hills 'friendly and frank', but on an official level, it was nearly impossible to get to know anyone other than the most senior leaders in government, and not in any personal way. Kathy was far from the only person who encountered this difficulty. In the weeks before the Yalta Conference, the State Department had submitted a request to the American embassy, asking for biographical profiles of the Soviet bureaucrats with whom they would be working. George Kennan, Averell's chargé d'affaires at the embassy and one of the few Russian experts in the Foreign Service, responded that the request was impossible to fulfil. The Soviets never shared any kind of personal information about their bureaucrats with outsiders, except in obituaries, when 'they can no longer be of use to the foreign world'. Friendship, expressions of mutual interest, or acts of kindness counted for nothing. As Kennan explained, if a Soviet bureaucrat 'does a kind or obliging act, it is because he finds it in the interests of his government to do so', as 'the personal views of a Soviet official have little or no influence on his behavior ... The views of a Soviet official are manufactured for him.' When it came to shaping policy, 'individual relations could therefore not possibly have – except possibly in the case of Stalin himself – much effect on such decisions.' As much as Kathy and even Kennan knew about the Soviet Union, there remained expanses of ambiguity and oblivion, as vast as the Soviet Union itself, which lay beyond the grasp of even the most informed outsider.

When Kathy was in her teens, her mother, Kitty, used to worry that if the governess did not handle her carefully, Kathy would turn out to be nothing more than a 'sporting woman'. (The comment did not lack irony, as Kitty had herself been an expert equestrian and crack shot.) In London and Moscow, Kathy's life had certainly evolved beyond riding, shooting and skiing. Her stepmother now had a tendency to worry about Kathy's 'state of spinsterhood', despite the fact that in London, Kathy had no shortage of ardent suitors and often found her calendar booked two weeks in advance – though appropriate dates in Moscow were a bit more difficult to come by. Most of the women in Kathy's social set, including her sister, Mary, who was only eleven months older, were married and settling down with husbands and children. But for Kathy, there would be plenty of time for that later.

Averell may have once predicted he and Kathy would become the closest of friends, but in many ways, the necessities of wartime made their relationship less like that of a father and daughter and more like one between business partners or colleagues. Even though much about life in Russia was unpleasant, Kathy had no intention of leaving her father's side before the war was over. As one of her most persistent admirers, General Ira Eaker, the American commander in chief of the Allied Air Forces in the Mediterranean, had prophesied in a letter to her, 'You are going to be in the USSR for a long time, if you continue to be your Dad's ablest Lieutenant.'

The ablest lieutenant now had just seventy-two hours left before the American delegation arrived at Livadia, and everything around her was still in an alarming state of extremes. There was more than enough caviar to feed a small city, but scarcely enough lavatories for a large family; the bed linens that had been acquired from one of the finest hotels in the world now covered hard, thin mattresses riddled with bedbugs.

But that was Russia, a land of extremes and contradictions, a place where perception often had no relation to reality. Where Moscow shops beckoned passers-by with tempting displays, yet inside there was nothing to purchase. There were luxuries that no American would ever expect in wartime at the embassy residence, such as champagne for breakfast and bouquets of irises and dahlias for Kathy's bedside table, yet no glass in the south- and east-facing windows for more than two years after nearby bombings of the Battle of Moscow had shattered them to pieces. And here, in this vestige of empire on the Black Sea, the three most powerful men in the world would gather in a tsar's palace that, save for some furniture and a coat of paint, otherwise would have been condemned.

TWO

February 2, 1945

Sarah Churchill stood on the deck of the HMS *Orion*, looking out over the cruisers anchored in the fingerlike inlet that formed Malta's Valletta Harbour as the walls of the ancient city bore down from above. Malta was a rocky fortress of an island off the southern tip of Italy, the city of Valletta seemingly carved directly from the local limestone. The city walls spiralled upward, and within each spiral the buildings fitted together like pieces of a three-dimensional jigsaw puzzle. The first time Sarah had come to Malta with her father, a year and a half earlier, she was struck by the colour. As an aerial reconnaissance intelligence analyst in the Women's Auxiliary Air Force, or WAAFs, as the women's branch of the Royal Air Force was known, she had spent two years scrutinising photographs of Malta and the Mediterranean so closely, she knew them as well as London. But those pictures were black and white. In reality, these homes, churches and buildings of state glowed with blushing warmth in the morning sunlight; everything was pink.

It was not yet 9.30 a.m., but excited crowds had gathered on both sides of the narrow harbour wherever they could get a view of the ships moored below, even piling onto the rooftops of buildings that had miraculously survived more than three thousand air raids during the enemy's relentless two-and-a-half-year bombardment. By the middle of 1942, Malta was the lone speck of an Allied stronghold between Italy and North Africa. This island, just one-fifth the size of London, had become the most bombed spot on earth. In honour of the Maltese people's fortitude, Britain's King George had awarded them the George Cross, and President Roosevelt had presented them with a hand-drawn scroll of honour. Now another prize lay in wait – the chance to catch a glimpse of the meeting of the two great leaders for whom they had fought and endured. The moment was imminent. The ship for which they were all waiting would soon steam into port.

Usually, crowds made Sarah anxious – which was ironic, considering that before the war she had been a stage actor. But today the onlookers were the least of her worries. Her father was pacing the deck beside her. As he puffed on his long cigar, little white clouds of smoke followed in his wake. The British delegation had been waiting nearly half an hour for the American ship to appear on the horizon. Half an hour's delay was nothing in the context of transatlantic sea travel, but given her father's multi-month ordeal in securing this meeting, patience had long since worn thin. Across the harbour, the rest of the delegation was gathered along the rail of the *Orion*'s sister ship, the HMS *Sirius*. The British and American military chiefs of staff were there, as well as Averell Harriman; Harry Hopkins; the American secretary of state, Edward Stettinius; and the British foreign secretary, Anthony Eden (who had experienced a rather rude awakening that morning, when the military band assembled on board had kicked off the day's festivities a trifle early, jolting Eden from his bed with a rousing rehearsal of 'The Star-Spangled Banner').

There were arguably better ways to spend one's morning than waiting for a ship to appear, but at least the day was warm. Back in England, seven inches of snow had fallen, but here the Mediterranean climate was so pleasant and mild that Sarah could leave her greatcoat behind in her cabin. In her neatly tailored WAAF uniform, she cut a striking figure beside her father, who was smartly attired as an officer of the Royal Yacht Squadron.

Though her ensemble, a blue wool skirt and jacket, was just one of many uniforms on display along the harbour that morning, it was nearly impossible for Sarah to melt into the sea of navy and olive, not least because of her red hair, which was tucked in tidy waves under her uniform cap. Once, she had a mane of red hair the very same shade as her father's – though he was now practically bald. When Sarah had arrived at the WAAF recruiting office in the autumn of 1941, the greatest concern of the woman conducting her interview was not Sarah's fitness to serve. Rather, she was broken-hearted to inform Sarah that her hair, the most beautiful red hair she had ever seen, would have to be cut. But Sarah hadn't cared. All she wanted was to get into the war as quickly as possible. Still, the recruiter had made Sarah promise she would visit a fashionable London hairdresser before departing for training, rather than place herself at the mercy of the camp barber.

Even if her hair colour had not prevented her from hiding in plain sight, her name made her instantly recognisable. Sarah was listed on personnel rosters as Section Officer Oliver, but by the time she joined the WAAFs, her ill-fated marriage to Vic Oliver was over, save for the technicality of obtaining a divorce. Regardless of what the personnel papers said, everyone knew Section Officer Oliver by her maiden name. Sarah Oliver was one Sarah Millicent Hermione Churchill, the prime minister's thirty-year-old daughter. As they stood side by side on the deck, any observer would have noticed her close resemblance to her father. She was slender and tall like her mother, with a delicate nose and chin, but she had her father's eyes and upturned smile. Father and daughter stood together along the rail of the *Orion* in the February sunshine, waiting for the president of the United States to arrive.

President Roosevelt was nearing the end of his 4,883-mile journey from Washington. The plan was for the British and American delegations to rendezvous in Malta and confer on military and political strategy throughout the afternoon and evening. Then, in the early hours of the next morning, they and their contingents would all leave Malta together and fly 1,375 miles over the Greek islands, the Aegean Sea and Turkey, to the Crimean Peninsula on the Black Sea. There, at the end of an eighty-mile drive, their host for the conference, Joseph Stalin, would be waiting.

Sarah had been granted special leave from her Royal Air Force base – RAF Medmenham – west of London, to join her father for this trip. It was the second time Winston had asked Sarah to accompany him to a major international conference. In early November 1943, Sarah's commanding officer had summoned her to his office and informed her that he was granting her leave, as the prime minister had requested her presence on an important but unspecified voyage. It was thrillingly hush-hush, every bit as dramatic as the start of a novel by G. A. Henty or H. Rider Haggard, and Sarah had 'walked on air'. Soon she was on a plane bound for Tehran, for the very first meeting of Churchill, Roosevelt and Stalin. The Tehran Conference, a triumph in Allied cooperation, solidified the leaders' commitment to the D-Day landings at Normandy, which finally relieved the Soviets of the concentrated brunt of Nazi aggression on the Eastern Front. Tehran had left Sarah optimistic. Goodwill seemed to flow among the three leaders, and Sarah felt inspired. 'Whatever follows,' she had written to her mother, 'one couldn't help but feel that a genuine desire for friendship was sown.'

Since then, the Allied forces had routed the Nazis at Normandy and slowly begun to push them east towards Germany. In the wake of Allied victories across Europe that summer, the three leaders called for another meeting to coordinate plans for what they hoped would be the end of the war. The code name for this conference would be ARGONAUT, as Churchill suggested, after the Greek mythological heroes who had accompanied Jason in his search for the Golden Fleece on the shores of the Black Sea. In early January, Sarah learned that she too would be an Argonaut. Once again her commanding officer had summoned her and told her to pack her bags. Her father required her for another 'Top Secret' journey. Asking a trusted friend at Medmenham to cover for her, she put out a rumour that she was ill, so no one would suspect the real reason for her absence. On the night of January 29, she met her father at RAF Northolt. Soon they were underway.

Despite the sense of optimism as victory in Europe became more tangible with every passing day, Sarah felt disquiet about this conference. It had started with the weather. They flew from RAF Northolt with a blizzard chasing their tail. They had raced to take flight before the gale truly set in, but new problems emerged once they were airborne. The pilots had trouble controlling the temperature inside the plane. The unpressurised cabin was so hot and uncomfortable that Sarah and her fellow passengers felt like 'tomatoes screaming for air', while her father looked just like a 'poor hot pink baby about to cry'. Not only did he have to suffer in the boiling cabin, but he also had developed a 102-degree fever. Despite Winston's stalwart constitution, it seemed as if every time he left for an overseas conference, he managed to fall ill. Every time he had willed himself to recover, even from a serious bout of pneumonia on the way home from Tehran, which had left him grounded in Carthage for two weeks; but cracks in his resolute nature were beginning to show. This time, the prime minister told his daughter, as they flew through the night towards Malta, he was absolutely certain he was 'in for something'.

Between the blizzard that had chased them east and her father's premonition, Sarah could not help but feel superstitious, experiencing something like an actor's qualms before opening night, as the start of the conference approached. She had begun to ponder the idea of fate. During a conversation with her father's doctor, Lord Moran, who had travelled with them to Malta, Sarah posed an unusual question. Was it possible, she asked, for the lines in one's hand to be used to predict one's future? Sarah's comment threw the man of science off balance. Surely not, he assured her. The distinct patterns in each person's palm were entirely the result of anatomy and genetics. 'You think there is nothing in it?' she asked, with a hint of disappointment. But Lord Moran could not give her the answer she sought and quickly changed the subject.

Fortunately, after several nights' sleep Winston had fully recovered his health, as well as much of his usual buoyant demeanour. He even had made up a rhyming couplet on the way to dinner the previous evening to reassure Sarah that all was well: 'My temperature is down, my tummy ache gone, my functions have resumed their norm: in fact I'm in the best of form!'

But by the time the British contingent gathered on deck to wait for Roosevelt, the cheerful atmosphere was gone. At eight that morning, they had received dreadful news. During the night, a plane transporting several Foreign Office experts to the conference had crashed into the sea near Lampedusa, a small Italian island. According to early reports, of the nineteen passengers and crew, seven had survived, but no one knew who those survivors were, nor if seven was an accurate number. The British delegation was stunned.

Winston was filled with trepidation as he paced the deck. Ever since he and his allies had begun planning the conference, he had harboured grave concerns about holding the meeting on the Black Sea. As the date drew near, he became even more convinced that his concerns were justified. Averell Harriman had reported that the Soviets had relayed inaccurate information about the runway at the airfield where the British and Americans were scheduled to land the next morning. It had not been lengthened, as promised, to accommodate the delegations' C-54s and Yorks. Instead, the planes were to land at a different airfield altogether, where the runway was two thousand feet shorter than normally required. The drive from the airfield to Yalta looked similarly troubling. An RAF officer who had arrived at Yalta with the advance team described a six-hour journey through a blizzard over nearly impassable mountain roads. Not only was the airfield six hours away from their lodgings, but the HMS *Franconia*, which contained the secure communications centre for the British and had dodged the floating mines on its way into port, was anchored in Sevastopol Harbour, a three-hour drive east from Yalta. As a British Army major in the advance contingent told a colleague, it was like 'running a conference with three focal points, one at each corner of Wales, linked by bad mountain roads covered with snow, ice and slush'.

The prime minister also had deeper concerns, particularly regarding his relationship with Franklin Roosevelt. Churchill and Roosevelt had developed a genuine friendship over the course of the past four years. The visit to Malta itself was a heartening reminder of that partnership. In the early days of the war, Italy and Germany controlled the Mediterranean and North Africa, save for this one tiny island outpost. From Malta, the British could attack the Italian navy and target enemy supply lines, thus keeping General Erwin Rommel and the Wehrmacht from unchecked domination in North Africa. But by May 1942, Malta was nearly on its knees. The enemy sank convoy after convoy of supplies from Britain, driving the population to the brink of starvation. Meanwhile, with no materials available to fix the planes engaged in a near-constant series of dogfights, the Allied fighting force was crippled. At one point, the RAF was down to a mere five functioning fighters to defend Malta. The British aircraft carrier ferrying Spitfire replacements to the island was so badly damaged, it was not seaworthy, and without more fighters to ward off enemy bombers, the island would surely fall, and soon. Desperate for help, Churchill had cabled Roosevelt. The president responded immediately, sending an American aircraft carrier loaded with new British Spitfires to the Mediterranean not once but twice, thus saving Malta from annihilation and the British forces from a fully supplied German army in North Africa.

In recent months, however, Roosevelt seemed increasingly ambivalent towards Churchill's opinions, convictions and concerns as they tried to arrange a tripartite conference. This stung Churchill acutely. Throughout January he repeatedly pushed Roosevelt to meet with him in Malta ahead of their conference with Stalin in order to outline a united Anglo-American position on the issues up for debate at Yalta. Churchill was particularly concerned about Polish independence. He thought the Americans failed to fully appreciate the matter's delicate complexities, while the Soviets understood them implicitly. Stalin was a merciless and wily autocrat, but Churchill was willing to believe he would be a man of his word. 'If only I could dine with Stalin once a week, there would be no trouble at all,' he once declared. In October 1944, Churchill and Stalin met in Moscow. During that meeting, the two men had reached a secret bargain whereby the Soviets agreed they would not interfere in liberated Greece, where the British had long held influence, and the British would largely stay out of Romania and Bulgaria. So far, Stalin had kept his promise. However, Churchill remained wary of the people surrounding Stalin and the historical forces that had shaped Russia for hundreds of years. Like the tsars in the imperial era, the Kremlin sought to control Eastern Europe. The entrenched national paranoia about security on Russia's western border, where open plains left the vast nation exposed to enemy invasion, retained a strong grip on the minds of Soviet leaders. Hitler's 1941 assault on the Soviet Union – Operation Barbarossa – was only the most recent example of such an invasion, and it might have been successful, had not an especially cruel winter taken the Nazis by surprise and halted their progress just outside the gates of Moscow. In pursuit of their national interest, the Soviets would be looking to exploit even the smallest points of disagreement between the two western partners. Poland had long been the object of Russian desire. But it was the guarantee of Polish sovereignty that had led Britain to declare war on Germany in the first place. On that issue, perhaps more than any other, it was imperative that the British and the Americans iron out their differences well in advance.

Roosevelt, by contrast, was far more concerned that meeting with Churchill in Malta would make Stalin feel as if the western powers were plotting behind his back. In response to Churchill's many requests for such a meeting, Roosevelt consistently demurred on the grounds that neither he nor his secretary of state would be able to arrive in sufficient time to hold any meaningful discussions. Pressing matters in Washington prevented them from leaving for Malta until the last possible moment. Besides, Roosevelt preferred to keep discussions with his counterparts 'informal' and saw no need to prepare an agenda.

Roosevelt wanted to commit to meeting at Yalta for a mere five to six days. But the end of the war presented deep ideological questions about the future of Europe, and Churchill adamantly believed that the answers would be too complex to resolve in five or six days. After all, he scoffed, 'Even the Almighty took seven.' Churchill was haunted by what he called the 'follies of the victors' after the Great War. The triumphant nations believed they had secured peace for generations, but they had failed to craft institutions strong enough to guarantee it. Old wounds continued to fester, and victory proved an illusion that led to further disasters: a global financial crisis, the failure of the League of Nations, German national humiliation, and ultimately another, bloodier war. This time, the Allies would have to proceed carefully; otherwise, Churchill wrote to Roosevelt, 'The end of this war may well prove to be more disappointing than was the last.' Cooperation between the Allies was crucial. As Churchill told Foreign Secretary Anthony Eden several days before leaving for the conference, 'The only hope for the world is the agreement of the Great Powers . . . If they quarrel, our children are undone.'

. . .

Because the prime minister was seen by so many, including the throngs of Maltese who had turned out to catch a glimpse of him, as a giant among men, it was easy to forget that just like so many of his countrymen, he was also a father, one with children in uniform – a father standing with his daughter on a sunny February morning.

To the woman standing beside him, Winston Churchill was simply 'Papa'. But Sarah had always known, long before her father became prime minister, that something special set her father apart from other men. He had an aura of greatness that sent dinner guests scurrying out of the room in search of pen and paper to take down his every word. But for all his lofty, imposing rhetoric and force of personality, he was also a doting father who let his children climb on his back and used his mastery of the English language to compose an ode, for 'Poor Puggy-Wug', his daughters' beloved dog that had fallen ill. When Sarah was home from school, she loved nothing more than to spend hours in the garden below the family's country home, Chartwell, engaged in one of her father's favourite, if unusual, pastimes: bricklaying. This work was the furthest thing from politics, and Winston found the manual labour relaxing. He built hundreds of yards of brick walls around Chartwell's gardens. While he did have a professional bricklayer on call, Sarah was his chosen 'second mate'. They established a perfect system. Sarah handed him bricks and maintained a ready supply of mortar, and while Winston laid the bricks on the wall, he entrusted her with the crucial responsibility of making sure the plumb line running along the top kept the bricks straight and even. Together, the mason and his assistant passed many pleasant hours anticipating the other's every move in quiet, contemplative harmony.

Twenty years later, she was at his side once again. There had been long periods of separation in the years when Sarah was touring with theatrical productions. For a man of his age and class, it was surprising that Winston did not wholeheartedly object to her decision to pursue a career on the stage, but his own mother, the wealthy American debutante Jennie Jerome, had been something of an unconventional woman for her day. She wrote plays for London's West End, was rumoured to have scores of lovers, and had a snake tattooed on her wrist.

By comparison, Sarah's way of bucking convention was quite tame. There had been tension between father and daughter when she ran away to New York to marry the much older actor Vic Oliver, a decision Winston did not condone and from which he had persistently tried to dissuade her.

But the war had brought Sarah and Winston back together. Early in the conflict, Winston and his wife, Clementine, had decided that someone from the family should accompany him as aide-de-camp and all-round protector, supporter and confidant on his travels. The various Churchills were not equally suited to the task. Clementine was terrified of flying. Diana, the oldest, was married, with three young children, and she cared less for politics. Randolph, the second child, the only son, and a major in the British Army, was brilliant like Winston, and while he sometimes joined his father, his drinking made him brash and arrogant, a liability in the delicate role of supporting Winston during stressful, high-stakes negotiations. Mary, the youngest, had travelled with Winston and Clementine to Quebec for Winston's meeting with Roosevelt in 1942, but though bright and capable, and an officer in the Auxiliary Territorial Service, Mary was eight years younger than Sarah and still a bit too inexperienced. Sarah was the ideal choice. She was the right age, had a sharp intellect, and was keenly aware of the military and political issues at stake, thanks to her work at RAF Medmenham.

But more than that, the deep connection between father and daughter confirmed the rightness of the decision. Since childhood, Sarah had felt like something of a 'loner'. Nervous and shy, she formed few friendships with the other girls in her social circle. As a teenager she spent much of her debutante season hiding in the bathroom, playing cards with her cousin Unity Mitford, to avoid making small talk with her peers. Even at home, from the time she was a little girl, she had felt timid and awkward in her father's presence. Whenever she worked up the nerve to speak to him, she had been sure to 'tidy' her mind before she opened her mouth. If her message was important, she would instead write her thoughts in a note. Though she always felt her father was much more eloquent and quick-witted than she was, she did believe that she understood him and, even in her silence, that he understood her. Others in the family would tease her for her reticence, but he would stay their tongues in an instant, saying, 'Sarah is an oyster, she will not tell us her secrets.'

During the quiet hours spent laying bricks at her father's side, Sarah studied him as a naturalist studies a species. She observed that when he was 'with a trusted audience he would let them see his mind leaping and ranging around a problem in a breathlessly spectacular way.' Sarah desperately wanted to be part of this trusted audience, to be 'in the league of people, who if they could not help, understood where he was trying to go with an idea'. So she decided to 'train [her]self to think; not the things he thought, but the way he thought, and would apply it to certain problems as a practice'. Even if she did not speak, she wanted him to know that she was 'in silent step with him'. Now perhaps no one, aside from her mother, knew Winston Churchill's mind better than Sarah.

It was for this reason that Sarah now found herself in Malta, watching her father as he impatiently paced the deck. Other than his protégé, Anthony Eden, there was no one else within the British delegation to whom he could confess his deep concerns about the upcoming conference, particularly his frustration with his American ally. But even Eden had his own agenda and political future to look after. Winston needed someone at his side who could share his inner burden while asking only to be allowed to help. Someone who could temper the linguistic torrent he unleashed behind closed doors, but one who could also interpret his feelings in the words left unsaid. At home, this task fell to Clementine, who had carefully honed her ability to channel her husband's energy and prod his impassioned speech and deepest convictions in a positive direction. Sarah did not have her mother's forty years of experience managing Winston Churchill, but she had experience enough. Just as she had maintained the plumb line on the brick walls at Chartwell, she could maintain the plumb line here, and help him adjust course when emotion tempted him off the narrow path he had to walk between his partners in the tripartite alliance.

At 9.35 a.m. the president's ship, the USS *Quincy*, finally appeared on the horizon. Ever so slowly, it eased its way into the harbour, carefully avoiding the submarine nets at the entrance. A squadron of six Spitfires raced across the sky, and the bands amassed on shore sprang to life, greeting the cruiser with a soaring rendition of the U.S. national anthem, followed by a rousing round of 'God Save the King'. With the aid of a tugboat, the thirteen-thousand-ton warship inched towards its berth. The two ships were so close together in the narrow inlet that Sarah could see the face of every person on the *Quincy* as it passed. The ship's crew was splendidly turned out at attention on deck. Sarah had to admit, the American sailors, soldiers and airmen looked to be 'very superior creatures'. The prime minister had stopped pacing and positioned himself on the landing, at the top of one of his ship's ladders facing the water. He had promised Roosevelt he would be 'waiting on the quay' when the president arrived. This would do just as well.

As the *Quincy* drew even with the *Orion*, a hush suddenly fell over the crowd. There, on the ship's bridge, was the president of the United States, sitting with a dignified posture in his wheelchair, along the rail. The president and the prime minister regarded each other. Churchill, standing firmly at attention, slowly raised his hand to his cap. Each man gave the other a firm salute. Just for an instant, the past few months' tension and pent-up frustration melted away as the two old friends were reunited. Even to Sarah, who had spent a lifetime surrounded by dignitaries and statesmen, it was a 'thrilling sight'. Across the harbour, on the *Sirius*, the British foreign secretary, Anthony Eden, was standing with the American delegates Harriman, Hopkins and Stettinius, observing the encounter. It was a moment, Eden later professed, when the world 'seem[ed] to stand still', making one 'conscious of a mark in history'.

Finally, the *Quincy* docked in its berth and lowered its gangplank. Harriman, Stettinius, Hopkins and General Marshall boarded first to greet their boss. Shortly thereafter, a formal announcement was made and the prime minister was 'piped aboard'. Sarah soon followed. Arriving on deck, she was ushered to a group of four wicker chairs arranged in the sunlight, where her father and the president sat side by side. They made an incongruous pair. With his Royal Yacht Squadron uniform, Churchill appeared dressed for a military parade, while Roosevelt was attired simply in a dark, striped suit and a tweed flat cap, as if he could not decide whether he was ready for a business meeting in the city or a country picnic at his beloved Hill-Top Cottage in Hyde Park, New York.

Like Churchill, Roosevelt had not come to Malta alone. Given his physical limitations, he often travelled with one or more of his sons, who helped him to stand and move between his chair, his car and his bed. At Tehran, both his son Elliott and his son-in-law John Boettiger had accompanied him, but this time he had left them at home. In early January, Roosevelt had cabled Churchill with an unexpected message: 'If you are taking any of your personal family to ARGONAUT, I am thinking of including my daughter Anna in my party.' FDR had never brought Anna, the oldest of his five children and his only daughter, on an official trip abroad before. It was a surprising, albeit welcome change to his retinue. 'How splendid,' Churchill replied. 'Sarah is coming with me.'

Winston and Clementine had met the 'first daughter' during their visit to Washington in 1943, and Sarah had spent time with Anna's husband, John Boettiger, at Tehran, but simply by reading the newspapers Sarah would have learned about Anna. The president's daughter was thirty-eight and had three children: a teenage daughter and son from her first marriage, to a stockbroker named Curtis Dall, and a five-year-old son with John. Before John had joined the army in 1943 as a captain in the Civilian Affairs Division, Anna and John had lived in Seattle, where they edited a newspaper, the *Seattle Post-Intelligencer*. With her husband deployed to North Africa and the Mediterranean, Anna had moved from Seattle to the White House in early 1944. After years of relative obscurity out west, she had become an increasingly visible figure in Washington; she frequently stood in for her mother as surrogate First Lady during Eleanor Roosevelt's numerous trips.

Now, here Anna was, sitting across from FDR. The two daughters were introduced. Anna was tall and blonde; her fine, straight hair, set in a permanent wave, had become frizzy in the sea air. Like her father, she wore a simple civilian suit and hat. Immediately Sarah was struck by just how much Anna looked like Eleanor. 'Although,' Sarah noted conspiratorially in a letter to her own mother, Anna was 'so much better looking'. Then another amusing thought occurred to her. She supposed strangers thought she and her older sister, Diana, looked much like Clementine, except in that case, 'not so good looking!' Appearances aside, Anna seemed an easygoing, pleasant person. Sarah decided she liked her very much. However, she observed that in spite of Anna's casual manner, she seemed to be 'quite nervous about being on the trip'.

Settling in, Sarah turned her attention to the president, who was seated to her left. Winston's frustration with Roosevelt aside, Sarah was glad to see him again. At Tehran, she had found him a warm and charming man. He was so full of life that at times he seemed ready to leap out of his chair, as if he had forgotten he could not walk. Looking at him now, Sarah was taken aback. This vitality so evident at Tehran was gone, the life sapped from his slackened face. It seemed he had aged a 'million years' over the fourteen months since she had last seen him, and his conversation, once sparkling and witty, wandered and meandered.

Something had definitely changed. Even the president's ever-present group of friends and advisers had notably altered. From what Sarah observed on board the ship that morning and learned during conversations with the Americans who had arrived the day before, Harry Hopkins, once inseparable from Roosevelt, no longer held the position of influence he had long enjoyed. Poor Hopkins had been seriously ill for some time. He had been treated at the Mayo Clinic in Minnesota for the side effects of stomach cancer, which he had been battling for the past six years. Hopkins had willed himself to make it to this conference, but an unfamiliar distance had arisen between him and the president. In place of Hopkins, Edward Stettinius, who had been secretary of state for only two months, had become Roosevelt's primary 'buddy'. Perhaps Sarah was wrong, but based on her first interactions with him, Stettinius had seemed rather 'wooden headed'. Worst of all, John Gilbert Winant, the American ambassador to Britain, was thousands of miles away. Although all the other American, British and Soviet ambassadors had been included (with the exception of Lord Halifax, Churchill's envoy to the United States, who had remained in Washington and had not attended previous international wartime conferences), Roosevelt had left Winant in London. Sarah desperately wished Winant, or Gil, as she knew him, was there. This was not just a selfish wish. When Winant was present, Sarah knew her father had a strong, true friend among the Americans. But with Winant in London and Hopkins in a diminished role, the president's inner circle at Yalta would be distinctly less pro-British.

The joy Sarah had felt as she watched her father and Roosevelt salute each other passed quickly as Winston's anxiety about the state of the relationship between Britain and the United States crept into her mind. What had happened to Roosevelt since she had seen him in Tehran? 'Is it health,' she wondered, 'or has he moved away a little from us?'

THREE

February 2, 1945

Perhaps it was because Sarah had an actor's ability to summon a wide range of emotions or simply because she had a natural ability to read people. Within moments of sitting down across from the Roosevelts on the *Quincy*, Sarah sensed what Anna was desperately trying to hide. Anna was indeed nervous about the trip, but not because she was new to the world of tripartite conferences, nor because she was, for the first time, seeing firsthand the furious destruction left by war. Anna was anxious not for herself but for her father. Sarah's perception had been acute: Franklin Roosevelt was seriously ill. He was dying of congestive heart failure. Other than the doctors, Anna was the only person who knew just how grave the situation had become.

In the winter of 1944, after her husband joined the army, Anna had moved back to the White House, with her four-year-old son. Shortly after her arrival, she began to notice small changes in her father. He had a persistent cough, his skin looked ashen, and he appeared far more exhausted than a man of sixty-two years should be. Granted, twelve years in the White House, including two at war, would have taken a toll on the fittest man in his prime, but this condition hinted at something more than fatigue. The signs were perceptible to only the most attentive observers. His hands shook when he lit a cigarette. Once, while writing his name at the end of a letter, he seemed to draw a blank, dragging the pen across the page in an unintelligible black squiggle. Sometimes in the dark of the White House movie theatre, as the family watched an after-dinner film, the light coming from the screen would be just bright enough for Anna to glimpse her father's mouth hanging open for long stretches of time, as if he could not muster the energy to keep it closed.

Anna's mother, Eleanor, attributed much of FDR's increased fatigue to concerns about their troublesome middle son, Elliott. He had recently announced that he was divorcing his second wife, Ruth, in order to marry a film starlet. But Anna's observations, taken together with a remark by FDR's secretary, Grace Tully, that he had either fallen asleep or briefly lost consciousness while signing papers some months earlier, compelled Anna to take action. She summoned her father's doctor, Vice Admiral Ross McIntire, an ear, nose and throat specialist. He tried to tell her that the president was simply suffering the prolonged effects of earlier bouts of influenza, sinus infection and fever, but Anna was unconvinced. She insisted that FDR have a comprehensive medical evaluation.

A thorough examination by the young cardiologist Howard Bruenn, at Bethesda Naval Hospital in late March 1944, revealed that Anna's suspicions had been correct. The president was breathless after moderate exertion, there was fluid in his lungs, and his blood pressure was 186/108 mmHg – a systolic number indicating a hypertensive crisis. Cardiology was a relatively new field – a professional organisation of American cardiologists had convened for the first time in 1934 – but to Bruenn, the results were clear: the president was suffering from acute congestive heart failure, a disease for which there was no cure. Bruenn could try to prolong his patient's life by using digitalis to temporarily clear the fluid in his lungs and by advising him to shorten his work hours, sleep more, maintain a strict diet, and lose weight to reduce the strain on the heart. But it was just a waiting game. Treating heart failure was beyond McIntire's capabilities, so he begrudgingly agreed to have the thirty-eight-year-old Bruenn take over the president's primary care on one important condition: Bruenn was not to tell anyone about FDR's diagnosis – no one in the Roosevelt family, and especially not the president himself. Surprisingly, Bruenn faced no resistance from the patient. FDR never asked what was wrong with him.

But Anna was no fool. There had to be a reason why her father was taking new medications, why his diet now closely resembled that of her toddler, and why the new doctor insisted FDR work no more than four hours a day. Before long, Bruenn broke McIntire's rule and took Anna into his confidence, revealing FDR's diagnosis in enough detail to ensure that his recommendations were given serious attention. Anna read whatever she could about heart disease and followed Bruenn's instructions to the letter. Aside from her husband, she told no one, not even her mother.

Though Roosevelt asked Bruenn no details about his health, he must have sensed that something was seriously wrong and that Anna was protecting him. Her presence at Yalta represented an abrupt change from the situation at Tehran. Then, Anna had begged to accompany her father, but he had flatly refused, for no logical reason. Instead he chose her brother Elliott and her husband, John. This rejection had stung Anna. Yes, her brother and husband could help support Roosevelt physically in a way she could not, but his Secret Service officer, Mike Reilly, could have done that. Not only had Elliott accompanied FDR to Tehran, but both Elliott and Anna's younger brother Franklin Jr had joined their father at the Atlantic Charter Conference with Churchill in August 1941, at which they had outlined the common principles that united the free world, as well as the Casablanca Conference in January 1943, which solidified the Allies' commitment to a German unconditional surrender. It was only fair that she should at last have a turn. At the time, Anna had also been desperate to see her husband, whose letters from his posting in Italy had taken on an anxious, depressed tone. She needed to see him to give him some reassurance. As she told FDR, if it was a problem that she was not in uniform, she could join the Red Cross. Still, her father refused to budge: in keeping with the age-old maritime superstition that women on board ships brought bad luck, no women were permitted to sail on navy vessels. (Never mind that, as the commander in chief, Roosevelt easily could have granted her an exception. Or she could have flown.) That old superstition did not seem to bother Winston Churchill, who was bringing Sarah to Tehran. No matter what argument Anna made, FDR would not acquiesce. In a rare fit of frustration with her father, Anna fumed to her mother that FDR was a 'stinker in his treatment of the female members of his family'. She blazed with anger at the injustice: 'Pa seems to take for granted that all females should be quite content to "keep the home fires burning," and that their efforts outside of this are merely amusing and to be aided by a patronising male world only as a last resort to keep some individually troublesome female momentarily appeased.'

But when she approached her father about joining him at Yalta, he simply responded, 'Well, we'll just see about that.' She expected to be disappointed once again. Then, in early January, he surprised her. Winston was bringing Sarah again, and Ambassador Harriman was bringing his daughter, Kathleen. Anna could come along if she wished.

When FDR told Eleanor he had decided to bring Anna, it was her turn to feel hurt. She had commiserated with Anna about being left behind for Tehran, and Anna knew how much Eleanor was hoping Franklin would ask her to join him for this conference. Instead, he put Eleanor off, saying it would be 'simpler' if he took Anna, as Churchill and Harriman were bringing their daughters rather than their wives. If Eleanor went, people would feel they had to go out of their way to make a 'fuss'. Eleanor pretended to understand.

While bringing Anna as his aide-de-camp did indeed simplify logistics, it did not fully explain the larger reason why FDR wanted to bring his daughter, rather than his wife, to this conference. Eleanor either could not see or could not accept that her husband of forty years was truly sick. Meanwhile, for all her good intentions, she did not help alleviate Franklin's exhaustion – she added to it. Anna admired her mother's relentless energy – she poured her heart and soul into causes such as advocating for the rights of women and providing opportunities for the poor. Yet she had never been a naturally warm and nurturing person. Anna had clear childhood memories of entering her mother's room while she was working. Without lifting her head from her papers, Eleanor would say, in a deep, chilling voice, 'What do you want, dear.' She did not phrase it as a question. Eleanor lacked a sense of timing as to the propitious time or place to voice her opinions on Franklin's policy decisions. And her opinions tended to be strong. Though he valued her perspective – in fact, he considered it one of his great assets – she often failed to appreciate the many competing demands on the president's time, particularly during a time of war. His moments of rest were few and far between. During those precious intervals, he was not especially receptive to being subjected to a family member's interrogation. At one particular dinner party, Eleanor began quizzing him about some decision or other that he had made. After a trying day, he had been looking forward to a relaxed, sociable evening and did not appreciate Eleanor's probing questions. Noticing that he was about to reach boiling point, Anna jumped in as mediator, lightheartedly heading Eleanor off by saying, 'Mother, can't you see you are giving Father indigestion?' In his public and private life, FDR was constantly surrounded by a crush of people clamouring for his favour and attention. Anna thought he liked to keep people around him all the time because as a boy, he had grown up with no neighbourhood children to play with and only a much older half brother for occasional company; thus, he always wanted to be 'one of the gang'. But even if he did not like to admit it, FDR's energy was not what it once was. It would have been a kind gesture to bring Eleanor to Yalta, but could he be blamed for trying to ensure that a gruelling trip would be as peaceful as possible?

Anna knew how much her father's decision had wounded Eleanor. In part Anna felt guilty, as if she were betraying her mother – and not for the first time. But Anna also knew that if Eleanor went, she would have to stay at home. So Anna kept her mouth shut, convinced herself that her presence really would keep things 'simpler', and blocked the guilt from her mind.

There was another, more nuanced reason why FDR wanted Anna to come with him. She might not have appreciated this rationale, had she allowed herself to consider it for a moment; instead, she breezed past it, another difficulty swept from her thoughts. FDR was able to thoroughly relax in Anna's presence because he felt that, as a woman, she had 'no ax to grind'. Unlike her brothers, who could and did use their time with FDR as an opportunity to meet people who might advance their careers, FDR assumed Anna would not be 'with him because she was inclined . . . to meet a lot of people to help her get into something else later on'. She existed to serve her family, especially the men, and to keep them tranquil and content.

No matter how hard Anna and Dr Bruenn worked to extend FDR's life, he would soon die. Going to Yalta was almost certainly Anna's first and last chance to experience being needed by her father, to become part of his world, which had long been closed to her. So she accepted his reasons for wanting her at his side and chose to interpret them as an affirmation that finally she was a person of value in his life.

Anna had long wished to be the person her father most wanted by his side. Some of her fondest childhood memories recalled the afternoons when she and Franklin had mounted their horses for long rides through the woods and glens surrounding their home in Hyde Park. As they rode, he would point out trees and birds to teach her about different species; he explained how to farm the land in a way most in keeping with the natural environment. Anna imagined that someday they would manage the Hyde Park estate side by side.

FDR indeed loved the natural world, but he loved politics just as much, if not more. He spent countless hours cloistered behind a heavy wooden door, strategising with his political colleagues, the cigar smoke spilling out from the crack under the closed door into the hall. Desperate for his attention, Anna would write him notes, asking him to please come and say good night. She tried to make the prospect more appealing with the promise of pulling a prank on her brother. To the 'Hon. F.D. Roosevelt,' she wrote. 'Will you please come and say goodnight . . . I am going up now to put something in James' bed and you may hear some shreiks [*sic*] when you come in.' One evening when FDR was shut in his office with his associates, Anna decided to sneak in and hide. Moments later she began to choke on the cigar smoke that filled the room from floor to ceiling, and her eyes started to burn. She had no choice but to give herself up and retreat, coughing and spluttering in utter humiliation. That air was clearly not intended for little girls.

Once, her father had invited her into his library to help him with some books. Anna trembled with nervous excitement at finally joining him in his sacred enclave. She must have trembled too hard, for the instant he handed her a stack of books, they slipped from her arms and crashed to the floor. Anna felt so completely ashamed, she wished she could melt into the ground. Terrified that her father would be furious, she burst into tears and ran away.

When FDR contracted polio, Anna thought her dream was lost for good. It was 1921, Anna was fifteen, and the Roosevelts were at their home on Campobello Island, in New Brunswick, Canada, for the summer. The day had started carefree and beautiful, the kind of day made for sailing and swimming. That afternoon, Franklin had begun to feel chills and a growing discomfort in his lower back. Two days later, he was paralysed from the waist down. He was only thirty-nine, but he would never walk unaided again. Gone were the horseback rides through the woods, and with it the dream that someday Anna would join her father as the custodian of Hyde Park. Anna was soon sent away to the Chapin School in Manhattan, and for the rest of her childhood she rarely saw her father without other people in the way – her omnipresent grandmother, the doctors and nurses, and FDR's political colleagues, who now had to come to him. All she could do was watch as he struggled with his new crutches and steel braces. He swore each day that today he was going to walk the one thousand feet of the driveway. He would strain on the crutches, swinging his legs as the sweat ran down his face, but each day he would fail as Anna stood helpless and broken-hearted at the top of the drive, watching the man who had so often carried her on his shoulders, who had for so long stood as the infallible hero at the centre of her universe, as he struggled and failed, over and over again.

In a way, FDR's heart failure, a terrible condition that no one wished upon him, was also a gift – a gift that Anna could not refuse. She quickly realised that she needed to take on a larger role in her father's life if he was to live to see the end of the war. She and her father never discussed her role at the White House; she just naturally stepped into ever-expanding responsibilities. People across myriad military, government and civic institutions were constantly clamouring for an audience with the president. Given Dr Bruenn's stipulation that FDR was to work no more than four hours per day, he could not possibly take all of the requested appointments; face-to-face interactions were exhausting. So Anna became his gatekeeper, determining who really needed time with the president and who could be fobbed off on somebody else. Sometimes she took the meetings herself and later gave FDR a summary of the discussion. She also tried to ease his burden in ways he was not aware of. After he went to bed, for example, she would sneak to the night pouch and remove whatever papers and requests she felt others could handle, so that he need not be bothered with them.

Had the public known what Anna was doing, there surely would have been an outcry. As it was, some people criticised her simply for living in the White House. One woman wrote Anna a scathing letter, scolding her for 'grafting on the taxpayers'. It was bad enough that Anna was living in the White House at the taxpayers' expense, the woman sniped – she had better not have the nerve to be taking a salary, too. The writer also implied that Anna was running the risk of turning out like her mother, whose excessive involvement in her husband's administration was unseemly. This woman was clearly no admirer of FDR, but 'at least *he* was elected', she spat. No one had elected Eleanor; she was 'only a meddlesome private person' who had no place interfering in political affairs.

This woman's vitriolic assault on the Roosevelt women aside, she did raise a valid concern. Surely Anna knew that taking papers out of her father's pouch was inappropriate, but still she did not stop. She was desperate to do anything to help him. If she could have kept him from going to Yalta, she might have. The entire journey would take weeks; the conference itself would be gruelling. It might very well kill him.

The long voyage to Yalta had begun in darkness. At 10 p.m. on January 22, Roosevelt and his delegation made a furtive escape from Washington. Newspapers across the country were predicting that the Big Three would soon have another conference, but for the sake of security, no one in the United States, Britain or the Soviet Union would confirm where or when it would take place. The president had a secret train depot in the basement of the Bureau of Printing and Engraving annexe, an innocuous-looking concrete-and-limestone building on 14th Street SW, one block south of the National Mall; there, he boarded his armoured train car, the *Ferdinand Magellan*. In this way he avoided the prying eyes at Union Station, along with its steps, which impeded his progress by wheelchair. From Washington, FDR, his aides and his daughter travelled to Newport News, where the USS *Quincy* was waiting. For weeks the ship had undergone secret renovations to make it fit for the president, though it was almost impossible to conceal the work completely. In November Roosevelt had received a letter from a retired U.S. Army soldier, warning FDR that he had overheard two men in a restaurant in Middleburg, Connecticut, talking about a toilet bowl on the *Quincy* being raised nine inches to accommodate a certain person on an upcoming trip. The saying 'Loose lips sink ships' never seemed so appropriate. It became even more difficult to suppress the rumours that something was afoot when Roosevelt held his birthday party on January 21, nine days before his actual birthday, January 30. Having successfully evaded any local Nazi spies and paparazzi en route to Newport News, the entourage set off on the eleven-day, 4,883-mile voyage to the rendezvous with Churchill at Malta.

Among the few in Washington who knew Roosevelt was bound for another tripartite conference, the choice of Anna as his aide was a bit of a surprise. Labor Secretary Frances Perkins had assumed he would take one or more of his sons to assist him physically. General Edwin 'Pa' Watson, FDR's longtime adviser, appointments secretary and close friend, who was often included in Roosevelt's coterie, was among those the president had included in the Yalta delegation. Watson often had the task of helping the president stand in his heavy leg braces. While he could provide FDR with physical support, Anna provided something less tangible. As Watson explained to Perkins before departing, 'Anna can do things with her father and with other people that the boys can't . . . They can't manage him . . . She can tell him, "You mustn't see people. You mustn't do that. You mustn't talk with them. It tires you out. You'll be no good tomorrow." And she can also handle the other people. Without alarming them, she can handle them, and that's why they're going to take her.'

Shortly after they left Washington, John Boettiger wrote to his wife. 'I HATE your being away,' he told Anna, 'but I am so thrilled that you are getting a chance to really be on the inside of a most historic meeting.' He knew how valuable she was to her father and how much this trip meant to both of them, personally and for the future benefit of the world. The sense of being part of history was by no means lost on Anna. When she had moved back into the White House, she had promised not to keep a diary, so that all she heard and saw would remain confidential. But for this conference, she decided to make an exception, so she could later share her experience with John.

But before the next pages in history could be written, FDR would have to survive the trip. Much could go wrong even before they reached Yalta. For eleven days, FDR would be under the close observation of those travelling on the *Quincy*. These included not only personal friends like Watson, who were devoted to Roosevelt, but also some with their own distinctly political aspirations. The president's party had hardly been at sea more than a few days before someone started asking about Roosevelt's health. Jimmy Byrnes, a former South Carolina senator and Supreme Court associate justice, now serving as the head of the Office of War Mobilization and attending the Yalta Conference in this official capacity, quietly mentioned to Anna that FDR did not look too well. In his opinion, the president's haggard appearance and open-mouth stares seemed to indicate that something more than FDR's frequent sinus trouble was amiss. Anna had brushed him off, saying of course it was just his tricky sinuses. Sitting with his mouth open was merely a way to breathe more easily. Byrnes remained sceptical.

If Byrnes was already suspicious, others likely soon would be. The sinus explanation was unlikely to pass muster if FDR's condition deteriorated further, so it was vital that Anna shield her father as much as possible. No one could know just how sick he was: not Byrnes, nor anyone else in the American delegation, but least of all Churchill and Stalin. The continued success of the alliance of Roosevelt, Churchill and Stalin was precariously balanced on the strong personal relationship among the three men. With victory so close at hand, it was imperative that nothing upset that balance.

Fortunately, the voyage to Malta allowed FDR time for plenty of rest. As the ship was travelling under radio silence, he was not obligated to respond to anything but the most urgent messages, to which he would reply via a complex system of couriers. Except for spending some time reading the briefing materials the State Department had prepared for the conference, he was free to relax in the sunshine on deck, nap in his cabin and organise his beloved stamp collection. Once they arrived at Yalta, Bruenn's four-hour rule would have to be suspended for the duration of the conference. It would be impossible for Roosevelt to miss any of the multi-hour plenary sessions or the formal dinners, filled with toasting and speeches, which inevitably would last long into the night. Anna could try to make her father rest as much as possible during the mornings and early afternoons, but with the Americans all under one roof, it would be difficult to stop Secretary of State Stettinius, Harry Hopkins, or other Americans from wandering in to chat. Churchill posed another problem altogether. During their journey on the *Quincy*, he continued to bombard Roosevelt with cable after cable. Some dealt with important military and policy concerns, but mostly they consisted of complaints about the journey to Yalta and the accommodation there.

If the prime minister could wear a person down by cable, he was positively enervating in person. Churchill continued to insist on scheduling private audiences with FDR, but Anna could not allow them. It would not be an exaggeration to say that if Churchill pushed Roosevelt too hard, the president could very well die of exhaustion or stroke. Despite their alliance, Roosevelt had concerns greater than Churchill's wounded feelings. With whatever energy he had left, he had to prioritise American interests as his principal object at Yalta. He could succeed only with cooperation, not just from the British, whose global power had waned considerably over the course of the war, but also from the Soviets.

First, Roosevelt was determined to save American lives, particularly in the Pacific. His generals projected that though their island-hopping strategy – the attacks on small, poorly defended Pacific islands that were well-positioned to serve as air bases midway across the ocean and support an eventual attack on the Japanese home islands – had thus far proved a success, even with recent victories in the Mariana Islands and the Philippines, they could not confidently envision launching a full-scale invasion of Japan itself for at least a year. Furthermore, fighting on the Japanese home islands would likely become a war of attrition. They believed the Allies would eventually win, but if the as-yet-untested wonder weapon failed, the cost of victory could possibly be as many as a million American lives over at least eighteen months of war. If FDR could draw the Soviets into the fight against Japan and thus hasten its conclusion, he could potentially save hundreds of thousands of American soldiers.

Roosevelt's second objective was strategic, and somewhat personal. The Soviet Union had exponentially increased in power under Stalin's leadership; it could no longer be perceived as a distant, mysterious hinterland on the fringe of Europe. Now it was imperative that the Soviets become part of the world order. In Roosevelt's mind, the way to do this was by securing their participation in a global fraternity united by a commitment to peace. FDR's hero Woodrow Wilson had tried to form such a fraternity: the League of Nations. As Wilson's assistant secretary of the navy, Roosevelt had attended the 1919 peace conference in Paris and had seen first-hand the political jockeying and deal-making that ultimately doomed the league. Where Wilson had failed, Roosevelt was determined to succeed. In his vision of a world peace organization that would unite all nations, Soviet participation was crucial. As much as Roosevelt viewed Churchill as a longtime friend and partner, Stalin was the person Roosevelt believed he needed to woo at Yalta. He was confident that Stalin could be swayed by Roosevelt's personal powers of persuasion.

Anna liked Winston Churchill well enough. She had met him when he had come to Washington in May 1943; she had been in Washington then to see her husband off to war. She found him a witty conversationalist, undoubtedly bright, yet also something of a rotund, comical eccentric whose liberal use of snuff produced enormous sneezes that 'practically rock the foundations of the house'. It was, however, one thing to enjoy his company personally and appreciate the value he brought to the wartime partnership, but quite another to embrace his old-fashioned, imperialistic worldview. As Eleanor said in a letter to Anna only a month after the Americans had entered the war after the attack on Pearl Harbor, 'I like Mr. Churchill, he's loveable & emotional & very human but I don't want him to write the peace or carry it out.'

FOUR

February 2, 1945

Averell Harriman had travelled two thousand miles from Moscow to Malta and was prepared to brief Roosevelt on all matters related to Soviet-Polish relations, Soviet demands for reparations, and the cost of Stalin's intervention in the war with Japan. After serving nearly a year and a half as ambassador to the Soviet Union, he had a better understanding of the internal workings of the Soviet regime than perhaps any other American. And yet, when lunch was announced and the president and prime minister headed to FDR's suite on the *Quincy*, with Anna, Sarah, Ed Stettinius, Anthony Eden, Jimmy Byrnes and FDR's chief of staff, Fleet Admiral William Leahy, Averell Harriman was not invited. Clearly it was not intended to be a working lunch.

For days, Harriman had been taking the blame for agreeing to hold the upcoming conference in such a remote, inhospitable location – to make matters all the more irritating, he had twisted his ankle badly on the rocky terrain of Malta. In truth, once Roosevelt had indicated he would agree to a meeting on the Black Sea, there was little Harriman could do to intervene. As he told Sarah Churchill, after nearly running her over with his car while racing to meet Stettinius's plane at RAF Luqa two days earlier, 'Well, it was there, or two worse places.' For the man who had led a charmed life since birth, the conference was off to an inauspicious start.

Handsomer than many of the movie stars who frequented his resort and heir to one of the largest self-made fortunes in America, Harriman had never encountered an obstacle – in business, in sports or in the form of an actual mountain range – that he could not surmount through tenacity, ingenuity, a talented staff and sound investment. He had grown up in a mansion atop a mountain overlooking the Hudson River Valley. In the vast parkland below the house, the three brown bears that his father had captured on the scientific expedition to Alaska lived as pets in spacious cages, and there was a barn filled with several scores of polo ponies next to the base of a funicular. This mechanism transported everything from food to cars to ponies from the bottom of the mountain to the house. From the Union Pacific Railroad, to international shipping lines, to mining companies, to *Newsweek* magazine, to Brown Brothers Harriman, his banking firm, he had found success in nearly every business endeavour he attempted. He approached leisure with the same focus and drive. Rejecting time-consuming rounds of golf in favour of the speed and aggression of polo, he had become one of the top-ranked players in the nation; his team defeated the world-class Argentinians in the 1928 Cup of the Americas. It was only natural that he would eventually turn his attention to government. As Roosevelt's Lend-Lease expediter, he took his relentless energy and business savvy to London, where he oversaw the distribution of more than $30 billion in aid to the British Empire.

Unfortunately, as the past few months had shown, working with the Soviet government was nothing like his previous business dealings, not even the investments he had made in the Soviet Union after World War I, when most businessmen had preferred to leave money on the table than do business in a country suddenly led by the Bolsheviks. There was a saying that Harriman and his staff used at the American embassy in Moscow: when 'trading with the Russians you had to buy the same horse twice'. Over the past six months, Harriman had tried desperately to convince Roosevelt to change his approach to negotiations with the Soviets, but Roosevelt had resisted. If the luncheon snub in Malta was any indication, the president was not about to reconsider.

The lunch ended, but still Roosevelt did not summon Harriman.

Instead of sitting down with his advisers or with the British delegation, as Churchill had intended when he suggested the rendezvous in
Malta, Roosevelt and his daughter set off on a tour of Malta, scheduled to last an hour and a half, with the island's governor general and
his family. Anna invited Sarah Churchill to come along. Making the
rounds of the island was a kind gesture to the local people, but time
was running short. The American and British contingents were leaving for Yalta that night, and still the two delegations had had no substantive discussion about the conference. As Roosevelt drove away for
his afternoon tour, Churchill returned to his ship to take a nap. For all
the influence Harriman was able to exert, he might have remained at
Yalta with Kathy.

It was not the first time during the war that Harriman felt that FDR
had failed to address a problem head-on. Early in the conflict, Harriman thought that Roosevelt did not truly recognise the scope of the
Nazi menace, namely, in the form of the German navy, the Kriegsma-
rine, which Harriman believed was capable of knocking Britain out of
the war. Lend-Lease was a brilliant plan, but it was not enough. The
Americans could send food and materiel across the Atlantic, but if
German U-boats sank the convoys, the British would be left with next
to nothing. If its people were starving, the government would have to
surrender to Hitler. In the spring of 1941, Roosevelt knew American
public opinion did not support a declaration of war on Germany, but
Harriman was frustrated that the president was 'unwilling to lead public opinion or force the issue'. The ambassador feared that the president was once again choosing to downplay a grave danger to American and Allied interests, thus revealing a naive understanding of the
Soviet leadership's true power and ambition.

It was convenient to forget that the Soviet Union had been in league
with the Nazis for a year and a half at the beginning of the war. Averell Harriman had only recently begun his tenure as Roosevelt's Lend-
Lease envoy in London when the Nazis invaded the Soviet Union, in
June 1941. By breaking the Molotov-Ribbentrop non-aggression pact of
1939, the Nazis drove the Soviets into alliance with Britain. Although
the American public held a similarly hostile view towards both the
Communists and the Nazis, there were undeniable benefits to this

new alliance. With the Red Army fighting alongside the British, the Americans might not need to enter the war at all. Roosevelt extended $1 billion in Lend-Lease aid to the USSR. Averell supported Roosevelt's decision wholeheartedly and looked at the alliance with the Soviets as a positive development for both the British and the still neutral Americans. He took a practical stance towards the situation, unconcerned with the Soviets' beliefs about the structure of society, industry and the economy. All that mattered was that they opposed Hitler. 'To put it bluntly, whatever it costs to keep this war away from our shores, that will be a small price to pay,' he explained. (Self-interest may have bolstered his opinion: in July 1941, he still owned $560,000 in Soviet government notes from manganese contracts liquidated in 1928.)

Almost from the outset, however, Kathleen, then just twenty-three, was less convinced than her father that an alliance with Stalin would ultimately be worth the price. As a reporter in London, Kathy had quickly gained a perspective different from her father's. Though most of the time the International News Service assigned her stories with titles like 'Girl's Cheery Song Helped Londoners Forget Their Woes' or 'Girl Reporter Finds Women Hang out Laundry as Usual', her boss slowly began to give her war-oriented beats, at least those that senior reporters had neither the time nor interest to cover. Among them were press conferences with leaders from exiled European governments, from countries such as Czechoslovakia, Yugoslavia and Poland; their prime ministers and kings had fled to London when the Nazis invaded. Just three years earlier, Kathy had been a student at Bennington College, writing her junior thesis on Nazi Germany's increasingly hostile behaviour towards Czechoslovakia. Suddenly she found herself reporting on the tragic results of what she had pondered in theory. At these press conferences, the issue that raised the most immediate concern was not Nazi aggression, but rather Britain's new alliance with the Soviet Union. The exiles were not pleased with the sudden rush of support for Stalin in Britain and the United States.

Neither Kathy nor her father particularly valued rest. In their suite at the Dorchester Hotel, father and daughter would stay up talking about the state of the world long into the night. Sometimes these conversations turned into healthy debate. 'Since I've been [g]oing around in the free-gov't circles,' Kathy wrote to her sister, 'I've found a very different Stalin feeling. (Different from Averell.) They distrust him and fear him and figure he's doing a good job of out-smarting the Americans and the British.' The exiled Polish leaders were particularly vocal. They argued that Stalin would look for any opportunity to seize Poland and install a de facto Soviet regime. Kathy believed them. Not until the late summer of 1944 would Averell realise that Kathy had been right to listen.

In October 1943, Roosevelt appointed Harriman ambassador to the Soviet Union. Despite the Poles' continued warnings that Stalin could not be trusted, Harriman remained convinced that the Soviets' objectives aligned with those of the West. Logically, the Soviets' historical desire to have friendly neighbours made sense, especially on their vulnerable western border, where they had sparred with Poland since the reign of Catherine the Great and been attacked by invading forces, from Napoleon in 1812 to the Wehrmacht in 1941. But Harriman did not think Stalin would go so far as to impose Communist puppet governments in countries such as Poland, or take over completely. He believed the United States should be prepared to take a firm stance if the Soviets stepped out of line, lest the Americans risk 'storing up trouble for the future'. However, like many westerners, including Churchill and Roosevelt, he believed in the power of strong personal relationships with Soviet leaders. Harriman was a businessman, and people liked to do business with people they liked. Did that not apply to Soviet politicians as much as to American industrialists or financiers?

For nearly a year, Harriman persisted in this assumption, until a much crueller reality became apparent. What Kathy had heard in London from the exiled Polish leaders was borne out in August 1944.

Throughout the war, the Poles had maintained an active resistance network, especially in occupied Warsaw, where they waged a guerrilla battle against the Nazis against heavy odds. For a brief moment in the summer of 1944, conditions tilted in the Poles' favour. The Nazi troops in Warsaw were weaker, and the Red Army was quickly approaching. The Poles knew they could not expel the Nazis from Poland entirely without Soviet assistance, but they also realised that the Soviet Union would eagerly absorb Poland if given the chance to put boots on the ground, especially with the Americans and the British distracted with their own battles raging across Western Europe and the Mediterranean. If the Polish resistance could secure Warsaw before the Red Army arrived, they could make a compelling case to the western Allies that the Poles were a formidable force worthy of an independent place in the world, not a dispensable people to be cast off to the Soviets the moment they were free of the Nazi yoke. The Warsaw Uprising began on August 1. At first, the plan looked promising. The Polish resistance secured central Warsaw, but food and ammunition quickly dwindled. The fighters expected the Red Army to arrive any day, bringing supplies and reinforcements. However, the Soviets, now just miles from Warsaw across the Vistula River, suddenly stopped. With no ammunition, the Poles became sitting ducks for the Nazis. Their courageous uprising became a mass slaughter. Over 200,000 Poles, mostly civilians, were killed, and the city was almost completely destroyed.

When Harriman discovered that the Red Army was simply sitting and watching from the banks of the Vistula as the Nazis destroyed the Polish resistance, he was shocked. Unable to comprehend why the Soviets would allow the Nazis to retake the upper hand in Warsaw, he lobbied the Soviet government to allow American and British planes to use Soviet airfields to resupply the Polish resistance. Stalin refused. No amount of personal persuasion could move him. Harriman began to realise the West had sorely miscalculated. They had misunderstood the man they had jocularly referred to as 'Uncle Joe'. Churchill defied Stalin and ordered the RAF to airdrop whatever supplies it could. Meanwhile, Harriman anxiously tried to convince Roosevelt, who at the time was campaigning for re-election, that it was imperative for the Americans to take a hard line with Stalin before the Soviets ran unchecked across Eastern Europe. But Roosevelt and the State Department had other priorities. They were more concerned that such intervention would jeopardise future American-Soviet cooperation, both in military terms and in the Soviets' commitment to an international peace organisation. Representatives from the three Allied nations would be convening to discuss this organisation at Dumbarton Oaks in Washington, D.C., on August 21. Roosevelt would allow nothing to derail those plans. While tragic, the resistance in Warsaw was simply another wartime casualty.

As Kathy told her sister in a letter, it was a 'very bloody time' for their father. By the middle of August, anxiety over Poland had taken a heavy toll on him. A tall, athletic man, Averell lost an alarming amount of weight, his frame dropping to a mere 160 pounds, and he developed stomach ulcers. Kathy became gravely concerned for his health. But, casting Kathy's worries aside, he continued to press his case, arguing through the night with Stalin's deputies, sometimes until 6.30 in the morning. As Averell waited for the inevitable call from the Kremlin every evening, he needed something to calm his racing mind. The only thing that helped was games of bezique. Kathy would sit with him and play trick after trick. Averell usually beat her handily. Over the first seven months of 1944, Kathy accumulated a 100,000-point deficit. Suddenly, in the late summer of 1944, she began winning. She triumphed so often that she nearly drew even, but she knew her victories had little to do with her ability. Averell's mind was elsewhere.

The ambassador was desperate for help. He could not fight the Soviets on Poland by himself. Finally, Harriman appealed to Harry Hopkins, urging him to make the president understand the severity of the situation, not just for Poland, but also for the United States: 'The policy appears to be crystallizing to force us and the British to accept all Soviet policies, backed by the strength and prestige of the Red Army ... The general attitude seems to be that it is our obligation to help Russia and accept her policies because she has won the war for us. I am convinced that we can divert this trend but only if we materially change our policy toward the Soviet Government ... They have misinterpreted our generous attitude toward them as a sign of weakness ... Unless we take issue with the present policy there is every indication the Soviet Union will become a world bully.'

Harriman asked permission to come to Washington to brief Roosevelt in person. His request was denied. Meanwhile, the Nazis continued to ravage Warsaw. In September, Stalin finally agreed to aid the Poles, but by then it was too late. One-quarter of the city's population was dead.

While the Warsaw Uprising fundamentally altered Harriman's view of the Soviets, it also drove a wedge between the ambassador and the president who had appointed him. Though Harriman and Roosevelt were the patriarchs of two of New York's elite families, they did not always see eye to eye. In fact, the Harrimans and Roosevelts had clashed long before either FDR or Averell Harriman rose to prominence. In the early 1900s, Averell's father and FDR's cousin Teddy Roosevelt developed a fierce political rivalry in New York State, prompting Teddy Roosevelt to launch an antitrust investigation into E. H. Harriman's way holdings. And though Averell Harriman had joined FDR's New Deal administration partly out of the sense of civic duty inherited from his liberal-minded father, he was not initially a true believer in its progressive agenda. Formerly a Republican, he had shifted his allegiance to the Democrats in part out of pragmatism. But it required a nudge from his sister, Mary Harriman Rumsey, the founder of the Junior League and Roosevelt's appointed chairman of the Consumer Advisory Board, for Harriman to join the New Deal. At the time, the newspapers mocked him, dubbing him one of the administration's 'tame millionaires', but he formed an unlikely and genuine friendship with Harry Hopkins, who had risen from his early days as a poor Midwestern social worker to become Roosevelt's closest adviser. It was Hopkins who had convinced FDR to appoint Harriman as his Lend-Lease envoy in London at the end of 1940.

But the deeper problem between Harriman and Roosevelt had to do with control. Averell Harriman's fortune outstripped FDR's by orders of magnitude. With such wealth came both purchasing power and a certain degree of political independence. Unlike the rest of FDR's inner circle, who depended on the president for position and prestige, Harriman did not need proximity to FDR to gain influence, nor did he rely on government funds. He took no salary as Lend-Lease envoy and paid for much of the Moscow embassy entertainment for the Soviets out of his own pocket. Roosevelt therefore lacked the necessary tools to rein in Harriman, save for one. FDR could control him by granting, or refusing to grant, access. Before the Atlantic Charter meeting with Churchill in 1941, Harriman had to seek the president's permission to attend multiple times before FDR finally agreed to bring him.

FDR similarly refused to dispatch Harriman to represent American interests at the Moscow Conference in 1942, forcing Harriman to appeal to Churchill to send Roosevelt a message requesting Harriman's presence at the meeting. Churchill did so happily. Eventually, FDR relented.

Though the two were never overtly at odds, relations between Roosevelt and Harriman reached a low point in October 1944 – with Warsaw already reduced to rubble – when Harriman was finally allowed to return to Washington to brief Roosevelt on Eastern Europe. During their first meeting, Harriman quickly found his efforts frustrated. It was nearly impossible to speak with the president alone. Harriman had much experience with FDR's ever-present coterie, but a new individual now seemed to be his mainstay: Anna was never far from his side. Harriman had no personal grievance with Anna, but her presence did cause complications. Harriman had travelled five thousand miles to brief the president on the desperate situation in Warsaw and to update him on developments in the Pacific. But at their first meeting, he could not fully disclose all information, as he did not know if Anna had clearance to hear classified reports. Then, during another meeting, Anna's son Johnny wandered in with his Labrador retriever. The president stopped to chat with the boy, so Harriman's briefing had to wait until Johnny ambled off to the garden.

When Harriman was finally able to describe the alarming developments to Roosevelt in detail, he was sorely disappointed by FDR's response. 'The President consistently shows very little interest in Eastern European matters except as they affect sentiment in America,' Harriman wrote in his minutes, noting that FDR had 'no conception of the determination of the Russians to settle matters in which they consider that they have a vital interest . . . on their own terms,' particularly in Poland. Ten months earlier, when the subject had turned to the beleaguered country at the Tehran Conference, he had callously joked, 'I don't care two hoots about Poland . . . Wake me up when we talk about Germany,' before pretending to fall asleep. Frankly, he told Harriman in May 1944, he 'didn't care whether the countries bordering Russia became communized', as it had little impact on U.S. public opinion.

But perhaps even more concerning was the fact that FDR remained convinced that Stalin would bend to American will through personal persuasion, just as Harriman had once naively believed. Roosevelt had previously told Churchill, 'Being brutally frank . . . I think I can personally handle Stalin better than either your Foreign Office or my State Department. Stalin hates the guts of all your top people. He thinks he likes me better, and I hope he will continue to do so.' After so many failed negotiations during the Warsaw Uprising, Harriman had painfully learned that such confidence in candour and apparent friendship was futile. Harriman would not go so far as to forcefully express his opinions; that would risk alienating Roosevelt. He had seen Gil Winant, the United States ambassador to the United Kingdom, do this as he strenuously advocated for the exiled Polish government living in London. The result, of course, was that Winant found himself iced out of the upcoming conference. Harriman enjoyed his position at the heart of geopolitics and had political aspirations that reached beyond serving as an ambassador in the Roosevelt administration. Still, he returned to Moscow in late November 1944 thoroughly disheartened and dejected. 'I do not believe that I have convinced the President of the importance of a vigilant firm policy in dealing with the political aspects in various Eastern European countries when the problems arise,' he concluded in his memorandum.

By the time Averell left Kathy in Yalta as he departed for Malta, his dire outlook had not changed. Though Poland's postwar borders and governance were to be a major topic of discussion at Yalta, like Churchill, Harriman feared it was already too late. The Americans had failed to truly challenge the Soviets on Poland throughout the latter half of 1944, and now the Red Army controlled Polish territory up to the Oder River, just miles from the German border. Regardless of what the western Allies argued at the conference, it seemed that Soviet designs on Poland were, as Harriman warned the new secretary of state, Edward Stettinius, 'virtually a *fait accompli*'. Not even the famous Roosevelt charm could change that.

When Roosevelt returned from his tour of the island at 4.30, Harriman finally learned that his services were required – only it was not the president who required them. As soon as FDR had arrived back at the *Quincy*, he went straight to a military briefing with his Joint Chiefs of Staff. The Roosevelt who needed Harriman's help was Anna. FDR had given her seventeen dollars to shop for gifts to bring home to the White House staff, as there would be no souvenirs to buy at Yalta. There were two problems with that. First, seventeen dollars was not nearly enough. Second, the shops would close in less than half an hour. The normally stoical ambassador took pity on Anna. FDR did not want his advice. He had nothing better to do. He might as well help her.

Averell Harriman was one of the wealthiest, most powerful people in the world, an expert across many areas of business and government. But he did happen to know a particular detail about shopping in Malta: the world-renowned Maltese lace was just the gift required. As Averell never carried a wallet, he had already asked a local administrator's wife to collect some for him. He generously told Anna she could take her pick from his own selection. They could go to the woman's house and look at it right away. Anna readily agreed, so the ambassador and the president's daughter went off together to examine piles of lace.

FIVE

February 2–3, 1945

Shortly after 11 p.m., Sarah, Anna, and their fathers arrived at Malta's RAF Luqa. Official cars were descending on the airport in droves, and the British and American delegates now spilled out of the vehicles onto the tarmac and made their way to their assigned Yorks and C-54 Skymasters, their path illuminated by one lone spotlight in the blackout. 'The Russians had been told that we were bringing 35 people a piece,' Sarah had remarked to her mother the day before. 'The total complement of souls is now 535!' Some were already based in Russia or had travelled there by ship, but the majority now stood on the airfield. Thousands of pieces of luggage and supplies were being loaded onto the planes: personal bags marked with white labels, hand luggage with buff labels, and cases containing secret documents bearing distinctive yellow labels with black bands. Roosevelt and his party looked on at the bustling activity as their bags were ferried away to their aircraft. Standing near the president was the forty-four-year-old secretary of state, Edward Stettinius, his customary Homburg covering his prematurely white hair, which contrasted starkly with his heavy, dark eyebrows. The president joked to Stettinius that the combined western delegation was so large that it might appear to the Russians to be 'a minor invasion'.

Sarah Churchill knew what an invasion looked like. She had spent the autumn of 1942 at RAF Medmenham preparing for Operation

Torch, the Allied invasion of North Africa. As a section officer in the aerial reconnaissance division, Sarah and her fellow intelligence analysts worked around the clock scrutinising pilots' aerial photographs of German and Italian shipyards, railways, troop movements and factories – vital information that informed Allied naval invasions, ground assaults and bombing strategies. The training was intensely difficult for men and women alike. They had to look at photographs taken from ten thousand feet above ground and discern whether an area of grass had been disturbed by troop movements or grazing animals. They learned to differentiate between types of ships solely by the shadows they cast, and how to layer images to create three dimensions, use complicated slide rules, and compute logarithms.

For Sarah, Operation Torch represented one of the triumphs of her war experience – but not because of the invasion itself. During a weekend leave that November, Sarah had driven to Chequers, the country estate of British prime ministers north of London, on an army motorcycle. When she arrived, she immediately went up to see her father, who was dressing for dinner. While meticulously brushing the two or three hairs that remained on his otherwise bald head, he conspiratorially turned to Sarah and said, 'At this very moment, sliding stealthily through the Straits of Gibraltar under cover of darkness, go five hundred and forty-two ships, for the landings in North Africa.'

It was rare that Sarah knew any military subject better than Winston, but on this occasion, she did. 'Two hundred and forty-three,' she corrected him, unable to help herself.

'How do you know?' he shot back.

Sarah had spent the past three months poring over images of the region. She had analysed the locations where the ships would drop anchor and knew exactly how large a fleet would land along the French Moroccan and Algerian coasts.

Impressed, her father demanded to know why she had not told him what she had been working on. Sarah retorted, 'I believe there is such a thing as security.' Instead of erupting in a 'blaze of anger' at this apparent impertinence, Winston chuckled. Later that night, he proceeded to regale his guests with the story. He also repeated it to Eleanor Roosevelt, who was in England, visiting British women engaged in war work. Amused, she in turn told the tale to the American press.

Several days later, Sarah found herself summoned to the Air Ministry. Officials there accused her of breaching security by divulging the details of a major Allied invasion. 'Who told Mrs Roosevelt this story?' they insisted.

Sarah could only reply, 'My father.'

Her superiors were simultaneously frustrated and amused. There was nothing the Air Ministry could do about it.

This evening, however, there was little room for humour. As Winston and Sarah bid their delegates from the Foreign Office a temporary goodbye as they were shown to their respective aircraft, neither the prime minister nor the foreign secretary yet had any concrete information about the fate of their colleagues and friends whose York had crashed into the Mediterranean Sea. Surely the tragedy cast an air of unease over the flight ahead – one that was, objectively speaking, far more dangerous than the trip from Britain to Malta. The transport planes were unpressurised, so the two delegations would fly to the Crimea at a low altitude – no more than six thousand feet – leaving them exposed to the smattering of Nazi anti-aircraft units that remained on the Aegean Islands. There was also a real risk of Turkish anti-aircraft fire. Still technically neutral, the Turks did not intend to fire at Allied planes, but they had mistakenly shot at a British plane carrying part of the advance team from Malta to the Crimea ahead of the conference; the attack left the tail riddled with shell holes. Roosevelt's and Churchill's planes would each travel surrounded by six P-38s for protection, but for the dozen remaining transports, the only safeguard was to fly under the cover of darkness. It was imperative that each aircraft take off at a precisely scheduled moment. Once the planes reached the Crimea, further complications could arise. It was reported that heavy fog was expected to hover over the Saki airfield for most of the day, leaving a narrow window of time for the VIP-laden planes to make a safe landing. Soviet airfields lacked the technological support a pilot needed to land a plane using instruments alone in conditions of poor visibility.

Danger aside, Anna Roosevelt was relieved to be getting under-way as she boarded their C-54 – nicknamed the *Sacred Cow* – the first plane ever custom-made for the president of the United States. She enjoyed being her father's girl Friday, but he did not make the job easy. She had spent the past eight hours in a frenzy. Her father seemed to assume that Anna could read his mind. After the tour of Malta and the potential souvenir debacle, which Harriman had sorted out for her, FDR had instructed Anna to make arrangements for dinner. He did not tell her whom he wished to invite, nor even how many people would attend, and as he had already left for the military briefing, all she could do was make an educated guess. Then she 'frantically' raced around, distributing invitations. Meanwhile, she was fretting about her father's condition after the strain of the long, exhausting day – with dinner still ahead. After the briefing with the chiefs of staff, she thought FDR would finally be able to take a short break, but Stettinius and Eden slipped into his room for a pre-dinner chin wag when she was not looking. Then an unannounced visitor appeared out of the blue: Randolph Churchill, the prime minister's son. Churchill decid-edly had not asked him along for the conference. Randolph, who was stationed in Yugoslavia, had come to Malta en route to Italy to have some dental work done, which just so happened to coincide with his father's visit. Having heard that Randolph 'annoy[ed] his father', Anna tried to keep him out of the way. She invited Randolph and Sarah for drinks in her cabin while she plotted the most diplomatic way to get rid of him before dinner. After all, Sarah had explicitly been invited, but Randolph had not. ('We had a visit from Randolph,' Sarah cryp-tically reported to Clementine, knowing just how much her brother could frustrate Winston. 'I will tell you about that in another letter.') Randolph quickly realised he was getting the brushoff; fortunately he excused himself, without making a scene, for a 'pressing engagement' back on the *Sirius*.

Dinner finally came and went, and just when Anna thought she had a few minutes to quickly throw her things into the appropriate cases and bags before leaving for the airfield, a peeved Harry Hop-kins – who had just had a run-in with Anthony Eden – turned up at her room, looking for a drink. Anna begrudgingly opened the case she had finally finished packing and offered him a dram of the scotch she had brought along. But when her back was turned, Hopkins walked off with the bottle. She was not terribly upset to lose the scotch itself. However, the bottle was packed in a special box her husband had carried with him while serving in the Mediterranean; keeping it with her made Anna feel as if some small piece of him was nearby. Hopkins had taken it without a thought.

At 11.30 p.m. the engines of the planes scheduled to leave first roared to life. The noise was thunderous. They took off at ten-minute intervals and soared eastward into the night, blue flames trailing behind them. One by one over the next four hours, the planes disappeared into the dark sky until just two transports and their fighter escorts remained. At 3.30 a.m., the *Sacred Cow* took flight, followed minutes later by the prime minister's Skymaster.

Much to the chagrin of Dr Bruenn and the chief of the president's Secret Service detail, Mike Reilly, Roosevelt refused to use a safety belt while he slept in his bed during the flight. Concerned that the president might roll out and injure himself if the plane braked suddenly on takeoff, Dr Bruenn had crept over to FDR's berth and lain down along the side. The young doctor thought he had managed to sneak in without Roosevelt's realising he had an uninvited bunkmate. The doctor was wrong. FDR later told him, with a wink and a smile, 'It's lucky I recognized you as you came in.'

At 8.30 a.m. local time, the planes began to break through a low ceiling of clouds, landing at Saki with perfect choreography. Everything around the airfield was carefully staged for their arrival. The Soviets had erected tents brimming with refreshments beside the runway, a resplendent Red Army band stood ready to burst into triumphant martial music, and a long line of black armoured Lend-Lease Packards and Russian-made hearselike ZiS limousines were poised to take the delegates off to Yalta, once they had been feted properly.

Between the planes' cinematic entrance and the lavish cornucopia the Soviets seemed to conjure out of thin air on the barren steppe, it seemed the delegates had landed on a film set. But as they emerged from their planes, they stepped not into the Technicolor world of Oz, but into Dorothy's sepia-toned Kansas. Gone were the sun-drenched, rosy limestone buildings and the cerulean waters of Malta. From the concrete tarmac to the snow-covered fields stretching towards the distant, overcast horizon, the land was flat, featureless and colourless. Robert Hopkins, Harry Hopkins's twenty-two-year-old son and a photographer with the U.S. Army Signal Corps, was travelling with the American delegation as the principal American photographer. He had brought a few precious rolls of colour film, but to use more than one at Saki would have been a waste. The crimson on the three Allied flags, flying from masts along the airfield, presented the only contrast to various tones of grey, which dominated the landscape.

Harriman, Stettinius, Hopkins, Eden and General George Marshall were among the earlier arrivals at ALBATROSS, the code name the Americans irreverently assigned to Saki and its dangerously short runway. The landing strip was just a path of concrete slabs pitted with shell holes, which the Soviets had smoothed as well as they could. The whole thing was covered by a layer of ice. Stettinius remarked that it was like landing on a slippery 'tile floor'. Miraculously, there had been no mishaps. General Aleksei Antonov of the Red Army had arrived promptly to greet General Marshall. As Marshall stepped off the plane, Antonov invited him to sample the lavish breakfast beneath the tents. Entering the feast-laden pavilion, the humble Pennsylvanian was pleased to find a tumbler full of what looked like fruit juice. Upon closer inspection, Marshall, a teetotaller, discovered that he was wrong. The tumbler was brimming with Crimean brandy. Unflappable as ever, Marshall stepped away from the noxiously sweet digestif. Without a backward glance, he turned to his men and muttered, 'Let's get going.' They departed promptly for Yalta, along with Hopkins, who had become seriously ill during the flight. Stettinius, Eden and Harriman were left to wait in the damp cold for the president and the prime minister. Among them, only Harriman, dressed in a custom-made calf-length leather flight jacket, with fur lining, looked both rakish and at least somewhat prepared for the change in weather. The others had to be content with steaming glasses of sweet Russian tea to stave off the chill seeping through their woollen overcoats.

At ten past noon, the *Sacred Cow* touched down at Saki and came to a rest on the side of the runway. While FDR readied himself to disembark, Anna hurried off the plane in time to see Churchill's Skymaster emerge from the clouds. The crowd gathered as the prime minister's plane taxied to a halt. Soon the door of the fuselage opened and Churchill emerged, dressed in a military greatcoat and an officer's cap, with a mischievous smile on his face and an eight-inch cigar clenched between his teeth. He gave the assembled crowd a little salute before carefully waddling down the stairs. Sarah followed moments later and joined Anna off to the side. Sarah was once again in uniform and no worse for wear after the overnight flight, while Anna seemed to be getting into the Russian spirit, having changed out of her simple tweed coat into a fur. The Soviet minister of foreign affairs, Vyacheslav Molotov, had been waiting for the distinguished visitors and now greeted the prime minister. The puglike Molotov was dressed all in black, from his double-breasted overcoat to his *ushanka*, a traditional Russian fur cap with the earflaps tied on top, which accentuated what Churchill described as Molotov's 'cannon-ball head'. Surely Molotov, who as a young Bolshevik had chosen that moniker, which meant 'hammer', would not have appreciated the teasing. Churchill knew that despite the amusing headwear, the Soviet foreign minister was ruthless and calculating, with his penetrating eyes and a 'smile of Siberian winter'. Shaking hands with Churchill, Molotov explained through his interpreter, the sallow, shrewish Vladimir Pavlov, that Stalin had not yet arrived in the Crimea. In the meantime, Molotov would be representing the general secretary.

Together, Churchill and Molotov stood waiting for Roosevelt to emerge from the *Sacred Cow*. Normally, FDR was carried down the steps of an aircraft, but the *Sacred Cow*'s engineers had installed an elevator that lowered him and his wheelchair from the belly of the fuselage to the ground. There, an open Jeep, one of the thousands of American vehicles that Harriman had negotiated to send to the USSR under Lend-Lease, was waiting. The Soviets had thoughtfully retrofitted it, so that the seat put Roosevelt at the same height as those walking along-side him. Everyone, from Churchill and Molotov to the Red Army sol-diers, looked on as Mike Reilly hoisted FDR out of his chair and into the Jeep. It was one of those rare moments when Roosevelt, always so protective of his public image, had no choice but to display his physi-cal vulnerability. In that instant, Churchill could not help but pity the man. The illusion of strength faded ever so briefly, revealing Roosevelt, in Churchill's sentimental mind, as a 'tragic figure'. The Soviets had covered the seat of Roosevelt's Jeep with a Kazak carpet, which lent him the appearance of an elderly maharajah as he moved forward, with Churchill and Molotov walking alongside, to review the troops. (Churchill's doctor, Lord Moran, described the scene less charitably, comparing the president to an elderly Queen Victoria in a phaeton, with the prime minister in the role of a lowly attendant trailing be-hind.)

As Roosevelt, Churchill and Molotov watched the white-gloved So-viet soldiers in knee-high boots stomping resolutely through the oily puddles, their rifles with fixed bayonets held over their shoulders in precise position, Sarah and Anna took in the scene together. The Red Army band began to play the Soviet national anthem. As she listened to the tune, Anna thought it strangely melancholy. And yet its sad air seemed appropriate in this place. As Sarah observed, they were stand-ing in the midst of 'a great wide open blank space of nothing covered with snow'. Any buildings that had once stood within view had been destroyed in the war.

While Sarah took in the barren horizon, Anna pulled out her cam-era. She had brought it to take some keepsake snapshots to share with her husband when she returned. She noticed a group of official Soviet photographers and a film crew standing nearby. Through the view-finder of her camera, she caught a glimpse of her father, which intro-duced yet another worry. At home, FDR and the American press had formed a gentleman's agreement. Newspapers refrained from printing pictures that revealed his wheelchair. Many Americans did not even realise Roosevelt did not have the use of his legs. It was unlikely that the Soviet photographers would be quite so accommodating.

It was not just Roosevelt's disability that concerned her. Churchill seemed amused by the review, while Molotov looked on with a scowl, as if secretly irritated to be standing out in the foul weather for yet another parade. By contrast, Anna's father appeared only half present, as if pasted into the tableau from a different scene altogether. Anna knew that the long day at Malta, followed by a short night of sleep on the plane, had left him more haggard than usual, but the difference between the prime minister and her father was striking. Though more than seven years younger than Churchill, FDR looked older: his cheekbones were sunken, and the lines around his mouth and jowls appeared weatherworn. He was dressed in his customary Brooks Brothers naval boatcloak, but instead of lending him the air of a dapper yachtsman, the garment seemed to swallow him, making him look more gaunt than he was. Just as Byrnes had noticed on the ship to Malta, he sat with his mouth hanging open for long stretches, sometimes staring off into the distance, his skin waxen. To a sick man, the camera lens could be incredibly unforgiving. But there was nothing Anna could do. The Soviet photographers continued to snap away.

The procession of Packards and ZiS limousines snaking across the Crimean steppe towards Yalta had only begun their journey, but Sarah could already sense they were off to a 'sticky start'. The rough, slushy roads, pockmarked by winter and war, rattled the passengers' bones as the convoy crawled along at a mere twenty miles per hour. At this rate, the final eighty miles to Yalta would take almost as long as the fourteen-hundred-mile flight from Malta.

The Crimea had long been a crossroads of conflict and imperialism. Since antiquity, Taurians, Greeks, Persians, Venetians, Genoese and the Tatar Khanate, a Muslim state of the Ottoman Empire, had lorded over the Crimea until, in 1783, the Russians annexed the khanate in the name of Catherine the Great. Each coloniser had left the Crimea with vestiges of its heritage; the local culture presented a mix of Mediterranean, Moorish and Russian influences. Cities such as Sevastopol derived their names from the Greek language, while the Uchan-Su waterfall, on the southern coast, took its name from the Tatar words for 'flying water'. The natural environment was every bit as diverse. The south, known for its rich greenery, beachfront resorts and sub-tropical temperatures, resembled southern France, but the Crimea's likeness to the Mediterranean quickly disappeared as one travelled in-land. Behind the beaches, the Crimean mountains rose suddenly like waves thrust skywards from the depths of the Black Sea. North of the mountains, the dramatic peaks gradually gave way to the flatlands of the steppe. In summer, the steppe was like a prairie, filled with flow-ers and lush grasses, but in winter, a cycle of frosts and thaws left the bleak expanse shrouded in thick fog. The steppe swept less than a hundred miles north to the Kherson Oblast, where a natural border between the Crimea and the Ukrainian heartland was formed by the Sivash, a series of salt-rich lagoons nicknamed the 'Rotten Sea', for the putrid odour emanating from their shallow waters. Microalgae turned the Sivash a startling deep red, as if the blood spilled by thousands of soldiers over two centuries of wars fought across the peninsula had collected and pooled in the lagoons. The Crimea was one of Russia's, and later the Soviet Union's, most prized lands, but it always stood slightly apart from Mother Russia. The Isthmus of Perekop, a four-mile strip of land between the crimson Sivash and the Black Sea, was all that connected the Crimea to the mainland.

After what felt like 'an eternity', Winston grumpily turned to Sarah and asked how long she thought they had been driving.

'About an hour,' she replied.

'Christ,' he muttered sharply under his breath, 'five more hours of this.'

Sarah knew it was hardly Averell Harriman's fault that Yalta had been selected as the conference location, but as they drove along through the barren steppe, she could not help but join the chorus of criticism. 'Really!' she thought. 'Averil [sic] must be mad' to force Roo-sevelt to suffer through such a drive. As their car crawled along, Lord Moran, who was driving with Winston and Sarah, noted that the miles and miles of frozen, foggy steppe reminded him of northern England's haunting moors covered in snow. It was an appropriate comparison. Perhaps recalling Emily Brontë's *Wuthering Heights*, Sarah scribbled in a letter to her mother that the expanse of countryside looked 'as bleak as the soul in despair!'

Once, this desolate land had been dotted with cooperative farms. Though neither Sarah nor Anna knew it as they drove south, the destruction the Nazis had wrought in the Crimea masked the brutality the Soviets had already inflicted on their own people there. The charred cooperative farms, which Stalin had organised in response to a grain shortfall in 1928, were vestiges not of agrarian prosperity destroyed by war, but of state-sponsored famine. Between 1928 and 1940, Soviet collectivisation led to the deaths of millions of peasants. Nowhere was the death toll worse than in Ukraine, where the famine disguised another objective – the Holodomor – the Soviets' genocide of ethnic Ukrainians. And in the depopulated city of Simferopol, the Nazis had given the Soviets the conditions they needed to eliminate another ethnic minority supposedly hostile to the state. The Soviets wanted unobstructed access to the Dardanelles and Turkey, but in their way stood the Crimean Muslim Tatars, with whom the Turks shared religious and ethnic ties. Stalin tasked his ruthless NKVD chief, Lavrentiy Beria, the same man in charge of preparations at Yalta, with their removal. Beria accused the Tatars of collaborating with the Nazis, and over the course of three days in May 1944, he loaded nearly 200,000 Tatars on cattle trains and forcibly deported them to Uzbekistan, where many died in exile.

Now their farms stood abandoned. Nearly all the buildings lay in scorched ruins alongside charred remains of trains, tanks and other instruments of war, as if General Sherman had risen from the dead for an encore march to the sea halfway across the world. The only people the travellers saw as they rolled slowly southwards were Soviet soldiers, many of them women and teenage girls, who stood at attention along the road every several hundred feet. It appeared that an entire infantry division had been pulled off the line to guard the route, though the presence of these careworn soldiers could hardly have been more than ceremonial. Few carried rifles. More striking than their gender or their lack of arms were their faces. The soldiers had been drawn from the many ethnic groups that made up the

Soviet Union – Russians, Ukrainians, Byelorussians, Georgians, Armenians, Azerbaijanis, Uzbeks, Kazakhs, Chechens and more. Each soldier, bundled in a long, padded coat, was intended to be a nameless copy of the preceding soldier, an identical cog in the wheel of the state. But their faces betrayed individuality.

Not until the convoy reached Simferopol did any signs of daily human life appear, albeit scenes more reminiscent of black-and-white newsreels than humanity in the flesh. Simferopol was once a thriving city under Catherine the Great, but by 1945, describing it as a city was generous. The few buildings that remained standing had no heat or electricity, and the inhabitants barely seemed to belong to the modern world. Their clothes were colourless. 'Neither gray nor brown – just plain drab,' Anna observed from the window of the Packard she shared with her father and his Secret Service agent, Mike Reilly. The women's skirts were voluminous, shapeless sacks, and it had clearly been years since the children had any new clothes. Over that time, they had grown. Their trousers and skirts were all too short, exposing their ankles and shins to the cold. At first, Anna thought they looked surprisingly healthy, considering the circumstances, but upon closer inspection, she saw their faces. She realised that the children, and especially the mothers, looked remarkably old. The women's skin was deeply wrinkled, and their lower backs were permanently curved from carrying heavy burdens.

After the convoy left Simferopol and began its ascent into the mountains, the Americans briefly pulled to the side of the road to eat the sandwiches they had brought from the *Quincy*. But the British pressed on. Harriman had assured them that a rest house stood only forty-five minutes away, and they were eager to find it – especially Sarah, who was experiencing one of the uncomfortable realities of being one of only two women present. 'The rest house,' Sarah wrote with amusement to her mother, was 'most necessary for more reasons than resting'. But the forty-five minutes passed, and it did not appear. Stale ham sandwiches and sips of brandy mollified her appetite, but they had been driving for nearly four hours, and the call of nature was growing more urgent with every passing minute. At one point, she desperately considered finding a clump of trees along the side of the road: 'I scanned the horizon – Cars in front – press photographers behind!! Obviously no future in that!' she told Clementine. Finally, when Sarah's 'hope had nearly died', they stopped. Mercifully, they had found the house.

Sarah and Winston expected to stop only a few minutes to use the facilities, but their Soviet hosts apparently had other plans. When they finished washing, they were led into a small room. Molotov had beaten them to the rest house and now stood, grinning, beside a table 'groaning with food and wine'. Like the overwhelmingly indulgent display of food beneath the tents at Saki, here was bounty strikingly incongruous with the dismal montages of subsistence living that the western travellers had observed over the past four hours. Ever the gracious hosts, Molotov, his deputy Andrey Vyshinsky, and the Soviet ambassador to Britain, Fedor Gusev, beckoned for them to sit. The table clearly had been laid for the three Soviet politicians, the prime minister, the president and the daughters to enjoy a sumptuous private luncheon. The Soviets had anticipated their every need. They had even constructed a ramp, covered in rugs, at the front door so Roosevelt could enter in ease and comfort.

But when he arrived a few minutes later, Roosevelt was fixated solely on the fact that several hours of driving still stretched on before them, mostly over dangerous mountain roads. As it was, they would barely reach Yalta before dark. He was exhausted and eager to press on. Observing the appalling destruction from the windows of the Packard had left him in a dark frame of mind. As they drove, he had turned jto Anna and said that he wanted 'to exact an eye for an eye from the Germans, even more than ever'.

Anna, however, was desperate to get out of the car, even just for a moment. Facing the same problem as Sarah, she 'begged' her father 'to be allowed to stop' just for a moment for purposes other than dining. He could hardly deny her. But as she was the one getting out of the car, she would be the one to 'pave the way with Mr. Molotov with a refusal' from FDR.

When Anna entered the rest house, she discovered with 'horror' the spread of delicacies assembled on the table: 'vodka, wines, caviar, fish, bread, butter – and heaven what was to follow'. FDR had never cared for lavish Russian delicacies; he had brought his own chefs to the Tehran Conference so he could eat the food he preferred. Harriman had once again arranged with Molotov for FDR to bring his own food, along with his longtime Filipino mess crew, to Yalta, but now it was not simply a matter of culinary preference. Dr Bruenn had placed FDR on a severely restricted diet to reduce his dangerously high blood pressure. Heavy, salty foods like those piled high on the table and copious amounts of alcohol were expressly prohibited. Anna knew that her father's blood pressure had been extremely high the night before. Even small deviations from his strict diet could put him in grave danger. Even if FDR had wanted to stop for lunch to be polite, he simply could not eat the caviar, cured fish and meats that lay before her.

Anna spent the next few minutes running back and forth between her father in the car and Molotov in the house, trying to decline the invitation to lunch as graciously as possible. She had no Russian vocabulary, so she had to enlist Pavlov, the Soviet interpreter, to help her. Finally, after several awkward minutes, Anna managed to put Molotov off without sparking an international incident. She hopped back into the car, and the Americans continued on to Yalta, leaving Churchill and Sarah to feast with the Soviet foreign minister. 'That tough old bird,' as Anna somewhat rudely dubbed Churchill in her diary, 'accepted with alacrety [sic] – and I left them all to go at it!'

As the Roosevelts drove away into the mountains, Anna saw neither the chagrin nor the dissatisfaction stamped across the Soviets' faces – nor did she witness how their departure had thrust the British into an awkward position. Like FDR, Churchill had already eaten lunch in his car and wanted to travel over the mountainous roads in daylight, but for both the western leaders to depart without acknowledging the Soviets' hospitality would have been rude, and deeply embarrassing to Molotov and his party. Trying hard to conceal their lack of appetite, Sarah and Winston dug into the feast. Only then did the look of disappointment fade from the faces of Molotov, Vyshinsky and Gusev.

The lunch was delicious, and the Churchills soon wished they had forgone their ham sandwiches. But they would not quickly forget the Americans' hasty departure, their tail-lights growing fainter as

Roosevelt drove southwest into the setting sun like the hero of an American western. Nor, for that matter, would the Soviets forget. Once, the British and the Americans had moved as a synchronised unit; each party's words and actions perfectly complemented the other's. But lately it seemed that a rupture had formed in this show of unity, for which the lunchtime encounter offered further evidence. The Soviets would be only too happy to exploit that rupture in the days ahead.

SIX

February 3, 1945

At six o'clock, the wheels of the American delegates' cars could finally be heard crunching over the gravel of the drive. Kathleen stood on the threshold of Livadia Palace, ready to greet them. Roosevelt's car emerged from the darkness and came to a halt in front of the palace, which still retained its stately elegance, despite the soot and grime that the conscripted labourers were unable to polish off. As the light spilled out around Kathy, it was as if she was the chatelaine of a great manor, ready to welcome guests into her home. No one had explicitly given her authority, yet no one questioned her either. She held no official title, but with her father riding in the car behind the president's, she was, for the moment, the most prominent American present in the tsar's palace.

As Roosevelt emerged from the car and entered the palace, Kathy laid eyes on him for the very first time. She had already met the other great Allied leaders. Stalin she had first encountered at the ballet in Moscow in October 1944, and she had long counted the Churchills among her dearest friends. Kathy had even been presented to the queen at a press conference two weeks after arriving in London, in 1941. And yet she had never once seen Roosevelt. How ironic, Kathy thought, that Russia was where she was meeting her own president for the first time. Meanwhile, the maître d'hôtel from Moscow's luxurious Hotel Metropol was buzzing around him, bowing excessively and addressing him at every turn as 'Your Excellency,' as if he could receive no greater pleasure than seeing to FDR's every need.

The delegates continued to clamber out of their vehicles, and Kathy ushered them into the cavernous reception hall. Fires blazed in the hearths, much to the travellers' delight, after the frigid drive. To the right was the white ballroom, where the conference plenary sessions were to take place. To the left were Roosevelt's quarters, in what had once been the tsar's private suite of office and dining rooms, which were more accessible by wheelchair than the tsar's official bedroom upstairs. Though the tsar had his imperial bedroom, legend held that he had slept in a different room in the palace every night, to outwit anyone who might try to murder him in his sleep.

While Kathy was waiting for everyone to arrive, she had begun a long, newsy letter to her best friend, Pamela Churchill, to keep her apprised of all the gossip and the goings-on, just as she wrote to Pam from the embassy residence in Moscow. Kathy's sister, Mary, was Kathy's foremost correspondent, but there was something particularly comfortable about writing to Pam. The prime minister's daughter-in-law could always be relied upon to understand the political issues and personalities involved in Kathy's reports from Russia. Pam was intimately familiar with nearly all of the key figures in the British and American delegations. She and Kathy were in fact two of the few young women accepted into this elite circle and were frequently invited to dinners and other gatherings that included the wartime leaders, both in London and at Chartwell. Sarah was another, but she spent most of her time at RAF Medmenham. Pam, though not physically present at Yalta, was there in spirit. Later, after the conference had ended, Kathy could take her pick of the numerous people who would jockey to deliver her letter to Pamela back in London.

As Kathy had written to Pam, the person she was most keen to see, after the president, was Anna, who had just followed her father into the palace. Anna and her husband, John, had once visited Sun Valley, though only after Kathy had moved to London, so she had not yet had a chance to meet Anna. Perhaps it was just as well that the two daughters were not introduced on that occasion, as the Boettigers' visit to Sun Valley may not have left the most favourable first impression.

While out hunting with Ernest Hemingway at the resort, John Boettiger somehow managed to accidentally shoot the foot off one of Averell's dogs. Averell had seen Anna during his most recent trip to Washington and assured Kathy that the president's daughter was 'a "peach" to quote exactly', as Kathy told Pam. 'I'll let you know when we meet.'

As the new arrivals thawed, Kathy made her way to Anna. Ever lighthearted and familiar in her manner, Kathy welcomed the mother of three to Livadia. Off to the side, the maître d' was still bobbing up and down before the president. As they watched this amusing scene, Kathy shared a conspiratorial chuckle with Anna. The maître d', Kathy told the president's daughter, had 'set and unset' the dining room table '3 or 4 times a day for the past week . . . experimenting with glassware and china effects' to ensure everything was just right. The Soviets had also repeatedly hung and rehung the pictures on the walls to create the proper atmosphere for their American guests, leaving Kathy 'to wonder if they would ever make up their minds!'

Before the Roosevelts arrived at Livadia, Kathy was unquestionably the doyenne of the palace, but within minutes of Anna's arrival, the dynamic abruptly shifted. Anna had barely removed her coat before she began to dispatch a flurry of instructions. Seeing no reason to change FDR's customary practice of having martinis before dinner (despite its being contrary to doctor's orders), she sent one of the Secret Service agents to see if there was any gin and asked Kathy where they could find some ice. Kathy told her there was 'supposed to be a Frigidaire hidden away somewhere'. Then Anna got out a pad of paper and a pencil and began drawing up a list of names for dinner. Though she knew nothing of Livadia, the Soviet workers, or the extensive efforts they had made on the visitors' behalf, Anna relieved Kathy of her duties in an instant and asserted herself as the ranking daughter.

While Anna saw to the drinks, the rooming assignments Kathy had fastidiously organised were doled out to the guests. Blissfully ignorant of the state in which the Harrimans had found Livadia Palace just days before, Roosevelt seemed pleased with the accommodation. Only Robert Hopkins, Harry Hopkins's photographer son and an unexpected addition to the party, dared to complain about the last-minute billet Kathy had found for him, in the enlisted men's quarters in the eaves. 'A bit thick' of him, Kathy thought. Meanwhile, Averell had joined Anna and Kathy. Turning to Anna, he told her that the one billet he was not entirely satisfied with was hers – as if he had made the arrangements himself. Her room was on the first floor, near her father's suite, but it could be better described as a 'cubicle'. If she liked, he told her, she was welcome to share Kathy's room instead. It was larger, but farther from FDR. Valuing privacy and proximity to her father over space, Anna chose the cubicle, though she would have to share a bathroom with Kathy. Her tiny bedroom was indeed Spartan, with just a rickety iron bed and a skimpy mattress 'a foot shorter than the springs' for furniture, but at least it was a room of her own. It was more than any of the colonels could claim.

As the delegates settled in, Anna 'sent someone scampering' in search of the select individuals she had invited for a private dinner with the president, in what had once been the billiard room. Kathy and Averell made the cut, as did the secretary of state, Edward Stettinius. Anna also included several of the president's closest friends – the reliable Pa Watson and FDR's chief of staff, Admiral Leahy, the first naval officer ever promoted to a five-star rank – to give the dinner the feeling of a relaxed family gathering. Harry Hopkins did not join them. He was still ill and confined to his bed. The dinner the Soviets had prepared was elaborate: cocktails, white wine, red wine, champagne, caviar, cured fish, potatoes, a variety of meats and game, two types of dessert, and dessert liqueur. Each time one of the diners passed on a dish, the maître d' looked as if he had been struck a mortal blow. FDR, eating the food his own chefs had prepared, remained genial throughout dinner, but he was exhausted and in no mood to linger. As soon as the meal was finished, he went straight to bed.

After the dinner plates had been cleared and everyone had retired to their rooms, Averell Harriman's work began. He had barely set down his luggage, and already he was leaving Kathy behind at Livadia once again. He had two errands to complete before he could sleep. He set off into the darkness, bound for the Koreiz Villa, to confirm the following day's agenda.

Just before midnight, he arrived at the villa, the erstwhile home of Rasputin's assassin. With him he had brought Chip Bohlen, one of only three State Department officials and the lone Soviet expert in the American delegation. Despite his expertise, the forty-year-old Bohlen had not been asked to the conference for his unparalleled knowledge. He was there to serve as Roosevelt's interpreter. The two men waited patiently as the Soviets checked their credentials at three separate checkpoints outside the villa, one of which was guarded by dogs.

Ten minutes after midnight, Harriman and Bohlen were finally admitted. Molotov was waiting, along with his own interpreter, Vladimir Pavlov. Harriman's midnight meetings with Molotov were by now routine. When Harriman had arrived in Moscow as ambassador, in October 1943, the Soviet foreign minister had welcomed him with a peculiar greeting, saying the Soviets understood Harriman was 'a very tough man to deal with'. When Harriman objected, saying that he had come as a friend, Molotov replied that he had meant his comment as a compliment. The two men had since developed a guarded mutual respect.

After a brief exchange of pleasantries and affirmation that the president found the accommodation to his liking, Harriman got down to business. Roosevelt, the ambassador informed the foreign minister, wished to begin the conference with a discussion about military affairs. The Allied armies were quickly approaching Berlin from their respective fronts, and the three nations' chiefs of staff desperately needed to coordinate, lest the armies inadvertently slaughter each other.

Determined, as ever, not to accept an American proposal on the first pass, Molotov countered that Stalin wished to discuss Germany first.

The two topics, Harriman pointed out, were essentially one and the same. As a compromise, he proposed that they discuss military coordination in Germany first, followed by a conversation about German political concerns. Molotov agreed.

With that settled, Harriman extended an invitation on Roosevelt's behalf for Stalin and Molotov to join the president and his party for dinner at Livadia Palace the following evening, after the first plenary session. The British would of course be invited as well. Molotov replied that he was sure Stalin would be 'delighted' but would confirm the arrangements the next morning.

Harriman had one final message to convey to Molotov on Roosevelt's behalf. Setting the agenda and issuing a dinner invitation were hardly controversial, and agreement benefited all three delegations; but this final request was different. FDR had refused to meet privately with Churchill at Malta for fear that Stalin might feel they were conspiring behind his back. That concern apparently did not extend in the other direction. Churchill would have been furious, had he known what Roosevelt had dispatched Harriman to ask. Would Stalin consider coming to Livadia Palace an hour before the first plenary session for a private visit with Roosevelt? The meeting would be 'purely personal,' but Roosevelt would be much obliged.

Molotov replied that he 'knew the Marshal's mind'. He was sure Stalin would be glad to have a private, personal meeting with Roosevelt. It was something Stalin desired, as well. Stalin would call on the president at 4 p.m.

Leaving Molotov, Harriman carried on down the dark coastal road to Vorontsov Palace for his second meeting that night. Earlier that evening the prime minister had sent word to Livadia, through his private secretary, enquiring after the plan for the next day. The British still did not know what exactly the president intended to discuss at the first meeting. Bohlen had replied, saying the details were in the process of being arranged and that he would telephone in the morning with the logistical details. Harriman could himself now give the prime minister some general information about the first plenary session, but his post-midnight visit to the prime minister was not entirely about business. Rather, it was a personal call on an old friend.

The British had not reached Vorontsov until the Americans were already sitting down to dinner. Molotov, Vyshinsky and Gusev had detained them for an hour and a half of feasting and toasts at lunch, so that by the time they had begun their journey through the mountains, the sunlight was waning. The prime minster spent the rest of the journey reciting Lord Byron's *Don Juan* to Sarah as they crawled along in darkness, past the soldiers still lining the roads, their anonymous figures illuminated by the cars' headlamps. Though it was pitch-black by the time the Churchills arrived at Vorontsov, there was enough light spilling from the windows to illuminate the outline of the villa, which was guarded by great lions carved from white stone. The architecture was bizarre. It was as if a mosque had swallowed a Swiss chalet, which had already consumed a Scottish baronial hall. The oddities continued inside. Unlike the situation at Livadia, the Germans had left the original owner's furnishings largely intact, and on the walls on either side of the dining room fireplace hung the portraits of some familiar faces. Count Semyon Vorontsov, an eighteenth-century Russian ambassador to Britain, had a daughter who had married George Herbert, the 11th Earl of Pembroke. The Herberts' portraits made the prime minister feel oddly at home.

Whereas Kathleen Harriman had overseen the Soviets' arrangements for both the conference rooms and the Americans' private quarters at Livadia, Churchill's chief military adviser, Pug Ismay, had dispatched his assistant, Joan Bright, to attend to the details for the British lodgings. She would not be living in Vorontsov Palace during the conference, but she had stayed long enough that evening, before disappearing into the background, to show the top delegates to their quarters. When she showed Churchill his suite, he was not entirely happy with it. 'But where is Sarah?' he insisted. 'I said she was to sleep in my quarters.' He wanted her safe and sound right near him in an adjoining room. Miss Bright explained that she was aware of his request, but to fulfil it was impossible. The only place in the suite to put Sarah's bed was in the hall outside the door to the prime minister's bedroom, where she, while she slept, would have been in full view of the Royal Marines and Russian soldiers guarding Churchill's door. Miss Bright had instead placed Sarah in a room down the hall. By then, Churchill was quite irritated, so his naval aide, Commander Tommy Thompson, told Miss Bright to clear out and went to find Sarah before the prime minister lost his temper.

Though it was late, Churchill was still wide awake when the

ambassador arrived at Vorontsov. During Harriman's years in London, he frequently found himself summoned to Downing Street for late-night card games and discussion of the cares of the world. Churchill told Harriman that while it was inappropriate for him, as prime minister, to engage in card games with his own British colleagues, it was quite all right for Harriman, as Roosevelt's envoy, to play with the prime minister. Harriman thought the real reason Churchill enjoyed his presence, as he wrote to his wife, was 'because I am blunt & outspoken on every subject – even if he doesn't agree he likes the stimulation of different ideas.' The same, Harriman had discovered during his tenure as ambassador, could not be said for Roosevelt.

This evening, Harriman found the prime minister cloistered with his privy council: Sarah, Anthony Eden and Lord Moran. Churchill's earlier irritation had subsided, but it had been replaced by something darker. The British had finally received a full report explaining what had happened to the transport plane that had plunged into the Mediterranean Sea. Due to some sort of navigational error and poor weather, the crew had lost radio contact with Malta. As the weather worsened, they became disoriented. After spending hours circling the area where they thought the tiny island should be, they began to run out of fuel. At long last, they identified a small dot of land. Believing it was Malta, they again attempted to make contact, but all they heard was static. The dot of land they had found was not Malta; rather, it was Lampedusa, a rocky Italian island more than a hundred miles away. The pilot spotted a small bay and attempted a desperate landing. Remarkably, he managed to bring the plane down safely on the water, but in the darkness, he could not see that immediately below the surface lay a shipwreck. As the plane skidded across the water, it hit the mass of sunken steel. The wreck shredded the belly of the plane's fuselage. Water instantly filled the cabin, drowning all but four of the passengers and crew, including three Foreign Office experts who knew the materials prepared for the conference down to the minutest detail.

Churchill's grief over the deaths soon gave way to his pent-up frustration about the almost entirely useless day at Malta. He was convinced that Harriman's boss was severely underestimating the complexity of the issues at stake, as well as the amount of time it would take to negotiate with the Soviets. The notion that they could, in five to six days, settle matters as complicated as German partition, reparation payments, the structure of Roosevelt's international peace organisation, Soviet participation in the Pacific war, and free elections in Eastern Europe was pure folly. Of all the issues up for debate, nothing upset Churchill more than the Americans' complacency about the future of Poland and what the nation's independence represented. 'We can't agree that Poland shall be a mere puppet state of Russia, where the people who don't agree with Stalin are bumped off,' he fumed. 'The Americans are profoundly ignorant of the Polish problem. At Malta I mentioned to them the independence of Poland and was met with the retort: "But surely that is not at stake."' If that was true, it was only because it was already too late. And if the western Allies failed to secure Polish independence, Churchill was the one who would have to look the exiled Polish leaders in London in the eye and tell them they no longer had a sovereign nation while the Americans scuttled back to Washington. Worst of all, Churchill realised that because of Britain's weakened position on the world stage, he was powerless to compel the Soviets to do what was right without Roosevelt's full support.

When Harriman returned to Livadia Palace half an hour later, his sobering meeting with the usually ebullient prime minister prompted him to seek out his own trusted confidante, the one on whom he could always rely to understand his deepest concerns.

During the Warsaw Uprising, Averell would summon Kathy for nightly games of bezique. The mindless rounds of cards and unguarded conversation with his daughter were cathartic. For now, there would be no cards, just weary talk. As Averell spoke with Kathy in private for the first time since returning from Malta, he described his troubling visit to Vorontsov Palace. Churchill, he told her, was in a thoroughly 'discouraged state of mind'. In the simplest terms, FDR was 'all set for the best' with this conference, a triumphant meeting of the minds. By contrast, Churchill was clearly 'all set for the worst'. The fate of Poland weighed on him, as it did on Averell; so did the news of the plane crash and the deaths of the young, brilliant people from the Foreign Office. The loss had hit the British party hard. Beyond the foreign policy expertise that had been lost, the prime minister and his party had also lost dear friends. Among the dead were Anthony Eden's beloved bodyguard, Sergeant H. J. Battley; Miss Patricia Sullivan, secretary to the permanent undersecretary for foreign affairs and conference delegate Alexander Cadogan; the diplomat Peter Loxley, whose wife had given birth to a stillborn child just the day before; and Alan Brooke's aide-de-camp, Colonel Barney Charlesworth. Brooke's last words to Charlesworth, as he departed from RAF Northolt, had been 'We shall meet in Malta.' Now those words haunted him. It was an ominous start to the week at Yalta.

The day that had begun for Averell some thirty-six hours earlier was finally over. At long last, he took himself off to bed.

Just as Kathy was the person to whom Averell turned to ease his burden, Kathy too needed a confessor, and for her that was Pamela Churchill. From her earliest encounters with Pam, she considered her to be 'one of the wisest girls I've ever met'. Together, the two women had braved London's blackouts in search of music and dancing. They had witnessed pivotal moments of the war at the prime minister's dinner table. They had also made and lost many friends, especially pilots stationed near London who never came home. Through letters, Kathy shared with Pam amusing gossip and witty observations about Russian life, along with concerns about the challenges she and Averell had faced in the Soviet Union since bidding London goodbye. Whenever Averell returned from Allied conferences or late-night tussles with Molotov at the Kremlin, Kathy wrote to Pamela about the worries she and her father shared. If anyone was in the position to understand, it was Pam, who heard about many of the same anxieties from her father-in-law and his inner circle. Though Kathy's Yalta letter, begun five days earlier, was peppered with quips about the less-than-ideal accommodation at Livadia, including the lack of indoor plumbing, her nonchalance was the shield from behind which she could write about the tragedy and destruction of war from her vantage point in Russia. Now, she wrote bleakly, 'At this point everyone's crossing their fingers & hoping for the best.'

There was another reason why Kathy was writing to Pamela. As the meeting in Yalta approached, all energy was focused on the aftermath of the war and how it would affect all nations involved. At the same time, Kathy knew, her father's reunion with the Churchills in Yalta had forced him to think about the future in especially personal terms. If the Allied victory at El Alamein in Egypt, in 1942, had marked, as Churchill called it, 'the end of the beginning', when the Allies had finally turned the tide against the Nazis, the winter of 1945 looked like the beginning of the end. At long last, the conflict was drawing to a close, and it was forcing Averell to confront the fact that as soon as it was over, he would have to make a difficult choice, one that affected not just Kathy and him, but Pamela too.

It was almost impossible not to be swept away by the heady nights of London in 1941. Though sandbags, rubble, and drab uniforms made the city dreary by day, at night, amid the danger and destruction, London radiated an otherworldly, romantic magic. Transfixed, Kathleen felt as if she were living in a wartime version of Walt Disney's *Fantasia*. London's stark white buildings glowed in the soft light cast by the dimmed headlamps of silhouetted black taxi cabs, which continued to rumble through the city in defiance of the Germans. Their drivers transported the young and reckless to underground clubs and swanky hotels, such as the Dorchester, the Ritz and the Savoy, where some of the era's greatest jazz orchestras performed nightly. At the Dorchester Hotel, supposedly the safest building in London, the resident American guests such as Averell Harriman lived in regal style. They forgot about rationing – it seemed like a figment of the imagination. The Americans were also wildly popular. One day, Kathy met a young soldier on Fleet Street. 'Just wait 'til I get back and tell them I've met an American,' he told her. As Averell mentioned to his wife, Marie, 'If it weren't for her Spartan upbringing (for which I take no credit) she would become unbearably spoiled.' The British felt an enormous sense of gratitude towards the Americans who had come to stand with them while the United States remained neutral – especially Americans like Kathy, who had come to Britain purely of their own volition. As Roosevelt had told Averell, Kathy was one of just two American women whom he had granted special permission to live in Britain that spring. Ambassador Winant's wife was the other, but unlike Kathy, she did not stay.

For many people, the jazz orchestras, the elegant hotels, the admiring praise and the danger would have added up to the thrill of a lifetime, but for the Harrimans, friendship with the Churchill family stood out above everything else. Winston Churchill had instantly pulled Averell Harriman into his inner circle, inviting him to meetings of his War Cabinet – unprecedented access for a foreigner – and to weekend country gatherings at Chequers. When Kathy arrived in May 1941, she too was promptly invited for the weekend. 'It's rather a shock meeting someone you've seen caricatured so many times,' she wrote to Mary after meeting the prime minister. He was smaller than she had anticipated and 'a lot less fat', but he was even more impressive than she had imagined: 'I'd expected an overpowering, rather terrifying man – he's quite the opposite – very gracious – has a wonderful smile & isn't at all hard to talk to.' Churchill, Kathy realised, seemed to speak to each of his countrymen individually. One day, Kathy met a battle-scarred pilot who had been in the RAF for twenty months. He had shot down eleven enemy planes and had been shot down four times himself. He was one of only two men left in his original squadron. Just twenty-eight years old, he was sure he would soon die, but he had made peace with his mortality. 'He showed me something he carries to cheer him up when he feels he can't go on any longer,' Kathy told her sister. 'Churchill's bit about the RAF – "Never in the history of the world has so much been owed by so many to so few."'

The warmth Kathy felt for the prime minister quickly extended to the whole family. Kathy admired the quiet, gracious Clementine, describing the prime minister's wife to her sister as 'a very sweet lady – She's given up her whole life to her husband – & takes a back seat very graciously. Everyone in the family looks upon him as God & she's rather left out & when anyone pays any attention to her she's overjoyed.' 'Don't get the idea she's a mousy Mrs. Winant,' Kathy observed. 'Not at all. She's got a mind of her own.' Kathy befriended the three Churchill daughters, especially Sarah and Mary, who were closer to her in age. Kathy thought Sarah was 'a terribly nice girl', though did not much care for Sarah's husband, Vic. While she found Sarah a surprisingly good actor, Kathy confided in her sister that she thought Sarah's marriage was not a happy one and believed that 'going on stage is the one way [Sarah] can keep from going mad.' When Kathy wrote to Mouche with lists of clothes and other necessities she could not obtain in London, she often asked her former governess to include in the package extra nail polish, stockings, makeup and accessories for the Churchill girls. Kathy's stepmother, Marie, also sent over a 'loot suitcase' for Kathy and her new friends. But of all the Churchills, Kathy's closest friend was Winston and Clementine's vivacious daughter-in-law, Randolph's wife, Pamela.

Pamela was two years younger than Kathy, and Averell had promptly introduced them, hoping that the two young women would become friends. Kathy soon wrote glowing remarks about Pamela in her letters to her sister, praising her as the 'nicest, sanest girl'. Pamela seemed to know everyone of importance. But Kathy also pitied her new friend. Beneath Pamela's playful, lighthearted demeanour, she faced serious problems. It was no secret that Randolph was unfaithful to her and had built up considerable gambling debts. Now he was away with the army, leaving her to scramble to pay creditors while also raising their new baby, little Winston.

The longer they lived in England, at the heart of British power and society, the more the Harrimans felt adrift between the two shores of the Atlantic. Over time, they found it harder to identify with friends back home. In August 1941, Kathy received a letter from Mary, who relayed their New York friends' opinion that the United States would enter the war only to save the British. 'Perhaps by now you've heard Averell on the subject – It's one of his pets,' Kathy replied. 'When will they understand that it's their own skins – not the English ones that they'll have to save?' 'They' and 'their' referred to Americans – as if she did not consider herself and her father members of that group.

The friendship between the Harrimans and the Churchills deepened over the summer and fall of 1941. The Churchills even hosted a dinner in honour of Kathy's twenty-fourth birthday: Sunday, December 7, 1941. Clementine mistakenly thought the birthday was December 6, so the official party took place at Chequers a day early; but Kathy and Averell were still there on Sunday, dining *en famille* with the Churchills and Ambassador Winant, who had also come for the weekend, when the news broke that the Japanese had attacked Pearl Harbor. Kathy watched as the prime minister 'danced a jig' in his silk, dragon-print robe, while her father stood near the fireplace, with a look of grim but satisfied relief. Britain could not hold out against the Nazis forever, and the Red Army appeared to be close to breaking point as Hitler's army charged east towards Moscow. Averell had long believed that American entry into the war was inevitable, and though it meant that the immediate future would be grisly, it gave hope that the Axis of Germany, Italy and Japan would eventually be defeated. To be sure, the attack in Hawaii had been horrific, but the Harrimans understood that if the United States did not enter the war, death and destruction worldwide would be much worse. 'I wonder,' Kathy mused to Mouche, revealing a grim understanding of this reality, 'if any event has ever made me happier?'

It was understandable that the Churchills and the Harrimans had forged a close friendship by sharing such remarkable experiences, but it complicated Averell's role as intermediary between Downing Street and the White House. Though officially in London to represent American interests, Averell found that his professional priorities sometimes became a bit murky. For example, in the summer of 1941, Churchill asked Harriman to serve as his personal representative on a tour of the Middle East to assess supply needs. Kathy did not think she had ever seen her father 'so excited about anything'. Technically, assessing supply requirements fell under Harriman's broad Lend-Lease mandate, but in this instance he would be travelling as Churchill's representative rather than Roosevelt's. Randolph Churchill, serving at British Army headquarters in Cairo, was Harriman's guide. 'I have been tremendously impressed by Harriman, and can well understand the regard you have for him,' Randolph wrote to his father. 'He has definitely become my favourite American.' Randolph also made a somewhat daring observation: 'He clearly regards himself more as your servant than R's,' he wrote conspiratorially. 'I do hope you will keep him at your side, as I think he is the most objective and shrewd of all those who are around you.' Though Harriman never openly claimed to feel more allegiance to Churchill than to Roosevelt, the relationship between the families had become tangled in every conceivable way – professionally, socially, and even romantically.

Shortly after Kathleen arrived in London, Averell was called out of town on business. As Kathy was unaccustomed to the nightly bombardments that Londoners had come to take for granted, Averell worried about leaving her alone. Since he was often absent, he thought perhaps Kathy would like to have a friend in their suite to keep her company. Pamela lived on the top floor of the Dorchester Hotel, the most dangerous floor, but it was the only room that she could afford. If Pamela moved into the Harrimans' suite, she would be out of harm's way, and she could look after Kathy during an air raid. Averell also offered to rent a country house in Surrey, where the two young women could spend weekends. Pamela could even leave baby Winston there with a nurse during the week, to keep him safe. Kathy thought it a sweet gesture. With people like Pamela looking after her, she felt 'rather like a prize cow'.

Before long, Kathy learned that her father's intentions were not purely selfless. Nor was her new best friend all she seemed. Averell had first met Pamela during a luncheon at Chequers two weeks after he arrived in England. Though not classically beautiful, the round-faced, red-haired Pamela exuded life and sensuality. Randolph Churchill had proposed to her on their first date, and they married just three weeks later, in October 1939. Their son was born one year later. Any number of British girls would have given anything to be in Pamela's position, but she aspired to more than simply being the wife and the mother to the next generations of the Churchill dynasty. Like her nineteenth-century ancestor Jane Digby, notorious for her string of lovers ranging from English aristocrats to Bavarian and Greek kings to a Syrian sheikh, Pamela saw herself as an irresistible courtesan. She had a remarkable gift for making anyone she met – particularly men – feel like the most fascinating person in the room. Averell Harriman was no exception.

Though Averell was forty-nine and Pamela twenty-one, there was an instant attraction. With black hair, tan skin, and a lithe, athletic physique, Averell was a striking man. He was also the wealthiest American in London. Never deliberately ostentatious, he spoke sparingly and deliberately; his verbal restraint lent him an air of aloofness, which only added to his appeal. He was decidedly serious, his gleaming smile a rare gift that was enchanting when he chose to bestow it. He also inexplicably seemed to succeed in every endeavour, whether multi-million-dollar business transactions or games of croquet. He was, quite simply, the most 'beautiful' man Pamela had ever seen.

Shortly after their first meeting, Averell and Pamela found themselves together at a dinner at the Dorchester in honour of Adele, Lady Cavendish, the woman Kathy would later insult in her *Newsweek* column. After a sumptuous meal, the mood suddenly turned; the worst bombing raid of the Blitz thus far was suddenly exploding around them. Soon all of London was ablaze. It was like a hellish version of the New York theatre marquees on 42nd and Broadway, sending searing light into the night sky and creating an artificial day so bright that one could read outdoors. From 9 p.m. until dawn, bombs rained down on central London: from St Paul's Cathedral to Parliament to the National Gallery. On Oxford Street, fires ravaged the chic Palm Court Restaurant at Selfridges department store. Vulnerable in her room on the top floor of the hotel, Pamela took refuge in Harriman's third-floor suite. Like so many couples thrown together in the frenzied atmosphere of the London Blitz, they spent the night in each other's arms. The next day, Averell wrote a letter to his wife, Marie, in New York, describing the bombs falling on London. 'Needless to say,' he wrote with ambiguous nonchalance, 'my sleep was intermittent.'

By the time Kathy arrived in London, a month later, the affair between Averell and Pamela was firmly established and an open secret. Churchill's friend Lord Beaverbrook, the Canadian British newspaper magnate who was then Britain's minister of supply, knew of Pamela's conquest and used it to his advantage. He paid off Randolph's debts. In return, Pamela passed on information about her conversations with Harriman, a key source of insight into American attitudes towards the war. Sarah and Diana Churchill knew about the affair, as did Diana's husband, Duncan Sandys, but Randolph remained oblivious.

After chaperoning Harriman in the Middle East, he wrote to his wife, 'I found him absolutely charming . . . He spoke delightfully about you & I fear that I have a serious rival!'

It was, however, unclear whether Winston or Clementine knew just how far Pamela's friendship with Harriman had gone. Only once did the prime minister give the slightest indication that he suspected anything. 'You know, they're saying a lot of things about Averell in relation to you,' he told Pamela. She countered that most people had nothing better to do than gossip, to which Churchill replied, 'I quite agree,' and duly closed the matter.

With so many people whispering about Averell and Pamela, it was only a matter of time before Kathy found out about the affair. She never told Pamela how exactly she had learned about it, but one day, when the two women were alone, she confronted Pamela. 'You know,' she told her friend, 'I am not a total fool.' Pamela tried to feign ignorance, but Kathy would not be put off. Though Kathy had grasped the situation, she decided not to tell anyone about it. She looked at the situation with pragmatic, transactional detachment – an ability she no doubt inherited from Averell. Yes, he was cheating on his wife, but Marie was Kathy's stepmother, with whom she was friendly but not close. Marie was also rumoured to have more men in her life, including the literary agent Mark Hanna and the bandleader Eddy Duchin. If Kathy revealed the affair as a matter of principle, she would injure her father's reputation. Self-interest was also involved. When Kathy had first moved to London, it was unclear whether the American government would allow her to remain permanently. As the United States was then still neutral, it was wise to keep only the most essential personnel in London to minimise casualties. She did have legitimate employment as a journalist, but if the situation in London became more dangerous, she could be sent home. Her friends believed that she was off on an 'adventure' for her own amusement and would leave London when the novelty wore off. But as Kathy told Mouche, she had absolutely 'no intention' of doing so. As long as Averell had a job in London, Kathy was determined to remain at his side. To avoid being packed off to New York or Sun Valley, she had to become indispensible to her father. Covering for his affair was a convenient way to do it. She told

Pamela, 'I had to decide whether I would go home or whether I would stay and protect my father, and I figured it was important to stay and protect him.' Kathy accepted the fact of her father's relationship with Pamela, shut any discomfort or moral qualms about the situation out of her mind, and moved on.

In the spring of 1942, the Harrimans moved out of the Dorchester and into a flat adjoining the American embassy in Grosvenor Square. Pamela moved with them. For a time, the arrangement worked suitably for everyone, but that summer, Randolph returned to London on leave. The trio quickly worked to cover Pamela's tracks. In an effort to keep the peace, Sarah Churchill temporarily moved into the Harrimans' flat herself and gave her own London flat to Pamela and Randolph during his leave.

But rumours about Pamela's special relationship with Averell had finally reached Randolph in North Africa. He was furious with her, and with Averell, whom he had trusted as a friend. For a time, Randolph and Pamela tried to maintain a public appearance of happiness so as not to publicly embarrass the prime minister, but the marriage was over. Soon Randolph returned to active duty, conveniently pushing the matter of divorce into the future. Several months later, Averell was summoned to Washington, where FDR informed him that he was to become the next ambassador to Moscow. Uncomfortable with confronting emotions as always, Averell wrote to Kathy from Washington and asked her to break off the affair with Pamela for him. 'Help Pam straighten herself out – poor child,' he told Kathy. 'She is in a tough spot. Tell her I am sure she will do the right thing if she follows her own instinct.' He instructed Kathy to burn the note or keep it locked away. In October 1943, the Harrimans moved to Moscow, but not before Averell gave Pamela the deeds to his Ford and a new Grosvenor Square flat. He also discreetly arranged to provide her with a hugely generous annual allowance of £3,000, for an indefinite period. Kathy was aware of this arrangement – if not in detail, at least in principle.

Meanwhile, in her seemingly insatiable desire for intimate attentions, Pamela carried on with a string of rich and powerful lovers; she had begun affairs with some of them even before Averell ended their relationship. She had a special appetite for Americans – they were arriving in London in droves – though she threw in some Brits for good measure. Her slate of lovers included Jock Whitney, who was married to James Roosevelt's ex-wife, Betsey Cushing, and who had supplanted Harriman as London's wealthiest American; Whitney's brother-in-law and the founder of CBS, Bill Paley; the CBS broadcaster Edward R. Murrow; Major General Frederick Anderson, one of the most senior figures in the U.S. Army Air Force; and the head of the RAF, Air Marshal Sir Charles 'Peter' Portal, who was utterly besotted with her.

Surprisingly, despite everything, Pamela and Kathy managed to maintain a friendship and kept up a regular correspondence between London and Moscow. Hundreds of pages of letters crossed between them. Sometimes Averell would add a postscript to Kathy's letters, but Averell and Pamela also occasionally wrote to each other directly. Even with so many other paramours at her beck and call, part of Pamela remained devoted to Averell. Nor was the stoic ambassador able to forget her.

Now, nearly a year and a half after their parting, memories of Pamela still played in Averell's mind, even as he became increasingly burdened with concerns over Stalin's intentions towards Eastern Europe and Roosevelt's naiveté in his relationship with the Soviet dictator. Not only would Averell's reunion with Sarah and Winston evoke memories of Pamela, but also two of Pamela's other paramours, Fred Anderson and Peter Portal, had arrived in Yalta as part of the military contingent.

Kathy was well aware that her father's feelings for her best friend persisted. She almost never made any overt reference to the affair in her letters to Pamela, rarely even hinting at it, but at the end of the first instalment of her letter from Yalta, she described another late-night conversation she had had with her father shortly before departing for the Crimea. As ever, it was in those late hours that Averell was most willing to untangle his personal feelings, which he usually suppressed. 'One evening Ave & I sat up for hours & hours talking about you & he & Marie,' she wrote to Pamela. 'He was more or less thinking out loud & needless to say got no where [*sic*]. He just can't make himself make a decision while the war's on & life's so unsettled.' Her father's affair, seemingly a wartime fling like thousands of others, was far from over.

SEVEN

February 3, 1945

While Averell Harriman was holding his private meetings late into the night, back at Livadia Palace Anna Roosevelt made her way down a long hall, her footsteps echoing as they struck the polished parquet floor. While her father slept, she was going to pay a call on his longtime friend and adviser Harry Hopkins.

Anna had never been particularly fond of Hopkins, but she was especially irritated with him now. After dinner, Edward Stettinius had found Anna. Stettinius had taken it upon himself to go to the room of the president's ailing special adviser, to consult with him on preparations for the next day. No one knew the details of the president's policies better than Hopkins – not even the secretary of state or the president himself. While the two men were conferencing, Stettinius had noticed Anna's bottle of scotch in Hopkins's room and rescued it. Now he handed it back – its contents somewhat depleted.

Scotch aside, Stettinius confided to Anna, he was concerned about Hopkins. Harry was not at all well. He had been sick for the past twenty-four hours and showed no signs of improvement. The scotch had not helped. Unless Hopkins recovered significantly overnight, he would be in no state to attend the conference sessions. This presented a problem. Roosevelt had brought very few State Department experts to Yalta – just H. Freeman Matthews from the European Affairs Division; Stettinius's special assistant, Wilder Foote; and the relatively unknown but rising star Alger Hiss – to assist with matters related to the international peace organisation. Hiss had been a late addition to the party, selected after FDR had refused to take Jimmy Dunn, the assistant secretary of state for European and Far Eastern affairs. Roosevelt had never been particularly keen on the State Department, the most conservative-leaning agency in Washington. Dunn particularly provoked his ire, even more than the usual 'old maids', 'cookie-pushers', and 'pansies' at State, as Hopkins called them. Dunn, one of the foremost experts on European and Japanese foreign policy, was deeply sceptical about the Kremlin's intentions. 'I won't take Jimmy Dunn,' Roosevelt insisted to Stettinius. 'He'll ball it all up.'

Stettinius had been secretary of state a mere two months and desperately needed help. Hiss, a young man with all-American charm, looked like a cross between Frank Sinatra and a handsome young professor sporting a bow tie. He was a graduate of Harvard Law School and a former clerk for Supreme Court Justice Oliver Wendell Holmes Jr; he had also worked for President Woodrow Wilson's son-in-law. Stettinius assumed he would be a strong addition to their party. But none of these men could influence the president like Hopkins, nor could they ease FDR back into a productive line of argument with the Soviets when his unbridled belief in his own charismatic powers as his chief instrument of foreign policy threatened to lead him astray. So now, despite the fact she had not properly slept in two days, Anna, who thought Hopkins something of a 'prima donna', strode down the hall to his room to assess his physical state for herself.

Even in Livadia Palace's dim evening gloom, anyone looking at Harry Hopkins would know that Stettinius had not been exaggerating. The overnight flight and long drive had not been comfortable for anyone, but no one had a more wretched trip than Hopkins. Ever since the president's longtime special adviser had three-quarters of his stomach removed after being diagnosed with stomach cancer in 1939, he had suffered serious problems with digestion. Unable to process food and absorb nutrients properly, he experienced frequent bouts of dysentery, particularly after eating heavy foods and drinking alcohol. Hopkins had been travelling on Roosevelt's behalf since January 21. He had first flown to London for a visit the prime minister, and then carried on to Paris and Rome for further meetings with the Free French leader, Charles de Gaulle, and the pope. Finally he had convened with his colleagues at Malta. On the way to the Crimea, he had suffered a particularly nasty bout of his recurring affliction. He was in such a dismal state by the time the American delegation reached Saki that, rather than make him wait in misery for the president, Stettinius sent him ahead to Livadia Palace.

A journalist once described Hopkins as having the appearance of 'an ill-fed horse at the end of a hard day', but he looked particularly frail and wan tucked under the covers of his bed. Nicknamed 'Skinny' by his classmates at Grinnell College, he had always been thin. As of late, he had become nearly skeletal. His jowls were sagging, and his thin brown hair was receding. He had lost so much weight that his eyeballs looked oddly large for his head, and he was swimming in his striped pyjamas, even with a layer of long underwear underneath. The fact that he was alive at all defied his doctors' expectations. They had given him weeks to live after his cancer diagnosis, but thanks to plasma transfusions, regular visits to the Mayo Clinic and sheer willpower, he had managed to survive another five years. If he looked like a workhorse ready to keel over, perhaps it was because his mind was still driving him forward at an astonishing pace. He had been Roosevelt's legs throughout the war, travelling to London, Moscow, Paris and Rome. As long as the war continued, he was simply too busy to die. But two days before he left Washington in January, he frankly faced the reality that he very well could die on this trip. He wrote a letter to his twelve-year-old daughter, Diana, saying that if anything should happen to him, Eleanor Roosevelt would be her guardian and would see to it that Diana 'got a good education and . . . a little money'. He also gave his daughter a copy of his will, though he had few assets to bequeath.

When Anna arrived at Hopkins's room, she found him 'in a stew'. He had had plenty of time to ruminate over the past forty-eight hours as he lay sick in bed, and he had decided he was not at all pleased with what had transpired. In London he had spent several days with Churchill, trying to assuage any doubts the prime minister had about the strength of the Anglo-American relationship after the terse back-and-forth between London and Washington concerning plans for the conference. But it seemed that Hopkins's efforts had been in vain. By refusing to meet with Churchill other than in a social capacity, the president had simultaneously devalued the goodwill Hopkins had been dispatched to repair and had undermined his longtime adviser's credibility in the space of one day. A visit from Hopkins used to be a signal of FDR's sincere commitment. He had sent Hopkins to London to meet with Churchill in the wake of Pearl Harbor. At that time Hopkins had been an extension of the president himself. What was his word worth now?

For nearly a decade and a half, Roosevelt and Hopkins had been inseparable. They made an unlikely pair: Roosevelt from New York nobility and Hopkins a nobody from Iowa. Many within the Washington elite were suspicious of Hopkins, who had somehow managed to bewitch the president, as Rasputin had charmed Tsarina Alexandra. And yet, for all their differences, the two men were united by their shared vision for a more progressive America in the wake of the Great Depression. Their relationship stretched back to 1931, when Roosevelt was the governor of New York and Hopkins was on the board of FDR's Temporary Emergency Relief Administration. Hopkins followed Roosevelt to Washington, serving in various roles as a key New Deal administrator and eventually as FDR's secretary of commerce. After Hopkins's second wife, Barbara, died of breast cancer in 1937, the two men became even closer. Barbara's death left Hopkins to raise then five-year-old Diana on his own and provide for his three sons – aged twenty-three, sixteen and twelve – from his first marriage, which had ended in divorce. When Hopkins stepped down as secretary of commerce to become FDR's special adviser in 1940, Roosevelt invited him to move into the White House with little Diana. With nannies to look after his daughter and no wife to keep him company, the special adviser was ever present and devoted almost entirely to FDR. The two men could be found locked deep in conversation in Roosevelt's study almost every night.

Strains began to appear in 1942, when Hopkins met Louise Macy, a glamorous editor from *Harper's Bazaar*, at a gathering at Marie and

Averell Harriman's home. They quickly fell in love and married that July, in a small ceremony at the White House. FDR urged Hopkins to continue living at the White House with his new wife and daughter, but the happiness Hopkins now found in his marriage left less time for friendship with his boss. Roosevelt began to feel neglected by his old friend, whose undivided attention he had taken for granted. Hopkins's friendship with Eleanor Roosevelt also became stressed. Eleanor made no secret of the fact that she looked down on Louise, who had what Eleanor considered excessively materialistic interests. The White House quickly became a very unwelcoming environment for the new Mrs Hopkins.

By December 1943 the close quarters had become so uncomfortable that the Hopkins family decided to move to a home of their own, on N Street in Georgetown. Throughout the next year, Hopkins continued on as FDR's special adviser, but a distance grew between the two men. In part, this was the result of remarkably bad fortune. In stark contrast to the joy Hopkins had found the previous year, when he married Louise, the first half of 1944 was devastating. His youngest son, Stephen, was killed in the Pacific. At the same time, Hopkins's health sharply declined. He was so sick that he spent the first six months of the year convalescing. He went first to the naval hospital, then to the sunshine in Miami, then to the Mayo Clinic – where he had yet another operation – and finally to White Sulphur Springs in West Virginia.

The unintended but inevitable consequence of those six months away from the White House was the loss of shared experience that binds friendships. After witnessing the momentous events of the past decade at the president's side, Hopkins was not in Washington that June to celebrate the Allies' victory in Rome or to pray with Roosevelt on the eve of the invasion of Normandy. Though Roosevelt had no conscious intention to injure their friendship, by the time Hopkins returned, others – Admiral Leahy; the war mobilisation director, Jimmy Byrnes; and the Treasury secretary, Henry Morgenthau – had started to take his place. Roosevelt's attention had also begun to pivot east, as he believed friendly relations with the ascendant Soviet Union could blossom in the postwar world order while the British Empire's influence waned. Hopkins, however, was sceptical. The relationship with the Soviets might not be quite as warm as Roosevelt expected. He also continued to have great personal respect for Churchill. While Britain was no longer the superpower it had once been, there remained great value in the Anglo-American alliance.

On the ship en route to Malta, FDR made some disparaging comments about Hopkins to Anna. He criticised him for freelancing with his opinions in conversation with journalists about the rumoured upcoming conference among the three Allied leaders. Hopkins had promised he would remain strictly off the record if asked about it. A report from Rome cited him as saying that, although he 'once was a firm believer in a "win-the-war-first" policy ... he now was convinced the problems of the peace would not wait upon the conclusion of the war.' Nor could Hopkins's decision to relay Churchill's aggrieved retort, that if the Allies had 'spent ten years on research we could not have found a worse place in the world than Yalta', have made him more popular with the boss.

Perhaps it was in everyone's best interest that Hopkins was too unwell to join FDR for dinner that first night at Yalta, for Hopkins was in no mood to be cordial. Now, with Anna standing at his bedside, he launched into a litany of complaints. 'FDR *must* see Churchill in the morning,' he insisted. Roosevelt may have avoided any kind of meaningful exchange with the prime minister at Malta, but now it was absolutely 'imperative' that Roosevelt and Churchill make some 'prearrangements' before anyone met with Stalin the next day. Otherwise, both the British and the Americans were setting themselves up for trouble.

Hopkins was still one of the most powerful voices in Washington, but Anna was not so easily swayed. She was not a naturally assertive person; it was a behaviour she had had to learn. When Anna was little, she was often at the centre of power struggles between her mother and grandmother, Sara Delano Roosevelt. Eleanor did not find motherhood easy, and Sara would criticise the way she raised her children, even going so far as to tell Anna's brother James, 'Your mother only bore you, I am more your mother than your mother is.' Later, when Eleanor became active in politics, Sara would try to provoke jealousy, regularly reminding Anna that her mother was spending her time with political people, and not with her. Not until Anna was sixteen did she realise that she had to stand up for herself; otherwise she would always be her grandmother's 'football'. Anna now put that assertiveness to use. Annoyed more than offended by Hopkins's tirade, she repeated the line her father had been using to put Churchill off for the past month. Didn't he think, she asked Hopkins, that such a meeting would 'stir up some distrust among our Russian brethren'?

Hopkins would have none of it. He dismissed her argument out of hand.

In that case, she suggested, perhaps Hopkins could convene with Ed Stettinius and his British counterpart, Anthony Eden? The three could strategise and report back to Roosevelt and Churchill. Surely that was sufficient.

Hopkins emphatically disagreed. A discussion between the foreign ministers would not be adequate. The two heads of government simply must meet.

Anna was not about to admit why she was so devotedly helping her father avoid meeting with the prime minister. Even if she did choose to confide in Hopkins, the very ill but still doggedly engaged man would have little sympathy for the idea that Churchill was too exhausting.

Anna's refusal to bring Hopkins's argument to FDR was driven by more than a desire to protect her father's health or a petty grievance over a bottle of scotch. Men like Leahy, Byrnes and Morgenthau were not the only people vying to succeed Hopkins as FDR's closest confidant. Anna was a dark-horse candidate for the position. While Hopkins was moving into his new Georgetown home, on December 21, 1943, Anna and her children had just arrived at the Roosevelts' Hyde Park home from Seattle, for a four-week holiday. Throughout the Christmas break, Anna showered her father with care and attention, beginning to fill the Hopkins void. Roosevelt was delighted to have someone nearby who wanted nothing more than to sit with him, talk with him, and see to his every comfort. He suggested that Anna extend her vacation. A month passed, and she remained. And when the president returned to the White House, Anna went too, moving into the Lincoln Bedroom suite that had long been Hopkins's private domain.

It was an ironic turn of events. After FDR was struck with polio when Anna was fifteen, his then chief political strategist, Louis Howe, had moved into Franklin and Eleanor's house in Manhattan. They decided to give Anna's room to Howe, relegating her to a tiny back bedroom on the fourth floor previously reserved for lesser guests or servants. Howe had been dead for nearly ten years, but Anna was at last getting her revenge. Too often her father's political colleagues had displaced her. By March, it was clear. Anna would not be returning to Seattle.

Throughout that year, Anna's influence in the White House and with her father steadily grew, while Hopkins became marginalised. When he returned from his convalescence, the relationship between Anna and Hopkins quickly turned tense. To Hopkins, Anna seemed excessively protective of her father. Anna in turn was quick to note when Hopkins's transgressions irritated FDR, and she callously maintained that his dysentery was a misery of his own making, as he took so little care with his health. She was also suspicious of Hopkins's loyalty to FDR. Hopkins had developed a close, genuine friendship with Churchill during his wartime visits to London, and the depth of that connection concerned her. She also surmised that Harry Hopkins had considered 'deserting' FDR and running for president himself in 1940.

As the Americans prepared to depart for Yalta, it became abundantly clear, not just to Roosevelt's coterie but also to the public, how rapidly Anna had ascended at Hopkins's expense. Just before FDR's fourth inauguration, the controversial journalist and radio commentator Drew Pearson, who frequently splashed embarrassing stories about the Washington elite across his nationally syndicated column, 'Washington Merry-Go-Round', wrote that the 'closest person to the President as he stands at the threshold of his fourth term is no longer Harry Hopkins ... but his attractive, vivacious daughter, Anna Boettiger ... She has come to be not only hostess but her father's confidante, friend and adviser. More and more personal appointments, more and more private reports dealing with important policy now pass through Anna's hands. Sometimes during a conversation in his executive office, the President will pick up the phone and call his daughter in the residence ... to ask her the status of a certain problem.' Hopkins used to be Roosevelt's first call. Now the man who for a decade had enjoyed unlimited access to FDR had to go through Anna to see his closest friend.

Weakened both physically and politically, Hopkins was fed up. His frustration partly was focused on Anna, who was not challenging her father's poor judgment in his dealings with his Allied counterparts. But she was just a proxy for his irritation with FDR, who was using his daughter's lack of political experience to shield himself from the difficult but vital conversations he preferred to avoid. Hopkins believed it was Roosevelt's duty as the president of the United States to have those conversations.

Had he not been so sick (and possibly slightly inebriated), Hopkins might have held back, but instead he lashed out at Anna. 'FDR,' he told her with cold sarcasm, 'asked for this job . . . Now, whether he like[s] it or not, he ha[s] to do the work.'

If he had hoped to persuade Anna to advance his argument, questioning Roosevelt's commitment to his office was perhaps the worst possible approach. Anna found his remarks thoroughly 'insulting'. The most she would do, she told him, was 'discuss it with FDR in the morning'. She bid him goodnight, leaving him to sleep off his misery.

Back in the privacy of her cupboard of a room, Anna reflected on the curt exchange. Both Stettinius and Roosevelt's cardiologist, Howard Bruenn, had told her Hopkins was truly ill. That much was evident. But perhaps his maladies were not limited to the physical. 'Certainly it didn't seem to me that his mind was clicking or his judgement very good,' she recorded in her diary. 'Or maybe,' she concluded subversively, 'it's just that I had never quite realized how pro-British Harry is.'

As the last light in Livadia Palace was extinguished and the Americans settled into a much-needed sleep, a telegram lay unanswered. It was from their ambassador in London, Gil Winant. Two thousand miles away, the man who had been kept from attending the conference was doing his best to advocate for a people who likewise had been brushed aside. Though Poland's future as an independent nation was one of the foremost matters facing the Allies at Yalta, not a single representative from Poland had been invited to the conference. Winant remained sympathetic to the legitimate Polish government in exile in London having worked with its representatives at length over the past four years. At 9.30 that morning, he had dispatched an urgent telegram on to Yalta from the Polish prime minister, Tomasz Arciszewski:

'Mr. President,' Arciszewski wrote. 'At this time the fate of many nations rests in your hands and in the hands of Prime Minister Churchill. The whole world expects that these important discussions ... will result in the creation of foundations for a future peace, a peace which should bring to nations the freedom of conscience and speech and secure for them freedom from fear and want. I trust that these essential freedoms will also be granted to our nation which has been fighting unflinchingly for their realization at the side of the great American and British democracies.'

The Poles had been fighting valiantly against the Nazis since the enemy had invaded in September 1939, but it was not just the Nazis who wanted to deny Poland its right to exist as an independent nation. As the Red Army pushed west towards Berlin, Arciszewski had good intelligence that the supposed liberators were arresting and deporting members of the Polish underground who were resisting the Soviets' attempts to subjugate the Poles. The Molotov-Ribbentrop non-aggression pact between the Nazis and the Soviets had long since been torn to shreds, but Poland seemed like an alternative reality, where a pact between enemies was still alive and well. If the Americans and the British failed to guarantee Polish sovereignty now, Britain's original declaration of war against the Nazis, as well as the sacrifices of the Polish soldiers who had fought steadfastly against the Nazis, would have been in vain.

The Poles had much to be proud of: their pilots had fought alongside the RAF in the Battle of Britain, and without them Britain might have fallen to the Nazis; their soldiers heroically assaulted Germany's defences in the victory at Monte Cassino; their mathematicians' invaluable contributions helped crack what was thought to be an unbreakable Nazi code; their underground resistance fighters remained in Poland, and their spirit had never flagged in the face of near-certain execution. Poland's future as an independent nation now hung in the balance. Its leaders could do nothing more than beg to be remembered.

PART II

'As if . . . the Conference
isn't so much more important
than anything else.'

EIGHT

February 4, 1945

When the Churchills arrived at Vorontsov Palace, Sarah could tell it was clearly suited to the tastes of an eccentric aristocrat, but it was not until the next morning that she could appreciate the hodgepodge of architectural styles to full effect. It was as if two completely different buildings – a Scottish nobleman's estate and Delhi's Jama Masjid mosque – had been set on lorries and smashed into each other at high speed. However, the back, Islamic-style side of the house boasted an impressive view. A large veranda gave way to wide stone steps, which led down the shrub-covered slope to a lower terrace; farther below crashed the waves of the sea.

Though the house's curious design and its mountainous setting had clearly been selected to impress visitors, Sarah sensed that something about the environment was off. 'There are views and valleys it is true,' she wrote home to her mother, 'but the whole landscape is rather like a woman who has all the attributes of beauty, yet no charm – no power to move one.' She found the looming mountains and precarious crags 'oppressive and ominous', even in the warm winter sunshine. 'Everything is too big – I feel swallowed up,' she told Clementine. 'I don't like it!!'

Sarah was not the first to feel something hostile in the beauty of the Black Sea coast. As the one-time Yalta resident Anton Chekhov wrote nearly half a century earlier in his short story 'The Lady with the

Dog', Yalta had long been associated with legends of 'conquests . . . of a swift, fleeting love affair, a romance with an unknown woman'. And yet those clandestine liaisons and secret passions were but a mirage obscuring the intangible air of unease that shrouded the coastal gardens. 'The town with its cypresses had quite a deathlike air,' the playwright wrote with mystical detachment, 'and the monotonous hollow sound of the sea rising up from below' put one in mind of 'the eternal sleep awaiting us'. Perhaps the palpable disquiet sensed by Chekhov – and now Sarah – emanated from the Black Sea itself, which, in addition to being filled with mines, was largely devoid of life due to the black sulfurous mud that coated its floor.

As Sarah contemplated the unsettling forces at work at Vorontsov, Kathleen and Anna were facing more immediate concerns, namely, the armed Soviet guards who were questioning them in the Livadia Palace gardens. In the days leading up to the conference, the U.S. Navy advance team had issued a 'General Information Bulletin' to all American delegates bound for Yalta. First and foremost, the advance team reminded everyone, 'Throughout your stay in the Soviet Union you are guests of the Soviet Government.' Having laid out that proviso, the document went on to list a number of useful facts, such as the exchange rate for rubles, where to find the incinerator to destroy sensitive documents, and where to purchase beer – available only when the canteen was open, between noon and 2 p.m. and then again between 5 and 7. Most important, it advised the delegates on what to expect from Soviet security. There would be numerous armed sentries posted throughout the Livadia Palace complex. Never mind one's rank or the urgency of one's business – under no conditions were the Americans to 'try to bulldoze the guards' if asked for their 'documente', 'proposk', or 'bumagy'. They were to produce them at once, as the guards had 'strict orders'. (The briefing sheet did not specify what those 'strict orders' were.) Nor were the Americans to offer the sentries cigarettes, candies or gifts – not even out of kindness – or attempt to photograph them. Failure to comply could be 'extremely injurious', not least for the poor sentries, who would undoubtedly be punished 'by extreme penalties'.

Kathy had no desire to put these warnings to the test as she gave Anna and Dr Bruenn (one of their few fellow conference attendees under forty) a walking tour of the grounds. With the first plenary session of the conference now just hours away, up at the palace FDR had finally convened his advisers in the Sun Room for a pre-conference discussion. While the president consulted with Harriman, the military chiefs, Stettinius, and the secretary of state's two deputies, Freeman Matthews and Alger Hiss, on the handful of topics most likely to arise in conversation over the next several days, Kathy, Anna and Bruenn knew their presence would not be required. Taking advantage of this free hour, they had gone out to the garden to get some exercise. But their plan had been thwarted. Armed sentries stopped them at seemingly every twenty-five feet, demanding to see identification. Each time, they produced their green American identity cards and their white Soviet passes, while Kathy calmly explained in Russian that they were simply taking a morning stroll. She had hoped to take her visitors down to the water to show them the black pebble beach, but the guards informed them it was off limits. One claimed it was because of the land mines that still washed up on the beach from time to time, though it seemed a weak excuse; the village of Yalta was also closed to them for no apparent reason. The three Americans were essentially trapped – in a large, airy and pleasant place, but trapped nonetheless. At least there was plenty to see around the palace grounds, including Rasputin's staircase leading up to the tsarina's boudoir, which Kathy made sure to point out. The American delegation was taking particular delight in teasing its current occupant, Admiral King, about his billet. As the fleet admiral had about as much personality as a 'snapping turtle', he surely did not find the jokes terribly amusing.

Though the two American women had dined together the previous evening, their walk around the grounds was their first opportunity to get to know each other. Kathy was grateful that Anna had come to Yalta. It would have been inappropriate for a mere ambassador's daughter to play hostess alongside the prime minister's daughter, regardless of how much Averell wanted to include her. But because Anna was part of the delegation, Kathy too was allowed to 'come & stay for the show'. So far, neither the show nor its actors had disappointed, least of all the leading man. Exhausted as Roosevelt was, he had come to life before a table of admirers during dinner. Kathy wrote to her sister that FDR was 'absolutely charming – easy to talk to with a lovely sense of humor'. Anna clearly shared her father's naturally sociable manner. Kathy thought the thirty-eight-year-old mother of three was 'great fun'. No doubt it was something of a relief to have a female friend by her side, especially one who spoke her language and was neither the immature teenage daughter of a foreign ambassador nor an American reporter's paid companion. Anna had endeared herself to Kathy almost immediately by telling her the story of Randolph Churchill's unexpected appearance in Malta, news that Kathy did not hesitate to relay to Pam in her letter.

Unbeknownst to Kathy, Anna did not reciprocate her new friend's warm feelings. They had known each other less than eighteen hours, but Anna had already formed a strong opinion of the poised ambassador's daughter who was guiding her around the palace grounds. 'I like Kathleen, but not as much as Sarah,' Anna wrote to her husband. 'The former is so damn self-assured, and to me, she lacks warmth of personality.'

It was a rather harsh comment to make after such a short acquaintance, perhaps more indicative of Anna's insecurity than Kathy's character. Objectively, there was much to envy about the beautiful, capable and bright girl standing toe-to-toe with armed Soviet guards. The Roosevelts may have been America's historic aristocracy, but the Harrimans embodied the unabashed American boldness of the twentieth century, a quality that had grated on the Roosevelts for three generations. Like her father and grandfather, Kathy was unquestionably independent and forthright, and she seemed to succeed in everything she attempted. Shortly after arriving in Moscow, Kathy had decided to compete in the Moscow Slalom Championships. She had once been considered for the U.S. national ski team for the 1940 Winter Olympics, which were ultimately cancelled due to the war; but aside from a few easy runs down the Lenin Hills, she had not worn a pair of skis since leaving for London in 1941. She had none of her own equipment, not even appropriate clothes. In a borrowed U.S. Navy sweatshirt large enough to fit a grown man and an old pair of ski pants held together with pins, she had taken third place against a field of the Soviet Union's best female skiers – many of whom were in the Red Army.

By comparison, Anna had struggled with a lack of self-confidence since she was a teenager, a trait she shared with her mother. Anna felt she had to secure Eleanor's approval before moving into the White House the previous spring, so as not to make her mother feel she was being pushed aside. But more important, compared to Kathy, Anna was an outsider. Though she was eleven years older and the president's daughter to boot, Anna was the novice. Nearly all the senior members of the three Allied delegations already knew and admired Kathy, thanks to their time together in London and Moscow. They naturally deferred to her as the ranking female at the conference, an honour that according to protocol should have been Anna's. No one meant any harm, but this was Anna's first, and likely only, turn to take top billing. She had waited so patiently, always standing behind her brothers, her mother, her grandmother, and a long list of political advisers. And yet, after waiting so long to receive the recognition she craved from her family, her father's inner circle, and especially FDR himself, there was someone else whose star shone brighter than hers.

It was some small solace to receive a useful scoop about Kathy from an unlikely source – Harry Hopkins. Before she went in to check on FDR that morning, she had gone back to Hopkins's room. Anna was uneasy with how she had left things with him the night before and realised it would behoove her to smooth things over. Hopkins clearly thought she was trying to 'save FDR too much'. Now, rather than let him think she was interfering in business beyond her experience, she decided to 'augment' her '"buttering" processes in [that] direction'.

Fortunately, Hopkins had calmed down and appeared to be 'responding nicely' to her efforts to reach a detente. Recognising the advantage of making her an ally rather than an adversary, he too extended a peace offering in the form of a bit of gossip about the lovely and talented Miss Harriman. 'Harry tells me that she and one F. Jr. [Anna's younger brother, Franklin Delano Roosevelt Jr] had a heavy romance about a year and a half or two years ago,' Anna wrote to John. With thick, dark blond hair and an enormous smile, Franklin Jr was by far the most handsome of the four Roosevelt brothers (and the only one with any semblance of a chin). He was also married to the heiress Ethel du Pont. Harry told Anna that Kathy and Frank's brief, punch-fuelled fling had occurred when he passed through London on navy business while the Harrimans were based there, likely in June 1942. The affair was not just idle gossip. Harry knew it was true, as 'he used to have to carry letters between them!' Perhaps Kathy was not quite as correct and forthright as she wanted people to believe.

As Kathy led her charges about the garden, she remained oblivious to Anna's feelings towards her. Even if she sensed that Anna was not terribly fond of her, she probably would not have cared. Back in London, there had been one other woman on the INS reporting staff, Inez Robb, who had decided she loathed Kathy after meeting her but twice. Inez convinced herself that Kathy was trying to steal her stories and tried repeatedly to get her fired. Despite Inez's histrionics, Kathy remained unruffled. 'I suppose women must be jealous,' she wrote to her sister, 'but it all seems too stupid to me.'

NINE

February 4, 1945

Molotov had lied to Churchill and Roosevelt at Saki airfield when he told them that Stalin was not yet in the Crimea. The Soviet general secretary had already arrived from Moscow by armoured train and was safely ensconced within the Koreiz Villa. The mansion had recently undergone some improvements. Under Lavrentiy Beria's watchful eye, labourers had constructed a bomb shelter, complete with a concrete ceiling two metres thick, which could survive the direct blast of five hundred kilograms of explosives. From the Koreiz Villa, Stalin had carefully monitored his allies' arrival by means of telephone updates from Molotov. He had also stationed several doctors incognito at Saki; their job was to observe FDR from the sidelines and report whether rumours about the president's declining health were believable. They reported in the affirmative.

That afternoon, after his visitors had a night of sleep and had settled into their residences, the elusive Stalin finally decided to show himself, beginning his performance with a visit to Vorontsov Palace to welcome the prime minister. The British expected Stalin to arrive at three. Thinking she had a few minutes to spare, Sarah dashed to her room to freshen up, but, as if determined to keep the westerners off balance, Stalin arrived early, before the British delegation had even finished assembling in the foyer to greet him. Sarah missed his entrance entirely. Winston barely made it in time.

Stalin's visit with Churchill was largely social; the general secretary was simply fulfilling the duties of any good host. He officially welcomed the British to the Crimea. During the visit, Churchill showed Stalin his cherished Map Room, the dynamic hub from which he followed military progress. The original Map Room was part of the Cabinet War Rooms, a secret bunker deep below the Treasury building in Whitehall, safe from the blast of Nazi bombs. Churchill's staff had created a portable Map Room for the prime minister to take on his travels, so he could continue to track the Allied armies' progress. As Churchill showed off his maps, the two men had 'an agreeable discussion' on the general state of military affairs in Germany, where the Wehrmacht's strength was quickly collapsing, but they refrained from addressing any specifics or any topics more political in nature. Half an hour later, Stalin said his goodbyes and continued down the road for his second, more important meeting.

Though under the guise of a social call, the meeting Harriman had arranged with Molotov between Roosevelt and Stalin at Livadia Palace at 4 p.m. had a very different tone. Stalin brought his foreign secretary, Vyacheslav Molotov, and his interpreter, Vladimir Pavlov, to the meeting, but Roosevelt decided against including Harriman or his secretary of state and brought in only Chip Bohlen, to translate. As Roosevelt had told Churchill, he believed he had a strong personal rapport with Stalin and did not want anyone from the State Department to get in his way.

Like Churchill, Roosevelt had some general military matters to discuss with Stalin, but he preferred to save those details for the 5 p.m. meeting, which would include the combined chiefs of staff. Instead, Roosevelt wanted to use his private audience with the Soviet leader to address a different agenda. While Churchill was already looking ahead to the postwar world and imagining demons emerging from the Soviet Union, Roosevelt had not forgotten that the western Allies and the Soviets remained united by facing a common enemy. He now looked to that enemy to remind Stalin of the forces that continued to bind the Americans and the Soviets together. Roosevelt's confession to Anna on the drive to Yalta – that the destruction in the Crimea made him feel more bloodthirsty than ever towards the Germans – was a rehearsal for what he would say to Stalin. He repeated those words almost exactly before adding that he hoped Stalin would once again 'propose a toast to the execution of 50,000 officers of the German Army', referencing a comment Stalin had made at Tehran, about executing the top 50,000 officers in the German high command. Churchill had objected, vociferously, to such bloodletting, no matter how evil the perpetrators. At the time, Stalin insisted it was just a joke, but Churchill was never quite 'convinced that all was chaff and there was no serious intent lurking behind'.

Having emphatically defined the common enemy in a way that subtly reminded Stalin of Churchill's opposition, Roosevelt then revealed that he was about to say 'something indiscreet', which he did not want to say in the presence of the prime minister. The British, Roosevelt told Stalin, 'were a peculiar people and wished to have their cake and eat it too'. For the past two years, they had been trying to convince the Americans to work to 'artificially [build] up France into a strong power' as a hedge against future German aggression. Once the war was over and the Americans went home, the British would reassume 'political control' over the French. One of the ways the British sought to do this, Roosevelt suggested, was by securing an administrative occupation zone for the French in postwar Germany, which the British would quickly dominate. As France had done so little of the work to defeat the Nazis on the battlefield, after its army's rapid collapse in 1940, Roosevelt was not sure they deserved a zone. The only reason to give them a zone, he joked, was 'out of kindness'.

Stalin agreed that the subject of a French-controlled zone in postwar Germany was one that required careful consideration but went no further. As it was nearly 5 p.m., the two leaders concluded their conversation on that note. Though they had made no concrete agreements, Roosevelt had achieved what he wanted. He had offered Stalin an important signal: the Americans were not simply going to walk in lockstep with the British this time. The Americans and the Soviets could negotiate without them.

• • •

Just before 5 p.m., the delegates from the three nations began to arrive at Livadia Palace for the first plenary session. It would be the first of eight tripartite meetings among the Allied leaders and their advisers scheduled over the next eight days. Soviet soldiers armed with tommy guns now stood on the Livadia Palace roof, and the nearby roads were closed to everyone except the delegates travelling from Vorontsov Palace and the Koreiz Villa. Stalin arrived with Molotov, surrounded as ever by his cadre of brass-buttoned guards. Generals and admirals from the three delegations soon appeared at the front door, strutting past two sad-looking potted palm trees as they entered the grand hall to join their political counterparts for the opening discussion on the state of military affairs in Europe. It was the first time the joint chiefs of all three Allied nations had gathered since Tehran. Now that the Ardennes had been cleared in northwest France and Belgium, the combined American and British offensive under Dwight D. Eisenhower's command had resumed their rapid advance on Berlin from the west; the Soviets had crossed the Oder River forty miles east of the German capital just days before. Though there were many thorny political considerations to discuss about the end of the war in Europe and developments in the Pacific, everyone agreed that, first and foremost, it was imperative for the Allied military chiefs to execute a united strategy to avoid chaos when their respective armies converged on Berlin.

When Sarah arrived at Livadia with Winston, Anna, in her short fur coat, was positioned at the front door, the first to greet them. Acting as her father's representative as he waited inside in his wheelchair, Anna said hello to Sarah, who hopped out of the car first. Anna then gave the prime minister a firm handshake, just as her father would have. She also shook hands with Anthony Eden, who arrived just after the Churchills. The British party was small compared to those of the Soviets and Americans, whose principals were flanked by an omnipresent, imposing security detail. Churchill, by contrast, had no phalanx – just two men in suits who melted into the background. As everyone moved inside, Anna invited Sarah to stand with her and Robert Hopkins among the pool of photographers snapping pictures of the historic gathering. Two British, sixteen American, and more than thirty

Soviet photographers jostled for position, their flashbulbs constantly blocking one another's shots of the leaders. Anna snapped a few photos of her own to share with John. Nearby, Kathy and Secretary of State Stettinius exchanged pleasantries.

Once everyone's coats and hats had been taken and the requisite photographs had been snapped, the delegates were ready to enter the ballroom. Before going in, Winston went over to Sarah, who was looking at him, eyebrows raised with hope and concern in equal measure. He gave her arm a reassuring squeeze. Then the dignitaries and delegates filed into the stark white ballroom, with its enormous round table and chairs carted in for the occasion. The photographers took a few final pictures, and the enormous double doors swung shut. The conference had officially begun.

Behind the closed doors, twenty-eight men took their positions around the table. Roosevelt's interpreter, Chip Bohlen, though dressed neatly in a grey suit and crisp white shirt, was ready for his profession's version of a marathon. Bohlen and his British and Russian counterparts, Arthur Birse and Vladimir Pavlov, were called interpreters rather than translators for a reason. If translation was a science, interpretation was an art. It required someone who was both a polyglot and an actor; the job involved much more than putting the words of one language into another. An interpreter had to translate intent, matching the tone and inflection of the voices being represented, emphasising certain words, minimising others. They intuitively had to understand when their principals were pausing to collect their thoughts or searching for a precise word to make their meaning exactly clear, or when they were deliberately trying to obfuscate or to play for time. Today, however, would be more of a biathlon than a marathon for Bohlen. Harry Hopkins had made the interpreter's job significantly more complicated by assigning him a second task. Hopkins, who had once again willed himself out of bed to make it to the meeting, had remembered, with some alarm, that FDR often kept no record of vitally important meetings.

Not only would Bohlen have to interpret; Hopkins insisted that he also take copious notes for the official conference record as he translated English into Russian.

As Bohlen prepared to handle two tasks, both requiring speed and precision, he sat down, with his papers and pencils, immediately to FDR's left. In a less formal or social situation, he would have sat just behind the president, but he needed the table surface to take his notes for translation and for the record. Bohlen likely did not realise it, but this had left Averell Harriman with no place at the table. While Bohlen arranged his papers, the ambassador dragged a chair from the corner of the room, his hand thrust nonchalantly into the pocket of his double-breasted suit as if to say he did not care. He placed it in the back row of chairs that formed an outer ring, while his fellow British and Soviet ambassadors, Archie Clark-Kerr and Fedor Gusev, had seats at the table. ('Bad luck on A,' Peter Portal later wrote acidly regarding his rival, in the continuous, nearly thirty-page letter he had been writing to Pamela Churchill since leaving London.)

Stalin asked Roosevelt to open the conference, as he had at Tehran. FDR eagerly complied. He began by expressing his desire that the 'talks be conducted in an informal manner in which each man would speak his mind frankly and freely'. When Roosevelt finished, Bohlen put his words into Russian. For the sake of clarity, translation at the conference would be sequential, rather than simultaneous, though it made everything take twice as long. Buoyed by FDR's message of good faith and optimism, the formal proceedings began with General Antonov's analysis of the Red Army's recent significant successes on the Eastern Front. In turn, General George Marshall, the chief of staff of the U.S. Army, summarised activity on the Western Front, estimating that the combined Anglo-American forces would cross the Rhine shortly after March 1. Stalin was pleased with the report and Churchill found the atmosphere 'most cordial', even if Admiral Cunningham, Britain's First Sea Lord, was a bit miffed that Marshall had taken it upon himself to provide the British military briefing as well. Over the next three hours, the three interpreters worked furiously as the combined chiefs and the heads of government discussed the technical and strategic aspects of the advance on Berlin. Their military staffs would then be prepared to sort out specific details of the coordinated plans at their own meeting the next day.

As the discussion unfolded, Stalin said little, interjecting only short questions or highlights of Soviet military strength, such as statistics that proved the artillery's supremacy. Just before the meeting adjourned, he indicated that he had something to say, prompting Pavlov to begin the process of putting the general secretary's thoughts into English. Stalin was a difficult man to interpret. He spoke Russian with a heavy Georgian accent, the equivalent, Churchill's interpreter Arthur Birse observed, of a Scot from the remote Highlands speaking English. He was impatient and often berated his interpreters to get on with it. Fortunately, Pavlov was stoic, even in the face of humiliation, but for now Stalin behaved himself as he delivered a crucial remark. The Red Army's winter offensive on the Eastern Front, he said, was not a result of any agreement the Allied powers had made at Tehran. Rather, it was a gesture of Soviet good faith and commitment to their alliance. Stalin assured his counterparts that in making such a statement he simply wanted to 'emphasize the spirit of the Soviet leaders who not only fulfilled formal obligations but went farther and acted on what they conceived to be their moral duty to their Allies'.

Turning to Stalin, Churchill responded in a seemingly friendly yet pointed fashion, which he relied on Birse to capture: 'The reason that neither the British nor Americans had made any attempt to bargain with Marshal Stalin,' to launch a winter offensive in the East, he stated, 'was because of their faith in him and in the Russian people,' for 'they could be depended on to do the right thing.'

As Bohlen recorded the minutes, he kept his personal opinions out of the official record. Though at Yalta to serve as Roosevelt's interpreter, Bohlen was actually one of the State Department's foremost experts on the Soviet Union, small in number though they were, and had served at the American embassy in Moscow in the 1930s. Bohlen had more extensive contacts among the Russian people and government, and a better understanding of the Russian language and culture, than almost anyone in Washington. He was by no means persuaded that 'an era of good feeling' was on the horizon, as Roosevelt hoped. It was true that the Red Army had taken the brunt of Nazi hostility on the

Eastern Front for nearly three years before the British and the Americans opened a second front in France. The Soviets' sacrifices, however, were hardly altruistic. If it served Stalin's objectives to act in accordance with what he could argue was a 'moral duty' to his Allies, he would do so, but the instant it no longer suited his interests, he would not hesitate to follow his own path.

The previous evening, Bohlen had received a sharply worded telegram from his colleague and friend of more than a decade, George Kennan, Averell Harriman's deputy chief in Moscow. 'I am aware of the realities of this war, and . . . I recognize that Russia's war effort has been masterful and effective and must, to a certain extent, find its reward at the expense of other people in eastern and central Europe,' Kennan began. Then he offered a word of caution: 'Although it was evident that the realities of the after-war were being shaped while the war was in progress we have consistently refused . . . to name any limit for Russian expansion.' In his opinion, any attempt to negotiate with the Soviets over territory the Red Army already occupied was entirely futile, and the Red Army was pushing farther north and west every day. The Americans might as well divide Europe into spheres of influence now and save everyone's time and energy. As Kennan asserted, at this point, any negotiation over territory was 'simply an attempt . . . to lock the stable door after the horse was stolen'.

In theory, Bohlen did not disagree. The Soviets were unlikely to make any significant concessions to the western Allies, no matter what the president optimistically but naively believed about his personal relationship with Stalin. But, Bohlen maintained, as Roosevelt was the leader of the world's strongest democracy, he had an obligation to try.

With the principal delegates sequestered behind the double doors, the hall soon grew uncomfortably quiet. From time to time a Russian servant or an underling from the British Foreign Office would enter the ballroom with silent footsteps to clear away glassware or deliver fresh cups of tea. They moved in and out so quietly and carefully, it was as if they were trying not to disturb those holding vigil for one who was ill and soon to die behind the ballroom doors.

While their fathers deliberated, Sarah and Kathleen were free to relax, knowing they would not be needed until after the dinner following the plenary session broke up late that night. As the two friends had not seen each other since the fall of 1943, they looked forward to their own dinner that evening – the 'children's party', as Kathy dubbed it – with Anna and some old pals from London, such as General Fred Anderson, one of Pamela's old flames, who had not made the list for the official dinner that night. Someone from the advance team had even managed to rig up a movie theatre for them on the second floor.

Meanwhile, Anna continued to suffer the headaches of being her father's trusted aide-de-camp. While the two younger women enjoyed a brief respite, Anna was 'sitting on tacks'. FDR was hosting the official dinner for his British and Soviet counterparts that evening. Once again, he had failed to give her a list of the people he wished to invite, and now that the Soviets were involved, Anna had to be particularly careful not to slight anyone by leaving him out. She could have asked Kathy for assistance. The younger woman had plenty of experience managing the intricacies of Soviet diplomatic dinner parties, but Anna intended to manage on her own, despite being out of her depth.

Before the plenary session, Averell Harriman had noticed that Anna was agonising over the dinner invitations. He reassured her that it was perfectly normal, at meetings like these, for dinner invitations to be issued off the cuff. Once again he offered to help her so that she need not trouble FDR. He told her that during a break in the conference, he would sort out the details, then come and find her to give her the list of names. Finally, after almost three and a half hours of discussion – nearly the time when dinner was scheduled to begin – the ambassador emerged from behind the double doors with his list. He offered Anna some advice on seating arrangements, then left her with FDR's aide, Lieutenant Rigdon, to work out the correct spelling of each person's name for the place cards.

Just as Anna completed those cards, the double doors of the ballroom opened and the conferees spilled into the hall, finished with their discussion for the day. They milled about, making conversation;

some went to freshen up for dinner. Just at that moment, Dr Bruenn suddenly appeared at Anna's side with an urgent message. Anna had to go to Jimmy Byrnes's room straightaway. Bruenn had just escaped from there, but poor Pa Watson, Steve Early, Dr McIntire and Rear Admiral Wilson Brown were still trapped. Byrnes 'was having a tantrum' and refused to attend FDR's dinner. Between Byrnes's probing questions about FDR's health during their voyage on the *Quincy* and now this, it seemed as if the man was determined to make Anna's time in Yalta a misery.

'A tantrum was putting it mildly!' Anna thought as she arrived at Byrnes's room. 'Fire was shooting from his eyes!' Byrnes was accustomed to wielding power. A former senator from South Carolina who had served a brief stint as an associate justice of the Supreme Court, Byrnes had become head of the Office of War Mobilization, an independent government agency FDR had created in 1943 to coordinate the activity of all other government agencies on war-related matters. This role gave Byrnes broad powers in Washington. Many referred to him as the 'Assistant President'. Used to being included in all war-related meetings at the highest levels, he had found himself that evening on the wrong side of the door to the first plenary session. FDR believed Stalin would be more willing to speak candidly about military issues if the number of civilian participants was held to a minimum, so he had decided not to invite Byrnes. Eventually, FDR took pity and told him to come to the ballroom at 6 p.m., but, as Anna gathered, after 'cooling his heels outside said doors for 45 minutes . . . nobody said boo to him', so he sulked away, frustrated and embarrassed, outraged that Harry Hopkins, also a civilian adviser, had been included in the meeting. In retaliation for the blow to his pride, he now categorically refused to attend Roosevelt's dinner. He even threatened to leave the conference altogether.

While Byrnes was nominally at Yalta to represent the Office of War Mobilization, FDR had primarily asked his old friend along to lend the conference additional gravitas. Byrnes, with his droopy eyes, hangdog countenance and wisps of grey hair, was a longtime Roosevelt ally and looked the part of seasoned elder statesman, as if straight from central casting. The invitation was also a sort of consolation prize for Byrnes,

FDR holding Anna, age three, at Campobello Island in 1909, twelve years before his paralysis. *Courtesy of the Franklin D. Roosevelt Presidential Library & Museum*

FDR and Anna sit by the fire in Warm Springs, Georgia, in 1932. FDR rarely allowed himself to be photographed in a wheelchair and many Americans did not realize he was paralyzed. *Bettmann / Getty Images*

Winston, Clementine, and Sarah Churchill, age four or five, attend a parade of the Brigade of the Guards, 1919.
PA Images / Alamy Stock Photo

Winston and Sarah, age thirteen, laying bricks at Chartwell, 1928.
Fremantle / Alamy Stock Photo

Kathleen, age two, Averell, and Mary Harriman at Overhills, North Carolina, 1920.
Used by permission of the Mortimer family

Kathleen Harriman ski-racing at Sun Valley, ca. 1930s.
Used by permission of the Mortimer family

Averell Harriman at Sun Valley, ca. 1930s.
Courtesy of Library of Congress

The Boettiger family at home in Seattle, 1939 (L-R: Curtis, John, Ellie, Anna, and Johnny). *Courtesy of John Roosevelt Boettiger*

Section Officer
Sarah Churchill
Oliver, Photographic
Interpretation Unit, RAF
Medmenham, ca. 1943–1945.
*Photo from Sarah Churchill
Papers. Used by permission of
Churchill Archives Center.*

The tsar's bedroom at Livadia Palace, where FDR stayed for the duration of the Yalta
Conference. *Photo from U.S. Army Signal Corps. Courtesy of Newberry Library.*

Anna, Sarah, FDR, and Churchill chat aboard the USS *Quincy*, Valletta Harbor, Malta, February 2, 1945.
Courtesy of the Franklin D. Roosevelt Presidential Library & Museum

Averell Harriman greets FDR aboard the USS *Quincy*, Valletta Harbor, Malta, February 2, 1945. *Photo from U.S. Army Signal Corps. Accessed from the Averell Harriman Papers. Courtesy of Library of Congress.*

FDR's plane lands at Saki, February 3, 1945.
Provided from the personal archive of Boris Kosarev courtesy of his sole heir, Maria Kosareva.

Soviet military parade marking the conference delegates' arrival in the Crimea, Saki airfield, February 3, 1945.
Photo accessed from the Averell Harriman Papers. Courtesy of Library of Congress.

Livadia Palace, February 1945.
Photo from U.S. Army Signal Corps. Courtesy of Newberry Library.

View of the mountains from Livadia Palace, February 1945.
Photo from U.S. Army Signal Corps. Courtesy of Newberry Library.

whom FDR had passed over for vice president when he replaced Henry Wallace with Harry Truman on the 1944 ticket. Given that Byrnes had little of immediate value to contribute to the conference, Anna thought his churlish fit was completely ridiculous. She detested this kind of petty behaviour from sycophants competing for her father's attention – Byrnes's outburst was the second such episode that day. At lunch Anna had arranged a small table for her father and five people who would not pester him; Admiral Leahy had then burst in uninvited and awkwardly inserted himself into their quiet luncheon *en famille*, spoiling her plans. Anna quickly made room, but Leahy made it clear that he felt slighted at not having been included in the first place. Exasperated, Anna wrote in her journal that afternoon that she would 'have to watch certain people's feelings very carefully'. The principal conference delegates had risen to prominence by virtue of ambition, talent and force of personality, and many had become obsessed with their own importance. Byrnes was a prime example. Much like Harry Hopkins, Byrnes could be 'a real prima donna', Anna thought.

For more than twenty minutes, Anna and Byrnes argued, Anna insisting he attend FDR's dinner, and Byrnes refusing. Hearing the commotion, Averell Harriman came in to offer backup, but Byrnes would not capitulate. It turned into an outright 'free for all'. Several times Anna was tempted to shout, 'Who cares anyhow if you do or don't [go] to the dinner!' but forced herself to maintain composure. She knew FDR wanted Byrnes to be there.

Finally, Anna made one last, completely absurd appeal. FDR hated the number thirteen. If Byrnes refused to go, they would be left with the devil's number at dinner. Roosevelt would have 'ten fits' and it would be all Byrnes's fault.

For whatever reason, that broke him. At last Byrnes relented and wandered off to the dining room. Anna, temporarily released from her duties, went to join Sarah, Kathy, and some of the generals who were under forty, whom Kathy had 'corralled', including Anderson and his U.S. Army Air Corps colleague Laurence Kuter – 'a swell 2 starer', as Kathy called him. Anna had missed most of the 'children's party' dinner, but at least she was in time for the movie.

• • •

Later that night, Anna went in to see her father before he fell asleep. His dinner had been a terrific success. His chefs had prepared an array of chicken, vegetables and macaroni to balance out the caviar and sturgeon, and everyone seemed most satisfied with the evening. Byrnes in particular had made a very 'fine toast!'

Pleased but a bit surprised, Anna betrayed nothing about Byrnes's earlier antics as she bid her father goodnight. As she had done so many times, she tidied away any unpleasantness that might upset him. Roosevelt remained blissfully ignorant about what transpired between his closest confidants when his back was turned – though, Anna noted, with the right spin, the Byrnes story would make an amusing tale at some later time.

TEN

February 5, 1945

I f you were a spectator along the bedroom corridors here at about 7:30 in the morning,' Sarah wrote to her mother, 'you would see 3 Field Marshals queuing for a bucket! And really some Field Marshals will not go into a bucket!' The bathrooms at Vorontsov Palace were no more plentiful than at Livadia; a mere four had to do for the entire British contingent. Only one had a flush toilet, and that was exclusively reserved for the prime minister.

Each morning, the chiefs of staff preserved their dignity by sending their aides to secure a place in the queue, which formed earlier and earlier every day. Air Marshal Sir Peter Portal, however, had his own method of securing a bathroom. Portal's Christian name was Charles Frederick Algernon, but somewhere along the way he had picked up the nickname 'Peter', and it stuck. A motorcycle aficionado turned pilot during World War I, he had an irreverent sense of humour. Whenever he felt that someone was taking too long in the bath, he would jump up and down to get a view through the transom above the door to determine the identity of the offending party and call him out by name. Before long, an embarrassed field marshal would emerge, dripping in his dressing gown, to sheepishly retreat to his room. If that did not work, Portal was not above picking the lock and bursting in.

Kathy had mused to Pamela, after visiting Vorontsov during its preparation for the British delegation, that if the bathroom situation turned truly desperate, the men might be driven to bathing in the massive champagne cooler, which was as large as a tub. 'Papa is very sweet and insists on me sharing his bathroom,' Sarah told Clementine, but overall, the 'ablution question' was 'grim'. So was the bug situation. Winston awoke with bed-bug bites all over his feet.

At Livadia Palace, to bring some order to the chaos, everyone had been assigned to one of the nine bathrooms, and temporary latrines had been constructed outside; but it was still hardly sufficient for a delegation of well over a hundred people billeted at the palace or one of the outbuildings. Sinks, toilets and bathtubs were in different rooms. As a result, the dignified diplomats and senior officers who, as a matter of principle, refused to use bedpans found themselves holding impromptu conferences bright and early in the hallways, as they waited in the interminable queues. Once in the bathroom, a delegate quickly discovered, the challenges continued. Privacy appeared an alien concept to the Russian staff. To many an unsuspecting general's dismay, chambermaids wandered in and out while a bather was in the tub.

It seemed as if the basic functions of human life could not be performed without risk at Yalta. Even the drinking water posed a hazard. The conferees were offered tap water or mineral water. Though they had been told it was safe to drink the former, they remained sceptical. The mineral water seemed the smarter choice – until they found that it contained magnesium sulfate, a natural laxative. Given the shortage of bathrooms, this gave them pause. In the end, they decided to risk the known perils of the mineral water rather than the bacteria and parasites that might lurk in the tap.

Everywhere the delegates turned, they found opulence and primitiveness in stark juxtaposition. Those who survived the morning bathroom gauntlet were rewarded with a two-course breakfast of questionable allure served by waiters from Moscow's luxurious Hotel Metropol and Hotel National. First came the Russian course: cold cuts, goat's cheese, and sour-cream-covered curd cakes, which had a consistency like that of cottage cheese. This was followed by what the Russians considered an American breakfast course, featuring both Wheatena cereal and Cream of Wheat – inventively prepared with hot butter and garlic. Some delegates were more adventurous eaters. Admiral Leahy was not one of them. When a waiter 'speaking no known language' arrived, Leahy started gesticulating wildly and barking in a loud voice – as if to overcome the language barrier – saying that all he wanted was an egg, toast and coffee. Fifteen minutes later, the waiter returned with a tray of caviar, ham, smoked fish and vodka. 'For God's sake,' an apoplectic Leahy bellowed, 'send me someone who speaks English!' Lunch was little better. Of the three to four courses, two were invariably caviar served with Russian black bread and a variation on cabbage soup.

Anna, Kathleen and Sarah would generally join their fathers for luncheons, which were generally quieter, more intimate affairs. Churchill's lunch was really more like 'brunch', as the Americans called it. At Yalta, he and Sarah were staying up past 2 a.m., as the diplomatic pouch carrying urgent Downing Street business did not arrive from London until midnight. As a result, Winston woke up late and did not eat his first meal until 11.30 a.m., the only one he would eat until dinner in the evening, as he worked the whole afternoon before the plenary session.

Lunches with FDR were more of a party. 'Comparing those meals with the Chequers ones,' Kathy told Pamela, 'they couldn't be more different.' During dinners at Chequers, which Kathy remembered so clearly, dire news of the war trumped all other topics of conversation, and the prime minister would wax endlessly on the topic. By contrast, 'The Pres. is absolutely charming, easy to talk to on any subject – The war is seldom mentioned except on the lighter side – the conference discussions gets talked about briefly – but in the main it's politics, friends, with everyone swapping amusing stories.' Included in FDR's luncheons were his customary 'hangers on', as Kathy called them, including the New York Democratic boss and FDR's political adviser Ed Flynn (apparently at the conference for a 'joy ride'), Pa Watson (genuinely kind, but also at Yalta largely to keep the president company), Admiral Leahy, and the press secretary, Steve Early, who Kathy found 'very self-important & stuffy'. Kathy told Pam, 'It's amusing watching them play court.'

With the arrival of Churchill, Roosevelt and their 'courtiers', it was as if royalty had once again come to Yalta; the Russian servants stood at their beck and call to serve their every whim. In 1867, the writer Mark Twain had visited Tsar Alexander II at Yalta during a round-the-world excursion with a group of fellow American voyagers. After visiting Russia, Twain concluded, 'A Russian imbues his polite things with a heartiness, both of phrase and expression, that compels belief in their sincerity.' It seemed that even after seventy-eight years, two world wars and a revolution, little had changed. So overwhelming were the Russians' shows of hospitality that at times the experience became a bit unnerving. While eating one of the countless dishes of caviar, Sarah Churchill offhandedly mentioned to no one in particular that lemon would accompany the caviar quite nicely. The next day, a lemon tree suddenly materialised in the orangery. In another instance, Peter Portal was admiring a large, glass fish tank in the Vorontsov conservatory. A number of plants were living inside it, but no fish, he remarked with amusement to some companions. Soon after, a school of goldfish could be found swimming happily in the tank. Someone had overheard Sarah and Portal. Who, and how, they did not know.

Most unsettling was the Soviets' offer of 'bed warmers' to their western guests. This sounded like a thoughtful gesture until one realised that the hosts were not referring to hot-water bottles, electric blankets, or even the old-fashioned perforated-metal boxes filled with hot stones. No, the bed warmers were young Russian women, at the delegates' disposal to do with as they pleased. When Anna learned of this, she was hardly surprised, given what she knew about the largely inferior status of women in Soviet society. But it bothered her all the same. Fortunately, it appeared that no one accepted the offer.

The meetings on February 5 started on a high note – after a bit of requisite confusion. While all of the afternoon plenary sessions would take place at Livadia Palace, the daily military conferences and foreign ministers' meetings rotated among the three Allied residences. At noon, the British chiefs of staff arrived at the Koreiz Villa to continue the previous day's plenary discussion with their American and Soviet counterparts. But when they pulled up at the gate, the NKVD sentries refused to let them past the stable yard. Peter Portal, Field Marshal Sir Alan Brooke, Admiral Andrew Cunningham, Field Marshal Harold Alexander and General Hastings 'Pug' Ismay were, after Churchill, among the most recognisable British names and faces of the war, but the NKVD seemed to have no idea who they were. After 'much telephoning' the issue was resolved and the guards waved them through. Meanwhile, the Americans had their own morning debacle. They arrived to the meeting half an hour late, having first gone to Vorontsov Palace by mistake. Eventually, the chiefs of staff got down to business and had a productive three-hour meeting about military coordination across land, air and sea.

The cordiality continued at the 1.30 p.m. meeting of the three foreign secretaries and ambassadors, the first of what would be daily meetings of the primary foreign policy experts and their staffs. Averell Harriman soon interrupted the proceedings to make an announcement. He had just received word that General Douglas MacArthur's troops had defeated the Japanese at Manila. It was a decisive blow to the enemy, certainly marking the end to their three-year occupation of the Philippines. As was the Russian custom, triumphant toasts had to be drunk all around before business could continue.

Convivial as the atmosphere seemed, Harriman had little confidence that the euphoric cooperative spirit, buoyed by the victory, would last. The Soviets' negotiation strategy followed a definite pattern with which he was intimately familiar. In the beginning, the Soviets would be cordial, obliging, and cooperative to the extreme, particularly about issues that were not a priority. In the second phase, the mood would shift abruptly. This was when they dug in their heels on matters they cared deeply about. They would be brusque, gruff and even hostile, refusing to budge from a particular position while emphasising how accommodating they had already been. But by the end of the proceedings, they would revert to jovial amiability and send their guests off with a celebratory banquet, filled with toasts to the spirit of cooperation and the strength of the alliance. The Soviets had mastered this negotiation tactic and could adapt it as needed. They had demonstrated this at Tehran. Surely they would do it again.

≡

Before leaving Vorontsov Palace for the plenary session at Livadia that afternoon, Winston and Sarah took a walk down to the terrace for a better look at the sea in the winter sun. The day was mild, and the sun warmed the terrace so nicely that Sarah was able to leave her coat behind. She was beginning to regret having spent her precious clothing ration coupons on thermal layers to wear under her uniform. The temperature here was a welcome change from perpetually shivering in the damp cold and fog that enveloped RAF Medmenham, which left Sarah suffering from painful chilblains on her feet. On their walk they encountered three of the top British military representatives from the army and the RAF – Alan Brooke, Harold Alexander and Peter Portal – who had just returned from the meeting of the combined chiefs of staff at the Koreiz Villa. The three officers decided to join them.

As the party of five stood along the edge of the terrace, looking down at the water, they noticed a remarkable sight. In the slick, oily-looking grey water below, a slaughter was underway. A school of fish directly beneath them was being assailed on two fronts: a great pod of porpoises was attacking from the sea, while a flock of hundreds of seagulls assaulted from the air. For the predators, it was a feast.

Sarah watched the carnage, expecting the fish to swim away and save themselves. But as the feasting continued, the fish schooled closer together. Over and over again, the porpoises attacked like U-boats targeting a shipping convoy, while the formation of circling gulls dive-bombed from on high. Still, the fish huddled in tight formation, safety in numbers their only protection. They were willing to sacrifice many to protect the school as a whole.

The slaughter went on and on; the porpoises' and gulls' appetites seemed insatiable. Sarah stared in horror and fascination. To her dismay, the military chiefs failed to share her incredulity. Portal was daydreaming about what a lovely day it would be for a sail, while Brooke, who was the vice president of the Royal Society for the Protection of Birds, stood admiring the gulls, as well as the ducks, loons and cormorants that had joined the action.

Sarah turned to Brooke, shaking him out of his reverie. 'Surely,' she exclaimed, the fish were 'idiotic not to disperse.'

Brooke quickly dismissed the idea. 'Not at all,' he said. 'It is much better they should stick together.'

Hearing Brooke's comment, Winston immediately piped up. He agreed with Sarah entirely. It would be much better for each fish to take the offensive to preserve its own life than to allow the group to decide for it that it was just one dispensable fish whose life was worth no less or no more than its neighbour's. Brooke, he scoffed, had allowed his 'usual cool dispassionate judgment' to become 'badly prejudiced' because of his affinity for the feathered species.

Sarah and Winston soon headed back to the house to find the car that would take them to Livadia, leaving Brooke to admire his birds, but Sarah's mind lingered over the disturbing scene.

Earlier, Sarah had looked to the lines on a person's palm to divine the future. Perhaps now she had been given a genuine sign. The growing ideological divide over Europe's fate – whether the continent would be shaped by the Soviets' vision for collective action or the West's commitment to self-determination – had been starkly mirrored in that grisly ecological tableau.

At 4 p.m., twenty-three men sat down around the conference table, which floated like an atoll in the Livadia Palace ballroom. Birch logs blazed in the cavernous stone fireplace, bringing some warmth to an otherwise cold, hard and empty space, about as welcoming as a mausoleum. Once again, Harry Hopkins had dragged himself out of bed for the meeting. And this time Harriman made sure to secure his rightful place at the table.

For the past few days, Franklin Roosevelt had appeared alarmingly haggard, but today he looked markedly better. His mind was sharp and alert, and his colour had returned, his face animated by his customary vigour. This would be a crucial day for Roosevelt, one that could set the tone for the rest of the conference. The previous day had been devoted to military matters. Now was the time to carefully prod at the great geopolitical questions that lay before them. Just as he had done at the first plenary session, Roosevelt opened the discussion.

It was tempting, he began, to have a broad-ranging discussion that touched the four corners of the world, but today they would 'confine themselves' exclusively to the 'future treatment of Germany'. It was the subject he had broached with Stalin the day before, in their private conversation. Roosevelt then passed Stalin a map of Germany drawn by the European Advisory Commission. It depicted Germany carved into three zones: an American zone in the south, a British zone in the west, and a Soviet zone in the east. In the centre of the Soviet zone, Berlin was circled with a bold pen stroke. The three Allies would administer Berlin jointly.

Stalin stopped him almost immediately. Roosevelt may have assumed they were of like minds after their private discussion the day before, but Stalin followed no one's agenda but his own. He turned the conversation in a different direction. It was not enough to partition Germany into zones of occupation, Stalin insisted. After the past war, the victors thought they had rehabilitated Germany, but they were clearly mistaken. This time, Germany needed to be completely dismembered so that it could never rise up in violence again.

The issue of dismemberment had first been raised at Tehran, and at the time Roosevelt had considered it worthy of exploration, but it was not a path he wanted to tread at this meeting. Instead of taking a firm stance on breaking Germany into a number of smaller states, he sidestepped the matter with a diversionary tactic, steering the conversation back into calmer waters. He began to reminisce on the Germany he remembered from his European travels as a young student, more than forty years earlier, when he and his tutor had spent many happy days cycling across the German countryside. Back then, Germany had been a very different place. There was no Reich, but rather a loose confederation of provinces with their own local governments. As Roosevelt waxed poetic, the Soviets looked at him with indifference, as if waiting for a slightly senile relative to return from a tangential reverie. Churchill toyed with his cigar while Eden stared off at some point in the distance. No one was quite sure whether Roosevelt was exercising skilful diplomatic legerdemain or losing his marbles.

As Roosevelt knew, Churchill had strong feelings about dismemberment. The Americans would not feel the immediate effects of continental Europe's problems in the war's aftermath, but Britain would. At Tehran, Churchill had been willing to consider breaking Germany into several small states, but the balance of power had since shifted east. Europe needed a counterweight to the Soviet Union's growing influence. A rehabilitated, united Germany could eventually fill that role. Churchill kept this opinion to himself. Instead he stated, 'Dealing with the fate of eighty million people . . . required more than eighty minutes to consider.' He could not possibly agree to carve up Germany into two, three, four, five or more separate states without comprehensively studying the local history, culture and economies across Germany. They would have to appoint a special commission to consider the question at length. Besides, if the Allies made it known that they intended to dismember the enemy nation upon its eventual unconditional surrender, the Germans might fight on harder long after the battle was inevitably lost.

While at first Stalin seemed intent to drive a hard bargain on German dismemberment, he now took a step back. It was all part of Soviet posturing in the delicate dance of negotiation, minimising the important and magnifying the trivial to obscure true intentions. Weakening Germany was indeed vital to the future security of the Soviet Union, but there were other neighbours closer to Soviet borders that held even stronger interest for Stalin. If he appeared willing to negotiate in good faith now, on an issue that *seemed* to be a Soviet priority, Churchill and Roosevelt would have to reciprocate later. And that was where he would win the most important concessions. Stalin told Churchill that he 'fully understood the Prime Minister's difficulties in setting out a detailed plan', but he would find it acceptable if they could agree 'in principle that Germany should be dismembered'. The foreign ministers could appoint a commission to study the issue as Churchill described. In the meantime, he would be satisfied with simply adding a clause about dismemberment to the eventual German surrender terms. Roosevelt and Churchill agreed.

After a less than ideal beginning to the day's discussion, Roosevelt now sensed an opportunity to reassume control. He turned the conversation back to the zones of occupation. What were they to do about the French? Roosevelt was not keen on the French, particularly their leader. He found General de Gaulle pompous and irritating and had made sure he was not invited to the conference. De Gaulle was furious at being excluded, a fact he made no effort to conceal from Harry Hopkins when the president's special adviser visited him en route to Malta. Roosevelt was not eager to give France a zone of occupation, though he was not entirely opposed to it. He was concerned about a bigger issue. If France was offered a zone, surely de Gaulle would insist on a place on the Control Commission overseeing the administration of German rehabilitation – and FDR did not want de Gaulle to have any part in it. But the question of France had broader implications, and it was part øf the reason why Roosevelt had tried to engage Stalin on the topic in private the day before. The Soviet leader's reaction could very well be a bellwether as to his willingness to cooperate on the issues that remained Roosevelt's priority: the world peace organisation and Soviet entry into the Pacific war.

Stalin, however, was staunchly against giving the French a zone, he told his colleagues. He felt nothing but antipathy for the French. In his mind, they were weak. They had contributed almost nothing to the war effort; their near overnight collapse in 1940 had allowed the Germans to preserve their resources so they could turn around and attack the Soviet Union in 1941. Stalin had not forgotten. He was also concerned that giving the French a zone would allow other, smaller countries like Belgium and the Netherlands to argue that they should have a zone too.

But France was not the priority for Stalin that it was for Churchill. Like Roosevelt, Churchill had no personal fondness for de Gaulle, whom he found haughty and 'phlegmatic'. De Gaulle had gone to great lengths to be discourteous to Churchill, to prove to the French people that he was 'not a British puppet', despite the fact that the British government had given him protection in exile. But Churchill's conviction that a robust France, Germany's oldest adversary, needed to play an integral role in both the administration of a new German state and in keeping the balance of power tilted west was further bolstered by FDR's sudden announcement to the table that U.S. public opinion would not support keeping American troops in Europe any longer than two years after the end of the war.

Churchill and Stalin began to bicker over giving France a zone and a share of the Allied Control Commission of Germany, but Churchill remained a formidable adversary, and Stalin was not digging in decisively. Before the conversation could devolve further, Harry Hopkins leaned over and passed Roosevelt a note. 'Promise a zone' to the French, he had scribbled. 'Postpone decision about Control Commission.' Roosevelt did as Hopkins suggested. Churchill and Stalin agreed to have their foreign ministers continue to consider the issue in a separate meeting.

As the three Allied leaders traded views on France, Ivan Maisky, the Soviet deputy commissar of foreign affairs, had been sitting quietly at the table, biding his time. Maisky's presence was not unusual. Unlike Molotov, he did not often speak on Stalin's behalf in meetings, and he interpreted for him only on rare occasions, but he had been at the plenary session the day before and was a familiar face to many of the men around the table. From 1932 to 1943, he had lived in London as the Soviet ambassador to the United Kingdom. His English was nearly perfect and he had established a close professional and social relationship with Churchill and Eden in the years when optimism for Anglo-Soviet cooperation blossomed in London. With the seemingly tame Maisky as messenger, a controversial request might be better received.

As Maisky reminded everyone, the Soviets had suffered more destruction at the hands of the Germans than anyone else, and something must be done to compensate for this. It was only right, he stated, as both a matter of fairness and future European security, to strip Germany of its heavy industry and transfer much of it to the Soviet Union. Through in-kind payments of industrial materiel and other assets to be determined, the Soviet Union deserved no less than $10 billion from the country responsible for this war.

Across the table, Averell Harriman was taken aback. Harriman had long maintained that it was imperative for the western Allies to avoid making any semblance of a commitment to a specific reparations figure. The Soviets would interpret any willingness to consider such a number as a baseline for future negotiation, and Maisky was requesting an extraordinary sum. This staggering number came on top of what Molotov had already requested a month earlier. The

Soviet foreign minister had asked Harriman for a postwar loan from the United States in the amount of $6 billion, to be repaid over thirty years with an annual interest rate of 2 per cent, which would cover orders for industrial equipment and building material purchased from the United States at a 20 per cent discount. Harriman had written off the suggestion, figuring it stemmed from Molotov's utter lack of understanding of normal business practices, but he was concerned about the way the foreign minister had positioned it. As Molotov had explained, the Soviets considered generous postwar credits crucial to the success of future relations between their two countries.

The crushing reparations imposed upon Germany after World War I led not only to rampant inflation in Germany; it had nearly destroyed the entire international economy and had ignited a wave of resentment that sent the world racing towards another war. On this issue, Roosevelt and Churchill naturally fell into agreement, needing no prompting from Harriman. Keen to avoid another global collapse, the two men were cautious about seeking reparations from Germany. Punitive economic measures were not the answer. History had taught them that a revived German economy would benefit everyone in the long run. They quickly acknowledged that the Soviets had indeed suffered more physical destruction at the hands of the Nazis than anyone else, but their ally's demands would surely devastate the German, and potentially the broader European, economy. Who then would be left to bear the burden of feeding eighty million starving Germans?

'If you wished a horse to pull a wagon,' Churchill remarked, addressing his comment to Stalin, 'you would at least have to give it fodder.'

'There would be food for the Germans,' Stalin rejoined, 'but care should be taken to see that the horse did not turn around and kick you when you were not looking.'

Roosevelt was a master of political manoeuvring, but Churchill was an equally wily and experienced opponent. From his hours spent with Churchill in London, Maisky knew the prime minister could be a brilliant actor. He filled his speeches with lofty sentiments about preserving friendship between the Allies after the war, claiming to Maisky that Britain would 'spare no effort to help Russia heal its wounds as quickly as possible'. For generations, the Spencer line of the Spencer-Churchill family was known for its creative and artistic capacities, and it seemed that the prime minister had inherited this gene from his ancestors. Like a leading Covent Garden thespian, he would summon up genuine tears and lose himself in 'sudden bursts of feeling' that 'overwhelm[ed] him like inspiration overwhelms a poet'. (With such theatrical inspiration ever present in her family life, it was little wonder that Sarah had turned to acting as her chosen métier.) But promises made in the throes of passion were often the ones Churchill knew he would never fulfil. While the British might talk about doing everything in their power to assist the Soviet Union's postwar recovery, Churchill was adamant that the Allies not make any commitment to the figures Maisky had proposed. Instead, he suggested the foreign ministers assemble a committee to address the matter of reparations. Once again, Stalin reluctantly agreed.

Kathleen, Sarah and Anna were standing in the hallway outside the ballroom, waiting for the plenary session to break up for dinner. Promptly at 8 p.m., the doors opened and the men filed out in orderly fashion, as if to signal the negotiations were progressing productively and without incident – all except for Stalin. Kathy watched as the Soviet general secretary 'came out at a run'. Over the course of the four-hour meeting, many cups of tea and carafes of water had been distributed, and though his name meant 'Man of Steel', even he could not avoid the call of nature. Someone pointed him towards a restroom, but he came right back out. There was no toilet in that one, only a sink. There was another restroom nearby, but Churchill already occupied it. One of the American embassy secretaries who had come with the Harrimans from Moscow discerned the problem and discreetly escorted Stalin down a long hallway to the next lavatory.

Suddenly, a commotion broke out in front of the ballroom. In the shuffle for bathrooms, Stalin's two NKVD bodyguards had somehow lost sight of their charge. Their lives must have flashed before their eyes. Woe to the men who lost Joseph Stalin. 'There was havoc

– everyone running around whispering,' Kathy recalled with amusement in her letter to Pamela. In a panic, Stalin's security detail dashed about like goons in a Marx Brothers film. 'I think they thought the Americans had pulled a kidnapping stunt or something,' she wrote.

Several minutes later, Stalin reappeared. Order was quickly restored, bringing the brief absurd episode to a close. The Soviets and the British ambled out to the cars waiting in front of Livadia Palace, and all returned to their respective 'lairs', as Sarah liked to call them, for dinner.

ELEVEN

February 5, 1945

On the basis of physical appearance, Joseph Stalin seemed an unlikely choice for a national leader, let alone one at the helm of a nation of 170 million souls. Standing at just five feet six inches, he was far less imposing in person than he appeared in photographs. Photographers took his picture from a lower vantage point, making him appear larger than life. It was a clever illusion. As Harry Hopkins remarked upon meeting Stalin for the first time in 1941, in reality, the Soviet dictator was 'built close to the ground like a football coach's dream tackle'. He was plainly dressed, his grey marshal's uniform unadorned, save for the gold star medallion on his chest, designating him a Hero of the Soviet Union. His left arm was shorter than his right; his hand shrivelled from a childhood injury. After meeting him for the first time in Moscow, Kathleen Harriman noted that Stalin's 'face was pockmarked, he had sort of yellow eyes and terrible teeth' from smoking a pipe. His odd 'walrus mustache' was 'chopped off at the sides to cover up these terrible looking teeth'. Nor did his conduct impress her. 'He had rather a limp handshake . . . Sometimes he would look you in the eye and sometimes not,' Kathy remarked. She remembered Averell telling her what his own father had often said to him as a boy: 'Never trust a man who [does] not have a firm handshake and does not look you in the eye.'

In person, it was easier to imagine Stalin not as a ruthless dictator, who had orchestrated the murder of millions of his countrymen between 1936 and 1938 during the Great Purge, but rather as a simple Georgian, who, like his Allied counterparts, was also father to a daughter. Stalin had four children: Yakov, his only child from his first marriage, who had died under questionable circumstances as a POW in 1943; Konstantin, an illegitimate son whom he never acknowledged; Vasily, a colonel in the Red Air Force; and finally, his youngest child and only daughter, Svetlana. Svetlana was nineteen, lived in Moscow with her husband, Grigory Morozov, and was pregnant with her first child.

Unlike Churchill, Roosevelt and Harriman, Stalin never discussed his political life with his daughter and did not consider bringing Svetlana to Yalta. He had encouraged her to learn English, which could have been an asset to him at an international conference, as he knew little English aside from a few phrases, like 'You said it,' which he had picked up from the American cowboy westerns he enjoyed, but he rarely allowed her to engage with foreigners. She was something of a mystery to the outside world. Kathy never once met Svetlana during the time she lived in Moscow. In fact, Winston Churchill was one of the only westerners who had ever laid eyes on her. Stalin introduced his daughter to the prime minister at his dacha during Churchill's trip to Moscow in 1942. That night, as Stalin presented Svetlana 'with a twinkle in his eye', Churchill thought he made the introduction as if to say, 'You see, even we Bolsheviks have a family life.' Like Sarah Churchill, Svetlana was a pretty redhead. Churchill recalled that Svetlana had kissed her father 'dutifully', albeit 'shyly'. She remained by his side as he made small talk with the prime minister, but Stalin did not allow her to stay for dinner. During their brief, one-sided chat – Svetlana understood everything Churchill said but was much too nervous to respond – Churchill told Svetlana about his own red-haired daughter who worked with the RAF. This must have made an impression on Svetlana, for sometime after the meeting, she sent Sarah a brooch as a gift. (Sarah had intended to take the brooch to Yalta and wear it as a gesture towards Allied unity, but in her haste to pack, she forgot it. Her sister Diana found it for her and sent it in the pouch of the prime minister's papers via the overnight Downing Street courier.)

Svetlana's mother, Nadezhda Alliluyeva, Stalin's second wife, died when Svetlana was only six. Svetlana grew up believing her mother's death was the result of appendicitis or an operation gone wrong. The truth was much darker: Nadezhda had committed suicide by shooting herself in the heart with a Mauser pistol. Svetlana did not learn of her mother's suicide until she was sixteen. Over time, she came to believe that her father's cruelty and brutality, in both his personal and political life, had driven her mother to depression and ultimately to take her own life. Soon Svetlana began to have her own troubles with her father. When she was sixteen, she fell in love with Aleksi Kapler, a famous Russian Jewish screenwriter two decades her senior. Her father disapproved of their relationship and sentenced Kapler to ten years in a Siberian gulag. Svetlana was heartbroken. When she was seventeen and a student at Moscow University, Svetlana rebelled by marrying her classmate Grigory Morozov. Like Kapler, Morozov was Jewish. Once again, her father objected to the match. He refused to meet his son-in-law.

Stalin rarely paid his daughter any attention, and when he did, he treated her and those she loved with spite. And yet somehow he managed to convince Svetlana that her misfortunes were her own fault. He made her believe that she was a 'bad daughter'. She felt more like a 'stranger than a daughter'. Trapped in his web of illusions, lies and malice, Svetlana came to excuse her father as a 'lonely spirit', blaming herself for not being able to assure him of her love.

While Stalin had not brought any of his children with him to Yalta, one of his foremost deputies had. Lavrentiy Beria, the head of the NKVD and the man behind the transformation of Yalta into a site fit for a gathering of statesmen – as well as the cruel deportations of 200,000 Crimean Tatars whom the NKVD accused of collaborating with the Nazis – had brought his son Sergo to the conference. Already he was training Sergo in the family business.

Stalin had told Roosevelt and Churchill that he could not leave the Soviet Union because his doctors feared it would put his health at risk, but the real reason was that, like the tsars before him, Stalin was paranoid about security. He rarely left Moscow, and never without a massive security net. But it was not to the ostensibly all-powerful and omnipresent Red Army that Stalin turned for his protection. Ubiquitous and authoritative as it seemed, the Red Army did not have as much power as its generals might have liked to imagine. As Kathy had realised less than a year after arriving in Moscow, the army had a tendency to be 'jealously cold to the NKVD'. The NKVD, Kathy had explained to her sister, 'are the real power over here'.

Originally formed to conduct standard police work and oversee the administration of Soviet prisons and gulags, the NKVD was transformed into an elite force of terror under Stalin's leadership. The agency became the secret police and the assassination squad. It made supposed enemies of the people, whether political dissidents or an entire ethnic minority, disappear. During the war, some specialised units were deployed to the front lines, but most of its agents focused on internal security. Protecting Joseph Stalin was the NKVD's chief priority.

The agency had stationed four regiments in Yalta, as well as an additional twelve hundred agents, a 120-man motorcycle detachment, and fifty bodyguards to protect the numerous Allied VIPs. This, they decided, was not enough, so an additional six hundred special agents and troops were sent to police the area. Two patrol lines surrounded the Koreiz Villa, Livadia Palace and Vorontsov Palace during the day. After dark, they added a third.

Unlike officials such as Molotov, Vyshinsky and Maisky, who were among the most prominent public faces of the Soviet bureaucracy, Stalin kept Beria in the shadows. He remained on the edge of the conference, just out of sight. If the western diplomats saw the forty-five-year-old NKVD boss lurking around Livadia Palace, they would not have known who he was. At first glance, Beria was unremarkable. Just as Stalin looked like an unlikely dictator, Beria's physical appearance belied his thirst for power and his ease with violence. He was short, fat and balding, and had a sallow complexion. He wore a tiny pince-nez, with circular lenses, perched on the bridge of his nose, lending him the appearance of a quiet intellectual rather than an eager facilitator of death and destruction. His power emanated not from his physical stature, but from his manner. Like Stalin, he was from a poor family in Georgia. As a boy he wanted to become an architect, but the allure of power enticed him irresistibly to the Cheka, the first incarnation of the Soviet secret police. There, he gained a reputation as a brilliant organiser and manager, but also for his sadistic ruthlessness. As Svetlana described Beria, 'He was a magnificent modern specimen of the artful courtier, the embodiment of Oriental perfidy, flattery and hypocrisy who had succeeded in confounding even my father, a man whom it was ordinarily difficult to deceive.' One of Beria's underlings believed he would not have hesitated to kill his best friend. When Beria came to the helm of the NKVD in 1938, he applied his affinity for both organisation and brutality to tasks ranging from overseeing the conversion of industrial plants to war production facilities to the deportation (and deaths) of 'class enemies' and certain minority groups, such as the Tatars, the Chechens, the Inguishi, the Kalmyks and the Meskhetian Turks. Under Beria's leadership, NKVD agents also policed the Red Army, following along behind the soldiers and arresting or shooting any dissidents or deserters it left behind.

Alongside his desire for political power, Beria also lusted after sex. In his office he kept everything from sex toys to pornography to silk negligees to instruments of torture. Beria raped women with the fury of an addict. Colleagues tried to keep count of the number of women he had forced into his bed. By some counts it was thirty-nine. By others, it was nearly a hundred. No one knew for sure. Some of these women had come to him begging for the release of loved ones whom the NKVD had imprisoned. Others he simply kidnapped off the streets, whisking them away in his armoured Packard. Those he did not have killed, arrested, or sent to a work camp after he'd had his way with them he sent home with a bouquet of flowers, a grotesque mockery of chivalry.

Like his father, twenty-year-old Sergo Beria remained tucked away behind closed doors at Yalta. In a quiet room, he sat for hours, listening to Franklin Roosevelt's every word. Sergo Beria was at the core of a coordinated bugging effort the Soviets had engineered, first at Tehran and now again at Yalta. Unlike his father, Sergo had no known vicious qualities; rather, he was a quiet student at a Leningrad military academy with an affinity for electronics. Stalin had known the younger

Beria since he was a child and had personally asked him to join the security contingent at Tehran, assigning him the crucial role of listening in on Roosevelt's conversations. His exceptional performance at Tehran earned him the trip to Yalta. While Lavrentiy Beria spoke only Georgian and Russian, Sergo also spoke English and German. And he was far more attractive than his father. Some daughters of the most powerful men in the Kremlin inner circle, including Svetlana, fancied they were in love with him.

Though the Americans and the British expected the Soviets to bug the premises and therefore swept for listening devices when they arrived, many of the Soviet bugs contained no metal, so the sweeps failed to pick them up. In addition to bugs, the Soviets had directional microphones, which worked at a range of 150 to 200 metres out in the open. The visiting delegates would inevitably flock to gardens for private conversations, so the Soviets planted bugs there too. They steered FDR towards their listening devices in the Livadia gardens by tidying certain garden paths, so he could manage them in his wheelchair, practically guaranteeing that they could follow his every move. From their listening centre the eavesdroppers would write transcripts of conversations and pass them on to General Antonov, who would in turn summarise them for Stalin, giving him detailed insight into his western counterparts' thinking before each meeting.

Eavesdropping was not the most glamorous job. The Soviets fed Sergo and his colleagues, many of them women, on the scraps of the American and British security teams' daily feasts. Most of the information Sergo and his fellow eavesdroppers picked up were tidbits of little value, such as innocuous comments about lemons and goldfish, but a few of the conversations he overheard were much more substantive. They made the job worthwhile. With headphones clamped over his ears, Sergo began listening to FDR as soon as he landed at Saki, eighty miles away. Through powerful directional microphones, he listened in on the two western leaders' chatter at the airfield. Sergo smugly noted that Roosevelt refused to engage with Churchill in any kind of meaningful conversation. Observing the reverence and deference with which FDR's ever-present coterie treated him, the younger Beria developed a certain respect for the American president and his political acumen. It was not unlike the respect Molotov had developed for the hard-nosed Harriman. But to Churchill, Sergo extended no courtesy. He compared the prime minister to a pathetic 'poodle wagging its tail'. Sergo listened as FDR made derisive remarks about Churchill and the British. An ardent anti-imperialist, Roosevelt particularly mentioned that he was in favour of the inevitable breakup of the British Empire after the war. Comments like these left Sergo convinced that Roosevelt knew he was being bugged and was making such comments as a signal to the Soviets of his earnest desire to build a lasting working relationship after the war. Whether or not FDR's comments were part of a canny political strategy or simple carelessness, Sergo heard him loud and clear.

Though on the surface, some of the NKVD's efforts – such as eavesdropping – appeared excessive, almost farcical, revealing a national paranoia about security, the threat that Lavrentiy Beria's forces posed to those who fell into their clutches was terrifyingly real. Of the three daughters who accompanied their fathers to Yalta, only Kathleen could appreciate how dangerous they were. When Kathy wrote to her sister that the NKVD was the real power in the Soviet Union, she already had glimpsed some of its reach. But the extent of that power was so shocking, she did not fully comprehend it for quite some time.

In January 1944, Kathy and Averell had been in Moscow for three months when some disturbing information crossed the ambassador's desk. The Soviets, having finally pushed the Nazis west out of the Smolensk region, which was 250 miles west of Moscow, had sent an investigative commission to assess German war atrocities in the region. There, they discovered the remnants of grotesque inhumanity: mass graves filled with the bodies of thousands of Polish soldiers. The Nazis, who had occupied the territory since 1941, had apparently systematically executed Poles in the late summer of 1941 and buried them in what had once been a woodland picnic ground called Goat Hill, in the Katyn Forest, just ten miles from Smolensk.

Yet the Nazis claimed that they had found those very remains a year earlier. According to their account, in the spring of 1943, as the Germans clashed with the Soviets on the Eastern Front, the Nazis had stumbled upon something suspicious in the Katyn Forest: a patch of young pine trees planted on top of a mass grave containing the remains of Polish officers who had been missing since 1940. The Nazis seized this opportunity to sow discontent among the Allies. They announced what they had found, pinning responsibility for the atrocity squarely on the Soviets, in hopes that the British and the Americans would rebuke their partners to the east. The Soviets denied the Nazis' charge and reversed the blame, stating the Nazis must have killed the Poles during their drive into the Soviet Union. Determined to prove their innocence, the Soviets offered to take Moscow's foreign press to the site and show them evidence. The journalists could reach their own conclusions – but surely they would see that the Soviet account was the truth.

Though the Soviets' invitation was explicitly for journalists, Ambassador Harriman wanted one of his people to observe the proceedings and report back. If he asked permission for an American doctor or medical officer to make the trip to verify the information independently, surely his request would be denied. He needed someone he could trust, someone the Soviets could not refuse. He turned to his twenty-six-year-old daughter.

As an Allied ambassador's daughter, and one well regarded in Moscow's diplomatic community, Kathy could hardly be denied a place in the group. As a former war correspondent, she had seen enough wounded and maimed servicemen in London hospitals to be somewhat desensitised to carnage. She would also be in familiar company with the other seventeen western journalists representing countries ranging from the United States and Britain to Spain, Czechoslovakia, and even Poland – though she would be the only woman. Harriman sent a message to the Soviets, requesting they include her in the trip, along with one of his embassy secretaries, John Melby, who would accompany her. His request was granted.

Kathy took on this significant assignment with enthusiasm. Since arriving in Moscow, she had faced no shortage of work. Part diplomat, hostess, press officer and interpreter, Kathy had toiled tirelessly those first three months, filling in wherever she was needed as the short-staffed embassy waited for new personnel from the Office of War Information and the State Department to arrive. The work was rarely mentally stimulating, and she was itching to see what lay beyond the ring road that surrounded Moscow. Here was her chance to do something important and to see Russia as it really was outside the shadow of the Kremlin.

The train carrying Kathy, John Melby and the correspondents slowly pulled away from Moscow. Smolensk was only 250 miles away, but it took more than eighteen hours to reach it because of railway damage, which left the few navigable tracks highly congested. Supply convoys heading for the front took priority, and Kathy's train spent hours on sidings or at bombed-out stations, waiting for the convoys to pass. With short January days in this part of the world, Kathy's group travelled mostly in darkness and saw little of the countryside.

At long last the journalists reached Smolensk, where they were greeted by a shocking scene. The destruction made Blitz-ravaged London look like a nursery in which a toddler had thrown a tantrum. Of the eight thousand buildings that had previously stood in this small Russian city, only three hundred survived. 'Compared to bombed English towns,' Kathy wrote to Mary and Pamela, Smolensk 'gave the feeling of being completely dead and deserted.' Just one-sixth of the pre-war population remained in the ravaged city. They eked out a subsistence living, one day at a time, sheltering in cellars beneath ruined homes. The only signs of life came from 'stove pipes sticking out of ground floor windows', which spewed smoke into the streets.

At Smolensk, Kathy and the journalists were met by their guide, who had a title that even Germans would have considered long: the Secretary of the Special Commission to Establish and Investigate the Circumstances of the Shooting by the German Fascist Invaders of Captive Polish Officers. After a tour of Smolensk, he ushered the western observers into cars, and they drove half an hour towards the Western Front, then into a copse of recently planted pine trees. The Soviets' main 'show' was about to begin.

As the journalists emerged from their cars, an overwhelming smell nearly knocked them flat. Rather than the crisp aroma of pine trees in winter, the stench of decaying flesh filled the air. The Soviets had opened seven mass graves and had already exhumed more than seven hundred bodies. As the Soviet officials told Kathy, there could be as many as fifteen thousand buried in the frozen ground.

Perhaps Averell had thought Kathy would be prepared for such a morbid scene, having reported on and written articles with titles like 'Plastic Surgery Doing Wonders for R.A.F. Pilots Suffering Burns'. In this article, Kathy described the pilots, maimed by excruciating burns when their planes were shot down, whom she had interviewed. 'Last September, I basked in the sun on a Long Island beach,' Kathy wrote. 'A portable radio echoed reports from England. Far away voices told of the pilots who were shot down in flames, defending their country ... In America, we heard no more.' In England, she met those survivors. So as not to offend her readers' delicate sensibilities, she took an optimistic approach and emphasised 'the hope behind those eyes' looking out from scarred faces. But to her sister she wrote the whole truth about men whose faces had been totally disfigured or whose burned fingers had curled under and grown together – if they had any fingers left at all. 'It's not easy talking to an earless, eyelidless boy of about 21, who also has very little nose structure left,' she told Mary. 'You can't let him realize what you feel.'

Averell had also had his share of harrowing experiences as a young man – when he was much younger than Kathy, in fact. While travelling with his own father in Japan aged thirteen, after the Russo-Japanese War, he was nearly caught up in a violent protest. He watched as angry Japanese citizens threw stones at the heads of two of his father's American associates. The attackers felt that Teddy Roosevelt, who had refereed the peace treaty between Russia and Japan, had penalised Japan and left them with a raw deal. During the same visit, Averell saw a vicious mob burn the home of a Japanese government minister, apparently a representative at the peace proceedings, to the ground. The man barely escaped over the back fence.

But Averell was a business-minded person. He needed a reliable, respectable witness, and Kathy, both colleague and daughter, was the person he most trusted. Sending Kathy on this mission had one further benefit. As the ambassador's daughter, she carried an air of authority, so what she reported would be respected. She was not, however, an official representative of the American government and technically did not speak for it. If her report included anything that could jeopardise good relations with the Soviets – a key objective of the president – Harriman and the Roosevelt administration could maintain plausible deniability and contain the damage.

Whatever Averell's thinking, he sent his daughter to witness unimaginable horrors. Kathy stood at the edge of the pits the Soviets had dug in the sandy, orange-coloured soil. They measured roughly twenty-five feet square and three to ten feet deep. Looking down, she could see that some of the bodies were arranged in tidy rows, six to eight corpses deep, like stacked firewood, while others lay in heaps. They were in 'varying stages of decomposition', and unquestionably they had been dead for quite some time.

Their guide then led Kathy, John Melby and the correspondents into heated tents, where eleven teams of doctors were performing 160 autopsies per day. Hundreds of bodies were laid out on tables. Each doctor wanted the privilege of demonstrating his findings to the ambassador's daughter, so Kathy was made to witness more post-mortems than any of the journalists. One exhibition especially imprinted itself upon her mind. The doctor, as she described him to Mary and Pamela, 'looked like a chef in a white peaked cap, white apron and rubber gloves. With relish he showed us a sliced Polish brain – carefully placed on a dinner plate for inspection purposes.' The bodies, the doctors explained, were well preserved. The bluish-grey colour of their uniforms was still visible, as was the imperial Polish eagle on their brass buttons. Even in the freezing temperature, given the rate of decomposition in soil conditions found in Katyn Forest, the colour of the muscles and the amount of hair left on the bodies indicated that they could not have been in the ground for more than two years. Therefore, the doctors concluded, it was not possible for the Soviets to have killed these Poles nearly four years ago, as the Nazis claimed. Then the doctors pointed out the manner in which the Poles had been executed. At the base of every skull was a bullet hole. Powder burns indicated that the guns had been fired at point-blank range. In some skulls, there was a second bullet hole at the top of the forehead.

Next, their guide presented them with evidence collected from the pockets of the corpses. Before burying them, the Soviets explained, the Germans had stripped the Poles of their valuables and personal effects, but they had missed some letters and receipts. These were dated as early as June 1940 but only as late as June 1941.

Finally, the westerners were led into a nearby dacha, to hear the testimony of witnesses. The room was hot, and blinding lights were trained on the witnesses for the sake of the motion picture cameras that were capturing the proceedings. Kathy and the correspondents heard five testimonies, including one from a girl who had been forced to work as a maid at this dacha when Germans occupied it. She claimed that on several occasions she had heard a succession of single shots ringing out from the nearby forest. Another witness recalled a conversation he had had with a Gestapo officer. 'The Poles are harmful people and inferior', the German officer supposedly told the man; 'therefore, the Polish population can serve usefully only as manure and so create space for the widening of the Leibensraum [*Lebensraum,* 'room to live'] of the Germans'.

Kathy thought the witnesses' statements seemed 'glibly given, as though by rote'. When the journalists tried to question them, the Soviets begrudgingly allowed it, but the witnesses turned 'hesitant and stumbled until they were dismissed by the Commission'. At the stroke of midnight, the feeling of 'at least semi-cordiality' between the commission and the journalists 'disappeared', and the Soviets 'announced abruptly' that the train to Moscow would be leaving in precisely one hour. The visitors were quickly bundled back to the station and dispatched.

On the return trip to Moscow, Kathy weighed the evidence both for and against the Soviet argument that the Nazis had perpetrated the crime. As for the information from the post-mortem, Kathy had no medical training. She had no way to verify the doctors' claims, but she felt compelled to accept their word as objective scientists.

It was odd that the Poles had been buried in greatcoats and long underwear if they had been executed in the summer, but the Soviets had found letters on the bodies dated as late as the summer of 1941.

These could have been planted, but they certainly smelled as if they had long been buried with corpses. And then there was the manner in which the Poles had been executed: systematic single shots to the back of the head. It reflected an efficiency that, at the time, Kathy believed to be 'typically German'. It was not until the next summer, in August 1944, when a group of western correspondents returned to Moscow from an assignment reporting on war atrocities at Majdanek, a camp of unspeakable terrors that the Soviets had discovered and liberated on the outskirts of Lublin, that Kathy would learn that the Germans had implemented more horrific methods of mass execution.

When Kathy arrived back at Spaso House, Averell asked her to write a report of what she had observed and what those observations led her to conclude. 'It is apparent that the evidence in the Russian case is incomplete in several respects, that it is badly put together, and that the show was put on for the benefit of the correspondents without opportunity for independent investigation or verification,' she wrote. 'The testimonial evidence provided by the Commission and witnesses was minute in detail and by American standards petty. We were expected to accept the statements of the high ranking Soviet officials as true, because they said it was true. Despite this,' she reasoned, 'it is my opinion that the Poles were murdered by the Germans. The most convincing evidence to uphold this was the methodical manner in which the job was done.' Averell did not argue with her findings, or her interpretation of them. The information supported what he was willing to believe was true. He had been in Moscow a mere three months and was determined to build a working relationship with the Soviets, as Roosevelt desired. He transmitted Kathy's report to Washington, directly to the secretary of state. Kathy's observations and summary became part of the State Department's official record.

There was just one problem. Kathy was wrong. With a journalist's scepticism, she had become wary of the Soviet regime in the early days of the war, long before her father and his colleagues developed the same attitude. But like many others before her, she had been taken in by Stalin's deceit. Kathy never said when she knew for certain that she had been fooled. Not until eight years later, in an American congressional hearing, was she forced to admit publicly that she had reached the wrong conclusion that day in the forest.

The Nazis committed countless crimes against humanity, from the euthanasia of 'incurables' to the murder of millions of Jews, but the Katyn Forest massacre was one crime they did not commit. In September 1939, the Soviet Union and Germany, then allied under the Molotov-Ribbentrop non-aggression pact, had invaded Poland and divided it between them. The Red Army took thousands of Poles prisoner, including soldiers, intellectuals and aristocrats – anyone who might have the means and desire to actively resist Soviet rule. With so many 'enemies of the state' in their clutches, the Soviet leaders realised they had a prime opportunity. They could begin liquidating the Polish ruling class, thus making it easier to control the country once the war was over. Stalin turned to the NKVD. He ordered Beria to dispatch his agents to execute 21,857 Polish officers, political leaders and members of the educated elite. Three NKVD agents set to work, each killing 250 men a night, making sure to shoot each man in the back of the head with a German Walther pistol to create a scapegoat for the murders. The killings eradicated the Polish officer corps: half of its ranks lay rotting in graves. A secret of such proportions was too large to remain a secret for long. Soon rumours that half of the Polish officer corps had vanished began to circulate. The Soviets offered vague explanations – these officers were 'engaged in construction work' near Smolensk or 'had been sent to eastern Siberia but had since disappeared and presumably had crossed the frontier into Manchuria'.

As soon as the Red Army cleared the Nazis from the Smolensk region in the autumn of 1943, the Soviets rushed to conceal what they had done. They reopened the graves and tampered with evidence, removing letters dated from 1939 and 1940 and replacing them with letters and receipts from 1941 as incontrovertible proof that only the Nazis could have done the killings. Despite this supposed evidence, the exiled Polish government in London remained sceptical. When the London Poles ordered an independent Red Cross investigation, the Soviets broke off relations, calling their request an 'investigation comedy' and blaming the Poles for being in league with the Germans.

Soviet protestations aside, the British and the Americans had already received a bounty of evidence suggesting that their ally was lying – even before Averell sent his daughter to witness the aftermath of the atrocities committed in the Katyn Forest. Kathy's conclusions helped reinforce a lie that the Allies had chosen to believe. The western Allies desperately needed the Soviets to continue to absorb the brunt of German aggression on the Eastern Front until the British and American armies were sufficiently prepared to launch their own assault against the Nazis on the Western Front. The West faced a moral dilemma of titanic proportions. Should they avoid alienating Stalin at all costs while in dire need of his military contribution to the fight against the Nazis? Or should they hew to the moral principles of western democracy and put this cooperation in jeopardy?

With grave displeasure and reluctance, the British and American governments chose not to challenge the Soviets' claims. Those working directly with the London Poles felt the stark hypocrisy of the decision most acutely. As Owen O'Malley, the British ambassador to the Polish government in exile, wrote to Anthony Eden, 'We have in fact perforce used the good name of England like the murderers used the little conifers to cover up a massacre' for the sake of the 'immense importance of an appearance of Allied unity and of the heroic resistance of Russia to Germany'. Heartrending as the decision was, Churchill and Roosevelt felt they had no choice but to safeguard the future of the alliance with the Soviets, for it was vital to winning the war. No matter how much the British and the Americans abhorred the atrocities the Soviets committed, defeating the Nazis remained paramount. As Churchill concluded to Roosevelt, 'What other hope can there be than this for the tortured world?'

TWELVE

February 6, 1945

Anna awoke at 8 a.m. and made the long walk past the Soviet soldiers and American sailors guarding the halls to the bathroom she shared with Kathy Harriman. By this third official day of the conference, she had formed a routine. First, she had a quick 'every-other-day bath', followed by coffee, orange juice and a hard-boiled egg. (She had persuaded one of the Filipino mess men to deliver breakfast to her room, so she could avoid the caviar.) She would then make the rounds of Hopkins, Harriman, and press secretary Steve Early's rooms to gather news that had come in overnight, projections on the day's agenda, and whatever information she could glean about upcoming side meetings between the foreign ministers. By 'separat[ing] the wheat from the chaff', she could brief her father on whatever she felt he needed to know and thus decrease the number of visitors he would have to endure in his room each morning. But it was not all business. Father and daughter also shared a sharp sense of humour. In private, Anna was terrific at imitating people – especially pompous ones – mimicking their expressions, accents and signature gestures. It was a gift she had inherited from FDR, who was known to perform an impression or two, but only when it could be done discreetly. Anna also knew that her father loved nothing more than a good gab, so she made sure to keep her ears open for 'any gossip . . . which might prove amusing or interesting to him' to lighten the start of the day.

Mornings at Yalta were never leisurely, but for Anna, today there would be absolutely no lingering over breakfast. It had the potential to be a watershed day for the Allies. The Big Three would finally discuss forming an organisation meant to unite nations in a global commitment to peace – the project to which FDR was passionately committed. But they were also due to debate the matter of Poland's sovereignty, the very issue that had led Britain to declare war on Germany in September 1939. Now, four and a half years later, the concerns of 1939 seemed more pressing than ever. Poland remained a fulcrum: depending on how the Allies dealt with the issue, the world could tilt to a peaceful future or years of further conflict.

As much as Anna may have wished to remain at her father's side on such a critical day, she had to entrust the president's care to Dr McIntire and Dr Bruenn. The 'Little Three', as people had taken to calling the three daughters, had made arrangements for a tour of a historic city on the Black Sea, and Anna was not about to be left behind.

Anna 'worked like mad all morning', running to and fro to gather information, delegate chores, listen to her father's view on the day ahead, write him reminder notes to be left on his pillow, and make provisions for his lunch with Churchill that afternoon. It would be the two leaders' first private meeting since arriving at Yalta. Hopkins and Byrnes would join them, along with Sir Alexander Cadogan on the British side. Harriman was also attending, so he could see to any last-minute details (and provide ego-management services) if required. Finally, at 10.30, Anna was free to join Kathy and Sarah. The three daughters and their Secret Service guard, Guy Spaman, piled into the car with their Soviet driver. Bundled in overcoats – Sarah once again in her double-breasted WAAF standard issue, Anna in a sensible tweed, and Kathy in wool with a smart fur collar – they began their freezing, three-hour journey around the southern coast of the Crimean Peninsula to the city of Sevastopol.

Though fewer than fifty miles away as the crow flies, the route to Sevastopol called for a drive over some of the damaged roads and hairpin turns they had endured on the way to Yalta: 'really very tortuous',

Sarah told her mother. Carved through the natural peaks and troughs of rugged, forested mountains, the route was so impressively daunting that Kathy kept a photograph of it for her scrapbook. In that single image she counted no fewer than fifteen switchbacks snaking through the mountains ahead. Along the route, they passed near the Baydar Gap, where hundreds of German tanks lay rusting. The Soviets had destroyed them during the Nazis' Crimean offensive the previous spring. Many still contained the bodies of dead German soldiers, as the Soviets could spare neither the time nor the able-bodied workers to remove them.

Two-thirds of the way through the journey, the driver made a wrong turn. With no passers-by to give directions on the desolate mountain road, they quickly became lost. Eventually, they found their way to a little town off the main highway. Even to foreign visitors, there was something familiar about this ramshackle town. They did not realise it at first, but they had stumbled upon a place every British schoolchild knew. Its very name evoked the stuff of legend: Balaklava. 'I presume,' Kathy wrote to Pamela of this unplanned adventure, 'I don't have to check you up on British history.' Nestled in a long, narrow valley between steeply sloping hills, Balaklava was the site of one of the British Army's most famous battles, perhaps second only to Wellington's victory over Napoleon at Waterloo in 1815. But whereas Waterloo became immortalised through triumph, Balaklava was shrouded in the memory of defeat, and the deaths of the valiant and the brave.

It seemed that as long as blood flowed red, it was destined to be spilled across the Crimean Peninsula. The great empires of Europe had clashed in the Crimea, first in the nineteenth century and again in the twentieth, each time trying desperately to tilt the balance of power in their respective favour. Although Russia had the land, the resources and the population to become a great power, it lacked what had made comparatively tiny Britain the greatest empire in the world: easy access to the sea. Trapped by ice to the north, desert and mountains to the south, and the might of the Japanese navy to the east, Russia's only point of access to the Mediterranean and the Atlantic was the Black Sea – the key to projecting power beyond its borders. Protecting the

Crimea and its warm-water ports had been of vital strategic importance to the Russians for well over a century. And it had been their enemies' objective to deprive them of the access they so desired.

The Crimean War – remembered for Florence Nightingale's pioneering advances in frontline medicine and the advent of battlefield correspondents and photographers – was fought between the combined forces of the British, the French and the Ottomans against the Russians from 1853 to 1856. As Russia grew larger and stronger, Britain and France sought to contain the ascendant empire and preserve the international balance of power. For two and a half years, they sparred on the western rim of the Russian Empire, waging some of the most intense battles on the Crimean Peninsula.

The Crimean War was enshrined in British cultural memory because of a disaster that occurred on the morning of October 25, 1854, when 670 British light cavalrymen charged a Russian battery in the valley. Amid thunderous noise and confusion, the British commander's order to secure the retreating Ottomans' guns was misinterpreted as instructions to mount a direct frontal attack on the Russians' artillery battery. It was suicidal. As the Light Brigade charged across the open valley, Russian artillery cut the soldiers down like grain before a reaper. More than 40 per cent of the brigade were killed or wounded in the foolhardy assault before being forced to retreat. The battle was over in less than twenty minutes. Though the commanders never recovered their good reputation, the cavalrymen became national heroes in Britain six weeks later, when Alfred, Lord Tennyson, the poet laureate, hailed in memorable verse the cavalry's bravery in the face of near-certain death. Tennyson's lines reverberated around the world, and the men of the Light Brigade became almost mythic figures:

> *Forward, the Light Brigade!*
> *Was there a man dismayed?*
> *Not though the soldier knew*
> *Someone had blundered.*
> *Theirs not to make reply,*
> *Theirs not to reason why,*
> *Theirs but to do and die.*

Into the valley of Death
Rode the six hundred.

Like many boys educated at London's famous Harrow School and the Royal Military Academy Sandhurst, Winston Churchill had read Tennyson's 'Charge of the Light Brigade' as a child. No doubt he was inspired by these heroes of the empire in his own brave – and often reckless – exploits on the battlefield in Cuba, India, Sudan and, most famously, in South Africa, when he bolted from a Boer prisoner of war camp, evaded a countrywide manhunt, and escaped to freedom.

Perhaps, as his daughter and her two American companions looked out at Balaklava, Tennyson's words ran through their minds. Though the Valley of Death now looked no different than other scarred fields across the Crimea, it served as a reminder of heedless waste of life over centuries of conflict. All around were signs of the most recent carnage. Bomb craters pitted the ground. German anti-tank guns, the modern incarnation of the cannon, which had earlier been mounted on wheels to rain a barrage of bullets onto the advancing Soviet line, lay bent and crumpled like metal in a junkyard. A grave had been dug beside a crashed aircraft. There was even the occasional skeleton of a victim of the last Crimean conflict, which had been unearthed in the most recent fighting.

As the women observed these vestiges of battle, their driver got reoriented. Before long, he found his way back to the main road, and they set off on the last leg of their journey to Sevastopol, leaving the ghosts of Balaklava behind.

On a bay at the southwestern tip of the Crimea, an estuary had formed where the river met the sea, creating a natural harbour. That was where Sevastopol was situated. It had served as a crucial strategic port for the Russian navy since the reign of Catherine the Great. Its crown jewel was a once-grand fortress designed by the military leader and statesman Grigory Potemkin. But when Sarah, Kathy and Anna emerged from the car in the centre of Sevastopol, they found little trace of the bustling life usually found at a harbour. Everywhere they looked, they saw piles of rubble.

Like Balaklava, Sevastopol had been overrun during the Crimean War. In the winter of 1854, a twenty-six-year-old artillery officer named Leo Tolstoy found himself caught up in the Siege of Sevastopol; he later transformed his memories into a series of short stories based on this city that appeared 'to have undergone every sort of vicissitude and deprivation'. It seemed nothing had changed in the past ninety years. This time, Germany and its allies had delivered the first blow to the harbour city during the Siege of Sevastopol in 1941 and 1942, as part of Operation Barbarossa, their massive invasion of the Soviet Union, which reached the outskirts of Moscow. The second came from the Red Army itself, as the Soviets evicted their enemies from Sevastopol in April and May 1944.

A Soviet naval commander native to Sevastopol was ready and waiting to give the three daughters a tour of the city. Providing distinguished visitors with a guide of considerable rank was a Russian practice that stretched back to the days of the empire. During his travels across Russia in 1839, the Marquis de Custine, a French aristocrat, observed, 'Would you see the curiosities of a palace, they give you a chamberlain, with whom you are to admire all that he admires. Would you survey a camp – an officer, sometimes a general officer, accompanies you . . . a fortress, the governor, in person, shows it, or rather politely conceals it from you . . . They refuse you nothing, but they accompany you every where; politeness becomes a pretext for maintaining a watch over you.'

While the naval commander may have wished to show his city in its finest form to these visitors, even he could hardly mask the fact that the once grand seaport was no longer a sterling example of Russian civilisation. Practically every building had been demolished in the fighting. Kathy wrote to Pamela that of the thousands of buildings in Sevastopol, only six still had roofs. It was not just the buildings that had been smashed beyond recognition. 'Statues had been decapitated,' Kathy wrote grimly. 'Target practice.'

Having already seen so many ghost towns like Sevastopol, including dozens of razed villages on the train ride to Yalta alone, Kathy looked at Sevastopol with a certain detachment, but Anna was somewhat in shock. Perhaps she was repeating Kathy's spoken observation when she wrote to her husband, 'The Germans literally left six buildings standing in the whole city.' Other than the day in Malta, where reconstruction was already well underway, Anna's only exposure to the scenes of war before coming to the Crimea had been from newsreels and photographs. 'Honey,' she told John, 'I've seen well over half of the Crimean peninsula – and if I hadn't seen it I would never have been able to believe that such wanton destruction could be possible. Nothing is spared, even farm houses and barns which were isolated and off the beaten path.' To Anna, it seemed so spitefully wasteful.

Though Sarah had lived through the London Blitz and looked at images of flattened cities routinely as she analysed aerial reconnaissance photographs at RAF Medmenham, the destruction of Sevastopol, and its human cost, affected her profoundly. In their professional experience, Kathy the journalist and Anna the editor may have developed some ability to maintain a dispassionate distance when reporting on tragedy. (As Peter Portal had once written to Kathy about her remarkably stoic attitude towards the cruel realities of war, 'I suppose journalism is a fine training for anything so macabre.') Or maybe it was simply that Sarah was more naturally expressive than her companions. While Kathy's and Anna's letters conveyed a level of editorial detail about the magnitude of the wreckage, Sarah's lyrical observations reflected emotional gravity. Echoes of her father's famously eloquent prose and keen perception of human feeling resonated in Sarah's descriptions of Sevastopol, which she wrote to her mother.

Sarah was struck by the physical destruction but also by the local population's peculiarly sanguine attitude. The guide, Sarah wrote to Clementine, 'showed us round the town as though there were no ruins at all! "This" – he said with pride, "is a very beautiful Church." We looked at a scarred shell and nodded. "Oh yes" he said "Sevastopol is a beautiful city" ... We gazed dumbfounded at a devastated area – a square wilderness of broken trees and shell holes.' After showing them one destroyed house, monument, church and park after another, the naval commander stopped and asked Sarah, 'You like Sevastopol?' Sarah paused for a moment. What could she say? He interpreted her hesitation as a sign of dissatisfaction; his expression was crestfallen. Hoping to reassure him, she quickly stated that she did indeed like it very much, but that the scars that the war had left on the city made her sad. 'But somehow,' she told Clementine, 'it was the wrong thing to say. He saw Sevastopol like someone who really loves a person, still sees them, in spite of some terrible physical tragedy unchanged – unbroken.'

As moved as she was by the enduring love that bound the local people to the remains of their city, Sarah's heart broke most not for those who had lost their homes and livelihoods, but for another group of people, who received little sympathy. Towards the end of their tour, Sarah noticed a 'bedraggled queue' of Romanian prisoners of war. Throughout the Crimean Campaign, the Romanian Third and Fourth Armies had fought alongside their German allies against the Soviets for control of Sevastopol. When the Soviets reclaimed the port city in 1944, the Romanians took nearly as many losses as the Germans: twenty-six thousand of their soldiers were killed, wounded or reported missing. The POWs were lucky to escape with their lives, though some probably soon wished they had died. The Soviets organised them into labour gangs. As Kathy had observed in the days before the American delegates arrived at Yalta, some had been sent to Livadia Palace to clear the gardens of the debris the Nazis had left behind.

But this group in Sevastopol was condemned to the backbreaking task of restoring the city they had helped raze. Kathy watched as they moved, street by street, building by building, cleaning up the rubble 'stone by stone'. Sarah first noticed these haggard prisoners lining up for meagre rations served out of a bucket on a cart that was dragged by an emaciated horse. She could not identify the slop in the bucket as anything remotely edible. These men were clearly starving. Sarah knew what it felt like to be under siege and was well aware of the magnitude of the casualties of war, both from conversations with her father and through her work, but images of bombed factories and transport lines taken from ten thousand feet in the sky could not compare with seeing first-hand the consequences of five years of war on the ground. 'One has seen similar queues of hopeless humans on the films,' she wrote to her mother, 'but in reality it is too terrible.' In her compassion for the enemy, Sarah was much like her father. Near the end of the long and gruesome Boer War, Winston, just twenty-five, wrote in the *Morning Post*, 'The wise and right course is to beat down all who resist, even to the last man, but not to withhold forgiveness and even friendship from any who wish to surrender ... Therein lies the shortest road to "peace with honor." ' Evidently, the Soviets did not share this perspective.

Sarah's anguish over the POWs' misery was so striking that Kathy wrote of it to Pamela. 'I think Sarah was slightly horrified by their bedraggled state,' she said. It was not that Kathy was unsympathetic – she had simply witnessed scenes like this many times before. From her perspective, as she somewhat archly reported, the Romanians even seemed to be fulfilling their gruelling task in a 'leisurely fashion', as if showing passive resistance to their enemy by working as slowly as they could. Besides, Kathy added, 'They weren't the worst I've seen by a long shot.' Her experience in the Katyn Forest a year earlier had not left her. But while Kathy had learned to be dispassionate, such dispassion was not in Sarah's nature.

Kathy's remarks to Pamela about Sarah at Sevastopol reflected the broader opinion the two women shared about their friend and sister-in-law. Over the years, they had come to know Sarah as someone with a tremendous depth of feeling – a trait inherited from Winston – and fierce loyalty. Both Kathy and Pamela had witnessed her selfless and genuine generosity of spirit first-hand. Setting aside whatever feelings she had concerning Pamela's relationship with Averell Harriman, Sarah had given up her flat for Pamela and temporarily moved in with the Harrimans, in order to save her sister-in-law's marriage and the reputation of everyone involved in the affair when Randolph came home from North Africa. Randolph was not the easiest person to love, yet Sarah gave all her love to her brother, even after he once struck her in the face when she tried to quiet him during a drunken outburst at a dinner in London with their father and the chiefs of staff. But Kathy and Pamela knew that Sarah's love and optimism were not always returned, even by those who claimed to love her most.

Perhaps it was because Sarah was so much like her father that she was desperate to make her own life and her own name apart from his. As a young man, Winston had an insatiable desire to distinguish himself.

He pursued these ends on the battlefield, seeking out danger at every opportunity in imperial skirmishes across the globe, as both soldier and war correspondent. This risk taking paid off: he rose to national fame at twenty-five, after his dramatic escape as a POW in South Africa. In spite of the love Sarah had for her father, a part of her felt compelled to break free from the comfortable life into which she had been born and make something of herself on her own terms.

Like her father, Sarah was bright, capable and eloquent. Sarah, rather than her brother, Randolph, would have been the natural choice to succeed Winston in politics. But in the 1930s, for a woman of good family to pursue a career was almost unimaginable. There were a few exceptions. In 1919, the American-born Nancy Astor became the first woman to sit as a member of Parliament when she succeeded her husband in his seat, and though twenty women had since followed her example, it remained an almost revolutionary concept. Nor were women like Sarah encouraged to pursue the university degrees that could lead to careers in fields such as foreign service, medicine or the law. In fact, when Sarah looked at the world around her, there seemed to be but one path that might be open: the theatre.

For one who had grown up painfully shy, the theatre did not seem the most natural fit, but upon graduating from finishing school in Paris at seventeen, Sarah knew in her heart that 'the debutante world ... was not enough for me'. She knew one woman whose family had allowed her to take dance lessons at a prestigious dancing school. The girl's grandfather persuaded Winston and Clementine to allow Sarah to join her.

When Sarah was eleven years old, she was playing a game of blind man's bluff with her cousins in the valley below her family home, Chartwell. The house sat at the top of the hill, and the flat, mowed lawn was separated from sloping fields by a stone wall; it was a drop of twelve to twenty feet, depending on the location, into the grass below. When it was Sarah's turn to play the blind man, she reached the stone wall and could hear her cousins in the field just beyond her. She could have run along the wall to its end, where the slope was gentle, and safely chased after them, but by then, they would have been long gone. Instead, Sarah did something impulsive. Taking a great 'Nijinsky leap', she blindly flung herself off the wall and crashed into the field below. The distance to the ground was equivalent to the height of a one-storey building. She was injured, but not too seriously. Trying to break the fall, she tore the muscles in her shoulders. But she easily could have fractured her legs – or worse. Despite this experience, Sarah never lost the brave, even reckless impulse to fling herself headlong into the unknown, a trait she shared with Winston. She was desperate to forge her own place in the world. As soon as the door to theatre and dance opened a crack, Sarah dashed through without hesitation for what might lie on the other side.

Once again she landed hard, but it was not for lack of talent. For her very first show, newspapers gave her glowing reviews. Winston did not discourage her ambitions. Instead, Sarah faced harsh criticism from two people whose support she should have received unconditionally: her mother and her husband.

Clementine Churchill struggled with her role as a mother. She had had a turbulent childhood and may have suffered from postpartum depression after the birth of her children. She was devoted to supporting her husband, but she found being both a wife and mother exhausting, and frequently left the family for weeks at a time to rest and recuperate from 'high mental fatigue'. As soon as she was out of bed after the birth of her first child, Diana, she left her husband with the nurse to look after the newborn baby. Although Winston spent much of his time away from his family, fulfilling his public duties, he was far more attentive to his children than the vast majority of fathers in his station, even going so far as to give his babies baths. Meanwhile, Clementine's frequent absences were hard on her children, especially Sarah. When Sarah was away at boarding school in Kent, she yearned for her mother to visit her and counted the days until she could come home, writing, 'Oh Mummie darling I'm so longing to see you,' and 'I should simply adore you to come down ... please do, I should like it much better than any school treat.' But she was almost always disappointed.

Sarah adored her mother, but Clementine struggled to understand her headstrong daughter. When it came to Sarah's career, she did not hesitate to express her belief that Sarah lacked theatrical 'talent or even aptitude'.

It was shortly after entering the theatre that Sarah fell in love with the star of her show, Vic Oliver. This charismatic Austrian Jewish musician and comedian, eighteen years Sarah's senior, was divorced – possibly twice. Sarah had not found love easily. When she compared the men in her social set to her father, she found them terribly dull. For a time, she dated Dick Sheepshanks, the Eton- and Cambridge-educated Reuters correspondent who had somewhat radical, left-leaning views. This romance did not last, and Sheepshanks eventually went off to Spain to cover the Spanish Civil War, where he was killed when a shell struck a car in which he was sitting with another British correspondent, Kim Philby (later revealed to be a Soviet spy). Philby somehow survived. But if Sheepshanks had been just radical enough to raise eyebrows, Oliver was something else entirely. When Sarah announced to her family just before Christmas in 1935 that she was going to marry him, they were alarmed. And yet Clementine was not alarmed enough to cancel her Alpine skiing holiday. She left Winston to manage the crisis on his own. 'Here I am doing nothing to avert this disaster,' Clementine wrote to Winston from Austria, 'but I feel Sarah will pay more attention to your opinions & to the time & trouble you are taking over her & her affairs.'

Winston did his best to persuade Sarah to reconsider, arguing that if conflict with Germany was to come, she could find herself 'married to the enemy', unless Oliver gave up his Austrian citizenship. But Sarah, whose family nickname was 'Mule', could be every bit as stubborn as her father. For the first time, she found herself truly at odds with him. She ran away to New York, where she and Vic Oliver eloped.

The couple returned to London and continued acting together, but Sarah's happiness was fleeting. Rather than support his wife's ambitions, Vic criticised Sarah's acting, claiming he was trying to help her. Soon he found a new project, a teenage actor named Phyllis Luckett, whom he suggested they adopt so the girl could use the Oliver name to help her career. It was unclear whether Vic and Phyllis actually had an affair, but it was emotional betrayal enough.

One afternoon in April 1940, while touring with a production in Bath, Sarah went to the movies in search of some distraction. Before the film began, a newsreel ran, and she found her father's face staring at her from the screen. For the past several years, he had been warning the British public about the rising threat of German aggression. At first no one had wanted to listen, writing him off as an alarmist. Now the British people saw he had been one of the few with the foresight and the courage to speak with forthright honesty about the danger across the Channel. Emotion swelled in her. 'The buzz and excitement that swept through the theater . . . made me feel so inordinately proud that I was your daughter,' Sarah wrote to him. 'It suddenly occurred to me,' she confessed, 'that I had never really told you, through shyness and inarticulateness – <u>how much</u> I love you and how much I will try to make this career that I have chosen – with some pain to the people I love, and not a little to myself – worthy of your name – one day –.' Just over a month later, on May 10, 1940, her beloved father became prime minister.

Though Sarah had long tried to make her own way, the individual identity she had begun to form apart from her family disappeared almost overnight. People on the street raced to shake her hand, thrilled to meet the daughter of the man who was going to save Britain from invasion. For a time, she soldiered on in the theatre, but no matter what she did, no one saw her as Sarah Oliver, a moderately successful actor. Now she was and would forever be Sarah Churchill, Winston Churchill's daughter. She had not wanted to reject her father's world; rather, her father's world had been closed to her. But suddenly she was thrust into the heart of it. For now, the theatre could wait. Once again, Sarah made a rash decision, and this time it was a good one: she decided to enlist.

Life as a WAAF at RAF Medmenham gave Sarah a sense of purpose and belonging and the opportunity to excel. After her first six months as a section officer, Winston offered to help her transfer to Bomber Command HQ, a more prestigious and coveted assignment, but Sarah humbly declined. For the first time, Sarah truly felt valued. 'They have allowed me to understand at Medmenham, that I am beginning to be useful to them,' she explained. 'You know how happy it makes me feel that you are interested in what I do,' she told him, as if he would not naturally take interest and pride in her work for the sheer reason she was his daughter.

But of course he was proud of her. He was bursting with pride. He had bragged about her to Eleanor Roosevelt during Operation Torch, when Sarah knew the details of the invasion of North Africa better than he did, and about her younger sister, Mary, who had enlisted with the Auxiliary Territorial Service and was manning anti-aircraft guns in Hyde Park. 'Your sisters have chosen the roughest roads they could find,' Winston wrote to Randolph in North Africa. 'We think they are very heroic.'

But before Sarah could truly move on from her disappointment in love and in the theatre, she had to rediscover that pride in herself. 'I must say,' she wrote home, 'one feels ridiculously proud of one's uniform – and all it stands for . . . It is rather as if slowly and painfully' Sarah found she was 'beginning to breathe again'.

Still, from time to time, the old clouds would find her. The music that filled the airwaves reflected the feelings she carried inside. On the surface, the big band jazz of Glenn Miller and Benny Goodman was sunny and upbeat, but the harmonies were built on the tension of minor chords that took many measures to resolve. Because of her father's position, Sarah and Vic could not divorce without a public scandal, and they would occasionally make public appearances together. Shortly after meeting Sarah, Kathy had written to her sister that although Sarah seemed 'desperately unhappy . . . she's got guts enough to stick with Vic on account of her father.' From time to time Vic would call Sarah on the telephone at Medmenham, intruding on the little world of contentment she had carved out for herself. In those moments, Sarah tried to carry her sorrow discreetly, but tears sometimes dripped down her cheeks and fell onto the blotting paper on her desk, giving her away.

'Though I think like many of us that she is not very happy at times,' Pamela wrote to the Harrimans about her sister-in-law, 'she is the sort of person who won't give up easily, & is quite certain that things will turn out right in the end.' Unlike so many young people – including Pamela, who thrived during the war, living each day as if it were the last – Sarah did not 'seem to mind waiting patiently for the things she believes in'. In a rare moment of self-examination, Pamela concluded, 'I think I should take a lesson from her.'

The war had given Sarah fulfilment in work and a deeper connection to her father, but there was still something missing. Then she met Gil Winant. Like the Harrimans, the American ambassador to Britain was a frequent weekend guest at Chequers and an intimate member of Churchill's wartime circle. Winant, a two-time Republican governor of New Hampshire, had succeeded Joseph Kennedy as ambassador in 1941. Kennedy was an ardent advocate of Nazi appeasement and seemed to care only for the famous and wealthy, but Winant, a one-time schoolteacher, was Kennedy's antithesis.

Unlike the glamorous Harriman, the fifty-two-year-old Winant was not particularly handsome. He was warm and charming, but an air of melancholy seemed to hover about him, leading Kathy Harriman to quip that he might have been happier 'if only he could find some cause to be a martyre [*sic*] for'. Unbeknownst to Kathy, Winant carried his own private burdens. His wife, Constance, had left London to return home to New Hampshire, and their marriage was breaking down. Later, he learned that his son, John Gilbert Winant Jr, had been captured by the Nazis when his B-17 was shot down. The Nazis had imprisoned him in the notorious Colditz Castle, Germany's maximum-security camp for high-profile prisoners.

Maybe it was this mutual sense of melancholy and vulnerability that drew Sarah Churchill and Gil Winant to each other. Winant was even older than Vic Oliver, but he was part of the political world in which Sarah felt at ease. Soon a secret romance was born. Though previously, Winston had been the parent who had counselled her on the affairs of the heart, she could not speak to him about Winant. The ambassador was technically his official line to Roosevelt, and to confide in her father would have put him in an awkward position. Just like the relationship between Pamela Churchill and Averell Harriman, which Winston had hinted at but never openly acknowledged, Sarah's attachment to Winant became the 'love affair which my father suspected but about which we did not speak'.

Instead, Sarah turned to her mother. Clementine had taken little interest in Sarah's past romances and had gossiped unhelpfully about Vic Oliver with friends such as the playwright and society darling Noël Coward. But as Sarah grew older, Clementine found herself able to relate to her daughter in ways she never had before. Ever willing to forgive and forget, Sarah discovered a warm and loving friendship with her mother. It helped that Clementine also admired Winant enormously.

'Are you flirting with my Ambass?' Sarah wrote teasingly to Clementine from Yalta, as if she knew Clementine would show Winant her letter. 'If so – desist for one moment and give him my love will you?'

While Sarah and Winston were away at Yalta, Winant twice visited Clementine. On his second visit, he drove her out to a nearby farm, where they took a long country walk. Clementine took advantage of the private moment to broach the subject of his intentions towards her daughter. A wartime romance was one thing, but she needed to protect Sarah's reputation as well as her feelings. She subtly asked him about the state of his 'private affairs'.

'That will be all right,' he assured her. As soon as the war was over, he and his wife were headed for divorce.

Later, Clementine wrote to her youngest daughter, Mary, about her conversation with Winant. 'Sarah does not know he has told me,' she said to Mary. 'I feel it will happen. Except for the big difference in age they are absolutely suited.' Nothing in wartime was certain, but Clementine allowed herself to be cautiously optimistic about her daughter's future happiness. Neither Sarah nor Winant would be free until the war was over, but this time, with someone who was part of the political world where Sarah belonged and who understood and valued her place in it, Sarah might find her love returned in the way she deserved. In the meantime, as Pamela had so astutely observed, Sarah would wait and hope for more, just as she hoped for more for the people whose lives had been shattered by the war, ally and enemy alike. Time and again, through her depth of feeling, Sarah put herself at risk of disappointment, but such was her nature, and she was powerless to feel otherwise.

This was something she had in common with the Soviet naval commander who showed Sarah and her fellow daughters around Sevastopol that day – this ability to look with hope at what once was and what might be again. The current state of Sevastopol provided good reason to mourn the past without hope for the future, but the naval commander chose not to see it that way. Before the three women left Sevastopol, he looked out at the city and slowly said to Sarah, 'We will build it up again – in five years – you see. You will come back to Sevastopol, my Sevastopol and I will show you round again?' And Sarah promised they would.

After yet another three-hour drive in darkness over the mountain roads, sometimes passing mere inches from daunting cliffs, the three daughters arrived back at Yalta close to seven in the evening, freezing and exhausted. Anna and Kathy returned to Livadia and put the misery they saw that day behind them. Sarah, however, sat up late that night, penning a long letter to her mother, as if unburdening her soul of the images of Sevastopol and the starving Romanian POWs.

The harrowing experience brought to mind the conversation she had with her father the previous night. When she went in to bid Winston goodnight after he had finished with the business in the pouch from Downing Street, she found him in a pensive mood. Perhaps that day's debate about the postwar treatment of Germany had recalled painful memories of the aftermath of the past war. Or maybe it was the totality of the horrors of the past five years that weighed upon him. Just before he fell asleep, Winston confided in her: 'I do not suppose that at any moment in history has the agony of the world been so great or widespread. Tonight the sun goes down on more suffering than ever before in the world.'

Unable to put the full scope of her emotions into words, Sarah wrote to her mother with uncustomary sparseness. What she needed to express could only be implied by what she left unsaid: 'I've seen a little of that agony these few days in Russia.'

THIRTEEN

February 6–7, 1945

The next day, Kathleen Harriman perched outdoors on a cold stone slab, pen and paper balanced on her lap. Groves of cypress trees afforded her a bit of privacy as she dashed off another instalment of her letter to Pamela. General Fred Anderson of the U.S. Army Air Force, Kathy's friend and one of Pamela's flames, mentioned he might be leaving Yalta the next day and would be happy to play courier, so Kathy could circumvent the censor. 'I'm out in the garden – in the sunshine – sitting on a fountain. It's the only non-windy spot available. Uncomfortable but the sun is too good a treat to miss,' she told her friend. After the long winter in Moscow, Kathy had had enough darkness. 'Ave & Ed [Stettinius] are over with the Soviets & this afternoon I guess they'll meet again with the big boys [Churchill, Roosevelt and Stalin],' she wrote.

It was rare that Kathy found herself with few details to share with Pamela. Since returning from Sevastopol, she had barely had a chance to speak with her father about conference developments. Roosevelt still did not consult Averell on matters of policy with the Soviets, but the ambassador had no trouble making himself useful in other capacities. Between the daily morning meetings with Ed Stettinius and the foreign secretaries, the lunches with Churchill and Roosevelt, the afternoon plenary sessions, the requisite conversations after the plenary sessions among the American camp, and the personal assistance he offered to the president's daughter, Averell was perhaps one of the hardest-working members of the Allied delegations. The previous evening, after the three women had returned from Sevastopol, Roosevelt had sent Averell on another post-dinner mission to the neighbouring delegations, and Kathy had not yet spoken with him about it. From what she could tell, 'They've embarked on the political questions,' she told Pamela. 'As far as I can gather, so far each person has stated his case – but the big job of reconciling differences of opinion has yet to start.'

Perhaps Kathy let on less than she knew for the sake of security, but even in her vague description of events, she was largely correct. The first two days of discussion behind the closed doors of the Livadia Palace ballroom had indeed sparked some debate, but it had not been especially contentious. Military coordination for the march on Berlin was of course imperative, and German rehabilitation and reparations presented challenges requiring complex solutions, but these issues were tangible and transactional in nature. On these matters, there would be debate and negotiation, and ultimately a compromise.

However, it was not until February 6, while Kathy, Sarah and Anna were away at Sevastopol, that the three Allied leaders and their advisers had begun to wade into the realm of existential questions – not about how to efficiently end a war, but how to guarantee a lasting peace.

Franklin Roosevelt was not naive enough to think that periods of world peace were anything but fleeting. Two world wars had been fought in less than half a century. But now the Allies, he believed, had a unique opportunity to guarantee a peace longer than any other in modern history, particularly in Europe. As he fervently stated when discussion began on February 6, 'all the nations of the world shared a common desire to see the elimination of war for at least fifty years . . . Fifty years of peace,' he insisted, were 'feasible and possible.'

For FDR, the seeds of peace he sought were rooted in the legacy of President Woodrow Wilson's League of Nations, formed after World War I. But this organisation had been destined to fail, thanks to bureaucratic ineptitude and American retrenchment into isolationism.

Those seeds remained dormant, and if protected by the right conditions, they might once again grow and thrive. A lasting organisation of nations committed to one another and to world peace would be the crowning achievement of FDR's foreign policy. For him, it superseded all other postwar issues; under the auspices of such an international body, all conflicts could be mediated and peacefully resolved.

In the early autumn of 1944, leaders from the United States, Britain, the Soviet Union and China had gathered in Washington, D.C., at the Dumbarton Oaks estate to lay preliminary plans. This world organisation would initially be made up of the signatories of the Declaration of the United Nations – those allied countries that had formally declared war on Germany in January 1942. Within this organisation, countries both large and small would have a voice in the assembly, but peace would depend on the leadership of the world's four great powers represented at Dumbarton Oaks. They would be the permanent members of the Security Council. At Dumbarton Oaks, the four nations had in principle agreed to form such an organisation, but they had yet to come to a consensus on the means by which the members of the Security Council would vote to settle disputes that could lead to violence or war – particularly disputes that emerged among the great powers. Roosevelt believed that in order to guarantee peace, the Security Council's decisions had to be unanimous, thus giving any one member veto power over the others. He also believed that the voting structure must be decided at Yalta. It was imperative to secure the Allies' full commitment before the war ended; otherwise he risked a reprise of the failure of the League of Nations. Postwar apathy and isolationism could quickly replace the spirit of international cooperation.

Churchill was not opposed to this peace organisation, but he had far less faith in it than Roosevelt did. Perhaps it could mediate quarrels between smaller nations, but he did not believe it could ultimately 'eliminate disputes between powers'. That, he responded to Roosevelt, 'would remain the function of diplomacy'. Furthermore, he stated that he was concerned that, to smaller nations, it might appear that the 'Three Great Powers were trying to rule the world' rather than protect future generations from 'repetition of the horrors of this war'.

As of the afternoon of February 6, Stalin was not ready to voice a firm opinion on the subject. Though he had received a copy of the American proposal in December, he claimed he had not yet had a chance to study it. In his mind, however, there was a matter at hand more pressing than the minutiae of the voting procedure. As long as Stalin, Roosevelt and Churchill remained at the fore of their respective countries, he was confident there would be no war between any of the three great powers. But in ten years, all three leaders might be gone. How, then, to guarantee peace for fifty years among their respective nations?

The unity of their three nations was of course 'one of our first aims', Roosevelt replied. 'Should there unfortunately be any differences between the Great Powers, and there might well be, this fact would become fully known to the world no matter what voting procedure was adopted ... Full and friendly discussions in the Council would in no sense promote disunity, but on the contrary, would serve to demonstrate the confidence which the Great Powers had in each other.'

As if to illustrate his point, Roosevelt then proposed a new topic of discussion, the second matter on the agenda for February 6. It was a bold strategy, for this subject was perhaps the most divisive issue the three leaders had come to debate. It was a topic they had avoided in the conference room thus far, but it was the very issue that had triggered the initial declarations of war in Europe in 1939: the fate of Poland.

By virtue of geography alone, Poland was condemned to a fragile existence. The Polish national identity had been cultivated in the fertile plains between the Oder and Vistula Rivers, but the Polish people had been whipsawed between two avowed enemies for five centuries. The Polish state, in its many monarchical and democratic incarnations, had constantly been shunted east and west between Russia and Germany – first in the form of neighbouring duchies, then kingdoms, and finally empires – each nibbling insatiably at Poland's borders. Several times, these hostile neighbours had swallowed Poland entirely. After the Napoleonic Wars, European statesmen at the Congress of Vienna had re-formed Poland and given it new national life, but its neighbours promptly swallowed it again. From 1918 to 1939, the Poles proudly flew the flag of the Second Polish Republic, but on August 23, 1939, Germany and the Soviet Union partitioned Poland once more, under the terms of the neutrality pact formed between *Reichsminister* Joachim von Ribbentrop and the chain-smoking, stone-faced gentleman now sitting to Stalin's right, Vyacheslav Molotov.

The debate over the future of Poland was twofold. First, after so many territorial upheavals throughout its history, to what land could Poland truly claim sovereignty, and where should its borders now be fixed? At the Tehran Conference in 1943, the three Allied leaders had tentatively agreed that the Curzon Line, the eastern border proposed by the former British foreign secretary Lord Curzon during World War I, should roughly delineate Poland's eastern border with the Soviet Union. Both Roosevelt and Churchill hoped that Stalin would agree to a small deviation from this line as a 'gesture of magnanimity' so that the majority-Polish city of Lviv (Lwów in Polish, Lvov in Russian) in the territory the Soviets claimed for Ukraine could remain part of Poland, but this was a pipe dream. With the Curzon Line as the new border, the Soviet Union would absorb significant territorial concessions from what had been the interwar state of the Second Polish Republic. In exchange, the Allies proposed that Poland should be rewarded with new territory from what had been eastern Germany, potentially as far west as the Oder and Neisse Rivers, though this would mean significant displacement of ethnic Germans and continued hostility between Poles and Germans along this border.

As crucial as these boundaries were, another issue superseded them. For a nation to thrive, it must have sovereignty. Since 1940, Poland's legitimate government, recognised by Britain and the United States, had remained exiled in London. The end of the war would mean the end of strife for most Europeans, but for the Poles, the problems would continue. The hopes once buoyed by the 1944 Warsaw Uprising against the German occupation had been dashed; now the threat posed by the Poles' eastern neighbours had become a grim reality. The Red Army had replaced the Nazis, and in their wake emerged a new government made up of Communist sympathisers supported and controlled by the Soviet Union. Stalin now wanted his Allies to recognise this government, based in the city of Lublin, as legitimate. Winant's telegram from the Polish prime minister had vociferously warned against this. The telegram still lay unanswered. Thus far at Yalta, only the State

Department representatives, Freeman Matthews and Alger Hiss, had read it, and they had decided it was not worth replying while discussions regarding Poland were still underway. This lack of response notwithstanding, Roosevelt and Churchill had staunchly refused to recognise the Lublin government since it was formed. Britain had declared war to guarantee Polish sovereignty. Together, the two western Allies had vowed that all people had a right to self-determination, and to recognise the Lublin government would be hypocrisy. It would give the Soviets carte blanche over the fate of their longtime foe and make a farce of the idea of self-determination.

Once again, Roosevelt positioned himself as mediator between the British and the Soviets. On the subject of Poland, he began, the Americans had the benefit of distance, which could perhaps be of use as the Europeans sorted out their differences. They could start the conversation now with a point they all generally agreed on: the Curzon Line could suitably demarcate Poland's eastern border.

But Churchill did not want to begin there. A lengthy discussion about borders would push off the essential issue, and Roosevelt's prolonged obfuscation on the subject had become untenable. The prime minister decided to cut to the heart of the matter. Indeed, the British supported the Curzon Line as the eastern boundary; they had drawn it in the first place. 'However,' Churchill stated emphatically, 'I am much more interested in the question of Poland's sovereign independence and freedom than in particular frontier lines ... This is what we went to war against Germany for – that Poland should be free and sovereign ... Never could I be content with any solution that would not leave Poland as a free and independent state.' This was not to say he bore any hostility towards the Soviets, he emphasised. It was simply a matter of principle. The people of Poland must be able to choose their own government through free and unfettered elections. An interim government must be established, one composed of men who legitimately represented the will of the Polish people. Poland, he argued, must 'be mistress in her own house and captain of her soul'.

Churchill's feeling about defending Poland's sovereignty as a matter of honour was genuine, but his position was also a matter of strategy. The Soviets must not be allowed to control all of Eastern Europe.

As Stalin sat listening to his counterparts' arguments throughout this third plenary session, he quietly doodled on the paper in front of him. Stalin was a notorious doodler. Even people like Kathy Harriman, who had never sat with him at a conference table, knew of his habit. As Averell had told her, if discussions were proceeding in his favour, Stalin would smile and draw benign figures in red pencil, but if he became angry, his scribbles would take on a hostile air, and wolves or foxes would flow from the pencil's tip. On the afternoon of February 6, he was doodling more vigorously than usual.

Stalin usually left it to Molotov to quit his chain-smoking just long enough to articulate the Soviets' requisite knee-jerk intractability on any given subject, but now the Soviet leader broke from his doodling, stood up, and began to speak. 'The Prime Minister has said that for Great Britain the question of Poland is a question of honor,' he began, with Pavlov translating. 'For Russia it is not only a question of honor but also of security . . . Throughout history Poland has always been a corridor for attack on Russia . . . During the last thirty years our German enemy has passed through this corridor twice. This is because Poland was weak. It is in the Russian interest as well as that of Poland that Poland be strong and powerful . . . It is not only a question of honor but of life and death for the Soviet State.' As Stalin spoke, he paced back and forth behind his chair as if to emphasise his point.

He continued. 'They all say that I am a dictator but I have enough democratic feeling not to set up a Polish government without Poles.' But the London Poles were unreasonable, Stalin claimed. They publicly called their Lublin counterparts 'bandits' and 'traitors'. How were these two groups ever to be reconciled?

Words flowed from the reticent old Georgian at a rate not yet seen at this conference, and he seemed to have no plans to stop. The minutes ticked by as Pavlov translated Stalin's exhortations. Harry Hopkins checked the time. He leaned forward and slipped a note to FDR. 'Mr. President, why not let this wind up today when Stalin is thru – and say we will talk it over again tomorrow. It is 7:15.' The discussion had taken a decidedly negative turn, and it would behove everyone to return to this issue with cooler heads on the morrow.

But Stalin was not finished. He had one more grievance with the

London Poles. 'As a military man I demand from a country liberated by the Red Army that there be no civil war in the rear,' he continued. 'The men in the Red Army are indifferent to the type of government as long as it will maintain order and they will not be shot in the back.' The Lublin government had maintained order relatively well. The same, however, could not be said for the London Poles, 'who claim to be agents of the underground forces of resistance ... Much evil comes from these forces ... They have killed 212 of our military men. They attack our supply bases to obtain arms. We have arrested some of them and if they continue to disturb our rear we will shoot them as military law requires ... We want tranquility in our rear. We will support the government which gives us peace in the rear ... I could not do otherwise.'

Before Stalin could say more, Roosevelt quickly interjected and suggested they stop there for the day.

But, eager to have the final say, Churchill decided he had one more point to make before they adjourned. 'I must put on the record that both the British and Soviet governments have different sources of information in Poland and get different facts,' he stated. For some time, the British had had agents within Poland reporting back to them about the frightening behaviour of the Red Army as it drank, plundered – and no doubt raped – its way westwards across the country. Nor could Churchill or Roosevelt truly forget the information they had received about the Katyn Forest massacre, which they had chosen to put aside for the sake of maintaining the alliance. 'Perhaps we are mistaken but I do not feel that the Lublin government represents even one-third of the Polish people,' Churchill stated. 'I fear the effect on the whole Polish question. Anyone who attacks the Red Army should be punished but I cannot feel that the Lublin government has any right to represent the Polish nation.' As he closed, an air of hostility crackled in the room like static from a radio.

Chairs scraped and the usual muttering broke out as the gentlemen prepared to leave the table, but the American president decided to make one more remark, perhaps in the hope of placing the day's discussion in a broader context and recessing on a lighter note. 'Poland,'

Roosevelt commented, 'has been a source of trouble for over five hundred years.'

'All the more,' Churchill rejoined, 'we must do what we can to put an end to these troubles.'

As the night of February 6 closed in, Roosevelt found himself dissatisfied with the results of the day's discussion. After dinner, as Anna read the mail she had received from her husband and children, Roosevelt instructed Chip Bohlen to compose a letter on his behalf to the Soviet generalissimo. He hoped that by calling upon the rapport he had built with Stalin over the past three and a half years, he could convince the Soviet dictator to find room for compromise. FDR then sent Harriman to retrace his steps of the night of February 3 to carry his letter, first to Vorontsov Palace, where Harriman showed it to Churchill and Anthony Eden. The British largely agreed with the tone and contents, but Eden felt it was 'not quite stiff enough' and suggested some modifications. Harriman then returned to Livadia with the edited letter. Roosevelt accepted all of Eden's suggestions and dispatched the letter to Stalin posthaste. 'My Dear Marshal Stalin,' the final version began:

> I have been giving a great deal of thought to our meeting this afternoon, and I want to tell you in all frankness what is on my mind. In so far as the Polish government is concerned, I am greatly disturbed that the three great powers do not have a meeting of minds . . . It seems to me that it puts all of us in a bad light throughout the world to have you recognizing one government while we and the British are recognizing another in London. I am sure this state of affairs should not continue and that if it does it can only lead our people to think there is a breach between us, which is not the case. I am determined that there shall be no breach between ourselves and the Soviet Union. Surely there is a way to reconcile our differences.

He then proposed a solution: ask several representatives from the Lublin government to come to Yalta, as well as two or three other respected Polish leaders from within the country, including those from the church and academia, to serve as mediators between the Lublin and London Polish governments. If they could reach an accord on the composition of an expanded, representative interim government that would be in no way 'inimical' to Soviet interests, the United States and Britain would consider 'transfer[ing] their recognition to the new provisional government,' which would be responsible for overseeing the Polish elections. 'I know,' he closed, 'this is completely consistent with your desire to see a new free and democratic Poland emerge from the welter of this war.'

Just as on the first night at Yalta, when Roosevelt had dispatched Harriman to the Koreiz Villa to fix the first day's agenda and FDR's private meeting with Stalin, the American ambassador found himself making the midnight rounds on behalf of a strategy in which he had little faith and yet was powerless to change. Roosevelt's letter was an appeal to both the friendship he believed the United States had developed with the Soviet Union and the friendship that he himself had developed with Stalin personally. Harriman had long been a believer in the power of personal relationships – not that they determined the outcome of geopolitical affairs, but rather had the power to influence them. The personal relationship between Churchill and Roosevelt certainly had had that effect on the 'Special Relationship' between Britain and the United States. However, as Harriman's deputy in Moscow, George Kennan, had asserted earlier that week when asked to report on the personal profiles of the Soviet delegates, '[For a Soviet official to] do anything or say anything in deference to a personal relationship which one would not have done or said in a straight performance of official duties would be considered equivalent to acting in the interests of a foreign state.' While Stalin might very well have liked to maintain his relationship with Roosevelt, Harriman knew that for Stalin, friendly neighbours would always trump personal friendships, without question. When it came to Poland, Harriman knew Stalin 'wanted to dominate them, to make certain that they would never again serve as a pathway for German aggression against Russia'. Roosevelt's appeal would be as ineffectual as a glass hammer in moderating whatever behaviour Stalin felt was necessary to bring his neighbour into line. No inducement, 'short of going to war', was about to change that.

The afternoon following this fraught late-night diplomacy, as Kathy was sitting at the fountain in the Livadia Palace garden, writing to Pamela, Sarah Churchill was taking a walk at Vorontsov Palace. On the terrace the photographers were out in force. The three delegations had just agreed to release a joint press statement, simultaneously in each country, at 4.30 Eastern War Time, acknowledging the conference and explaining its objectives. The film crews that had travelled with the delegations had immediately sprung into action to capture newsreel footage of the participants at their respective lodgings, and of the surrounding area, to follow the press release. Now that the information was about to be made public, there did not seem much point in maintaining the charade at RAF Medmenham that Sarah was sick. She had written to her mother, asking that someone please ring her friend at the base who was covering for her, to tell her there was no need to 'hold the fort' any longer.

On the terrace, Sarah came upon the head of the RAF, Peter Portal. He had stayed behind for a meeting with Churchill's chief of staff, General Pug Ismay, and the representative of the U.S. Army Air Corps, General Laurence Kuter, while the rest of the British military chiefs, led by the zealous amateur historian Alan Brooke, set off for Balaklava, armed with maps, compasses, and books of military history. Sarah was always glad to see Portal. Once described by a contemporary as 'a man of granite and of ruthlessness', Portal also had an 'immense personality' and a sense of humour that could be simultaneously 'funny and malicious', as evidenced by the great pleasure he derived from bullying those who took too long in the bathroom. He was from an old, distinguished British family purportedly of French Huguenot origins – at least, that was how people accounted for his nose, which was of a scale different from the rest of an otherwise handsome face. A graduate of Christ Church College, Oxford, he had served as the head of the RAF since 1940 and was made a Knight Grand Cross of the Order of the Bath by King George in 1942, one of the foremost British Orders of Chivalry. Portal was a fixture of Churchill's wartime conference delegations and had been, like Sarah, at Tehran. He and Sarah also knew each other socially in London; he regularly featured in her father's professional circle and Pamela's entourage of eager swains. Beyond his devotion to the RAF, Portal also enjoyed the arts, which Sarah particularly appreciated; she had once invited him to join her for a concert in London.

Though Sarah enjoyed Kathy's and Anna's company and found them 'very kind and agreeable', as she had written to her mother, there was something perhaps more familiar and easy about being with a compatriot, especially one like Portal. Even though he was fifty-two and technically her commanding officer, since the WAAFs fell under the jurisdiction of the RAF, he was a delightful companion, full of amusing gossip and the closest thing to a 'buddy' she had at the conference. As they stopped to chat, the newsreel crews filmed them in earnest, and Portal jested that they would soon be starring in cinemas in London. Conversation then turned to the subject of local attractions. Neither had yet seen the thousand-foot Uchan-Su waterfall, reputedly remarkable, which Kathy had written about in her pamphlet on the Crimea. The two decided that if Winston did not require Sarah for the drive over to Livadia that afternoon, they would find a Jeep and driver to take them to see it. They bid each other so long, and Sarah carried on with her walk, making her way down the wide stone steps flanked by carved lions on the 'mosque' side of Vorontsov Palace, which led down to the sea.

Sarah had yet to see the shore up close, so she took advantage of a quiet moment to escape from the delegates and the film crews to explore the water's edge. The sun was shining, but the sea was a 'vivid angry blue flecked with white'. All along the shore, the water 'swirled and hissed among the gigantic boulders that fringe[d] the edge'. Something was weighing on her during this brief, solitary walk. Sarah knew that part of her duty, as her father's aide-de-camp, was to serve as family chronicler of events at Yalta – especially the personal details behind the pomp and circumstance. The Churchills were well aware of their place in history. Sarah's father would undoubtedly write a history of this war, just as he had done after the previous one. Offers from publishers had begun to pour in as early as September 28, 1939 –

exactly four weeks after the war began. Even Clementine had some literary ideas to pursue after the war. She often had her children's letters retyped to proudly share with family and friends; Clementine found Sarah's letters especially 'enchanting and entrancing'. Their quality, she told Winston, could 'rival any letters as literature of a very high level'. As Clementine catalogued these letters for the family archives, she mused that she enjoyed the wartime correspondence of Sarah and her sister, Mary, so much that she might someday compile a volume called 'Letters from My Daughters'.

But now, Sarah was having a crisis of conscience about one of these letters, the one she had written to her mother the day of the arrival at Yalta. She had been so foolishly indiscreet. Describing the Americans as they arrived at Malta, she had said that Roosevelt was either sick or turning his back on her father, that the new secretary of state seemed none too bright, that the president appeared to be holding his longtime confidant Harry Hopkins at an unfamiliar distance, and that Gil Winant was the only American who could be trusted. The British had never lost a courier at any of the wartime conferences, but God forbid, should something happen to the plane carrying the pouch back to London, her letter might fall into unfriendly hands. It could be deeply embarrassing to her father, for Sarah's ungracious opinions about Britain's closest ally could be interpreted as those of the prime minister. At this stage in the conference, such a misstep could jeopardise everything her father had been working towards.

Sarah had dashed off a frantic note to her mother, hoping that it would reach her before she showed Sarah's letter to anyone else. 'Darling,' Sarah wrote, 'I have had second thoughts and a pang of conscience, and you know what my pangs of conscience are! Will you *please* delete from my last letter the entire page concerning personalities here. It is most important that my impressions should go no further than you.' Clementine was of course savvy enough not to circulate anything that would cause trouble, but still Sarah fretted. 'I realise you know this, but feel it was *very* wrong of me – and unwise to have written it at this stage.'

When Sarah returned from her walk, she discovered that her father did indeed want her to drive with him to Livadia that afternoon.

He had been without her while she was at Sevastopol the day before, and as Stalin seemed to be revelling in the suspense he created as the hours crept by – there had been no reply to Roosevelt's letter – on this day in particular, Winston needed Sarah's reassuring presence. They did not need to speak about the burden he felt. Her work as a WAAF and her intuitive understanding of her father's mind told her all she needed to know. Her father had brought her to the conference because of these qualities.

She found Portal and told him their excursion to the waterfall would have to wait for another time. At 3.30, Sarah and Winston climbed into their Packard and began the thirty-minute drive back to the American compound for the second day of discussion about Roosevelt's peace organisation and the fate of the Poles. A chilling breeze was blowing from the east, but the afternoon sun was now out in full force, trying its 'best for the scene' as if to encourage a positive state of mind. Perhaps it was trying a bit too hard, for the sun reflected so brightly on the sea's ripples that Sarah had to blink.

Winston sat quietly staring out the window, looking 'stolidly' at their surroundings. After a time, he turned to Sarah and harrumphed, 'The Riviera of Hades!' That, Sarah thought, summed up the situation perfectly.

Kathy was about ready to close her long letter of February 7 so that Fred Anderson could take it to Pamela in London. But after dinner that night, she found herself with some concrete news of the conference – a true turn of events – to share. 'There was great rejoicing,' Kathy told her friend. That afternoon, there had been a breakthrough. After the conference that summer in Washington, months of correspondence, and two days of debate at Yalta, at long last, reported Kathy, 'They sold U[ncle] J[oe] on Dumbarton Oaks.'

A key factor that had been hindering a settlement on Roosevelt's peace organisation was Stalin and Molotov's insistence that the Soviets receive one vote in the General Assembly for each of the sixteen republics making up the Soviet Union. After negotiation that afternoon, Molotov magnanimously dropped the number to two or three. Ukraine and Belorussia had sacrificed so much in the war, he said. Surely 'it was only fair', to allow these two Soviet republics to join as charter members, with their own votes. After all, British Commonwealth nations like Canada would have separate votes, and Churchill was pushing for India, which remained a British colony, to have a vote as well. As soon as the British and the Americans indicated a willingness to agree, Stalin accepted the Americans' proposed voting structure for the peace organisation's Security Council.

Delighted with his success with Stalin, FDR was in the best of spirits at dinner. Admiral Leahy pronounced the agreement a triumph for his boss. Even Jimmy Byrnes, who, Kathy noted, had a habit of droning on 'boringly & at great length', could not dampen the mood. 'Lord save me from American politics!' Kathy joked sarcastically to Pamela, in reference to Byrnes.

With this victory in hand, Edward Stettinius and his assistant, Alger Hiss, were left with the happy task of choosing a date and location for the inaugural gathering of the new organisation later that spring. The president soon retired for the evening, but many of the Americans wanted to continue the revelry. There was no bar at Livadia, and the canteen was now closed. Fortunately, many delegates had brought their own provisions. Kathy invited a few close friends, such as Fred Anderson, to her room for drinks and spirited conversation, but word quickly spread that Kathy's quarters were the place to be. Before she knew it, a 'mob gathered', turning her bedroom into a late-night watering hole.

Kathy could not help but feel that the Americans' successes at the negotiating table thus far were in no small part due to Averell's efforts. She had established a 'spy system' among her friends in the British and American delegations at Yalta to report to her, to the extent that their security clearances allowed, what went on behind closed doors. Her agents were only too happy to extol the ambassador's achievements to his charming and attractive daughter. 'Ave's in there pitching as you can well imagine & reports so far are very favorable,' she boasted to Pamela.

Pride in her father was still a relatively new sensation for Kathy.

Growing up, she had been aware that he was rich, handsome and talented, but only after joining him in London did she realise that he had gifts of far greater importance. 'I only arrived last evening – but already I'm beginning to feel what Ave is,' Kathy had written to her sister after her first night in the Blitz-torn British capital four years earlier. 'He seems to stand for something secure that people can hang [on] to & believe in & they all have great faith in him . . . They all love him.' Roosevelt had sent Averell to London as his 'Expediter', a significant if not strictly defined role, and one that still seemed to define him after his official title changed to ambassador. But things were different in Russia. The Soviets could be obdurate, and often Kathy had seen Averell return late to Spaso House, disappointed because his efforts to reach an agreement had come to naught. It had been some time since Averell had wielded the level of influence that was his in London. After a long Russian winter, Kathy dared to hope that he was once again in a position to do so.

Perhaps Kathy's spies were not especially adept, or perhaps they enhanced their reports about Averell's prowess at the negotiating table in hopes of ingratiating themselves with the ambassador's daughter. Or maybe Kathy saw in her father only what she wanted to see, as Anna did in regard to her own father. Regardless of the reason, back in London, Pamela Churchill would soon receive a strikingly different report from Peter Portal, who had written to Pamela the night before: 'I am sorry to tell you that the general opinion among our people here is that A is not having great success with the Russians and that this is worrying him. He certainly looks older than when I last saw him. It must be one hell of a job, 90% frustration & 10% disappointment. I feel very sorry for him.' Whether the British air marshal truly felt any sympathy towards his rival for Pamela's affections was left to the lady to interpret, but to Portal, one thing was clear. Harriman may have been one of the shrewdest businessmen in the western world, but the Americans' man in Moscow was no match for Stalin when the strongman was determined to have his way.

That was hardly Averell Harriman's fault. He was playing a game he was practically guaranteed to lose. No matter how astute a businessman, no matter how deft his skills at the card table, he was always playing at a distinct disadvantage. This was because Stalin commanded a prime source of insight that the British and Americans lacked: real spies.

For nearly a decade, the Soviets had been infiltrating Britain's security services – MI5 and MI6 – and the Foreign Office. Among their most notable agents were the Cambridge Five – Kim Philby, Donald Maclean, Guy Burgess, Anthony Blunt and John Cairncross – a group of wealthy, gifted and ideologically committed gentlemen-spies recruited from Cambridge University. As they rose through the ranks of British intelligence, the Cambridge Five passed thousands of documents to Moscow, including those detailing the British position on Poland. Maclean, who was posted to the British embassy in Washington, provided one of the Soviets' greatest intelligence coups – crucial insights about the Manhattan Project, the Anglo-American mission to build the atomic bomb, an operation so secret that not even Vice President Truman knew about it. Meanwhile, Britain's foreign intelligence service, MI6, had a grand total of zero spies in the Soviet Union. The British Foreign Office had curtailed all efforts. Spying on one's ally was not the done thing in civilised nations.

In Washington, the Soviets ran similar operations, identifying and recruiting rising stars in government agencies who had Communist sympathies. Their efforts proved even more successful than they had anticipated when one of their American assets at the State Department unexpectedly secured an invitation to join Roosevelt's delegation to Yalta: Alger Hiss.

Much like the Cambridge Five, the svelte, bow-tie-sporting forty-year-old with the impeccable résumé appeared an unlikely traitor. And yet Hiss – code-named 'Ales' – had secretly been working for Soviet military intelligence (the GRU) since at least 1936, the year he joined the State Department. State could not say it had not been forewarned. Almost six years earlier, in 1939, a *Time* magazine writer named Whittaker Chambers, a former American Soviet asset who had since firmly turned his back on Communism and was now actively working against the Soviets, had approached a top State Department official, Adolph Berle, to warn him that Hiss was not all that he seemed. Chambers informed Berle that for many years Hiss had been a member of an underground Communist organisation and worked as a Soviet asset. Chambers knew this with absolute certainty – he had, after all, been Hiss's handler.

But through either negligence or doubt about this information, Berle failed to pass the message along. Hiss continued to rise through the State Department, ultimately landing as a trusted deputy of the secretary of state. Using his security clearance, he copied and sent countless documents to Moscow; as his access to confidential information widened, his value to the Soviets grew. With proximity to people like Stettinius, who had Roosevelt's ear, Hiss was also ideally positioned to act as a covert influence agent. His subtle yet effective comments and suggestions could steer discussions and decisions in ways that favoured the Soviets. (No doubt the Soviets would have been doubly thrilled had they known that Harry Hopkins had made a contingency plan in the event of FDR's death. Hopkins might then run for president in 1944, and if he won, he would look to appoint Alger Hiss as secretary of state.) At Yalta, Hiss was meeting regularly with Stettinius, preparing him for discussions about the world peace organisation and attending nearly all the plenary sessions, as well as the foreign ministers' lunch meetings. Sitting quietly behind Roosevelt in the plenary sessions, Hiss took his own set of notes on all the conversations that took place. They would become part of the official American record of the Yalta Conference, alongside the notes taken by Chip Bohlen.

When Hiss arrived at Yalta, he was working only for the GRU, but as the conference progressed, he came to the attention of one of the more powerful agencies in the Soviet Union, the People's Commissariat for State Security (Narodny Kommisariat Gosudarstvennoy Bezopasnosti), better known as the NKGB. Though their names were similar, the NKGB was an entity distinct from Beria's NKVD. The NKVD specialised in internal security, while the NKGB collected intelligence and performed counterintelligence both at home and abroad. Joining Roosevelt's entourage at Yalta elevated Hiss's profile and alerted the NKGB that Hiss might be someone worth cultivating. The Soviets wanted inside information on Roosevelt's world peace organisation. Hiss was just the man to get it.

≡

Espionage can take a variety of forms, and at Yalta, everyone was under close scrutiny all the time. The British may not have had any active spies in the Soviet Union, but they were not without watchful eyes entirely. Since arriving at Malta, Churchill's doctor, Lord Moran, had been observing Franklin Roosevelt intently at every opportunity and making notes in his diary. Rumours about Roosevelt's declining health had spread to Britain, though it was difficult to make a diagnosis based solely on the judiciously selected and carefully composed photographs in newspapers. At times, as on the night of his reelection, in November 1944, a moment when FDR should have been utterly exhausted, photographs showed a man in his prime – full of robust energy and ready to lead the nation through a fourth term. He looked so animated that Anna's colleague from the *Seattle Post-Intelligencer*, the renowned sports reporter Royal Brougham, cabled to say he could see that 'the champ hasn't lost the old wallop.' At other times, such as the day of his fourth inauguration, the president appeared minutes away from death.

In addition to serving as Churchill's doctor, Moran was president of the Royal College of Physicians. The day before he left England for Yalta with the prime minister, Moran had received a letter from his friend and American counterpart, Dr Roger Lee of Boston, the president of the American Medical Association and former president of the American College of Physicians. Lee disclosed to Moran what he had heard about Roosevelt's health: the president had been diagnosed with congestive heart failure the previous spring. It was difficult to say how far the disease had progressed based on the patient's appearance, for it could fluctuate significantly from day to day. But the symptoms Lee described indicated that Roosevelt's heart condition had reached an advanced stage.

From a doctor's vantage point, FDR clearly appeared to be a 'very sick man', Moran noted in his diary. 'He has all the symptoms of hardening of the arteries of the brain in an advanced stage, so that I give him only a few months to live,' Moran wrote that night. To someone with medical training, this would have been readily apparent, but in the doctor's opinion, FDR's deterioration was so evident that even a layman would notice. And yet none of Roosevelt's inner circle seemed to acknowledge what Moran felt was plainly obvious.

The person whose reaction surprised him most was Anna's. 'His daughter thinks he is not really ill, and his doctor backs her up,' he wrote. 'But men shut their eyes when they do not want to see, and the Americans here cannot bring themselves to believe that he is finished.'

FOURTEEN

February 8, 1945

Anna had been trying her best, she wrote to John, 'using all the ingenuity and tact' she could summon to stay informed about developments in the plenary meetings and to 'keep the unnecessary people out' of her father's quarters and 'steer the necessary one's [*sic*] in at the best of times'. But no matter how many notes she left for FDR, reminding him to rest, to eat only the prescribed food, or to not wear himself out with matters someone else could address, it was never enough. She could not shorten the gruelling sessions in the ballroom, nor could she dissuade her father from meeting with Stalin before the three Allied groups convened for the conference that afternoon; Anna knew little about the details of that session. It seemed that FDR had burned through the energy he had derived from victory concerning his world peace organisation the night before. By the time he returned to his private quarters after five straight hours of meetings on the evening of February 8, his skin looked ashen, his cheeks sunken. He was deteriorating even faster than Anna could have imagined, but still his workday was not over. Tonight Stalin was hosting a grand banquet at the Koreiz Villa, and the three daughters had been invited.

In the president's room, Dr Bruenn examined his patient. He was concerned about Roosevelt's pallor. Like Anna, Bruenn knew no specific details about what had been discussed that afternoon, but he could tell that this day had been 'especially arduous' and 'emotionally disturbing'. Roosevelt was 'obviously greatly fatigued'. The patient, Bruenn logged in his notes, 'has had a constant stream of visits from the time he awakes in the morning until lunch . . . has had no time to take his afternoon rest'. As Bruenn continued his examination, Roosevelt confessed that the afternoon conference had left him 'worried and upset about the trend of the discussions', namely, regarding Poland.

The last two days of meetings about Poland had been sorely disconcerting. First was Stalin's response to Roosevelt's letter of the night of February 6 – or rather, the lack thereof. When the three leaders arrived at the plenary session on the afternoon of the seventh, Stalin claimed he had only just received FDR's letter. He had little to say on the matter except that he had 'endeavored to reach the Lublin Poles by telephone', only to discover they were away from Lublin on other business. As for the other Polish leaders FDR had suggested including in the negotiations at Yalta, Stalin had no idea where to locate them, as he did not know their addresses. Averell Harriman thought it the 'flimsiest possible excuse', but before anyone could dispute it, Molotov had promptly changed the subject to announce the Soviets' support for the world peace organisation and their satisfaction with a mere two or three extra votes. It was a blatant obfuscation, but even Harriman could not deny that the Soviets had 'brilliant timing'.

At the meeting on this afternoon – February 8 – the battle over free elections in Poland had continued. True to form, Churchill made some sweeping pronouncements to the effect that they had reached the 'crucial point of this great conference', repeating his conviction that failure to reach an agreement regarding Poland would 'be interpreted all over the world as a sign of cleavage between the Soviet government on the one hand and the U.S. and British governments on the other'. Such a breakdown, he insisted, 'would stamp the conference as a failure'. Stalin then responded with histrionics of his own. Roosevelt had little patience for this.

Poland was the second weighty subject Roosevelt had addressed that day. He had already spent half an hour before the plenary meeting with Stalin, Molotov and Harriman to discuss the war in the Pacific. The British were not included in the meeting. For the Americans, it was crucial to walk away from Yalta with an agreement guarantee-ing that the Soviets would declare war against Japan. The Pacific con-flict might devolve into a war of attrition. Nothing but a total Allied victory would make Japan capitulate, and if the Manhattan Project proved a failure, victory in Japan would require overwhelming man-power. Even with General MacArthur's recent success in the Philip-pines, which Averell Harriman had announced at the foreign minis-ters' meeting earlier that week, the American leadership remained convinced that without Soviet intervention, the cost of victory in the Pacific would likely be another eighteen months of war and hundreds of thousands of American lives. That afternoon, Roosevelt agreed to the Soviets' desiderata in exchange for their promised entry into the war against Japan. After Germany was defeated, Roosevelt and Stalin agreed, the Soviets would declare war on Japan in exchange for access to warm-water ports and railway lines in Manchuria, as well as the restoration of the Kuril and Sakhalin Islands to the Soviet Union; the Soviets maintained the Japanese had taken the islands from them during the Russo-Japanese War, in 1905. Roosevelt assented without consulting the Chinese leader, Chiang Kai-Shek, despite the agree-ment's direct impact on China. Fearful of security breaches, the presi-dent decided he would inform the Chinese at a later date.

And if battling with Stalin and then Churchill was not enough to sap Roosevelt of whatever strength remained, he also had to suffer through infighting within his own camp. These difficulties included a sharply worded telegram from Gil Winant on the subject of post-war Germany, which began with the preamble 'Since you and Secre-tary Stettinius and Mr. Hopkins decided to exclude me from the con-ference –' It was little wonder Roosevelt looked decades older than his sixty-three years.

Bruenn now listened to the president's lungs. They sounded clear of fluid. His heartbeat was a normal rate, eighty-four beats per min-ute. But when Bruenn checked Roosevelt's blood pressure, he realised something was seriously wrong.

In the 1913 novel *Sons and Lovers*, D. H. Lawrence describes a scene in which a woman is dying as her son sits at her bedside. As she nears her end, her son puts his fingers to the sallow skin on his mother's wrist to feel her pulse. 'There was a strong stroke and a weak one,' Lawrence wrote, 'like a sound and its echo. That was supposed to betoken the end.' This sound and its echo was exactly what Bruenn heard. 'B.P. for the first time showed pulsus alternans,' Bruenn wrote on the president's health charts. He did not tell the patient.

The president's heart was beating at a regular rhythm, but every other contraction was weaker than the one before, due to fluid build-up within the left side of his heart and the progressively depressed function of his heart muscle. Bruenn knew that pulsus alternans could be temporary, and though it could not be treated with medicine or surgery, the heart could return to its normal pulse on its own. However, coupled with the diagnosis of left-sided heart failure months before, Bruenn also knew this could be evidence of a worsening of the president's condition. As D. H. Lawrence had ominously described it in his novel, this was a telltale sign that the end was near.

Anna had experienced one of her father's acute health scares before. She had made a short trip back to the West Coast with him in August 1944, where he gave a speech to thousands of workers at the naval yard in Bremerton, Washington, across Puget Sound from Seattle. While addressing the crowd from the deck of the USS *Cummings*, he had experienced sharp pain in his chest and shoulders. At first it seemed he might be having a heart attack, but Bruenn quickly realised it was the first time in months that Roosevelt had delivered a speech wearing his heavy metal leg braces while supporting himself with his forearms on the podium. All of this took place on a rocking ship, no less. It was not a heart attack, but angina, a temporary but painful tightness in the chest. A normal result from an electrocardiogram confirmed his diagnosis. In September 1944, Roosevelt experienced another episode while watching a film about Woodrow Wilson after dinner one night at the Quebec Conference, with Churchill and the Canadian prime minister, Mackenzie King. Anna was not with her father at the time, but Bruenn was. The film depicted Wilson embarking on a tour around the country, trying to rally support for the League of Nations, only to return to the White House, defeated. Shortly thereafter, Wilson suffered a stroke. 'By God, that's not going to happen to me!' Roosevelt exclaimed, his blood pressure skyrocketing to 240/130. Fortunately, it returned to normal by the next morning.

This, however, was different, and it confirmed what Anna had only just come to understand the day before. Months earlier, when Bruenn had broken the rule set by Admiral Ross McIntire, Roosevelt's White House physician, and had confided FDR's heart condition to Anna, Bruenn had not given her complete information. At Yalta, he finally divulged everything. 'I have found out thru Bruenn (who won't let me tell Ross that I know) that this "ticker" situation is far more serious than I ever knew,' Anna now disclosed to John. 'The biggest difficulty in handling the situation here is that we can, of course, tell no one.' She could not have revealed anything to Kathy or Sarah, as they surely would have told their fathers. Writing to her husband was security risk enough. She thinly disguised her father's identity with the initials OM – short for Old Man or Oscar Mann, the code name she and John used for FDR – but anyone remotely savvy would realise whom she was referring to. Still, it was too large a burden for Anna to carry alone. 'Better tear off and destroy this paragraph,' she hastily added in parentheses.

A very small part of Anna could not help but feel that FDR's turn for the worse was partly his own fault. He was happy to have her shield him from people like Hopkins and Churchill when he did not wish to see them, but instead of resting, he relished performing in front of a crowd. 'He gets all wound up, seems to thoroughly enjoy it all, but wants too many people around, and then won't go to bed early enough,' Anna fumed to John. Anna sometimes found it difficult in such moments to believe that her father was truly ill.

The only thing Anna and Bruenn could do in hopes of reversing FDR's pulsus alternans was to make him rest. Skipping Stalin's dinner that night was, however, not an option. Doing so would be seen as a slight to Stalin and also reinforce any suspicions the Soviets might have about his declining health. Most important, Roosevelt still firmly believed in the power of his personal rapport with Stalin, which was best fostered through unstructured social interactions free from the interference of State Department bureaucrats. FDR remained convinced it was his strongest and perhaps only means of inducing the Soviets to embrace the postwar international community. This dinner presented an opportunity that could not be missed.

Perhaps the thrill of performance would be enough to carry the president through, but within the walls of the Koreiz Villa that evening, every one of Stalin's men's eyes would be fixed on him. It was lucky that pulsus alternans was not visibly obvious. Roosevelt's colour was certainly paler than usual, and he did indeed look exhausted, but at this point in the conference, so did everyone. Some people, especially among the British delegates, had hoped they would not be invited to Stalin's banquet. They were weary of the excessive toasting and heaping portions of caviar and wanted nothing more than to get some sleep. Anthony Eden's deputy, Alexander Cadogan, was particularly thankful the three daughters had been invited that night. The dinner table had room for just thirty, and with Sarah, Kathy and Anna taking up three of those seats, Cadogan did not make the cut. For FDR, however, there could be no escape.

At half past eight Roosevelt's Secret Service officers helped him into his car. Anna, wrapped in her fur coat, slid in beside him. As they prepared to leave, the signal went out to close the road between Livadia Palace and the Koreiz Villa to all but the president's car and those travelling in his party: Ed Stettinius, Admiral Leahy, Jimmy Byrnes, the Harrimans, Chip Bohlen and Ed Flynn. Together, the Americans drove thirty minutes along the dark coastal road to the erstwhile villa of Rasputin's killer, where the Russian Bear and a twenty-course meal awaited them.

For the rest of the evening, Anna would smile, raise her glass as many times as was required, and pretend nothing was the matter, just as she had at White House dinners for the past year. As Anna had discovered, keeping her father's secrets was the price paid to be close to him, even when that meant keeping secrets from not just his colleagues, advisers, allies and potential adversaries, but from the people who cared for him the most.

Whether her father was afraid for his health or had been nervous about the dinner, Anna could not say. If he had consciously absorbed anything from Bruenn's examination, he had made no mention of it.

Anna was well aware that her father rarely discussed his true personal feelings with her, or with anyone, for that matter. This night was no exception. Just as, for the sake of security, he divided his papers among his secretaries so that none had a complete understanding of everything that occurred in the Oval Office, he compartmentalised the parts of himself he showed to others so that no one saw his whole being. From the public he hid his paralysis, rarely allowing himself to be photographed in a wheelchair. Much of the country did not even know he was paralysed. From Churchill he hid his private conversations with Stalin. By refusing to ask Bruenn or McIntire about his medical condition, he even hid from himself. 'He doesn't know any man and no man knows him,' Anna had confessed to her friend Assistant Attorney General Norman Littell, in the summer of 1944. 'Even his family doesn't know anything about him.' Living in the White House that year had made this abundantly clear to Anna. The closer she tried to get to him, the more she came to understand just how much of himself he had been concealing for a very long time.

When Anna was seven, a twenty-two-year-old woman named Lucy Mercer came to work for Eleanor while the family was living in Washington during Franklin's tenure as assistant secretary of the navy. Lucy came from a family of impoverished gentility. Her once well-to-do parents had lost their money in the Panic of 1893, and now that Lucy was an adult, she needed to find work considered appropriate for a young single woman of good family. Eleanor hired Lucy as her social secretary.

Anna knew nothing of Lucy's background. She knew her only as the young woman who 'sat at a desk and wrote on cards'. As a little girl, Anna felt an inherent wariness toward women who came to work at the house, such as nurses and governesses. Much like Clementine Churchill, Eleanor felt insecure in her ability to be a mother and left most of her children's care to the nurses, including one who was 'addicted to the bottle' and had an affinity for punishment. The cruel woman had once locked James, the oldest of the Roosevelt boys, in a closet for what must have been hours. In response, Anna and James rebelled. They dropped paper bags full of water on the heads of passers-by from the third-floor window of their house in Washington and lit stink bombs in the dining room before guests arrived for their parents' dinner parties. But Lucy had no part in teaching, minding or disciplining Anna or her brothers. She never locked anyone in a closet, nor did she cruelly yank Anna's hair while combing it before her grandmother's friends came to tea. Instead, as Lucy sat at the desk and worked on her cards, she radiated qualities that the Roosevelt household lacked: warmth and friendliness. And she smiled.

Anna had one particular memory of Lucy. One day, Lucy had greeted Anna good morning, not as if addressing an impish, misbehaving child, but as one young woman greets another. Anna decided she admired Lucy Mercer.

Then, one day, Lucy was gone. No one said why, and Anna heard no more about her for several years.

As Anna later learned, she was not the only person who had found something to admire about Lucy Mercer. During the summer that Anna was eighteen, she went to stay with her mother's cousin Susie Parish in Newport, Rhode Island, for Tennis Week. It was one of the many social obligations Anna faced during her debutante season, and she dreaded every minute of it. Like Sarah Churchill, Anna wanted no part of being a debutante. She was awkward and shy. She had no interest in the clothes, the dances, or the chaperoned outings with suitable young men. She felt she was being '*forced*' to make her debut, and she was furious with her grandmother and her parents for insisting on it. Franklin and Eleanor were remarkably progressive in their social and political views, yet none of that progressivism applied to their expectations for their daughter. Her mother's inconsistency particularly surprised Anna. Eleanor constantly criticised the silly rules and the vapid people who made up this part of society, and yet she was shoving her daughter into the system she claimed to despise.

Anna's anxieties about being a debutante were quickly replaced by even more painful feelings. Cousin Susie was a dreadful gossip. One day, Susie began to tell Anna about 'this horrible thing' that had happened several years ago. While Franklin was assistant secretary of the navy, he had had 'an affair' with 'another woman'. The affair was 'very much gossiped about at the time', and people suspected that this woman might run off with Franklin, but 'thank goodness, nothing had happened.' 'Nothing' meant 'no divorce'. Anna, Susie claimed, even knew the woman. It was Lucy Mercer.

Suddenly, certain uncomfortable things that had confused Anna for some time began to make sense, such as why Franklin began spending less and less time with the family at Campobello while he was assistant secretary of the navy. Or why her parents, who had once had, if not a great romantic love, certainly genuine warmth between them, suddenly seemed cold with each other. Or why her mother had abruptly decided to build a cottage of her own in the woods more than a mile away from their family home. Anna did not know what to do. Anna could not divulge to anyone the terrible burden that Susie Parish had imposed upon her. Not even to confirm whether it was true.

Anna harboured this miserable secret for months until one day, when Anna and Eleanor were alone together at home, Eleanor broke down in front of her daughter. What Susie Parish had told Anna was true. As Eleanor explained, after Lucy left her employment in 1917, she joined the women's branch of the navy, where she soon found herself working in Franklin's office. Whether this was by coincidence or by design Eleanor did not say, but unbeknownst to her, Franklin and Lucy had been having an affair for almost a year. Eleanor did not find out until 1918, when she discovered a packet of love letters to Franklin from Lucy while unpacking his suitcase after he returned ill from a trip to Europe. Furious and mortified, Eleanor offered Franklin a divorce, but a divorce would have ruined his political career. Instead, he swore he would never see Lucy again.

As a teenager, Anna had been constantly irritated with her mother, first for sending her away to school in Manhattan and then for insisting upon her making a society debut. Now that hostility quickly evaporated. For the first time, Anna was truly '*mad – mad* at Father' for the hurt he had caused her mother. She believed that she had to choose a side. Though she and Eleanor had never been close, she felt a natural solidarity with her mother as a woman. A niggling worry also planted itself in the back of Anna's mind. If a woman like her mother had been betrayed, she feared that someday, the same 'could easily happen to *me*'.

Though Franklin had promised Eleanor he would cut Lucy out of his life, he failed to keep his promise. In 1920, Lucy married Winthrop Rutherfurd, a wealthy widower with six children, but Franklin and Lucy continued to exchange letters from time to time. Franklin even made discreet arrangements for her to attend his first presidential inauguration, in 1933. Later, after Winthrop Rutherfurd suffered a stroke, in 1941, Roosevelt used his influence to help Lucy's husband receive treatment at Walter Reed Army Medical Center in Washington, D.C. Three years later, in March 1944, Rutherfurd died, leaving Lucy widowed at the age of fifty-three.

One night, about three months after Rutherfurd's death, Franklin approached Anna with a question. It was early summer, just a few months after Anna had moved back into the White House. Eleanor was spending nearly four weeks in Hyde Park, leaving Anna to attend to First Lady duties while she was away. Would Anna mind, FDR asked, if he 'invited a very close friend for dinner'. It was an unusual query. As president, he could invite anyone he wished, regardless of who was acting as hostess. But Anna quickly guessed who this mysterious dinner guest must be. And why her father had asked if she would mind. It was not her permission he sought, but rather her blessing. His intended guest was Lucy.

For more than twenty years, the memory of Lucy had hung over the family like a shadow. Now Anna found herself forced to confront a painful, long-repressed memory. The scene of her mother's devastation over the affair came rushing back, as did the anger she had felt towards her father. He was now putting Anna into an entirely unfair position. In essence, by asking if she would conceal a visit from Lucy from her mother, he was asking her to protect one parent over the other. He could have invited Lucy on a night when Anna was out of the White House, but perhaps subconsciously he was looking for someone to share the burden of guilt he carried for breaching his wife's trust. And yet he was so desperately ill. It was 'a terrible decision to have to make in a hurry'.

Anna tried to look at the situation dispassionately, shutting out the personal and emotional as she had always done when trouble arose among those she loved. Anna knew that married life was far from perfect. It could be ugly and complicated. Her first marriage, to Curtis Dall, had proved that, not least of all when, during an argument, he had thrown a kitchen knife, which landed in the wall just above Anna's head. Her brothers already had three divorces between them, and she had begun an affair with John Boettiger before she was divorced from Curtis. And as much as she adored John and was desperate for their marriage to be a success, she knew that John struggled with inner demons, which she did not know how to expel. His anxiety and depression while deployed were one manifestation, but the signs had been noticeable much earlier. Instead of facing them, Anna went on as if nothing was wrong.

To criticise her father on the grounds of the sanctity of marriage would have been hypocritical. Furthermore, her parents were in their sixties. Certainly, she felt, they were at an age when no one, least of all their children, had any right to say, 'You shouldn't do this' or 'You shouldn't see this person.' She decided that the 'private lives of these people' were not her 'business', as if 'these people' bore no relation to her.

But no matter how analytically Anna looked at the situation, the matter *was* emotional and intensely personal. Her father was dying, and she was willing to do anything to give him peace and comfort to ward off the inevitable. Looking at FDR, Anna thought to herself, 'Here was a man who never moved without being surrounded by people.' A man who could barely move under his own power. He had given his adult life in service to his country and confronted the most dreadful decisions, day after day, at the helm of a nation at war: Whose lives would be spared? How many soldiers were expendable? What was the relative value of an enemy civilian's life compared to that of an Allied soldier? He never had a quiet moment free from these terrible decisions and the competing interests of those who surrounded him, each looking to advance a particular agenda. Franklin was crippled and Lucy was a widow. Meetings between them would consist of little more than reminiscence of past happiness and some hours of cheerful, relaxed conversation. If it could give FDR some measure of joy in a joyless world, could Anna deny him?

So she agreed to make the arrangements. The dinner was set for the night of July 8, after FDR finished three days of meetings with the French leader Charles de Gaulle at the White House. Anna would see that Lucy entered via the Southwest Gate near the Executive Office Building, not the front door. The president's trusted butler, Alonzo Fields, would serve dinner. The guest list, which was often made public, would be kept private. Eleanor would never need to know. Anna convinced herself she had no reason to feel guilty.

At 6.30 in the evening on July 8, 1944, a dark car discreetly pulled up to a four-storey townhouse on Q Street situated just across Rock Creek from Georgetown. A man was sitting inside. An elegant woman with light brown hair and blue eyes emerged from the house and climbed into the vehicle. The car then drove southeast through the streets of Washington, where it passed through a gate on 17th Street NW and traversed the long, sweeping drive around the White House South Lawn to the door beneath the South Portico.

Anna and her husband, John, were waiting in FDR's study when the door opened for the president in his wheelchair. Lucy Mercer Rutherfurd was at his side. It was the first time Anna had seen Lucy since she was eleven years old. Franklin had once written to Lucy about his daughter. 'Anna is a dear fine person,' he said. 'I wish so much that you knew her.' Now Franklin reintroduced Anna to the woman who had caused her mother so much pain.

If Anna had any apprehension about this encounter, it quickly melted away. Lucy was every bit as attractive, warm and bright as she remembered. She was 'friendly' yet 'stately', with an 'innate dignity and poise which commanded respect'. It was impossible not to like her. They soon went in to dinner, where conversation was 'lighthearted and gay' as the butler served the meal. Nothing about the occasion felt untoward.

In spite of everything that had transpired many years ago, Anna soon realised that she was 'grateful' to Lucy. To Franklin, she represented fond memories of happier days: summer days spent sailing on the Potomac River and a time before the Depression, the war,

and perhaps most important, before polio. She was 'quiet and unob-
trusive', listening attentively to Roosevelt's stories, demanding no attention for herself. Unlike nearly everyone in FDR's world, Lucy wanted
nothing from Franklin. She sought only to give. In that way, she was
much like Anna. What Lucy could give was a precious few hours free
from the relentless pressure of the presidency. For all of Eleanor's ad-
mirable qualities, Anna realised that her mother was sadly 'not capable of giving him this'.

Eleanor was not a restful person. It seemed she saw rest as an indul-
gence, even the thirty minutes before dinner, when Franklin hosted
his nightly 'Children's Hour', playing bartender and mixing martinis
(heavy on the vermouth) for his friends. Eleanor would come in for
a few minutes at the end to have just one cocktail, which she would
'wolf' down. Anna remembered one night in particular. Her mother
had come into the room, determined to discuss a matter of business.
What the issue was Anna could not recall – she had 'permanently
blocked' it from her mind. Eleanor had sat down across from her husband with a stack of papers and said, 'Now Franklin, I want to talk
to you about this.' Instinctively, Anna thought, 'Oh God, he's going to
blow.' As if on cue, FDR erupted. He picked up the whole pile of papers and threw them at Anna, snapping, 'Sis, you handle these tomorrow morning.' There were so many papers, Anna felt she 'almost went
through the floor'. With unparalleled self-control, Eleanor stood up,
paused half a beat, said, 'I'm sorry,' and went to speak with someone
else. Franklin picked up his drink and began to tell a story. No one
said anything more about the incident, but tension hovered over the
rest of the evening.

Throughout that summer and autumn, Franklin secretly continued
to see Lucy. Sometimes she came to the White House for meals, where
either Anna or Franklin's cousins Daisy and Polly, two unmarried
women in their fifties, were often present and could be trusted to be
discreet. Or he would discreetly pick her up at her sister's house on Q
Street, and they would go for a relaxing drive. He even took her for a day
trip to the presidential retreat at Camp David, which FDR nicknamed
'Shangri-La'. Though the Secret Service had a cover name – 'Mrs.
Johnson' – for Lucy, Anna did not see these meetings as 'clandestine'.

In fact, she came to welcome and appreciate them. Anna and her father never discussed his association with Lucy as a 'relationship', only as a 'friendship'. Safeguarding it brought Anna closer to her father, the person she loved above all others. As the vault for his secrets, Anna had made herself indispensable.

By the time Franklin and Anna left for Yalta, Lucy was a firmly established presence in their lives. On the first day of their sea voyage, Anna was sitting alone with her father on the deck of the USS *Quincy* as it sailed down the coast of Virginia. As they drifted, Roosevelt told Anna about the many types of birds that could be found along the shore. Suddenly he broke off from this discussion and casually said, 'Over there is where Lucy grew up,' as if it was the most natural thing in the world. On January 30, FDR's birthday, he received a special surprise when the ship's steward brought him his breakfast tray. It was a gift from Lucy and FDR's cousin Daisy. They had scoured the slim pickings in the shops in Washington, D.C., for a birthday present for him and had come away with a package full of knick-knacks: cloth napkins for Warm Springs, pocket-sized combs, a room thermometer, and a nifty cigarette lighter that worked in the wind. It was an odd assortment, but Franklin was delighted. He told Anna he had forgotten all about his birthday 'until this package arrived'.

From Eleanor, by contrast, Franklin received not a birthday greeting but a missive about the difficulties his former vice president, Henry Wallace, was facing in his Senate confirmation as FDR's nominee for secretary of commerce. It was the only message he had received from Eleanor since leaving Washington.

Once at Yalta, another day passed, and then another, and another, and no further messages came from Eleanor. 'I haven't had a line from her since I left, and [FDR] hasn't mentioned hearing from her,' Anna wrote to John on February 7. There was not a problem with the mail. Anna had received letters from John and from her older children from her first marriage, Ellie and Curtis, who were at boarding school in San Francisco and Lake Geneva, Wisconsin, respectively. There was even a message from her five-year-old son, Johnny, who was having a grand time playing spelling games and reading books about giants and witches with his pops. Could she please, Johnny relayed through his father, send him a letter 'with funny pictures in it'?

By the time Franklin and Anna departed for Stalin's dinner on February 8, with FDR in the throes of pulsus alternans, they had yet to receive a word from Eleanor. It was 'a very sad situation', Anna told John. 'The only times he has mentioned her to me on this trip have been times when he has griped about her attitudes towards things he's done and people he likes.' Franklin and Eleanor were more than five thousand miles apart, and still Anna found herself playing referee between them. She told John, 'Gosh, how lucky I am to have seen all this – but how THRILLED I'll be to put both my arms around your neck and have you squeeze me so tight I can't breathe.'

Perhaps thinking about her parents' complicated relationship spurred Anna to close her letter on a sentimental note. She was determined to will her own marriage into being a lasting success, despite the anxieties she had for John. 'This seperation [*sic*] stuff is the unmitigated bunk, my Honey', she wrote, filling her letter with an abundance of love, desperate to bolster him – and herself. Yet again, Anna was taking on the burden of propping up those she loved. 'I long, so utterly, to be US in all our days and nights, all our experiences and work and play. After all these years, I WANT YOU more than everything or anything in this world – and in the next one, if I can arrange it.'

FIFTEEN

February 8, 1945

As Kathleen and Averell drove to the Koreiz Villa for Stalin's dinner, Kathleen was feeling 'horribly embarrassed'. She had been invited to the banquet along with Anna and Sarah, but she had not realised, until just before dinner, that her invitation had come at the expense of others. With Kathy attending, one of the chiefs of staff, either General Marshall or Admiral King, would be left out. As little as Kathy cared for deference to social and political hierarchy, it simply was not right that she should be at the banquet when the heads of the army and navy were not. Kathy knew how much 'bad feeling and upset pride' was 'caused by people left out of social gatherings', even more so than 'official ones'. She had hurriedly found Anna and told her, 'For God's sake,' please 'change . . . the list and leave me off.' Averell tried to intervene as well, but Anna refused to make any modifications. FDR wanted dinner to be a 'family party'. In his allotted ten people, he had also included Ed Flynn, the powerful New York Democratic politician and one of his closest advisers. Flynn had no part in the official business and had nominally been included in Roosevelt's entourage to serve as a Catholic representative for post-conference discussions in Moscow about religion in the Soviet Union. It seemed, however, that he was at Yalta chiefly to serve as someone whose company FDR enjoyed. Thus far, he had spent his time hanging around the room he shared with Dr Bruenn, drinking tea poured from an enormous samovar, and sitting on the Livadia Palace terrace as he looked contemplatively at the sea. With both Flynn and Kathy in, Marshall and King were out.

Like Kathy, Averell was uncomfortable with the arrangements. Whatever Marshall's and King's personal feelings were on the matter, they did not say, but the situation would look very odd if the British and the Soviets brought their military chiefs, as they surely would. As their car wound along the dark coastal road, Averell turned to Kathy and said that since she was coming to the dinner, she would 'damned well have to make a speech in Russian'. Neither Anna nor Sarah would be able to make a proper Russian toast, so the 'price' of her 'meal ticket' would be a toast on behalf of the three daughters.

Kathy felt her 'stomach sink'. A toast 'in English would have been hard enough to do', she thought. Having to toast in Russian – in front of Stalin, Molotov, the Soviet ambassadors, and the chiefs of staff of the Red Army, no less – 'made it that much more scarey [sic]'. Nerve-racking as it was, as they pulled up at the Koreiz Villa, she had to concede it was 'a good idea'.

While Averell had ventured to the Koreiz Villa several times that week, this was Kathy's first visit to Stalin's residence. Like Livadia, the Koreiz Villa was designed by the architect Nikolai Krasnov. It was built from grey stone in an Italianate style, with rectangular wings; its sharp edges were softened by arched terraces and windows looking out onto a lush green park. This building was smaller and more intimate than Livadia Palace and was better suited to a weekend house party than an international summit.

Once inside, it was evident why the banquet had been restricted to thirty people. Kathy observed that the long rectangular table in the formal dining room was nearly as large as the room itself, leaving space for just two tropical plants in pots and a marble fireplace for ornamentation. The table was set with fourteen places on each long side and one on each end. As young women were not customary guests at Soviet political banquets, Kathy was curious about where the Little Three would be seated.

As the guests mingled, it became clear to Kathy that, sure enough, the other delegations had brought their military chiefs. The British were represented by a full complement of the top brass: chief of the Imperial General Staff, Field Marshal Sir Alan Brooke; marshal of the Royal Air Force, Sir Peter Portal; admiral of the fleet, Sir Andrew Cunningham; Churchill's chief military adviser, General Hastings 'Pug' Ismay; and Field Marshal Sir Harold Alexander. Meanwhile, Admiral Nikolai Kuznetsov, General Aleksi Antonov and Marshal Sergei Khudyakov of the Soviet navy, army and air force, respectively, were in attendance. The British and the Soviets were confused as to why Admiral Leahy was the sole member of the American military present, and then only in his capacity as FDR's personal chief of staff. If Kathy had had her choice, she would have substituted General Marshall for Admiral Leahy. Marshall had quickly become one of her favourite attendees of the conference, as he told the best war stories. Meanwhile, she had grown to distinctly dislike Leahy. Kathy had overheard Leahy expounding upon the French the day before. 'My God he hates the French,' she had written to Pamela. 'He has the makings of a prime "hands off for America in Europe" ' advocate, she noted, 'which in my mind isn't far removed from isolationism . . . I couldn't agree with him less.'

Averell left Kathy to find Peter Portal, who was leaving for London in two days and had promised to carry a letter home from Averell to Pamela. Though he was Averell's rival in this matter of the heart, Portal might have felt confident that Averell would remain in Moscow for some time and thus posed little competition – and delivering the letter would give Portal an immediate reason to see Pamela in London. The trouble was, Averell had not yet written it. He told Portal he would write something after dinner and have it ready by morning. As there was no chance of the dinner breaking up before midnight, Portal very much doubted this would happen.

Kathy looked around the room. In addition to Churchill, Stalin and Roosevelt, the military leaders, the three foreign secretaries, the three interpreters, and Sarah, Anna and Ed Flynn, the remaining guests included Jimmy Byrnes (now apparently calm and collected); the British ambassador to the Soviet Union, Archie Clark-Kerr; his Soviet counterpart, Fedor Gusev; and Andrei Gromyko, the Soviet ambassador to the United States. Molotov's deputies, Ivan Maisky and Andrey

Vyshinsky, were also present. Harry Hopkins had once again retreated to his bed and would not be at dinner.

Kathy either knew or could recognise all the guests save for one man, who was hovering at the edge of the room. He was the head of the NKVD, Lavrentiy Beria, thus far a faceless name to the westerners. Stalin had finally released him from the shadows.

Beria's presence was enough to make any Soviet citizen shudder and second-guess every phrase he had ever uttered or every acquaintance she had ever met, for fear that anything from the past would be misconstrued and interpreted as treasonous. Even Beria's most powerful colleagues in the Soviet Politburo felt this threat. Nikita Khrushchev, then serving as the first secretary of the Communist Party of Ukraine, noticed that whenever Beria appeared in Moscow, 'the life of Stalin and the group that had formed around him took on quite a different character'. Stalin himself once remarked to Khrushchev that Beria 'invariably introduces some kind of fear or competition over who will drink the most'. At a gathering like the banquet at Yalta, the destabilising effects of alcohol could work to Stalin's advantage.

Kathy was well acquainted with some of Beria's underlings. During her first winter in Moscow, she had written a letter to Clementine Churchill about adjusting to life in the Soviet Union. As she told Mrs Churchill, 'Occasionally on Sundays we all go out ski-ing ... "We," of course means the two of us plus Averell's four NKVD boys. One dons skis and tries unsuccessfully to keep up with Averell and the others stand at vantage points along the hill.' Kathy liked to refer to them as Ave's 'angels', as they always seemed to be flitting around him, though, as she told the prime minister's wife, 'I can't figure out whether they're there to protect Averell, or protect people from Averell. At any rate, they're extremely useful to hold things, and ... they never seem to forget matches!' Though flippant, as ever, in her comments, she knew the NKVD was not to be trifled with.

Kathy was intrigued by Beria's sudden appearance. Looking at him now for the first time, she observed that he was 'little and fat with thick lenses which give him a sinister look', and yet, something about his countenance simultaneously made him appear 'quite genial'. To Kathy, Beria's presence was unsettling but not intimidating – after all, she was in a protected position. He could not directly endanger her. Nonetheless, she knew that he was indeed 'the most feared man' she had ever encountered. Beria thrived on the dread he almost universally instilled in people, and this ready creation of fear allowed him, and by extension Stalin and the Soviet regime, to control individuals and subjugate a population. When it came to manipulating westerners, the tactics had to be subtler. The NKVD could not overtly threaten Churchill, Roosevelt or Harriman through arrests, denouncements, or trials and convictions based on little to no evidence, which was their standard treatment of political enemies within the Soviet Union. But there were other ways to pressure men of such stature.

Unbeknownst to Kathy, several weeks earlier, in January, Averell had had an odd encounter with one of Beria's deputies, Pavel Sudoplatov, whom he had met during a meeting at the Ministry of Foreign Affairs. Sudoplatov was introduced as Pavel Matveyev from the Council of Ministers, who was supposedly overseeing conference preparations. After this meeting, Sudoplatov invited Harriman to lunch at a Georgian restaurant in Moscow to continue their conversation about the arrangements for Yalta. During this meeting, Sudoplatov hoped to induce Harriman to discuss the American position on the more delicate matters of the conference, particularly Poland. The NKVD taped the conversation in order to analyse, for Stalin, Harriman's psychological profile, but Harriman's responses revealed little.

Frustrated, Sudoplatov turned to an age-old tactic to persuade his target to cooperate. With all politeness, the NKVD man suggested that Harriman 'look closer at the adventures of his daughter in Moscow, because her relationships with certain Russian young men could lead her to trouble'. But Harriman, who had already deduced that 'Matveyev' was an NKVD agent, ignored the implication that Kathy had been consorting with inappropriate beaus. Kathy had many Russian acquaintances whom she had met skiing or at the ballet, but her relationships with them were purely platonic. She liked to joke about these people in letters to her sister, referring to sweeter members of Soviet officialdom as a Russian boyfriend or the like, but it was pure jest. Approved social outings with young Russians were opportunities to improve her language skills. Sudoplatov insisted to Harriman that his warning about Kathy was 'very friendly'. By no means was it 'a threat of blackmail'. Harriman was 'highly respected' by Stalin, he insisted. His 'purpose' in mentioning the matter was to show that the Harrimans were 'beyond any provocations by us' and that they should feel comfortable discussing 'any delicate matters, both personal and diplomatic'. Unfazed, Harriman waved him off and queried whether there would be adequate amounts of vodka and caviar for the delegates at Yalta, continuing the charade that Sudoplatov was responsible for such arrangements. At the end of the meeting Sudoplatov gave Harriman a tea service as a gift from the government and skulked away, having fallen short of achieving his objectives.

Though Beria and the NKVD had failed to intimidate the Harrimans, there were always new targets to pursue and a variety of ways to trip them up. Beria now turned to an individual conveniently standing just a few feet away from him, making small talk with the delegates.

Like Kathy and Anna, Sarah had arrived with her father at the Koreiz Villa a few minutes before 9 p.m. As always, she was neatly turned out in her blue uniform, her tie straight, her buttons gleaming. In a slight violation of uniform regulations, she had pinned to her lapel the brooch Stalin's daughter, Svetlana, had sent her as a gift. No doubt this minor infraction would be forgiven as a friendly gesture towards the British-Soviet alliance.

Kathy may have felt self-conscious about attending this party, but Sarah had no such qualms. At her father's table, she had grown up at dinners where she was surrounded by the lofty, the rich and the powerful, including the fabled British diplomat, officer and Middle Eastern expert T. E. Lawrence and the silent film star Charlie Chaplin. Sarah had already been present at similar feasts at the Tehran Conference. If Stalin's banquet was to be half as impressive as those her father and FDR had hosted there, an invitation was not to be refused.

As she waited for dinner to be announced, Sarah stood chatting with the 'very friendly' Ivan Maisky, whom she had known during his tenure as Soviet ambassador to Britain during the early years of the war. Suddenly, their party of two became three when a man appeared at her elbow. He was about her height, wore a pince-nez, and had yellow teeth; while not physically intimidating, he immediately cast a pall over the conversation. Sarah quickly realised this was Beria, the head of the OGPU, the old acronym by which she knew the secret police before they were rechristened as the NKVD.

While the conference was in session that afternoon, Sarah, together with her father's naval aide, Commander Tommy Thompson, and a man the Soviets had supplied as guide and interpreter, had driven out to visit Anton Chekhov's home, just as Kathy Harriman had done while waiting for everyone to arrive at Yalta. When Sarah and Thompson reached the White Dacha, as this 'State-maintained Cultural Institution' was known, they found it looking rather the worse for wear; the garden wildly overgrown. Inside was Maria Chekhova, the famous writer's sister. As Kathy had discovered during her visit, the elderly woman seemed anxious and unsettled when speaking in the presence of the Russian interpreter and minder. Sarah knew that French had been the language of the Russian elite before the Revolution, and she herself spoke excellent French, having attended finishing school in Paris. So she tried to communicate directly with Chekhova in that language, which the interpreter fortunately did not understand. Still, when fear is deeply ingrained, habits adopted for self-preservation are not easily set aside. Even while speaking French, Chekhova remained nervous and refused to say anything of substance within earshot of the interpreter, just in case.

Maria Chekhova's reticence was a prime example of the fear that Beria, and the troops he commanded, instilled in the hearts of the Russian people – even the esteemed sister of one of Russia's most celebrated sons. Now Stalin's spymaster was standing at Sarah's elbow, waiting for her to say something. But what could she possibly say? They had absolutely nothing in common, nor was he the type who engaged in friendly chitchat. She searched her mind for something appropriately bland to fill the awkward void. Then she recalled that the British delegates had unearthed some Russian phrasebooks. Over the past few days, Peter Portal had been studying them intently at mealtimes, and Sarah had picked up several useful words. For lack of other ideas for conversation, she began with the practical. She summoned an actor's deportment, ignored her nerves, and, with Maisky's assistance, recited to Beria the first handful of Russian words that popped into her head.

The first few phrases – simple things like 'yes', 'no', 'please', 'thank you', 'come in', 'don't worry', and 'tea and coffee' – elicited no particular reaction from Beria. But when she got to the last phrase she realised that, when dealing with Beria, even the mundane could quickly lead to trouble. Sarah's last line was, 'Can I have a hot water bottle please?' (surely a useful question in either Britain or the Soviet Union in February).

Though she said it in jest, these benign words triggered something in Beria that instantly transformed him from rotund academic type into an aggressor who used sexualised banter to achieve his political ends. Sizing up Sarah, from her red hair, to her slim figure, to her legs toned from years of dance, he leered at her from behind his round spectacles and said, with Maisky translating, 'I cannot believe that you need one! Surely there is enough fire in you!!'

Before Sarah could formulate a response to the salacious statement, dinner was announced. Unlike many of the luckless women that Beria set his sights on, Sarah was rescued from further interaction. Bemused more than frightened by the bizarre encounter, Sarah tested her water-bottle line on 'twinkly-eyed' Andrey Vyshinsky as she settled into the chair beside him at the end of the table. Sarah apparently delivered the line with 'great conviction', for Vyshinsky did not understand it as a joke. He replied 'with all seriousness and not a little surprise, "Why? Are you ill?" ' Sarah had to resort to charades to make him understand that she was only kidding. Evidently, for the man who, unbeknownst to Sarah, was the state prosecutor behind Stalin's show trials of the Great Purge in the 1930s, which condemned fifty of Stalin's critics and rivals to death, British humour did not translate.

At the same time, another futile conversation was quietly taking place on the other side of the room. Jimmy Byrnes, with his knack for causing trouble just before a tripartite dinner was to begin, quietly approached the president. Byrnes boldly told Roosevelt he thought that the western Allies had made 'a serious mistake' that afternoon by supporting Stalin's request for two extra votes for Soviet republics in the new peace organisation.

Roosevelt was not in the mood to hear what Byrnes had to say, especially not at a social gathering. He brushed off the former Supreme Court justice, telling him that he 'raised no objection' to Stalin's request, as he 'did not want to endanger the entire proposal for a world security organization' after the Soviets had finally decided to support it. Byrnes was welcome to join him for lunch with Churchill the next day. They could discuss Byrnes's concern at that time, but he 'feared it was too late to make a change'. That was all Roosevelt had to say on the matter. Byrnes was dismissed to find his seat on the other side of the long table.

The guests settled into their places where a list of courses awaited. Once again, the menu was extensive, intended to impress the visitors with the best of regional cooking: red caviar, herring, a dried and salted fish dish called *balyk*, cold pork, assorted cheeses, duck bullion, salmon in champagne sauce, grey mullet, fried horse mackerel, kebabs of lamb, veal tenderloin fillets, pilaf with quail, willow grouse, two different chicken preparations, cauliflower in breadcrumbs, fruits, and coffee. There was even a nod to Stalin's Georgian heritage in the form of *churchkhela*, a candlelike rod of candy made from nuts, chocolate and raisins strung together, then dipped in thickened fruit juices and hung to dry. Stalin sat in the middle of the long table, flanked by Roosevelt on the right and Churchill on the left, the three foreign ministers directly across from them. Sarah was seated down the row from her father; Anna was in the same position on FDR's end. The Soviets had placed Kathy across from Sarah and between Chip Bohlen and the Red Army's General Antonov. Averell Harriman was two places farther down from Antonov, beside Field Marshal Sir Alan Brooke.

As soon as everyone took their seats, their glasses were filled with vodka and wine. Molotov, serving as toastmaster, signalled for the speeches to begin. Stalin stood and opened the proceedings with a toast in honour of the gentleman sitting to his left.

'I propose a toast for the leader of the British Empire, the most courageous of all Prime Ministers in the world . . . who when all Europe was ready to fall flat before Hitler said that Britain would stand and fight alone against Germany even without any allies ... To the health of the man who is born once in a hundred years.'

Though he never made eye contact for more than a fraction of a second, Stalin's words rang true. Sarah generally found the Soviet leader to be 'a frightening figure with ... bear eyes,' in which light reflected with an intensity akin to 'cold sunshine on dark waters'. But he also had a 'great sense of humor as daunting and swift' as her father's. That night he seemed to be 'in terrific form'. Sarah thought his tone 'friendly and gay', and she was touched by his seemingly genuine magnanimity.

Churchill then stood to respond to Stalin's generous beginning: 'It is no exaggeration or compliment of a florid kind when I say that we regard Marshal Stalin's life as most precious to the hopes and hearts of all of us.' (No doubt the bodyguard thinly disguised as a shabbily dressed waiter standing directly behind Stalin agreed.) 'There have been many conquerors in history, but few of them have been statesmen, and most of them threw away the fruits of victory in the troubles which followed their wars ... I walk through this world with greater courage and hope when I find myself in a relation of friendship and intimacy with this great man.'

When Churchill finished, the diplomats rose from their places and walked around the table to clink glasses with him to second the toast. It was intended as a sign of respect, but it was a nightmare for the poor waiters, who were attempting to distribute the first of many courses between toasts before the food got cold. Meanwhile, Ed Flynn, a recovering alcoholic, passed on the drinks and made himself useful by beginning a tally of the banquet's numerous toasts and courses.

Stalin then turned to his right and toasted President Roosevelt. As had been the case for Churchill, Stalin's decision to go to war was an easy one, he claimed. Britain and the Soviet Union had been 'fighting for their very existence'. But in Stalin's opinion, Roosevelt deserved special commendation. 'Even though his country was not directly imperiled,' Roosevelt 'had been the chief forger of the instruments which had led to the mobilization of the world against Hitler.' Lend-Lease,

Stalin declared, was 'one of the President's most remarkable and vital achievements . . . in keeping the Allies in the field against Hitler'.

The president then signalled that he wished to respond to Stalin, raising his glass from his chair. Twenty-nine pairs of eyes turned in his direction, his daughter's among them. There was a time several months earlier, after FDR's health scare in Bremerton, Washington, during the 1944 campaign against Thomas Dewey, who was twenty years his junior, when Anna had doubted whether her father could still deliver a speech with the force and enthusiasm he once had been able to muster. Sam Rosenman, Roosevelt's speechwriter, had reassured her that everything would be fine. And sure enough, it was. Tonight FDR would not be making a proper speech, but his performance was every bit as important.

'The atmosphere at this dinner', he began, was like 'that of a family'. That was just how he felt about 'the relations that existed between our three countries'.

Listening intently from across the table, Kathy thought that it was perhaps going 'a little bit far' to call the Soviets and the western delegations 'a happy family', but the president's sentiment seemed sincere.

Roosevelt continued, emphasising that the world had changed significantly during the past three years, and that 'even greater changes would soon come'. Each in their own way, the three Allied leaders were working 'for the interests of their people . . . Fifty years ago there were vast areas of the world where people had little opportunity and no hope, but much had been accomplished.' There remained 'great areas where people [have] little opportunity and little hope'. It was the object of the three men now sitting together 'to give every man, woman and child on this earth the possibility of security and wellbeing'.

Peter Portal, like Kathy, was less than convinced; he privately thought Roosevelt's words were all 'sentimental twaddle without a spark of real wit'. But as the president was speaking, no one had noticed anything seriously amiss. From her place down the table to the right of her father, Anna surely breathed a sigh of relief. It had not been the most eloquent speech of FDR's career, but he had made it through, even going so far as to reaffirm that he had every intention of being part of the future, no matter what the rumours might say about his health. He would lead the peace just as he led the war.

The banquet progressed, the waiters distributed course after course, the glasses were refilled repeatedly, and the toasting continued. Flynn added to his tally. Molotov toasted Britain's armed forces, much to Churchill's satisfaction. Stalin remained in jovial form and even took to teasing Fedor Gusev, the Soviet ambassador to Britain, calling him 'a gloomy man'. Kathy watched as Gusev then had to 'struggle to his feet' and make a half-hearted toast of his own.

Two people were enjoying themselves even less than Gusev. On the other side of General Antonov, Field Marshal Sir Alan Brooke was becoming 'more and more bored' and increasingly irritated with the food. By the time each course reached him, it was cold. Brooke had not been eager to attend the banquet in the first place, and his dining companions could not spur him into good humour. He later recorded in his diary, 'On my right I had General Antonof who speaks just a little French, but not enough to be able to keep up a flowing conversation with him. On my left I had [Averell] Harriman, whom I dislike and who annoys me intensely.' Nor was Admiral Leahy in the best form. He was being eaten alive by mosquitoes, and who knew what else, under the table. Doctors McIntire and Bruenn had not considered giving typhus shots to the Yalta-bound Americans until it was too late for them to be effective. Surely Leahy was cursing the doctors as the bugs chewed his ankles to bits, praying the insects carried no diseases.

At the opposite corner of the table, Anna had been relatively quiet. Beria, seated across the table, had fixed his attention on her. Anna thought him 'a most sinister appearing gent', with thick lips and bulging eyes, and he seemed intent on making sure her glass was always full. Before long, Anna realized the head of the NKVD was trying to get her 'tight!'

Toast after toast ensued, and Anna knocked back round after round, keeping up with the men as Beria kept her under a watchful eye. Nearby, Admiral Leahy was growing alarmed as Anna continued to drink. She was enjoying the admiral's obvious unease, as she knew his concern was entirely unnecessary. She had things well in hand.

Though neither Leahy nor Beria realised it, when no one was looking, she was refilling her glass with soda water, not vodka.

Roosevelt may have noticed Anna's drinking or Leahy's concern – something caught his eye at Anna's end of the table. Midway through the meal he realised that an unfamiliar face was situated among the members of his happy Allied family. Turning to Stalin, he asked, 'Who's that in the pince-nez opposite Ambassador Gromyko?'

'Ah, that one. That's our Himmler,' replied Stalin through his interpreter, with more than a hint of gleeful malevolence as he referenced the head of Hitler's SS. 'That's Beria.'

There was much truth in the comparison. One of Beria's contemporaries remarked that the two ruthless men even looked similar, with their identical rimless eyeglasses. Beria heard Stalin's remark but said nothing. He merely smiled his yellow-toothed smile.

The Soviet leader's casual likening of Beria to Himmler left Roosevelt momentarily but visibly disturbed. Surely he would have been all the more so, had he realised the Soviet Himmler had been observing his daughter intently.

Stalin's remark about Beria seemed to spark an idea in the mind of the British ambassador to the Soviet Union, Sir Archibald Clark-Kerr, who had an affinity for lewd humour. Clark-Kerr was seated near Beria, and throughout the meal the two men carried on a bizarre and vulgar discussion about the sex life of fish. Rather worse for wear after a multitude of toasts, the unsteady British ambassador now stood up and proposed a toast of his own.

Having spent much time with Clark-Kerr on the Moscow diplomatic circuit, Kathy Harriman could predict some approximation of what was about to come out of his mouth, for the British ambassador 'always seem[ed] to get an obscene touch to his toasts'. This would be no exception. Clark-Kerr offered a toast to Beria, saluting him as 'the man who looks after our "bodies" '.

Churchill stood up immediately. Even if he was not fully aware of Beria's past crimes, the prime minister knew enough to realise it was a thoroughly inappropriate crack. He strode around the other side of the table to the ambassador, and instead of clinking his glass against

Clark-Kerr's to second the motion, he shook his finger at him in front of everyone, while muttering, 'Be careful, be careful.' It was more than obvious to Kathy and to everyone else in the room that Churchill really meant 'Shut up!'

Before those assembled could descend any further into their cups, Churchill decided he had more to say. At times, his loquaciousness bordered on rambling, and he had a habit of leaving his interpreter trailing perilously behind. But no one could restore dignity to an occasion quite like the prime minister. To counter the effects of the vodka on the gathering, Churchill began to speak again, this time on a sombre note, in case anyone had forgotten the purpose of their gathering.

'I must say,' he began, 'that never in this war have I felt the responsibility weigh so heavily on me, even in the darkest hours, as now during this Conference ... We are on the crest of the hill and there is before us the prospect of open country. Do not let us underestimate the difficulties. Nations, comrades in arms, have in the past drifted apart within five or ten years of war. Thus toiling millions have followed a vicious circle, falling into the pit, and then by their sacrifices raising themselves up again. We now have a chance of avoiding the errors of previous generations and of making a sure peace ... To defend one's country is glorious, but there are greater conquests before us ... My hope is in the illustrious President of the United States and in Marshal Stalin, in whom we shall find the champions of peace, who after smiting the foe will lead us to carry on the task against poverty, confusion, chaos, and oppression ... Otherwise the oceans of bloodshed will have been useless and outrageous. I propose the toast,' he concluded with a flourish, 'to the broad sunlight of victorious peace.'

Kathy had been watching Stalin throughout the speeches. All night, he had sat with calm satisfaction, 'smil[ing] like a benign old man', something she 'never thought possible'. Stalin was the first to answer the prime minster's words. The guests were accustomed to Churchill's verbosity and had come to expect it, but Stalin's remarks too had been eloquent and charming that night. Even Churchill had never realised Stalin 'could be so expansive'.

As Stalin began his response, he told the room that he was addressing them as 'a garrulous old man'. 'That,' he said, 'is why I am talking so much. But I want to drink to our alliance, that it should not lose its character of intimacy, of its free expression of views. In the history of diplomacy I know of no such close alliance of three Great Powers as this, when allies had the opportunity of so frankly expressing their views. I know that some circles will regard this remark as naïve.'

Thus far, his sentiments had been as benevolent as his smile. Now Stalin continued, choosing his words carefully as Pavlov translated with expert precision: 'In an alliance the allies should not deceive each other. Perhaps that is naïve? Experienced diplomatists may say, "Why should I not deceive my ally?" But I as a naïve man think it best not to deceive my ally even if he is a fool. Possibly our alliance is so firm just because we do not deceive each other; or is it because it is not so easy to deceive each other? I propose a toast to the firmness of our Three-Power Alliance. May it be strong and stable; may we be as frank as possible.'

Stalin may have appeared benign, his smile may have been authentic, and his feelings may have been sincere, but he still embodied the very phrase Churchill had used to describe the Soviet Union during a BBC radio broadcast in 1939: 'A riddle wrapped in a mystery inside an enigma.' Depending on what his audience wanted to believe, depending on what they hoped to see in the soul of the man they had no choice but to trust with the future of peace in Europe and the world, his words could be either a message of hope or a word of warning. A genuine commitment to cooperation or a threat so eloquent and subtle as to make Beria and Sudoplatov's fumbling attempt to blackmail Harriman look like the work of fools. Roosevelt and Churchill desperately wanted to believe that Stalin was a man they could trust and that any Soviet duplicity or capriciousness was the fault of an unseen higher Soviet power, a politburo to which Stalin was beholden – but no one from the West could know this for certain. Any agreements made at this conference were ultimately a leap of faith, just as an alliance with Stalin had been from the very start. Jimmy Byrnes soon broke the enigma's spell with a toast to the 'common man all over the world', but Stalin had placed his challenge before his partners, laying it on the table for all to see, interpret as they saw fit, and respond as they chose.

Waiters continued to bring plates of Russian delicacies; the food, inevitably, had gone cold; glasses were emptied and refilled again and again. One by one, guests began to tap out. Some had taken to dumping their vodka in the potted ferns. By the time the suckling pig was distributed, Sarah and her neighbour Vyshinsky could do little more than poke politely at their plates. With a wink, they joined Anna in swapping their vodka for mineral water. No one appeared to notice, as Sarah and the other two women seemed temporarily forgotten. But by the third meat course Stalin was on his feet again to make a chivalrous pronouncement, bringing the guests to attention. As if to assuage any doubts that he was a civilised man of honour (the man who mistreated his own daughter, who kept her from his sight until her presence was useful to him, who refused to meet her husband), Stalin now raised his glass to the 'ladies' who graced his guests with their presence that evening.

Each of the three daughters had come to Yalta conscious of the history she was about to witness. No three women in recent history had acquired such a seat at the table alongside the most powerful leaders in the world at a major international summit. Now Stalin walked around the table and touched glasses with each of the three women in turn, recognising each of them and the place they had earned.

Either unaware that the proper response was to stand and propose a toast in return or too nervous to formulate one, Anna and Sarah remained rooted in their chairs, but Kathy realized the time had come to pay her debt for the invitation to dine. Averell had been relatively quiet throughout the meal, but it suited him perfectly to have Kathy speak for both of them. At the table, he was just one man among twenty-four others serving their principals. His Russian-speaking daughter, however, could help him subtly reassert some of the authority and independence he had steadily been losing over the past six months. Though she would be toasting on behalf of the women at the banquet, she was also toasting on behalf of the Harrimans – who were, if not equal in stature to the Roosevelts and the Churchills, on a higher plane than any of the other civilians in their company. Sure enough, Averell now leaned over and whispered to her, urging her to 'get up.'

During the brief moments throughout dinner when Chip Bohlen

was not translating or taking notes, Kathy had consulted him on her Russian grammar. On her other side, General Antonov had taken 'great interest' in what she intended to say and offered some suggestions. Between her own Russian-language skills and the help of her neighbors, she was confident she had found the right way to phrase her message. 'Jesus,' she thought. She was still terrified. But with Bohlen and Antonov to her right and left and Averell just two places away, she felt she had 'both sides working' for her, so she stood up to speak.

'Replying for the three ladies present,' Kathy said in Russian, she would like to propose 'a toast to those who ... worked so hard in the Crimea for our comfort.' Kathy had seen this work firsthand. Politics aside, the sacrifices the Soviets had made to secure even the most basic necessities at Yalta was astounding. 'Having seen the destruction wrought by the Germans here,' Kathy said, she 'fully realized what had been accomplished.'

Kathy was concise with her remarks. Her nerves could hardly allow her to go on at length. But her words were gracious, personal, and not overtly political, as was appropriate for her role at the conference. By referencing the Germans, she had reaffirmed the Allies' bond by citing the deeds of their common enemy. It was simple yet effective soft diplomacy.

Anna made no remark about the woman who was speaking on her behalf, but Sarah thought Kathy had 'surpassed herself'. She could see that the Soviets were obviously 'delighted' by the gesture.

Kathy Harriman was not an official diplomat, but at twenty-seven years old, she had gained more access to the Soviet inner circle than any other American woman. And now she had addressed the Soviet dictator and his closest associates – unquestionably some of the most fearsome men in history – in their own language, according to their own customs, at one of the most important gatherings of the war, as a peaceful future hung in the balance. Of the forty-five toasts Ed Flynn counted that evening, Chip Bohlen, in the Americans' official minutes, recorded the words of only eight. Six had been offered by Churchill, Stalin and FDR. The seventh was Jimmy Byrnes's toast to the common man. The last toast Bohlen included in the minutes was Kathy's.

★ ★ ★

By the time the last course had been cleared away – the twentieth course, by Flynn's count – it was nearly one in the morning. Stalin raised his glass one more time, proposing a word of thanks to the men who had 'worked while we were enjoying ourselves'. He offered a toast to Chip Bohlen, Arthur Birse and Vladimir Pavlov: the interpreters. The three men conferenced quickly and nominated the American interpreter to respond on their collective behalf.

Emboldened by several glasses of vodka, Bohlen stood up and made an audacious proclamation: 'Interpreters of the world, unite; you have nothing to lose but your bosses.' The room fell silent for a moment, stunned that Bohlen had dared to make a joke of the Communist Manifesto. Then Stalin burst out laughing, signalling that it was appropriate for everyone else to laugh, and came around the table and clinked glasses with the plucky young man, heartily praising Bohlen for his 'wit'.

To round out the joke, Churchill offered an alternate version: 'Interpreters of the world, unite! You have nothing to lose but your audience!'

On that festive note, the party broke up. Everyone soon returned to their respective villas and headed off to bed in a pleasant, murky haze of wine and vodka. Many issues remained unresolved – France's role in the administration of Germany, reparations, and of course, Poland – but the banquet had relaxed the gridlock of the past few days, giving the participants hope that the Allied family could resolve its differences in the end. Even Beria's disconcerting presence had not dampened the jovial atmosphere. Once in the privacy of the Roosevelts' own (bugged) quarters, FDR joked to Anna that the NKVD boss had reminded him of some '"big business men" ' he knew 'in the U.S.A.!' (Whether Sergo Beria found that remark about his father to be a compliment as he eavesdropped on FDR would remain a mystery.)

Ten miles down the road, at Vorontsov Palace, Sarah put her father to bed a happy man. That night, for perhaps the first time at the conference, he seemed to look with hope towards the future. From the Map Room next door, one of the Downing Street secretaries swore she could hear the prime minister singing 'The Glory Song'.

SIXTEEN

February 9–10, 1945

'How do you want to handle this, Robert?' the president asked.

Robert Hopkins, the twenty-three-year-old son of Harry Hopkins and the Americans' designated photographer at Yalta, framed the scene in front of him through the lens of his Speed Graphic camera, in which he had loaded some of his precious colour film.

'First, Mr. President, I'd like to have Mr. Stettinius stand behind you, with Mr. Molotov behind Marshal Stalin, and Mr. Eden behind Prime Minister Churchill. Then I would like the others who participated in the deliberations to move in so that they will be included in the photographic record of the conference.'

Hopkins was having trouble corralling the three nations' statesmen and senior military leaders as he attempted to arrange them in a variety of appropriate combinations for the conference's official photographs. Three large oriental rugs had been laid out in front of an ornate well in the centre of the Italian courtyard at Livadia Palace, where Churchill, Roosevelt and Stalin were sitting in a row of chairs, waiting for the others to pose behind them. Churchill was on the left, looking cherubic in his greatcoat and furry Russian hat. Roosevelt sat beside him in the middle, smoking a cigarette, with a naval cape over his shoulders; his lined face looked especially weary in the overcast afternoon light. Stalin sat on the president's other side with his hands folded in his lap, seeming rather isolated without his interpreter beside him.

Stettinius, Molotov and Eden did as Hopkins requested, but others milling about in the background seemed oblivious to the young photographer's instructions and made no effort to get out of the frame of the shot. From the second-floor balcony, American motion-picture cameras captured the chaos. The delegates were like a group of unruly schoolchildren having their class picture taken. No one listened to instructions carefully enough to go where they were told the first time. There was such a pile of people waiting to be photographed that they spilled off the eight paths that radiated like spokes from the central hub of the courtyard.

After much jostling, Hopkins and the Soviet photographers Samary Gurary and Boris Kosarev got their pictures of the Big Three with their foreign ministers, but not without the American interpreter Chip Bohlen, the British Cabinet minister Lord Leathers, Averell Harriman, and the British diplomat Alexander Cadogan also in the frame. The senior military figures then filed in behind their respective heads of government to take their turn in front of the camera. From his chair, Roosevelt made an effort to joke with the commanders, but Field Marshal Brooke was not in the mood. This photography session was turning out to be 'a most disorganized procedure with no one getting the people in their places for the various military and political groups', he griped. It was a waste of a perfectly good half hour.

Thus far, this sixth day of the conference had been a disorganised, out-of-sorts affair. With only two days left to decide crucial matters, particularly Poland's future, no one could afford miscommunication and delay. First, Roosevelt had been more than half an hour late to his first meeting of the day with Churchill and the British and American combined chiefs of staff. He looked dreadful. Peter Portal, knowing nothing about FDR's health, assumed it was the result of a hangover from Stalin's banquet the night before. Then, Roosevelt, Churchill, Harriman, Admiral Leahy and the three daughters sat down for lunch. Jimmy Byrnes promptly appeared to continue the futile discussion he had begun with Roosevelt the night before, about the peace organisation. All he was able to secure was a general agreement from Churchill that Britain would be willing to give the United States as many votes as the British Empire, should colonies like India be admitted as independent members.

It seemed that Averell Harriman was the only person who had emerged from Stalin's dinner as his normal, superbly efficient self. Peter Portal was surprised when the ambassador, arriving for the meeting with FDR at Livadia Palace, handed the air marshal a letter to carry to Pamela. Portal had assumed that, after returning home from the banquet at one o'clock in the morning, at most Harriman would have managed a few cursory lines, if anything at all. Instead, Harriman gave him a thick envelope filled with numerous pages. He must have stayed up all night to write it.

While most of the photographers were training their lenses on the men in the courtyard, Army Signal Corps film crews were dispatched across Livadia Palace, collecting B-reel footage for news segments from the conference, which would be shown in theatres in the United States. One of the crews caught Anna, Kathy and Sarah as they chatted while strolling along the veranda, which surrounded the courtyard. It was a chilly day, with the sun behind clouds. Anna had traded in her tweed for her fur. Kathy and Sarah shivered, their coats over their shoulders, their arms crossed. Another cameraman captured a close-up of Kathy and Anna for the American audience. Aware that her actions were being recorded, Anna leaned over to Kathy, as if to share a witty observation. Kathy smiled broadly, looking natural, relaxed and glamorous.

Kathy had every reason to smile. She had now dispatched her responsibilities for the conference, and she had represented her father – and herself – with aplomb. But Anna's smiles for the camera that afternoon were a façade. Inside, she was seething. She was irritated with everyone and everything, starting with press secretary Steve Early and this photo session. Anna had had a low opinion of Early even before Yalta, and the past week had only confirmed her feelings. 'Steve is a poor organizer,' Anna griped in a letter to John. 'He will tell other people to make arrangements for him and then forget to check, and his plans will then fall thru.' Early had initially scheduled the official photographs for the second day of the conference, but he had forgotten to inform the military leaders. So of course none of them showed up, thus wasting everyone's time.

Anna had reason to be irritated with Steve Early, but her fixation on the press secretary had less to do with his incompetence than the fact that by this sixth day of the conference, she was feeling desperate about being sidelined. 'I hear lots of tidbits, of course, but no particulars,' she told John. It was not just the plenary sessions to which Anna was denied entry. 'There are "side" meetings every day, in addition to the regular Conf. meetings – and damn it all, I have access to nothing but "droppings" in the way of information!' Churchill and Harriman generally kept their daughters informed, to the extent possible, of political developments at Yalta and beyond in their late-night father-daughter conversations. Roosevelt, by contrast, was far less forthcoming. Anna had to fight to keep abreast of events. She was trying desperately to pre-empt calamities that could put her father's health at risk, but his lack of communication made her efforts that much harder. She took out her exasperation on FDR's band of followers; they seemed to be constantly in her way, and she found them completely useless: 'Most of the people that OM brought in his immediate party just sit on their fannies and play gin rummy . . . Ross [McIntire] goes nuts because he has had nothing to do but . . . worry about some of the things I last wrote you about,' Anna wrote to John, referring to FDR's heart failure cryptically. Those actually with the president at the negotiating table were little better: 'The only practical guy here, on our side, who is smart, is Jimmy [Byrnes]. But, he is not 100% loyal to the Boss. Harry [Hopkins] is a complete d-fool about his health; doesn't think straight when he is not well; and so can't be counted on.'

Anna's irritability was not assuaged by the fact that she had just learned from John that their five-year-old son, Johnny, had been sick for days with the flu and a fever. John had not told her at first; he had not wanted to upset her. At least FDR had finally received a letter from Eleanor, so Anna was spared from worry about the state of her parents' marriage for the time being.

That afternoon, after all the photos had been taken, perhaps the only person with more reason to fret than Anna was the Soviet photographer, Samary Gurary. He had accidentally opened his camera before winding the roll of film, exposing it to the light. He dashed to the dark-room, where, for the ten minutes it took for the film to develop, he felt his life '[hanging] by a thread'. He was the only photographer from the Soviet press at the official photo session, and if he had ruined all of the photos he had taken for the Soviets' official record, he was finished. At the end of the longest ten minutes of his life, he felt the noose loosen. The developed images showed Stalin, Roosevelt and Churchill looking back at him. The ruined film began two frames later.

The photo session wrapped a little before 4 p.m. Sarah departed with Peter Portal for their long-planned Jeep ride to the Uchan-Su water-fall, leaving the two American women to their letters and their walks while the leaders and delegates sequestered themselves in the ball-room once more.

Churchill was feeling the pressure of time. The triumphant atmo-sphere of the previous evening had dissipated. From the outset of the conference, Roosevelt had believed it would take no more than five or six days to reach an agreement on the various matters in front of them. Six days had already passed, and FDR still had no intention of staying later than Sunday, which was two days away.

Throughout the week at Yalta, the British and the Americans had been insisting that the Polish Provisional Government could not be a modified version of the Lublin government. Rather, it must be a new government and explicitly described as such in the official communi-qué expressing their agreements. The western Allies wanted it to be perfectly clear that they would not accept the Lublin government. But the Soviets were proving intractable, continuing to argue that the So-viet-friendly Lublin government was what the Polish people wanted. Stalin and Molotov were also fighting vociferously against Roosevelt and Churchill's demand that the British and American ambassadors and press be allowed to observe the election process in Poland, to guarantee that it was truly free and unfettered.

After Stettinius addressed the group with his report of the for-eign ministers' progress on the Polish issue that morning, of which there had been little, Churchill called for a pause. They needed more time to resolve this complex situation, which would affect the lives of more than twenty-five million people. When Roosevelt suggested the three delegations take half an hour to discuss their positions separately before reconvening, Churchill stopped him. 'I mean more than that,' he urged, underscoring that it would be 'better to take a few days of latitude than to bring the ship into port'. 'Of course you could all go away and leave me in the delightful spot,' he said. Then, shifting from sea to land in his metaphors, he continued. 'We should not put our feet in the stirrups and ride off.' He was adamant on this issue, not just because it was a matter of pride for Britain, which had gone to war over Polish sovereignty. Poland was a litmus test for the rest of Eastern Europe. If the British and the Americans failed to check the Soviets' efforts to seize control of the Polish government and undermine Polish self-determination, the Soviets were sure to do the same in every country in Eastern Europe where the Red Army had boots on the ground. The Soviets were not liberators. They were merely replacing the Nazis as the occupying power. Dropping all forms of metaphor, Churchill made his feelings perfectly clear: 'These are among the most important days that any of us shall live.'

Roosevelt, however, still refused to allow his relationship with the Soviets to turn antagonistic. Instead, he once again attempted to diffuse the tension Churchill's rhetoric had heightened. 'I find that it is now largely a question of etymology – of finding the right words,' he said. 'We are nearer than we have ever been before ... I want this election in Poland to be the first one beyond question.' Turning to humour, he quipped that the Polish elections should be as free of suspicion as 'Caesar's wife. I did not know her,' he joked, 'but they said she was pure.'

'They said that about her,' Stalin retorted darkly, 'but in fact she had her sins.'

When the ballroom doors opened again four hours later, the conferees had little to show for their efforts. There was still no agreement on Poland. Churchill had not persuaded his American colleagues of the need to stay longer to properly work things out. They were almost out of time. After a break for dinner, the three foreign ministers, plus Harriman, Alexander Cadogan from the British Foreign Office, Molotov's deputy Andrey Vyshinsky, the Soviet ambassadors Fedor Gusev and Andrei Gromyko, and their interpreters reconvened for a late-night session to see if they might make some headway before the sun rose, but a few extra hours were hardly the few extra days at Yalta that Churchill had failed to secure. Late that night Anthony Eden wrote in his diary, 'Found the Russians unprepared to even consider our draft, so I fairly let them have it, told them something of British opinion, said I would far rather go back without a text than be party to the sort of thing they wanted.' Roosevelt had hoped that this conference would represent the marriage between the Allies from East and West, but instead, they were in danger of devolving into Montagues and Capulets. As for the differences between the Soviets and the western Allies being simply a matter of words, Eden felt FDR was 'deluding himself'. They could change a few words and reach some semblance of a face-saving agreement with the Soviets, but, like Averell Harriman, the foreign secretary knew that as far as Poland was concerned, the Soviets' 'intention remained untouched'.

It had been four days since Sarah had spent the entire afternoon with Kathleen and Anna while their fathers were in session. The creeping divide between the British and the Americans perhaps subconsciously spurred Sarah to retreat into her own tribe rather than seek out the company of her fellow women. But the military chiefs had departed on this Saturday morning, February 10, Portal among them (Averell Harriman's letter to Pamela safely in hand), so Sarah was left without her friend. She was also left without her father. Winston liked to have Sarah drive with him to the meetings at Livadia, but this afternoon, he had departed from Vorontsov Palace in a huff, with Anthony Eden and his interpreter, Major Birse, in tow. He was supposed to be going to Livadia for a pre-session meeting with Roosevelt, but instead he sped off to the Koreiz Villa to have it out with Stalin over Poland. The three powers could reach no conclusions if the Soviets kept moving the finish line with their constant amendments to and new proposals for the language regarding the interim Polish government and eventual elections. Of particular concern were the Soviets' attempts to cut the clause in the document allowing the Allied ambassadors to supervise the elections. Otherwise, how could Churchill and Roosevelt possibly have any accurate information as to whether the elections were truly legitimate? For the sake of expediency, the Americans had indicated they were willing to cut a deal and drop the language, so long as it was understood in principle that the ambassadors would be allowed to be observers. But to Churchill, this was unacceptable. So off he went to confront Stalin on this 'highly unpleasant matter', forgetting all about his meeting with FDR.

So, while Winston continued to wage the battle of Poland, Sarah sought out Anna and Kathy. The three daughters were not going to leave Yalta the closest of friends, but Sarah did enjoy their company well enough to spend one last afternoon with them, especially as they had a final expedition to make before they bid the Crimea farewell. Over the course of the trip, the women had explored Sevastopol and the gardens surrounding their villas, and had made independent excursions to see the nearby waterfall and Chekhov's home, but they had yet to see the town of Yalta or meet the people who lived there. Kathy and Anna had attempted to walk to Yalta earlier in the week, but the Soviet guards surrounding Livadia Palace had stopped them. Today they had finally received permission to venture out into the village that lay just beyond Livadia, on the condition that a Red Army soldier accompany them. On leaving Yalta, Portal had jokingly compared such treatment to 'protective custody'. He was not at all sorry to leave the official escorts behind.

Sarah met Anna and Kathy at the American headquarters. Anna was back in her sensible tweed, with her purse over her arm, the hat she had worn on the *Quincy* on her head, gloves in hand, looking ready to forge on ahead, much like her mother. Kathy had pinned a small hat to her wavy brown hair and was wearing her fur. If not for Sarah being in uniform, they might as well have been three friends meeting for lunch at a fashionable restaurant in London or New York. As they were leaving, they stopped to say hello to Robert Hopkins and one of the Army Signal Corps cameramen filming extra footage. He had his film rolling and captured them just as they were about to head out the door. Anna was in the middle, with Kathy beside her on the left, and Sarah standing slightly apart to the right. Thinking the cameraman had what he wanted, Sarah started to walk away. As she turned, Robert pulled out his camera. He had photographed their fathers and their military and civilian advisers in various combinations the day before, but he had not yet taken the women's picture. Anna put her hand out to Sarah and pulled her back into the group. Robert pointed his camera at the three daughters and snapped.

Like Sarah, Anna and Kathy, Robert was also keen to see and photograph Yalta, so he decided to join them for their afternoon expedition. They set off for a walk into town, the armed Soviet soldier shadowing them twenty paces behind. As they made their way down the gradually sloping road, it was easy to see flashes of the Yalta that had once been a delightful coastal retreat. With elegant seafront promenades, lush vineyards in the nearby hills, and subtropical breezes in the summer months, Robert could see why it had been so popular among Romanovs and comrades alike. But now, like Sevastopol, it was a decrepit shell, a hollow reminder of its best days. Yalta was not damaged quite as extensively as Sevastopol, where but a handful of houses were left standing and a heartrending number of Orthodox crosses had been stuck into shell holes to mark graves of civilian victims. Still, Yalta's battering had been significant. Along the road, the visitors passed many ruined homes. Anna noticed that entire families had crowded into single rooms to survive; large chunks of walls and roofs were missing, where the damp and chill could seep in. Although it rarely snowed in Yalta, temperatures regularly reached freezing point and below.

Farther down the road, a large billboard was nailed to the side of a wooden hut. Robert took a picture of Anna and Kathy as they stopped to examine it, only to realise it was entirely hand-painted. In the United States, Coca-Cola and Kellogg had been mass-producing highway billboards promoting their sodas and cereals for nearly half a century, but it seemed that none of the local printers had the machinery to produce large-scale posters. The left side of the billboard was an anti-Spanish fascist propaganda cartoon. The Soviets despised Spain's Generalissimo Francisco Franco and his Falange party, which had sent nearly fifty thousand infantry volunteers to fight against the Soviet Union. The cartoon depicted a caricature of Franco standing atop a tower of Mussolini, Hitler and Japan's Emperor Hirohito. The enemy leaders were raising Franco up to the window marked 'Peace Conference', in hopes that he might squeeze in.

Anti-fascist propaganda was hardly surprising in this part of the world, but the right side of the billboard was more troubling. The cartoon showed three bourgeois Polish landowners. Two were fat and moustachioed, while the third was dressed in a western-style suit and tie. This man was likely meant to represent the Polish president-in-exile, Władysław Raczkiewicz, drawn in profile with a large, beaked nose, as if to suggest Jewish heritage. Beside him, the two fat members of the bourgeoisie react to the Soviet-supported Lublin government's land reform policies, meant to redistribute the private lands of the wealthy in the form of *kolkhoz*, or communal farms. 'Gentlemen, we are losing ground from under our feet!' one of the landowners exclaimed with alarm. But this was exactly what the Soviets wanted. Instead of the reviled bourgeoisie, the Polish peasant class – the supposed true voice of the Polish people – would control the land in harmony with their peasant brothers to the east, in the Soviet Union. For the past week, the fathers of these three women had been fighting to restrict the influence of this Soviet-supported Polish government, albeit to little avail.

Sarah found this immersion in local Russian culture both fascinating and discomfiting. Here was a country with a thirty-five-million-man army, a country that could mobilise the manpower and materiel for a massive drive towards Germany on the Eastern Front, and could within days turn a ravaged villa back into an emperor's palace to suit the whims of one man. And yet whole families who had once lived surrounded by Mediterranean splendour were reduced to subsistence living in shanties. 'I wouldn't dream of forming an opinion on these few days under these exceptional circumstances,' Sarah later wrote to her mother, 'but inevitably a strong impression is being formed – and not all of it, by a long way – makes sense.'

Sarah's feeling of disorientation was reinforced when her party came upon a crowd of children playing alongside the road. One of them could not have been older than four. The children were warmly dressed and looked healthy, and they eyed the four visitors with solemn curiosity. Anna had a bar of Hershey's chocolate with her. Taking an interest in the little four-year-old boy so close in age to her own Johnny, she took it out and offered it to him. Suddenly, the Red Army soldier following them appeared before the boy, gun and bayonet prominently displayed. He snatched the chocolate out of the boy's hand and forced it back at Anna. He barked at the children to clear out, then turned to Anna and snapped at her. Kathy translated his words, but his meaning had been perfectly clear: 'There is no need to feed our children.' Kathy knew well from her own early attempts to feed children in Moscow that they would never take food from a westerner while a soldier was watching. The Soviets were proud. They could look after their own children without outsiders' condescending pity. The children ran away and disappeared.

The group made a brief stop at the local newspaper office, where Anna picked up a few propaganda sheets to add to her collection of conference memorabilia. One, referencing Aesop's fables, depicted a Red Army soldier shooting a German frog, which had tried to puff itself up to the size of an ox; another offered a caricature of Adolf Hitler being crushed in a vice turned by Soviet, British and American hands; a third showed a grotesque German beast being run through by three Allied bayonets. FDR had told her that such souvenirs would be valuable someday.

The foursome decided they should soon be getting back. It was an hour's walk to Livadia Palace, and the sun was beginning to set. But just as they were about to leave, Sarah and her three companions found themselves standing in front of a small Orthodox church. There was a service beginning inside. For a moment, they hesitated while deliberating whether to go in. Timidly, they decided to take a peek. As they looked inside the church, they were met with a surprise. Robert said he had thought 'religion was stifled in the Soviet Union'. But this church was brimming with people.

Soviet society had an uncomfortable relationship with religion. The Russian Orthodox Church was considered a symbol of the tsarist era that needed to be eradicated, and the Soviet Union was officially atheist. For the Soviets, belief in the state supplanted belief in God, but during the war, they were forced to cede their war against religion to the larger needs of the war against the Nazis. Religion could rally the people and provide them with comfort in a way the government could not. Priests were allowed to return from prison and labour camps to preach to their congregations across the Soviet Union. As soon as they opened the churches' doors, the population that had been forced to renounce religion rushed in. Kathy had written to her sister about going to the Old Believers Church in Moscow for Easter Vigil. It was so crammed with people, she could not lift her hands from her sides. The whole congregation was swaying, and several times people fell down or passed out; there was a risk they might be trampled. Kathy could focus her attention on the service only half the time. The other half she struggled just to stay upright and out of the way of her neighbours' candles, terrified her clothes might catch fire.

Looking around in this little Crimean church, Sarah observed that the sanctuary was 'lit only by myriads of little candles which hardly pierced the gloom'. People's faces, as if painted by a Tenebrist, were illuminated in otherwise complete darkness. Compared to the streets outside, though, the church felt comforting and warm. Incense was burning, and a choir was singing. Sarah could not see the singers from where she stood, but the room echoed with the robust resonance of men's voices raised in song. There were no instruments to accompany their singing, no pews, chairs or benches. The entire congregation was made up of the very old and the very young – grandparents left to look after children while parents were gone, fighting in the war. Robert later noted that when it was time to pray, the congregation simply 'prostrated themselves on the smooth stone floor'.

Nobody knew if Stalin would allow religion to thrive after the war, or if the Russian Orthodox Church was simply living on borrowed time. In a sense, this little church faced a similar uncertainty about the future as the three young women standing in the doorway watching the service. Everyone, from Sarah, Anna and Kathy, to the children in the church waiting for their parents to come home, looked forward to the end of the war and the peace agreements that the conference at Yalta was meant to foster. After nearly five years of sacrifice, loss and heartbreak for soldiers and civilians alike, the world yearned for a return to normality. But was the pre-war state of normality a world to which they wanted to – or could – return?

Every day the three delegations stayed at Yalta without an agreement was a day that ended in frustration for their fathers, but for the three daughters, it was a chance to delay the inevitable and remain at their fathers' sides. In the Crimea, time stood still. It was a place trapped in a centuries-long cycle of peace and war, where progress seemed elusive. As they stood in the church that afternoon, the three daughters might have stepped back into any of the past three centuries. 'These trips are timeless for me,' Sarah later wrote to her mother. 'Wow.' The tableau before them was simultaneously tragic and hopeful. 'I wish I could describe how lovely it was,' Sarah wrote, 'how much it all suddenly meant. Here was the church being imaginative and helping. Outside everything was cold and grey and broken down. Here was warmth and time-tested security. Here was a palace everyone could go to and sing of their joy or sorrow . . . I knew that if I lived in this grey country, this is where I should go to, to escape.'

When the three daughters and Robert Hopkins returned to Livadia Palace, they were met with a surprise. The ballroom doors opened to reveal not frustration written on long faces, but rather a sense of real hope in the future – and relief. While the daughters had been at the church, it seemed that their fathers had experienced a divine intervention of their own.

All three delegations had arrived at Yalta a week earlier intending to secure resolutions on the future, and despite the discord of the past three days, this remained their objective. The deadlock simply could not continue, for reasons both practical and symbolic. Perhaps the festive banquet the previous evening had reaffirmed faith in their alliance, or perhaps the delegates were simply spent. Whatever the reason, that afternoon, it seemed that the three groups had finally remembered why they had come together at Yalta. At long last, they had reached an agreement. Each of the three leaders could walk away with something he considered a victory in Europe.

The afternoon's plenary session was a testament to diplomatic compromise. Much to Churchill's gratification, FDR dropped his opposition to French participation in the Control Commission for postwar Germany as a counterbalance to the East. Stalin could take comfort in the fact that discussions about reparations would continue in Moscow, with $20 billion as the basis for initial discussion. Half would go to the Soviet Union. Stalin could thank Harry Hopkins for that concession. During the debate Hopkins had passed FDR a note, saying, 'The Russians have given in so much at this conference that I don't think we should let them down. Let the British disagree if they want to – and continue their disagreement at Moscow.' (Churchill most certainly did disagree and made it clear on the record that he still objected to naming any figure. But, outnumbered, he could do no more than object.) And FDR had finally brought his two partners together on language they could all accept on the future of Poland. The Curzon Line would serve as the new eastern boundary, with some digressions of five to eight kilometres in Poland's favour. The new Polish government would decide on the western boundary for itself after Germany surrendered.

Most important, after six plenary sessions and numerous meetings of the foreign ministers, the three powers had agreed on the language that would bring that new Polish government into existence. With time running short, that afternoon the three delegations had finally settled on this phrasing: 'The Provisional Government which is now functioning in Poland should therefore be reorganized on a broader democratic basis with the inclusion of democratic leaders from Poland itself and from Poles abroad.' Over Soviet objections, the British and the Americans managed to retain the language about Harriman, Clark-Kerr and Molotov serving as a commission to oversee the formation of the provisional government and the forthcoming 'free and unfettered elections', which were to be held 'as soon as possible' and were open to 'all democratic and anti-Nazi parties'. Once a 'reorganized' provisional government had been formed, Britain and the United States would recognise this new body as the legitimate government in Poland and exchange ambassadors with it, thus ending their recognition of the exiled Polish government in London. On the whole, it was weaker language than Roosevelt, and especially Churchill, had hoped for; its strength was rooted in the promise of future free elections, not in a broadly representative interim government. It relied heavily on Stalin's willingness to fulfil his end of the agreement not to interfere in the Polish elections. But the language was a signal that the Soviets were willing to participate in the international post-war system.

However, amid the buoyant feelings brought about by successful compromise, the western statesmen might have been wise to keep the words of a forbearer in mind, especially in light of their daughters' visit to the Orthodox church that afternoon. As the French aristocrat and traveller the Marquis de Custine observed after visiting a Catholic church in Saint Petersburg in 1839, 'In Russia toleration has no guarantee, either in public opinion, or in the constitution of the state: like every thing else it is a favour conceded by one man; and that man may withdraw tomorrow what he has granted today.'

SEVENTEEN

February 10–11, 1945

Roosevelt's mind was made up. He was leaving that afternoon, just as soon as the final conference communiqué was signed. When he first agreed to come to Yalta, he had intended for the conference to last no longer than five to six days. It had already been eight, and he had pressing business elsewhere. FDR would fly from Saki to Deversoir, Egypt, and then drive to the USS *Quincy*, which was waiting for him at Egypt's Great Bitter Lake. There, he was to meet King Farouk of Egypt, Emperor Haile Selassie of Ethiopia and Ibn Saud of petroleum-rich Saudi Arabia, with whom he hoped to foster deeper ties.

Roosevelt had announced somewhat abruptly the day before, as the plenary session was breaking up, that he would be leaving the next day, Sunday, February 11, at three. During the private dinner Churchill was hosting for the three leaders, the foreign ministers and their interpreters at Vorontsov Palace following the breakthrough plenary session, the president said to his colleagues that he felt it important to finalise the communiqué publicly, summarising Yalta's scope. 'If we meet at eleven tomorrow,' he proposed, 'we can finish it by lunch.' This was a hefty task, as the report would publicise the matters discussed and agreements reached at the Yalta Conference, including everything from general language about the defeat of Germany and proposals regarding reparations, to an announcement of the first Conference of United Nations – Roosevelt's peace organisation – in San Francisco on April 25, to the controversial decisions about Poland's fate. It would also include the 'Declaration on Liberated Europe', reaffirming their commitment to the principles of the Atlantic Charter: that the people and nations around the world would be self-determinate. The document would not, however, publicise Roosevelt and Stalin's agreement on the Soviet entry into the Pacific war; that remained a closely guarded secret.

For once, Churchill and Stalin found themselves presenting a united front against Roosevelt. The nuances of the communiqué's language were much too important to be jotted off in haste, they insisted. It would place all of their agreements before the eyes of the world to scrutinise. Even though they had agreed on the issues in general terms, the precise wording of certain sections would require detailed attention, not to mention the additional time required for translation. Setting an artificial deadline of 3 p.m. the next day seemed very unwise, especially in light of this dinner at Vorontsov, Stalin insisted. He proposed they discontinue the dinner and resume their work instead. The tripartite drafting committee was already scrambling and would have little choice but to work through the night.

As a compromise, the three men might have converted the feast at Vorontsov Palace into a working dinner, as the small group present – the leaders, their foreign ministers and interpreters – all had clearance to hear matters of the utmost secrecy. For the final evening of the Yalta Conference, the three daughters were having a dinner of their own in another room at Vorontsov. But Roosevelt's mind was already three thousand miles away. As they sat down to dine on sturgeon in aspic, whitefish and wild goat, FDR soliloquised, with heavy-handed optimism, on the theme of overcoming differences by getting to know one's adversary. When he was a younger man, he told Churchill and Stalin, 'there had been an organization in the United States called the Ku Klux Klan that had hated the Catholics and the Jews.' For some reason, he decided to overlook the group that was the primary object of the group's hatred: African Americans. During a visit to 'a small town in the South', he had attended an event as 'the guest of the president of the local Chamber of Commerce'. At the event, he found himself seated next to 'an Italian on one side and a Jew on the other'. He 'asked the president of the Chamber of Commerce whether they were members of the Ku Klux Klan, to which the president had replied that they were, but that they were considered all right since everyone in the community knew them'. This, Roosevelt remarked with satisfaction, was 'a good illustration of how difficult it was to have any prejudices – racial, religious or otherwise – if you really knew people'. Churchill said nothing in response to this inapposite and insensitive story, nor did any of the foreign ministers. Stalin may not have understood enough about the Klan to fully appreciate the wilful naiveté of Roosevelt's remarks. He merely replied, 'this was very true,' before turning to Churchill to discuss British politics and the impending general election.

Later in the meal, after everyone had moved on to British staples, such as roast turkey, quail, partridge and green peas (the first vegetable of the feast), Stalin asked Roosevelt if he 'intended to make any concessions to Ibn Saud', subtly attempting to assess whether the Americans were trying to make a postwar oil-related agreement with the Saudis. Roosevelt replied with a smile, saying he had only 'one concession' in mind, and that was 'to give [Ibn Saud] the six million Jews in the United States', before trying to draw Stalin into a conversation about Zionism. This callous remark, doused in the casual anti-Semitism of the elite, was the only time over the course of the conference that the Jewish people, millions of whom had been murdered during the Nazi genocide that FDR and the other leaders were by then fully aware of, had been mentioned.

Stalin steered Roosevelt back to conversation about the conference and pressed him once again to stay longer at Yalta. Finally, Roosevelt relented, but only in part. He was willing to remain a few hours past 3 p.m. the next day, but only if it proved absolutely necessary.

Meanwhile, in one of the many smaller rooms at Vorontsov, the three daughters were having a conversation of their own. During their walk that afternoon, they had been friends exploring a community.

Once they returned to the conference grounds, they reverted to their roles as their fathers' aides. Well aware that their fathers had reached compromises with the Soviets that afternoon, they naturally focused on the end of the conference; their dinner conversation moved in parallel with their fathers'.

Echoing the words FDR had used earlier that evening, Anna informed her dining companions that they would be off the next day. 'The President,' she said, has 'appointments which he must keep.'

Sarah was incensed. Ever since Roosevelt had cabled to say he thought the conference would take no more than five or six days, Winston had been afraid that his American counterpart lacked appreciation for the gravity of the matters before them and would try to rush off at the earliest moment – to hold meetings in a region that had long been in the British sphere of influence, no less. Now it appeared his fears were entirely justified.

'As if,' Sarah shot back, 'the Conference isn't so much more important than anything else.' Her words were edged with a sharpness that her father could not afford to employ.

As the final conference session convened on February 11, a cautious optimism was in the air. No single party would return home with every goal achieved, but many delegates were willing to believe that the compromises reached over the week at Yalta were a harbinger of revitalised desire for cooperation among the three Allies. Some, like Harry Hopkins, had even higher hopes. Hopkins, who had initially sparred with Anna about her father's lack of attention to the need for Anglo-American coordination – and who had lost eighteen pounds over the course of their time at Yalta – had shed his early scepticism and now thought the conference would mark the dawn of a new era of diplomacy. From his sickbed, Hopkins declared that the Russians had 'shown that they will listen to reason' and that the president was sure he could 'live at peace' with his allies to the east. No doubt he thought his sacrifice of health was worth it. Even the usually reserved General George Marshall told Ed Stettinius that, despite the excess of alcohol and lack of indoor plumbing, 'For what we have gained here . . . I would gladly have stayed a whole month.'

Sarah drove from Vorontsov to Livadia with her father a little before noon. Anna had just returned from a Jeep ride with FDR around the Livadia Palace grounds. Neither made any further mention of words exchanged during dinner the night before. For the eighth and final time, the men filed into the ballroom, the double doors closing firmly behind them, once again leaving their daughters on the other side.

This last gathering was to be brief, no more than an hour. It would be followed by lunch in the tsar's billiard room, which was serving as FDR's private dining room. The remaining business of the three powers concerned not one but two documents that the drafting committees had raced to assemble in the sixteen hours since the end of their previous meeting. The first was the public communiqué, which would be simultaneously released in the United States, Britain and the Soviet Union the next day. The second document was officially titled 'Protocol of the Proceedings of the Crimea Conference', which was to be circulated only among the most senior members of the three Allied governments. It described some of the topics in the communiqué in more detail, such as the composition and voting structure of the United Nations organisation, which would not be made public until it was shared with the other members of its Security Council, France and China. The protocol included a paragraph to be added to the official German terms of surrender, calling for 'complete disarmament, demilitarization and the dismemberment of Germany'. The Allies feared that this language might inspire the Nazis to fight harder, and in vain, if they learned how severely they would be punished in the war's aftermath. The document also discussed reparations (as well as Churchill's objection to the figure of $20 billion as a basis of discussion), a matter that would soon be taken up by the Reparation Commission. It also briefly referenced a handful of topics that had been set before the three foreign secretaries for further discussion, such as the future prosecution of war criminals and issues involving postwar relationships with the Balkans, Iran and Turkey.

The three leaders were largely pleased with the drafts and ready to sign the papers at lunch, save for a few small amendments. Much to the relief of everyone, Churchill's outstanding objections on language were largely restricted to excessive use of the word 'joint' to describe tripartite agreements. In his mind, the connotation of the word 'joint' was 'the Sunday family roast of mutton'.

There was, however, one last settlement that appeared in neither document. It had been under discussion since the summer of 1944: an agreement on the repatriation of POWs. As the Red Army marched towards Germany, it encountered many POW camps where the Germans had detained captured British and American airmen and soldiers. The Soviets soon found themselves with sixty thousand western POWs on their hands. Meanwhile, as the British and American armies marched east, they liberated Soviet POWs. As German forces surrendered, the western Allies realised there were hundreds of thousands of Soviet nationals among them, both Red Army soldiers the Nazis had captured and Soviet men fighting against the Red Army in German uniforms – some by choice, some by coercion. Others were forced labourers the Nazis had captured or civilians who had become captives of chaos after being forced to flee their homes. Stalin had demanded the repatriation of these Soviet nationals. This, Churchill realised, could become something of an international 'embarrassment'. The western Allies feared that if they failed to repatriate the Soviet nationals, the Soviets might use the British and American POWs as a bargaining chip, by treating them poorly or by delaying their repatriation. Herein lay the problem: many Soviet nationals were begging not to be sent back. Some were so desperate they tried to commit suicide to avoid being repatriated. But for the British and the Americans, their own POWs remained their primary concern. On the morning of February 11, the three powers came to an agreement to exchange their respective prisoners of war. Beria would oversee the arrangements on the Soviet end. Anthony Eden signed for the British, while General John Russell Deane of the U.S. military mission in Moscow signed for the Americans. The State Department wanted no political involvement.

The British and American commitment to protecting the rights and lives of their POWs forced them to be utilitarian when faced with the fact that the Soviets did not see POWs in the same light. In the Soviet view, those who had been captured by the enemy were traitors to the nation; they should have fought to the death or committed suicide rather than allow themselves to be taken prisoner. Stalin's own son Yakov, who had been captured by the Germans in July 1941, was among this group. Not only did Stalin not free his son when he had the opportunity to exchange him for a German field marshal, but he also sent Yakov's wife to prison under Order No. 270, to share in her husband's shame of having supposedly defected to the enemy. The western Allies might have asked why hundreds of thousands of Soviet nationals had chosen to assist the Germans and fight against the Soviet Union. Many were Cossacks or came from other ethnic minorities that had been persecuted by the Soviet government. If they returned to the Soviet Union, the authorities there would use the Cossacks' so-called traitorous wartime activity as an excuse to execute them.

Two days earlier, Sarah had said she thought they would be at Yalta 'for a lifetime'. Now 'the merry-go-round was off again!' After the ordeal of travelling to Yalta and the days of stagnation instead of progress, the arguments, and the seemingly endless frustration, everything was suddenly over in the blink of an eye. By the end of lunch, the communiqué had been signed, the last changes to the protocol approved for the foreign ministers to enter into the draft and cable to their home governments. As the delegates gathered in the marble foyer of Livadia Palace, Sarah could see that they were in 'highest spirits', both pleased with the results of their work and ready to return to the comfort of their own homes.

Perhaps no one was more eager to leave Yalta than Anna; for the first time in days, she looked genuinely cheerful. She stood chatting with Ed Stettinius, her fur coat folded over her arm as if she was ready to jump in the car at the earliest opportunity. But the getaway would be incremental. Despite FDR's insistence on leaving Yalta that afternoon for his urgent meetings in the Middle East, he had decided that first the Americans would all go to Sevastopol and spend the night aboard the USS *Catoctin*, to thank the support staff for their efforts and boosting naval morale before flying to Egypt first thing the next morning. Anxious not to be left out of discussions impacting Britain's historic sphere of influence, Churchill had decided that he too would see Ibn Saud on the way home to London. He had hurriedly arranged a meeting with the Saudi leader. After their own brief stay on their logistics ship, the HMS *Franconia*, in Sevastopol, the British would fly to Athens for a day and then briefly reconvene with Roosevelt and his party at Egypt's Great Bitter Lake, which connected to the Mediterranean and Red Seas via the Suez Canal. Only then would Winston and Sarah finally bid FDR and Anna goodbye.

'I don't see how we can get home before the 26th,' Anna told John. 'I fear it looks more like the 28th.' Anna was anxious to get back, not just because of concerns about FDR's health. 'I find it almost impossible to get people to leave me alone so that I can write without having someone peeking over my shoulder! As I am always with OM the "someones" are always the same old gang from the W[hite] H[ouse].' As much as she wanted to escape FDR's cabal, they would be there to peek over her shoulder the whole way back to Washington. Anna found little point in writing to John about the Yalta agreements, she told him, for by the time her letter reached him, the communiqué would have been public for days. 'I have read the one suggested by our crowd, and written by the State Dept. It sounds like it, too. To my mind it is chuck full of too many glittering generalities, but Steve swears it's a wow of a story!' As usual, she directed her ire at press secretary Steve Early, never once considering that the 'glittering generalities' she disparaged in the communiqué could only have been approved by her father. 'Honey Darling,' she closed, 'I know that I've been a help to OM, and of course, the whole experience is a thrill, a terrific one.'

With the communiqué signed, all that remained was the requisite diplomatic gift exchange: watches and fountain pens for the Soviet officials and staff, and hundreds of pounds of caviar, champagne, vodka, fruit, liqueurs and Russian cigarettes for the British and the Americans to cart back to London and Washington. There was a particular gift waiting for Anna. It was from Averell Harriman. Ever the diplomat, he set his irritation with her father aside and offered her a thoughtful token. Acting upon the half-conceived plans FDR had dumped in Anna's lap the first few days of the conference would not number among his most treasured ambassadorial achievements, but this he did not blame on the daughter. Harriman had managed to find a small figurine

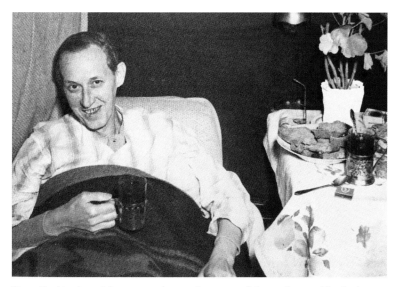

Harry Hopkins lost eighteen pounds over the course of the conference. The Soviets offered to transport him to Saki by train at the conference's conclusion, as he was too ill to make the long drive.
Photo by Robert Hopkins from Witness to History *(Castle Pacific, 2003)*

Pamela Churchill, spring 1941, around the time she met Averell Harriman.
Photo from Life of the Party *by Christopher Ogden (Little, Brown & Company, 1994)*

FDR and Stalin meet together with their interpreters at Livadia Palace before the first plenary session, February 4, 1945. *Courtesy of Newberry Library*

John Gilbert Winant
Courtesy of Library of Congress

Roosevelt, looking ill and exhausted, confers with Churchill in Livadia Palace's ballroom turned conference room.
Bettmann / Getty Images

Joseph Stalin and his daughter, Svetlana, ca. early 1930s.
Laski Diffusion / Getty Images

Lavrentiy Beria, 1938
Photo printed in Literaturuli Sakartvelo.

Winston Churchill has a pre–plenary session chat with Sarah at Livadia Palace, with Field Marshal Sir Harold Alexander (left), Kathleen Harriman and Edward Stettinius (center), and Robert Hopkins (right) in the background.
Photo from U.S. Army Signal Corps. Courtesy of Newberry Library.

The three daughters — Sarah, Anna, and Kathleen — at Livadia Palace.
Photo from U.S. Army Signal Corps. Courtesy of George C. Marshall Foundation.

Anna and Kathleen look at a propaganda billboard in the town of Yalta, February 10, 1945. *Photo from U.S. Army Signal Corps. Accessed from the Robert Hopkins Papers. Courtesy of Georgetown University.*

Preparing for the official photo session, February 9, 1945. Peter Portal stands behind Churchill, who chats with Roosevelt, while Stalin appears isolated without his translator. Sarah and Kathleen watch from under the colonnade.

Photo from U.S. Army Signal Corps. Accessed from the Robert Hopkins Papers. Courtesy of Georgetown University.

Anna and FDR take a Jeep tour of the Livadia Palace grounds, February 10, 1945.

Photo from U.S. Army Signal Corps. Accessed from the Robert Hopkins Papers. Courtesy of Georgetown University.

The Big Three and their advisors at the official photo session, February 9, 1945
(L-R: Winston Churchill, Anthony Eden, FDR, Edward Stettinius, Alexander Cadogan,
Vyacheslav Molotov, Joseph Stalin, Averell Harriman).
Photo accessed from the Averell Harriman Papers. Courtesy of Library of Congress.

Kathleen with Fact,
one of two horses
Joseph Stalin gifted to
the Harrimans, 1946.
*Used by permission of the
Mortimer family*

FDR addresses Congress to report on the Yalta Conference, March 1, 1945. It was the first time he had done so while seated. *Courtesy of the Franklin D. Roosevelt Presidential Library & Museum*

Winston and Sarah leave the memorial service for FDR at St. Paul's Cathedral in London, April 17, 1945. *Dave Bagnall Collection / Alamy Stock Photo*

of a woman in traditional Crimean dress, holding a baby. He thought Anna might give it to her daughter, Ellie. It was crudely made, like a lump of clay moulded and painted by a child, but Anna was touched, both by the gift and by Averell's kindness to her throughout the conference. He was one of the only people that week who had thought to make her life easier.

Averell and Kathleen Harriman would be leaving that afternoon with the Roosevelts to spend the night on the *Catoctin* before flying on to Moscow the next day. Ed Stettinius and his party from the State Department, including Freeman Matthews and Wilder Foote, would accompany the Harrimans onwards to Moscow as guests at Spaso House for the following two days. This would allow Stettinius and Harriman to discuss further Soviet-American issues, such as peacetime economic competition and trade, with Molotov and company. Once again, Stettinius decided to bring Alger Hiss to assist in these vital discussions. Ed Flynn, FDR's political adviser and tagalong, would be travelling to Moscow with them, as well. As far as Kathy could tell, the New York Irish-Catholic's amorphous assignment was 'to make the Russians pray.'

Kathy had fully imbibed the marked spirit of cooperation. 'All are going home very happy,' she wrote, as she closed her sixteen-page letter to her sister. 'It looks as though all 'round it's been a good conference – a hellova long one too.' And to Pamela she added, 'You can imagine how elated Ave is – though Lord knows what trouble his new job as Polish gov't conciliator will bring.'

It was as if Kathy and Averell had swapped places since the beginning of the war. Kathy had been an early sceptic of the Stalin regime and of the sincerity of the Soviets' commitment to the Allied cause, while Averell had been hopeful about the nascent working relationship between East and West. Now, Kathy was the optimist, while Averell had turned the sceptic. If Averell was elated, it was likely because of the welcome prospect of physically leaving Yalta. On matters of substance, however, he had grave reservations. As he said that morning to Chip Bohlen, who was working furiously to translate the final details in the protocol and communiqué for the leaders' approval, there would be 'trouble ahead', and soon. The language in the conference protocol promising a 'reorganized' Polish government, comprised of the Lublin Poles and an unspecified number of additional representatives from within Poland and abroad, was 'far too vague and generalized'. From his experience working with Roosevelt, dating back to his New Deal days, Harriman knew Roosevelt was not one to haggle over words. As long as he could derive his desired interpretation from a text, FDR did not 'much care what interpretation other people put on it'. But Harriman knew that unless the language was precise, the Soviets could manipulate it however they liked – they might add to the provisional government a mere one or two non-Communist individuals with no power – and still be able to claim they were acting according to the agreement. Recalling the oft-uttered expression about buying the same horse twice, Harriman was resigned to the fact that as far as Poland was concerned, the Yalta agreement had 'established nothing more than the machinery for renegotiation'. Bohlen concurred. Everything they had supposedly resolved would have to be redeveloped 'from the ground up'.

Harriman and Bohlen were two of a small minority of American delegates concerned about the language of the Polish agreement. Another was the president's chief of staff, Admiral Leahy. Leahy was no expert on eastern European affairs, but even he was not convinced about the deal Roosevelt and Churchill had negotiated with Stalin. Taking advantage of his trusted position within FDR's inner circle, Leahy even went so far as to express his frank opinion to Roosevelt directly, saying, 'Mr. President, this is so elastic that the Russians can stretch it all the way from Yalta to Washington without technically breaking it.'

'I know Bill – I know it,' Roosevelt had conceded. 'But it's the best I can do for Poland at this time.'

Harriman was similarly apprehensive about the Pacific agreement between Stalin and the president, particularly regarding the Soviets' increasing influence in Manchuria. The secretary of state, and particularly the Chinese, had yet to be informed of this, despite the fact that the concessions the Soviets would receive in the Pacific, especially the ports and railroads in Manchuria, were right on China's border. 'There is no doubt,' Harriman had conveyed to Roosevelt with concern two months earlier, when he had first broached the subject with Stalin in Moscow on FDR's behalf, 'that Soviet influence in Manchuria will be great, what with the control of the railroad operations and with the probability of Soviet troops to protect the railroad'. This agreement was essentially an invitation to the Soviets to expand their foothold significantly in the East. And, as with the Polish agreement, the language was alarmingly vague and unqualified. The ambassador had spent two and a half hours the previous afternoon driving back and forth between Livadia Palace and the Koreiz Villa as Roosevelt and Stalin traded drafts on the final language. When Harriman showed it to the Joint Chiefs of Staff – General Marshall, Admiral Leahy and Admiral King – for their comment, he hoped they would raise an objection so he could take the document back to Roosevelt and convince him to tighten the language. But they did not. Leahy may have sided with Harriman when it came to Poland, but his feelings about the Pacific agreement were entirely different. Leahy even went so far as to tell Harriman that the Pacific agreement 'makes the trip worthwhile'. And as Kathy overheard Admiral King declare, the joint chiefs believed Soviet intervention in the Pacific would save two million American lives.

Roosevelt had clearly made up his mind, and Harriman's mounting misgivings were of no interest to him as he was preparing to depart. That morning, the president had sent Harriman a note. 'My dear Mr. Ambassador, At this time I shall not attempt to comment on the far-reaching efforts of the [Yalta] Conference or on the part you have played in that historic meeting,' the note began. 'I do wish to comment, however, on the part you and your people have played in preparing a place where the conference could be held and in the highly efficient manner in which that preparation has been carried out on very short notice . . . We were all faced with a difficult problem to find an appropriate setting for the conference . . . I feel that we could not have made a more successful choice . . . I am also conscious of the great assistance given us by your daughter Kathleen. With my very best wishes to you all and confidence in your continued help to the nation, Franklin D. Roosevelt.'

It was a note of thanks, but it could also be read as a dismissal. By recognising only Harriman's contributions to the conference's logistical arrangements and breezing past his extensive, substantive efforts on behalf of Roosevelt's political and diplomatic objectives, both at Yalta and during his tenure of nearly a year and a half as ambassador, Roosevelt was indirectly communicating just how little weight Harriman's opinion had come to carry. The president was shaping the future in the manner he saw fit. Harriman's worldview concerning the relationship between East and West did not reflect that image.

Tyres crunched on the gravel in front of the Livadia Palace portico as Churchill's black Packard arrived to make one last drive back to Vorontsov. The full complement of photographers had turned out to capture his departure. Word had gone out to the Soviet security forces to close the road between Livadia and Vorontsov for a final time, while from the rooftops snipers scanned for potential threats. Churchill donned his greatcoat and furry Russian hat, put a new cigar in his mouth, and strode across the carpet that had been laid from the front door of Livadia to the car. A British officer opened the car door, saluting the prime minister as he approached. Churchill returned the salute with an expression somewhere between a smile and a grimace before stopping and gesturing to Sarah to come along. Sarah hurried out of the building to the car and ducked her head to climb into the proffered seat as her father playfully swatted her in. Then he turned, gave one last salute, and climbed into the car beside her. One of his aides shut the door firmly behind him, and they drove off down the drive, leaving Livadia Palace behind.

On the trip back to Vorontsov, Churchill quickly grew agitated. The British had planned to stay at Vorontsov for the night and set off for Sevastopol the next morning in an orderly fashion, but as they carried on down the road, Sarah noticed a wave of loneliness wash over her father, perhaps tinged with a hint of embarrassment. FDR and Stalin were departing from Yalta that afternoon. Churchill would be left behind.

'Why do we stay here?' he insisted to Sarah. 'Why don't we go tonight – I see no reason to stay here a minute longer – we're off!'

As soon as they arrived at Vorontsov, he jumped out of the car and blew straight into his makeshift private office like a great gust of wind, which threatened to scatter tidy stacks of paper everywhere. 'I don't know about you,' he announced to his staff, 'but I'm off! I leave in 50 minutes!' Sarah arrived behind him, in time to see everyone stare at him with 'a second's stunned silence'. The shock lasted only a moment, and they were 'galvanized into activity', packing up the boxes of papers and portable typewriters and scurrying to collect any personal effects, while Churchill wandered around in search of his aide and valet. 'Where's Tommy? Sawyers!' he shouted, 'Sawyers! Where is everyone?' Meanwhile, Sarah noticed that a pile of 'trunks and large mysterious paper parcels' had appeared in the hall. More gifts from the Russians, more packing for the beleaguered staff.

'Naturally,' Sarah told her mother, as she later described the scene, '50 minutes gave us time to change our minds six more times!' Winston paced as his staff raced to pack, firing off one new plan after another. 'We will spend the night here after all and leave to-morrow lunchtime – We will fly – We will leave to-night and go by sea – We will go to Athens – Alexandria – Cairo – Constantinople – We will not go to any of them – We will stay on board and read the newspapers!'

As plans were made, torn up, made, and torn up again, Churchill's valet, Sawyers, was nearing his wits' end. Tears welled up as he looked around at suitcases that remained partially packed and laundry that had arrived back clean but damp, as it had not had time to dry before the sudden pronouncement that they were leaving. He picked up a sponge bag and placed it in a suitcase, then took it out again, befuddled. Then he gently laid out Churchill's Lord Warden of the Cinque Ports uniform, changed his mind, put it back, and laid out the Royal Yacht Club uniform instead. 'They can't do this to me!' he exclaimed to Sarah, overcome by the trauma of the sudden, haphazard departure.

Meanwhile, Winston paced around, popping into rooms, 'genial and sprightly like a boy out of school, his homework done', oblivious to the stress he had thrust upon his staff as he urged everyone to move faster: 'Come on, come on!'

One hour and twenty minutes after Churchill had announced the imminent departure, 'a cavalcade of cars' filled the drive, 'groaning with bulging suitcases', ready to traverse the mountain switchbacks en route to Sevastopol. There were, however, a handful of items that had not made it into the suitcases: the prime minister's extra cigars, lighters and silver cigar boxes. It seemed some light-fingered members of the Russian staff had lifted them as souvenirs.

At 5.30 p.m., the last car door slammed shut and the cavalcade turned its back on the Black Sea to begin its long trek through the mountains. As remarkable an achievement as it was to pack and depart within eighty minutes, Sarah soon learned they were the last delegation to leave. The Roosevelts, the Harrimans and the rest of their party had left a full hour earlier, right on schedule, according to FDR's well-ordered plan. The Americans had suffered only one minor mishap. The car carrying Admiral Leahy and Dr Bruenn had a gas leak and began to fill with toxic fumes, forcing the two men and their driver to make the cold, dark drive to Sevastopol with the car windows completely open. Meanwhile, Sarah remarked, 'Stalin, like some genie, just disappeared.' The Soviets had turned their ransacked country inside-out to restore the tsar's derelict summer playground to at least a modicum of its former glory, but mere hours after the communiqué had been signed, 'Yalta was deserted, except for those who have to tidy up after a party.'

Those left to tidy up were the three foreign ministers, their interpreters, and the staff assistants. Back at Livadia, they put the finishing touches on the conference protocol, signed the document, and transmitted it home by radio. For the Americans, that meant sending it first to the *Catoctin*, whose radio operators would then relay it on to Washington. When the final sentence had been transmitted, Freeman Matthews turned to Stettinius and said, 'Mr. Secretary, our last message has been sent. Can I cut the connection to the ship?'

'Yes,' Stettinius replied. Matthews broke the connection, and with that, the Yalta Conference officially came to an end.

As the three foreign ministers walked through Livadia's grand foyer one last time, their footsteps echoing on the marble, something caught Molotov's eye. It was one of the lemon trees that had been shipped to Yalta, after the Soviets picked up on several of the westerners' remarks, like the one uttered by Sarah Churchill, that caviar and cocktails tasted nicer with a twist of lemon. The tree was still covered in lemons. It was a shame to let the precious fruit go to waste. Molotov suggested that Ed Stettinius and Anthony Eden each cut a branch from the tree and take it home as a small memento, like an olive branch. Someone found a knife and cut a branch for each of the foreign ministers. As there were still a number of branches left, these were cut and distributed among the remaining Allied staff, until only the skinny trunk remained standing in the pot, like a lance stuck in the ground. Then they bid one another goodbye until their next meeting in London, three months hence, and drove away with their lemons, oblivious to the irony, which would soon become apparent.

Night had long fallen by the time Sarah and Winston reached Sevastopol. For three hours, they had wound their way along the coast and over 'grey and indestructible mountains' in twilight, through passes and around the bases of limestone peaks. 'I'm so relieved to get this bloody thing off,' the prime minister growled to Sarah and Lord Moran as they drove along – the 'bloody thing' meaning the conference communiqué. 'Grand to get back to English fare after the sucking-pig and the cold fatty approaches to all their meals.'

When the road neared its zenith, they had stopped the car and got out to take a look. Sarah looked not down but up. A five-hundred-foot precipice shot up before them 'so straight, it seemed to lean over like the beetling brows of a giant'. Once over the peaks of the mountains, they descended through the alpine meadows, or *yaylas*, in the Crimean Tatar language. Red Army soldiers were once again out in force, lining the road every several hundred feet and saluting the prime minister's car as it drove by. As they neared Sevastopol, they drove through a small village. Though it was dark and not possible for the villagers to have properly seen the car, they broke out in a cheer as Churchill passed by.

Eventually, the *Franconia* came into view, the ship's lights reflecting off the surface of the water. The once luxurious Cunard ocean liner had been refitted as a troop ship during the war, but even in its modest state, it loomed like a sleek marvel of H. G. Wells's imagination against the backdrop of mid-nineteenth-century rubble that was Sevastopol. Nearby, the *Catoctin* was moored in its berth. On board, Roosevelt was having a steak dinner, while some of his party, including Anna, Kathy and Averell, had travelled into town where the band of the Black Sea Fleet had organised a concert for the visitors. The programme featured an eclectic mix of songs: everything from sea shanties to traditional Russian folk songs, accordion solos, and Strauss's 'Blue Danube' – even the American hit 'This Is the Army, Mr. Jones', by Irving Berlin. The concert was held in the Sevastopol theatre, one of first buildings raised from the rubble and ash after the fighting ceased. It had been rebuilt in just two months.

Sarah, arriving later to Sevastopol than the Americans, was in no rush to attend. Once she set foot on the *Franconia*, it would have been difficult to persuade her to leave again. After the last week in the Crimea, their ship was nothing short of 'astonishing'. She had done little more than walk the gangplank, but in the space of 'three short minutes', she felt as if she had 'left the bleak, grim world and stepped into gentle civilization'. She certainly 'wasn't expecting anything like it'. Her cabin – if she could even call it a cabin, it seemed as plush as a 'bridal suite' – had every comfort of home and then some. The stewardess soon arrived with a martini and chicken sandwiches prepared by the chef. Down a passageway was a hairdresser. 'It all seems – how to put it,' she queried Clementine, 'a little unreal? So close to Reality outside.'

As if to ease the jarring transition between the world of subsistence living outside and luxury within, Winston had lingered on the deck. He was standing silently in the briny February air, looking over the rail at the city that stretched before him. Sarah joined him and followed his gaze out towards Sevastopol. By day, the tragic remains of the city had overwhelmed Sarah. Her heart had broken for the families whose lives had been destroyed, some for the second time in three or four generations. But in the darkness, Sevastopol was nothing short of 'a revelation'. Sarah was transfixed. 'You remember I told you of the devastation, of not a house in view standing or unbroken, and how one wondered where or how they lived?' she later wrote to her mother. 'Well, at night one discovers. From nearly every ruin, wherever four walls of one room still stand, from behind boards that fill gaps, from basements, from piles of stones even, shafts and specks of light shine and twinkle. It's incredible! They are incredible!'

The lights of Sevastopol immediately brought the little church in Yalta to the forefront of Sarah's mind. Amid the cold, dark, broken surroundings, Yalta's survivors had emerged from the rubble and held fast together, the tiny halos of candlelight binding them to one another as they fought to see each new day, much like Londoners during the height of the Blitz.

Sarah had watched as her father spent the past weeks, months and years grappling with the Soviets, trying to bridge the gap between socialism and democracy in order to vanquish a common enemy. Despite the apparent success of the conference, it was clear that the Soviet Union was pulling farther and farther away from Britain and the United States, even as their armies – and their borders – moved closer together.

Breaking the silence, Sarah asked her father if he was tired.

'Strangely enough, no,' he answered. 'Yet I have felt the weight of responsibility more than ever before and in my heart there is anxiety.'

For all the political strife of the past weeks and months, the hours Sarah had spent with Kathy and Anna in Sevastopol and Yalta had allowed her to see a side of the Soviet Union that her father had not. She had seen the people on the poorest, most downtrodden outskirts of a vast empire. These people knew nothing of geopolitics, alliances or grand strategy, nothing of Marxist-Leninist doctrine or capitalist market forces. The war had taken everything from them, but still they were proud – of their city, their community, their homes and their children. Regardless of what her father had decided with Roosevelt and Stalin in the gilded palaces of Yalta, or whether they walked away as enemies or friends, these people would rebuild their city and their lives, just as they had done before.

Though there was every reason to despair as she stood alongside her father, looking out at Sevastopol at the end of one of the most remarkable, troubling and fascinating weeks of her life, Sarah found reason to look at the Soviet Union and see hope. Describing the scene to her mother, she wrote, 'It's no use saying "They're used to suffering. They're built differently from us. They don't expect much." Why are the churches so full, then? Of course they hope for more. Of course they dream in their darkened churches.'

PART III

'All this, and more
I have with me
forever.'

EIGHTEEN

April 12–July 27, 1945

You really have been in on the greatest meeting in history,' John Boettiger wrote to Anna as Roosevelt and his party made the long voyage home to Washington. Her brothers may have attended more conferences, accompanying FDR to the Atlantic Charter meeting with Churchill in 1941 and the Tehran Conference in 1943, and though it stung Anna to be left behind for those events, the wait had been well worth it to witness Yalta. 'The other meetings have all been tiddle-de-winks compared with this one, so you can say fiddle-sticks to your brothers,' John cheered. 'I am really thrilled beyond any words to tell it that you are on the trip, and I KNOW how tremendously valuable you are to OM. I only hope he realizes it at this time.'

Whether FDR realised Anna's value to him at Yalta or not, he did not say. He remained as detached and enigmatic as ever. As much as Anna might have liked to bask in both the sunshine and some praise as they commenced their journey on the *Quincy*, she could not. FDR's meetings on the Great Bitter Lake still loomed. The trip had begun well, save for the grumblings of Gil Winant, who was still smarting at having been left out of the conference when he joined the president's party in Egypt. Only once their journey home was underway did Roosevelt finally respond to the Polish prime minister. 'You may be assured that Poland's problems received most careful and sympathetic consideration,' he wrote tersely. 'I hope we may all work together harmoniously to find the correct solution in due time.' The Americans arrived at the Great Bitter Lake in the afternoon of February 12. On the thirteenth, FDR received his first two visitors, King Farouk of Egypt and Emperor Haile Selassie of Ethiopia. The next day, Ibn Saud arrived on the *Quincy* with a forty-eight-man entourage, including his astrologer, imam and royal coffee server. Because the battle-scarred Saudi leader would take offence at a woman's presence at such a gathering, Anna had to leave the ship and spend the day in Cairo.

FDR had high hopes for this meeting, as the Saudis could be a valuable ally in the postwar world – not least because of their vast reserves of oil. But he quickly found himself disappointed. When he broached the subject of working with the Saudis to create, in exchange for American technology, a Jewish homeland in Palestine for Holocaust survivors, Ibn Saud rebuffed him: 'Arabs would choose to die rather than yield their land to Jews.' Not even the Rooseveltian charm and a brand-new C-47 plane could persuade the Arab leader otherwise. For the first time in long weeks of wily negotiation and diplomacy, FDR came away empty-handed. The following afternoon, the Roosevelts reconvened with Winston, Sarah and Anthony Eden in Alexandria for a family luncheon before the prime minister's own meeting with Ibn Saud. Randolph Churchill had turned up once again, though Sarah was undoubtedly far more pleased to see Gil Winant. Anna smirked, noting that he had been most eager to see Sarah for obvious reasons. Several hours later, the Americans said their farewells and continued the journey home.

Throughout the rest of the trip, the Americans encountered one setback after another, each one worse than the one before. Roosevelt had intended to rendezvous with Charles de Gaulle in Algiers, but the French leader, who was furious that he had not been invited to the Yalta Conference, refused to meet. Also troubling Roosevelt was Pa Watson, his longtime friend and emotional and physical support; when FDR had to stand in public, it was often Watson who kept him upright. On the first night in Egypt, Watson had suffered a heart attack. He then slipped into a coma. If the British had made their human sacrifice to the gods of war and peace on the way to Yalta, the Americans made theirs on the way home. Watson died on board the ship eight days later. He was sixty-one, two years younger than Roosevelt.

Shaken by Watson's sudden decline, Harry Hopkins began to feel trapped on the ship. His health had deteriorated even further, and he was much too ill to sail all the way home. He decided he would leave the *Quincy* at Algiers and fly home from Marrakesh, taking his son and Chip Bohlen with him. Roosevelt was deeply irritated. He needed Hopkins's help to draft his address to Congress about the conference, which he was set to deliver immediately after arriving home. But Hopkins would not change his mind. Roosevelt accused his old friend of wanting to leave because he was bored.

Once again, Anna went to Hopkins to intervene. As before, she found him lying in bed. Please, she begged him, he must stay. It simply was not fair to leave her father to write the speech himself.

'Truly, Anna . . . I am too sick to work. I mean it . . . Tell your father to call Sam Rosenman in. He's in London and can fly down to Algiers and work on the speech all the way home.' She had to admit defeat.

'Hopkins won't budge,' she reported to FDR.

'Let him go,' he replied curtly.

Privately, Anna was seething on her father's behalf. She told John, 'I'm pretty well convinced now that Harry H. is a pretty dangerous guy.'

When they moored in Algiers, Hopkins came to take his leave. Roosevelt was engrossed in his papers. He looked up only long enough to extend his hand and mutter, 'Good-bye.' Hopkins had risen from humble roots as a social worker to become one of the most powerful individuals in America, as secretary of commerce and as the guiding hand behind two of the most ambitious and successful government programmes in history – the New Deal and Lend-Lease. Roosevelt had relied on Hopkins to be his legs, his eyes, his ears and his voice when he sent Hopkins to meet with Churchill and Stalin overseas in the darkest days of the war. For fifteen years, it was Hopkins, above all others, who had turned the president's lofty dreams into reality. He had given the last decade and a half of his life and his health in service to Roosevelt. Now he left the ship unceremoniously, with little more than a paltry acknowledgment at parting. He would never see Roosevelt again.

As Hopkins suggested, Sam Rosenman, a former judge and FDR's capable speechwriter, joined the *Quincy* at Algiers to help write the address to Congress. He had not seen the president for a month and was alarmed by FDR's appearance. The president had lost weight; never before had he looked so exhausted. Over the next few days, Rosenman worked to assemble a speech about a conference he had not taken part in and knew little about. When he tried to engage Roosevelt in the writing, the president was not interested. Instead, FDR sat on deck in the sunshine, his energy sapped, able to do nothing but read, smoke cigarettes and stare at the ocean. As he mourned the death of his friend Watson, Anna worked with Rosenman, diligently tearing into three drafts of the speech with her sharp pencil as if once again editing the *Seattle Post-Intelligencer.*

Finally, at 10.15 p.m. on February 27, they moored at Newport News, Virginia, the port from which they had set sail thirty-five days earlier. The next morning, in the rain, they buried Pa Watson at Arlington National Cemetery. The following day, Roosevelt made his address to Congress. Anna watched while, for the first time, her father allowed himself to be wheeled into the House Chamber. 'I hope that you will pardon me for an unusual posture of sitting down during the presentation of what I want to say,' he told Congress, 'but I know that you will realize that it makes it a lot easier for me in not having to carry about ten pounds of steel around on the bottom of my legs; and also because of the fact that I have just completed a fourteen-thousand-mile trip.' Labor Secretary Frances Perkins, the first woman ever to be appointed to the Cabinet, was sitting in the front row. In the three decades that she had known Roosevelt, she had never before heard him publicly acknowledge his infirmity or request an allowance for it. Still, he spoke clearly and forcefully from his wheelchair, extolling hope for a peaceful future. He was determined to be a part of it.

Immediately upon its conclusion, the American press hailed the Yalta Conference as a great achievement. The *New York Times* wrote that the tripartite agreements 'justify and surpass most of the hopes placed on this fateful meeting', while the *New York Herald Tribune* remarked that the 'Conference has produced another great proof of Allied unity, strength and power of decision'. The *Washington Post* applauded Roosevelt personally, stating, 'The President is to be congratulated on his part in this all-encompassing achievement.' But before the week of FDR's address to Congress was out, public sentiment about the Yalta accords began to shift. On March 5, *Time* magazine published a curious piece, one the magazine described as a 'political fairy tale'. It was written by *Time*'s Whittaker Chambers, the reformed Communist spy whose warnings about the conference delegate Alger Hiss had fallen on deaf ears at the State Department nearly six years earlier. In the piece, Clio, the Muse of History, and the ghosts of the slain Tsar Nicholas II and his family look down from the rafters of Livadia Palace as the Big Three confer below them. The ghost of Tsar Nicholas listens to Stalin with rapture: 'What statesmanship! What vision! What power!' the ghost raves. 'Stalin has made Russia great again!' This satire, printed in one of the nation's foremost publications, was a piercing rebuke of what Roosevelt hoped would be one of his finest achievements.

Meanwhile, in London, the reaction to the conference was negative from the start. Sarah, back at work at RAF Medmenham with the aerial reconnaissance division, could only listen from afar as her father faced a groundswell of criticism from his colleagues in Parliament. When he delivered his report on the conference in the House of Commons, requesting a vote of confidence on the Yalta resolutions, many honourable members immediately decried what they saw as an obvious capitulation to the Soviets, especially regarding Poland. After three days of debate, Churchill ultimately received his vote of confidence, but not without a written protest led by twenty-five MPs and the resignation of one member of his own party. Criticism was also pouring in from the outer reaches of the British Empire. Though Churchill tried, in public, to position Yalta as a success, he was more candid when responding to the prime minister of New Zealand, who had written in remonstrance over Poland: 'We are not in a position to get exactly the solution we should wish. Great Britain and the British Commonwealth are very much weaker militarily than Soviet Russia, and have no means, short of another general war, of enforcing their point of view. Nor can we ignore the position of the United States. We cannot go further in helping Poland than the United States is willing or can be persuaded to go.'

As critics of the Yalta agreements began to speak out, the White

House soon found itself with another public relations problem. The press had turned its attention on an unlikely individual: Anna. Since arriving at the White House a year earlier, Anna had deliberately avoided the spotlight. To the public, she maintained that she was just like any other daughter, wife and mother: a private person with no official mandate or political ambition. However, between Drew Pearson's January 'Washington Merry-Go-Round' column and the pictures of Anna seated beside her father on the *Quincy*, which appeared in the press after the conference, people began to speculate on just what sort of influence she was having on the president. On the way home from Yalta, John had written to Anna, warning her that both *Life* magazine and the Associated Press wanted to write about her. They would welcome her cooperation if she wished to speak with them or write about her impressions of Yalta, but if she did not, they would publish anyway. Anna and John decided it was best for her to 'have as little publicity as possible, and contribute toward none'. But public attention could no longer be avoided when *Life* published an eight-page feature about her the same day that *Time* published 'The Ghosts on the Roof'. *Life* did not overtly criticise her position or influence in the White House, but the story established that Anna was anything but a passive resident. The writer, John Chamberlain, went so far as to imply that Anna was indirectly responsible for the selection of Truman as vice president. 'For purposes of public consumption,' he concluded, 'she may continue to pose as someone living in the White House, in prolonged transit from and to a newspaper job. But no matter what the White House press agents may say, it is a fair bet that . . . Daddy's girl has her work cut out for her, running Daddy.'

For the next few weeks, however, Anna could not spend her time 'running Daddy'. By the time she returned home from Yalta, her son Johnny had developed a severe glandular infection and was admitted to the Bethesda Naval Hospital for treatment with a new, revolutionary medication – penicillin. Johnny was still in the hospital on March 29 when FDR left for Warm Springs for several weeks' recuperation. Every night FDR was at Warm Springs, he called Anna on the telephone. The evening of April 11 was no exception. 'Hello, girl,' he said. 'How is Johnny?' Much to Anna's relief, her son was finally improving.

Her father told her about the barbecue he had planned for the next day. He sounded relaxed and easy and full of life. The only problem, he said, was that he knew he was going to overeat, which would certainly make Dr Bruenn grimace, but he was determined to 'thoroughly enjoy it!' No doubt he would, as Anna knew Lucy was also at Warm Springs. She had summoned Lucy herself.

The next afternoon, Anna had not been at Bethesda Naval Hospital with Johnny more than twenty minutes when the head of the hospital came into the room. 'Mrs. Boettiger,' he said gravely, 'my car is waiting to take you to the White House.' FDR had collapsed. As she rode down Wisconsin Avenue, a swirl of thoughts raced through her mind. Was this what had happened to President Woodrow Wilson when he suffered his debilitating stroke? What if her father was incapacitated and could no longer serve? FDR had always been afraid of something like that happening to him. As soon as the car pulled up at the White House, Anna dashed up to her mother's sitting room. Eleanor was wearing a black dress.

Her father was dead. He had died just two weeks shy of the first meeting of the United Nations, in San Francisco. The organisation was his greatest source of pride, and he was determined to be there.

It was nearly two in the early morning of April 13 when Kathy became aware that the Spaso House telephone was ringing. Its shrill tones punctuated the fleeting moment of gaiety like an unwitting intruder who does not realise he's stumbled into the middle of a gathering to which he was not invited.

It had been a long few days. The Harrimans had been entertaining Clementine Churchill, who managed to set aside her fear of flying for one trip and travelled to the Soviet Union on a goodwill tour as chairman of the Red Cross Aid to Russia fund. As she left for Leningrad, Josip Broz Tito, the leader of Yugoslavia, arrived in Moscow for meetings. Averell and Kathy had of course been invited to all of the requisite festivities surrounding the visit. The Harrimans were now hosting a farewell bash for their colleague John Melby, the Foreign Service officer at the American embassy who had accompanied Kathy to the Katyn Forest. He was being reassigned to Washington to prepare for the United Nations conference. The sendoff was meant to express their admiration for their colleague, but it was also a chance to blow off some steam after eight trying weeks.

'The honeymoon after Yalta was short lived,' Kathy wrote to Pamela from Moscow, 'shorter in fact than even the more pessimistic hoped.' In the two months since Yalta, the goodwill between East and West had almost completely evaporated, even though nothing but news of success was coming in from the front lines. By the end of March, Allied forces had cleared all Nazi troops west of the Rhine and had begun pouring into the German industrial heartland after defeating the enemy at Remagen a full two weeks ahead of schedule. Meanwhile, in the East, the Red Army had snuffed out one last, desperate German offensive in Hungary. Even the Pacific looked promising. The U.S. Marines had prevailed at Iwo Jima, securing a prime staging area for the invasion of the Japanese home islands.

But in Moscow, though there seemed to be every reason to rejoice in the fruits of the three powers' joint labours, Kathy watched as the 'gallant' Soviet allies became 'most bastard-like', blatantly disregarding one Yalta agreement after another. There may as well have been no conference at all. The Americans could have followed George Kennan's advice and just stayed home. Kathy admitted to Pamela, 'Lord knows I fell for the Yalta atmosphere of good fellowship, brothers in arms etc etc hook line and sinker.'

The complications began immediately after the conference. As if an augury of things to come, the Spaso House boiler exploded the day the Harrimans returned from Yalta with the secretary of state. Later that week, on February 17, three American officers who had been held as POWs in northwest Poland appeared at the front door of the American embassy on Novinsky Boulevard. Two days later, the American officers were eight in number. They started appearing at 'the rate of several a day'. Then came the enlisted men. So many American POWs appeared at the embassy that Kathy and the staff had no choice but to convert the Spaso House billiard room into a dormitory until they could arrange to send the men home. These POWs were fleeing not only the

Nazis but also the Red Army. Each man who appeared told a similar story of the supposed liberators' brutality: of wandering through Poland, desperately seeking American authorities to help them; of being forcibly rounded up and sent by the Red Army to repatriation assembly points that were hundreds of miles from where the prisoners were liberated; of theft at gunpoint by Soviet soldiers. If not for the generosity of Polish peasants, many POWs would have starved to death.

As soon as these Americans were safely on their way home, the Soviets began stirring up trouble in neighbouring Romania. They manufactured a violent demonstration to force the resignation of the Romanian prime minister, Nicolae Rădescu, and installed a new Communist government, completely flouting the Declaration on Liberated Europe, which they had signed a mere three weeks earlier at Yalta.

And, as Kathy had predicted, the new Polish government was proving a nightmare for Averell. The Soviets had not 'reorganized' the Lublin government at all. Not only had they maintained it as the nucleus of the purportedly new government, but they had also blackballed every Polish leader in London and from the resistance within Poland, which the British and the Americans had proposed as candidates for the Government of National Unity. 'The Lublin Government every day is becoming more and more the Warsaw Government and the ruler of Poland,' Averell warned Washington on March 7. The free elections that Stalin had promised would be arranged within a month were nowhere in sight. By the end of March, rumours began to circulate that sixteen leaders of the Polish underground who had been invited to Moscow to discuss the new government had disappeared without a trace. Meanwhile, as tension mounted between the Americans and the Soviets, the Soviet employees at the embassy suddenly had their ration cards revoked without warning.

In London, Churchill was grappling with the stark reality of Britain's eroding power as he watched Poland's self-determined future slip away. Unable to force the Soviets to cooperate, the prime minister had urged Roosevelt to intervene. 'We are in [the] presence of a great failure and an utter breakdown of what was settled at Yalta,' he wrote to FDR on March 13, one month after the conference. 'We British have not the necessary strength to carry the matter further . . . The limits of our capacity to act have been reached. The moment that Molotov sees that he has beaten us away from the whole process of consultations among Poles to form a new government, he will know that we will put up with anything.' Again, Churchill aimed his frustration at Molotov, rather than Stalin, but he acutely understood that any window for action was quickly closing.

But when Roosevelt directed the western Allies' concerns to Stalin, he minimised the problem. For fear of jeopardising future cooperation, the president avoided directly accusing the Soviets of deliberately violating the Yalta agreements. 'So far there has been a discouraging lack of progress made in the carrying out . . . of the political decisions which we reached at the conference,' he wrote to the Soviet leader on April 1, in a message delivered by Harriman. 'I am frankly puzzled as to why this should be.' The Soviets gainsaid all of Roosevelt's indirect objections.

Harriman knew that the president's weak rhetoric would be ineffective. As he watched Romania and Poland fall to the Soviets and listened as American POWs condemned the dastardly actions of the Red Army, he understood that nothing short of retaliatory measures would stop the Soviets from taking what they wanted. He warned FDR on April 2, 'Unless we do take action . . . the Soviet Government will become convinced that they can force us to accept any of their decisions . . . We may get some temporary repercussions, but if we stand firm I am satisfied it is the only way we can hope to come to a reasonable basis of give and take with these people . . . We will get them to recognize our point of view only if we show them specifically that their interests are being adversely affected.'

Relations between East and West reached a crisis that week, when Stalin became paranoid, thinking that the Americans were attempting to negotiate a separate peace with the Nazis. This was related to events in late February, when the ranking SS commander in northern Italy indicated to the Americans that he wanted to surrender. The Americans were sceptical that this was a legitimate overture, but agreed to hold exploratory talks in Bern, Switzerland, to determine what the rogue commander actually intended. Due to faulty intelligence reports, Stalin believed the erroneous idea that the Nazis were considering surrendering the entire Western Front to the Americans alone. He accused Roosevelt of betraying Soviet trust. After a series of sharp exchanges with the Soviet marshal, which set Stalin straight, the crisis was fortunately resolved.

Once again, FDR took the high road and extended yet another hand of friendship to the Soviets. Early in the morning of April 12 in Moscow – exactly eight weeks from the day that the Harrimans had returned from Yalta – the ambassador received a message from the president to convey to Stalin. Roosevelt had sent it around dinnertime in Warm Springs, Georgia. When Harriman received it in his bedroom study, he could see that FDR clearly wanted to put the Bern incident to rest. There was, however, one line in the message to Stalin that stood out. Roosevelt had written, 'There must not, in any event, be mutual mistrust, and minor misunderstandings of this character should not arise in the future.'

Harriman disagreed with this phrase. Instead of taking the message directly to Stalin, Harriman cabled back, respectfully suggesting that the president reconsider the word 'minor'. 'I confess,' he said, 'that the misunderstandings appeared to me to be of a major character.'

Harriman heard no more from Roosevelt until nearly midnight; the party for Melby by then was in full swing, and jazz poured out of the Victrola. Roosevelt had cabled, 'I do not wish to delete the word "minor" as it is my desire to consider the Berne misunderstanding a minor incident.' There was nothing more the ambassador could say. He would relay the message to Stalin so the Soviet leader could read it in the morning.

When Kathy heard the telephone ringing at 2 a.m. she thought little of it. Late-night phone calls were not unusual, given the time difference between Moscow and Washington and the Soviet habit of working into the wee hours. But when Kathy went into the room next door and quickly picked up the receiver, before the ringing could deflate the festive atmosphere, she discovered it was neither the White House, nor the State Department, nor the Kremlin on the line. Rather, the operator informed her that it was a woman she knew from the Office of War Information in Washington. That was odd. The OWI was associated with the dissemination of anti-Nazi propaganda but not breaking news. Kathy took the call.

It was desperately urgent, the woman said. Over the background noise of the partygoers and the music at Spaso House, Kathy heard her say that she had just run into someone who had told her the dreadful news. Surely someone would have phoned the embassy by now, but just in case they had not, she decided to call.

The next thing the woman said left Kathy in stunned silence. It was the last news the ambassador's daughter expected to hear at 2 a.m., in the middle of a party. 'Jesus,' she thought. She had to find Averell and get rid of everyone else immediately. There was no way to soften what Kathy had to tell him: Franklin Roosevelt, the man who had led the United States through four years of war to a victory in Europe that was all but assured, was dead. He had died that afternoon, well before his last telegram had even reached Averell.

It was in some ways like the moment they learned about the attack at Pearl Harbor. News of world-shaking events seemed to find them late at night, in the middle of a celebration. Perhaps Kathy should not have been surprised. At Yalta, Roosevelt's face was haggard, grey and drawn. She knew that Averell privately suspected Roosevelt would not live to see the end of his term, but still she could not help but feel dazed. Roosevelt had been president since she was fifteen years old, and, before that, the governor of New York since she was eleven. He was a permanent fixture, a towering presence. His photograph stared at her from the green marble mantle over the Spaso House fireplace. What would become of the Big Three, she wondered. Without Roosevelt, 'that name no longer seem[ed] to have much meaning.'

When she wrote to Pamela two days later, Kathy was still unmoored: 'Somehow I never quite believed that the statesman who made our wheels move could die.' If the post-Yalta honeymoon was fleeting, perhaps Roosevelt's death spelled the end of the marriage too. 'There's no knowing what will happen,' she told Pam, 'our plans included.'

≡

Two days after the shocking news from Warm Springs, the Roosevelts brought FDR's body back to Washington on the presidential train. Eleanor had decided there would be no autopsy, despite the fact that Stalin made it known from Moscow that he thought they should have one, just in case the president had been poisoned. Roosevelt had asked to be buried in Hyde Park, in the rose garden beside his home, but first the nation had to say goodbye. After the funeral procession through the streets of Washington, from Union Station to the White House, Eleanor asked Anna to come into her room. Immediately, Anna noticed her mother's face was 'as stern as [it] could get when she was angry'.

Lucy Mercer had been at Warm Springs the day Franklin died, Eleanor said. Was it true she had come to the White House too? Was Anna the one who had arranged it? There was no reason to deny it; Eleanor already knew the truth. Yes, said Anna. One night, while she was with FDR taking notes, he had asked if she would mind if Lucy came to dinner. That was how it had started. 'It was all above board,' she insisted, reverting to the defensive. 'There were always people around.' But it did not matter. As Anna looked at her mother, she knew she had betrayed her. She feared Eleanor would never forgive her. Eleanor masked her feelings in a dispassionate expression, and the two women went back downstairs, where the service for FDR was about to begin. Anna had been issued an orange-and-white card etched with an image of the White House. At the bottom of the card were the underlined words NOT TRANSFERABLE. It was a ticket to her own father's funeral.

That night, Anna, Eleanor, and Elliott Roosevelt, who had managed to make it back to Washington from England, boarded the presidential train to take Franklin home to Hyde Park. James was racing the nine thousand miles home from Manila for the funeral, but Franklin Jr and John would miss it, as they were at sea. This would be Franklin Roosevelt's – and the Roosevelt family's – final journey home. Eleanor had promised the Trumans they would vacate the White House by the next week, and Franklin had donated the Hyde Park estate to the government for his presidential library and museum. These places that Anna had for so long called home would be home no more.

Anna had ridden this train countless times, all over the country, to take part in FDR's campaigns, to hear speeches, and to meet the regular people the president represented. Now, for the first time, her father would not be in the last car, the *Ferdinand Magellan*, which the Pullman Car Company had specially built for him. Its armoured doors were too narrow for the casket. It appeared that, for this final trip, the president's stateroom would remain empty. But when Anna looked at the Secret Service's list of berths and staterooms to find where she would sleep, she was surprised. Someone had assigned her father's stateroom to her. She would take his place there for one final journey.

As the heavy train lurched north towards the Hudson River Valley, Anna did not sleep. All through the night, she sat on the foot of what had once been her father's berth, staring out the window. Along the tracks from Washington to New York, people stood at attention. They were not soldiers, like those she had seen guarding the roads in the Crimea, but simply American citizens. Children, parents and grandparents lined the tracks the entire night – at eleven o'clock, at two o'clock, even at four – to pay their last respects to the president of the United States.

Three weeks later, Anna was back in Seattle. At last, Johnny was well again, and she and John had decided to return to the place that had once brought them so much happiness. Since her father's funeral, a piece of unfinished business had been tugging at her mind. She picked up the phone and placed a long-distance call to Aiken, South Carolina. To Lucy. Despite Anna's guilt over having betrayed her mother, she knew the grieving Lucy would appreciate this gesture. It was what her father would have wanted. And perhaps it was what Anna needed.

When Lucy picked up the phone, the two women soon found themselves laughing and reminiscing. Anna felt in her heart that she was doing what was right, that the relationship between Lucy and her father was 'an important friendship to both of them'. And with this phone call, she would set it behind her.

But several days later, a letter arrived for Anna from Lucy. 'Anna dear –' the letter began:

Your telephoning the other night meant so much to me. I did not know that it was in me just now to be so glad to hear the sound of any voice – & to hear your laugh – was beyond words wonderful. I had not written before for many many reasons – but you were constantly in my thoughts & with very loving and heart torn sympathy & I was following every step of the way. This blow must be crushing to you – to all of you – but I know that you meant more to your Father than any one and that makes it closer & harder to bear. It must be an endless comfort to you that you were *able* to be with him so much this past year. Every second of the day you must be conscious of the void and emptiness, where there has always been – all through your life – the strength of his beloved presence . . . I love to think of his very great pride in you . . . He told me so often & with such feeling of all that you had meant of joy & comfort on the trip to Yalta. He said you had been so extraordinary & what a difference it made to have you. He told me of your charm & your tact – & of how *every*one loved you. He told how capable you were & how you forgot nothing & of the little typewritten chits he would find at his place at the beginning or end of the day, reminding him of all the little or big things that he was to do. I hope he told *you* these things – but sometimes one doesn't. In any case you must have known – words were not needed between you.

Franklin had never mentioned any of these feelings to Anna. In her heart she had known she had been a help to him, that she had been invaluable in the last weeks of his life. Reading it stated now, in the letter from Lucy, it must have felt as if her father were speaking to her one last time, finally saying what she had yearned to hear for so long.

'The world has lost one of the greatest men that ever lived,' Lucy concluded. 'To me – the greatest. He towers above them all . . . It is a sad inescapable truth that you will now suffer in the sum & measure of your love which was so great. No one can spare you that . . . Forgive me for writing of things which you know so much better than I, & which are sacred, & should not even be touched on by a stranger. I somehow cannot feel myself to be that, & I feel strongly that you understand.

'My love to your husband – and to you – Anna darling, because you are his child & because you are *yourself.*'

Of all the letters Anna ever received, this one perhaps mattered more than any other. She would keep it close for the rest of her life.

Nine months after the early-morning call to Spaso House, Kathy and Averell left Moscow. In the mean time, as Kathy had anticipated, everything changed. The afternoon following the president's death, Averell gave a memorial service for Roosevelt; he read from FDR's D-Day prayer, the radio address Anna had helped craft. Red flags with black borders hung all around the city as a sign of respect for the fallen president, something Kathy had not expected. Averell had been planning to fly to Washington to brief the president on the situation in the Soviet Union – at long last taking Kathy for a much-needed visit home. Roosevelt's death changed those plans. On April 17, Averell did fly to Washington, to brief President Truman for the first time. He left Kathy behind to contemplate the uncertain future – for the world, and for the Harrimans – with a new president at the helm.

Averell promised President Truman he would serve in Moscow for the duration of the war, but he quickly found himself even more isolated in the new administration. If FDR took Averell's advice less often than he should have, the new secretary of state, Jimmy Byrnes, took virtually no advice from him at all. As Averell continued in his thankless task, the Harrimans' friends and family began to prepare for his and Kathy's homecoming. 'When I return to N.Y. I don't think my living at 18 E 68th will work,' Kathy told her sister, referring to the family apartment. 'I'd rather be independent.' Kathy was never one to dwell on memories or to try to force a moment to last. She had lived every day of the past four years for her father, an experience she would cherish, but the world was moving forward, and Kathy would move with it. The war had changed the social fabric of the United States – never before had single women had so much opportunity. Kathy's next adventure was to live for herself.

But Kathy discovered that her independence would have to wait a bit longer. Averell agreed to remain in Moscow several months more, to ease the transition between administrations; she would remain until they finished the job they had begun together. Then, just after the start of the new year, Averell and Kathy were able to leave Moscow.

In January 1946, after almost four years abroad, their extraordinary partnership was at an end. The Harrimans flew home via Japan, Korea, China, San Francisco, and finally New York. Just as they were settling into the new pattern of their lives, two very special, albeit unusual gifts arrived from Moscow. Stalin had sent them two of the Soviet Union's prized horses: Fact, an English-blooded stallion, for Averell, and for Kathy, Boston, a Russian cavalry horse that had heroically charged against the Nazis in the Battle of Stalingrad. Stalin's gift was excessively generous in material terms, but, true to form, thoroughly enigmatic. Did he intend the stallions as a sign of genuine respect? Or were they a gratuity for services rendered, a recognition of the assistance they had given – at times reluctantly, at other times unwittingly – to secure his international standing and his objectives in the postwar world? The Harrimans would never know. As Averell would later state, 'For me Stalin remains the most inscrutable and contradictory character I have known – and leave the final judgment to history.'

After Moscow, Kathy resolved to begin anew and live a life of independence. She rarely addressed her time in Europe during the war, yet, in the years to come, whenever she returned home to Arden House, Stalin's horses would be waiting in their stalls, alongside the polo ponies as a reminder of her former life. Kathy and Averell would mount their horses and ride out into the pastures and over the woodland trails. Though neither father nor daughter was the type to dwell on the past, Stalin's gift would remain a singular reminder of the partnership they had discovered and the extraordinary war years they had spent together.

≡

On the morning of April 17, 1945, the sun was shining through the windows of Sir Christopher Wren's glorious cathedral, St Paul's. Though blackened with ash and soot, its altar destroyed by a German bomb during the Blitz, this building, the pride of London, had survived. Surely it was a divine miracle. Throughout the war, it had served as an inspiration and a comfort for the people of London. Now, with the war in Europe nearly over, St Paul's was filled to bursting with mourners who had gathered to say farewell to Britain's great friend, Franklin Roosevelt.

Churchill had received the news of FDR's death in London, around midnight on April 13. He sat slumped in his chair the rest of the night. The colour had drained from his face; his voice lacked inflection or expressiveness. He wanted to travel to Washington for Roosevelt's funeral. But at the last minute, though a plane was ready and waiting, he decided not to go. With many Cabinet ministers already in the United States for the United Nations conference on April 20 in San Francisco, and with increasingly loud voices calling for a general election in Britain, the turmoil in domestic politics made it impossible to leave. Anthony Eden was going to America for the San Francisco conference. He would represent the prime minister in the United States; Churchill would attend Roosevelt's memorial service in London.

Among the dignitaries who gathered with the prime minister in St Paul's Cathedral that morning were four of the exiled monarchs of Europe – from Norway, Yugoslavia, Greece and Holland – as well as two of Churchill's dearest wartime friends, Ambassador Winant and the king, George VI. The king had brought the queen and their eighteen-year-old daughter, Princess Elizabeth, to pay their respects. Like her father, Princess Elizabeth was in uniform. He wore the simple yet stately regalia of the admiral of the fleet, and she the humble olive-green dress of a mechanic in the Auxiliary Territorial Services. Sarah Churchill, wearing RAF blue, sat beside her father. Clementine was still on her Red Cross goodwill tour of the Soviet Union, so Winston had again recalled Sarah from RAF Medmenham to be his comfort and support: Roosevelt's passing was nothing short of 'a bitter loss to humanity'. Towards the end, the two leaders had had their differences, but to Winston Churchill, Franklin Roosevelt remained 'the greatest American friend we have ever known'.

When the memorial service finished, Ambassador Winant escorted the prime minister down the black-and-white-marble floor of the nave to the door. Sarah followed, clutching the service programme. Once outside, her father stopped, holding the silk top hat of his formal mourning attire. As he stood at the top of the stairs in his frock coat, his famous silhouette framed between two great, blackened columns, a beam of sunlight suddenly illuminated his face. As the light shone upon him, something glinted on his cheek. The prime minister was weeping. After a moment he regained his composure, returned his hat to his head, bid farewell to his companions, and strode bravely down the stairs while Sarah trailed three steps behind. Winston was ending the war just as he began it: out front, and alone.

In 1940, when Churchill had steadfastly condemned the Nazi menace as his colleagues considered signing a peace treaty with their continental foe, the British people rallied behind him, determined never to give in. Now those who had once rushed to support him were deserting him, though the battle was nearly won. Many of his colleagues in Parliament had censured him for the geopolitical decisions made at Yalta, but Sarah knew that alarming developments a thousand miles to the east were not driving this desertion. Most people looked no farther than their own neighbourhood. Some looked no farther than their own home – if they were lucky enough to still have one.

After nearly six years of war, the British people were exhausted. Rationing left them perpetually cold and hungry, while German bombs had created a housing shortage throughout the country. The end of the war gave rise to fears of unemployment. Sarah sensed these concerns among her colleagues, who were not sure what peace in Europe would mean for their unit. Would they be transferred to Pacific work, or would they simply be demobilised? In the military, they could count on steady pay, a place to sleep, and three square meals a day. After demobilisation, what work would there be for the returning battlefield heroes and their unsung counterparts who had waged the war from home?

Sarah returned to RAF Medmenham after the London memorial service and for the next few weeks watched from afar as her father struggled. As the calls for a general election grew louder, support increased for Clement Attlee's Labour Party and the ideals of socialism.

On May 23, two weeks after the Nazis surrendered unconditionally and victory was declared in Europe, the Labour and Liberal members of the wartime coalition government officially resigned, leaving an interim Conservative caretaker ministry to bridge the gap until the July 5 General Election established a newly elected government. Churchill began his month-long campaign on June 4 with a fiery speech denouncing the rising popularity of socialism in Britain. He hoped desperately to convince Labour's followers of the perils that would follow what appeared to be a humanitarian, well-meaning form of socialist government. At Medmenham, Sarah listened intently that night as his voice poured from the radio. Under a socialist regime, he warned, the British democratic tradition of free speech and discourse would give way to a police state. As history had shown, such a government would inevitably lead to a totalitarian state, which would have to 'fall back on some form of *Gestapo*' to enforce its programmes and silence its critics. Civil servants would be 'no longer servants and no longer civil'. These were fierce words fuelled by Churchill's growing alarm over developments in Eastern Europe.

As she listened, Sarah noticed that this was a rare moment when her father's rhetoric was off-tone. Unlike him, she spent her days with working people who had a broad spectrum of views. He needed to speak to them. When the speech ended, she telephoned her father. He had a question for her. If she had been a supporter of the Labour Party, would his speech have persuaded her to change her views? Unfortunately the phone connection was poor, and Winston could not hear her response.

The next morning, Sarah awoke still eager to share her impressions of the speech. Over the course of the war, her confidence had grown, and now she did not shy away from sharing her frank opinions. 'You asked me if I felt influenced?' she began her treatise. 'If I were thinking Labour, I doubt it would have made me vote Conservative.' She understood her father's fears related to socialism, especially in the aftermath of Yalta. But though the speech may have encouraged people to think about socialism in the abstract and accept his viewpoint, abstractions were of little importance to people struggling to feed their children.

'The people I know who are Labour, don't vote Labour for ideals or belief, but simply because life has been hard for them,' she explained. 'They think that only by voting Labour will their daily struggle become easier ... Socialism as practised in the war, did no one any harm, and quite a lot of people good ... What milk there was, was shared equally, the rich didn't die because their meat ration was no larger than the poor; and there is no doubt that this common sharing and feeling of sacrifice was one of the strongest bonds that unified us. So why, they say, cannot this common feeling of sacrifice be made to work as effectively in peace.' She tempered her words a little. 'Don't think I am a rebel!' she urged. She was not becoming a socialist. She understood, though, that he needed to address two bases of Labour support. As for those of an academic, intellectual bent who had embraced Labour – she doubted he could change their minds. But, she said, 'I am worried about the vast unthinking or only superficially thinking public who I repeat are Labour because they believe that only by voting that way will inequalities of opportunity, the privilege of class and money be curbed. I doubt they think any deeper than that, nor do I believe they believe in the pipe dream of a completely equal world. But they do want more, a lot more of everything than they have hitherto had.' Just like the people of Yalta and Sevastopol, the British people held out hope that someday their lives would be a little bit easier and mean a little bit more.

A week later, Sarah received a note from her mother. 'Your Father showed me the excellent letter you wrote to him about his broadcast,' Clementine wrote. 'It made a great impression on him ... it is a very wise and good piece of political writing.' But sentiment had turned decisively against the government and the man who had brought the country through the war to victory. Ten days before the election, Sarah joined her father for a day of campaigning. What she saw and heard broke her heart. She was 'angry and bewildered at the violence and bitterness of the ... personal attacks' on her father, especially from those who had been part of his wartime coalition government. As the election drew near, the vitriol of a tired and hungry public increased. On the last day of his campaign, a crowd of twenty thousand people booed Winston at Walthamstow Stadium.

On July 5, the British people went to the polls, but the results of the election would not be known for another three weeks. Absentee votes from men and women serving in uniform on the other side of the world took time to arrive. In the meantime, Churchill left for Potsdam, a suburb of liberated Berlin, where he was to meet with Stalin and the new American president, Harry Truman. This was to be a longer conference – more than two weeks. The primary objective was to make concrete, specific arrangements for the administration of postwar Germany and the penalties to be imposed on it. This time Winston gave his youngest daughter, Mary, the chance to be his aide. 'I hope the meeting goes well and that you find Truman as good as his messages,' Sarah wrote to her father as he prepared to leave. 'It will be strange the first time you 3 sit down without F.D.R.'

Potsdam was an unusual conference, not least because of FDR's absence. After only a week, it was briefly adjourned, on July 25, so that Winston and Mary could return to Britain for the results of the election the next day. The prime minister was confident that, despite the hostility he had faced the last few weeks, his country would affirm that he would lead the peace as well as he had led the war. He expected to win the day, return to Potsdam, and get back to business without delay.

On the morning of July 26, Sarah was at the hairdresser. She had the day off to be with her family as the tally came in. She felt it an amusingly 'trivial' way to begin such an important day, but she wanted some distraction while anxiously waiting for the results. A radio played as the stylist set her hair, and the announcer was discussing the election. It was too early to make meaningful predictions. But by the time Sarah emerged from under the noisy hairdryer, the announcer's tone had shifted. Early poll numbers were showing 'an overwhelming victory' for Labour. When Sarah left the hairdresser, she glanced around at the crowds in the streets. Word had begun to spread that Labour was in the lead. People 'looked stunned, rather like a child that has pressed the fire alarm bell and is somewhat confused by the promptness with which the fire engine arrives'.

As soon as Sarah reached No. 10 Downing Street, she went directly to the Map Room. Now, instead of war maps, the walls were covered with maps of the British parliamentary constituencies. Her father was sitting at the head of the table; the rest of the Churchill family was gathered around him. As each result was announced and recorded, he nodded his head pensively, making no comment. Before long, it was clear that a Labour 'tidal wave' was underway. As Winston tried to accept the reality of a crushing defeat, he began making jokes, but no one else felt quite up to good humour. Lunch was soon served. Fortunately, the cook had thought to prepare something that could be more easily swallowed than the election results.

After struggling through forlorn conversation, Clementine spoke up and said, 'Winston, this may be a blessing in disguise.'

He looked back at her and replied, 'Well, it is certainly very well disguised.'

Later that night, with defeat firmly written across the election maps on the walls and his resignation tendered to the king, the prime minister gathered his family – Clementine, Sarah, Mary, Randolph, Diana and her husband, Duncan Sandys, and Winston's younger brother, Jack – and began to daydream about returning home to his beloved Chartwell and its idyllic pastoral charm. Perhaps, he mused, they might even keep the family together all the time. Each of his children and their families could have their own little cottage down the hill from the main house, he mused. They could call it the 'Chartwell Colony'.

For the rest of the evening they sat together, each struggling to come to terms with the overwhelming defeat. Sarah and Mary had changed into fashionable evening gowns at dinner to infuse the gathering with some cheer, but the trimmings did little to brighten the moment. As ever, Clementine maintained a dignified composure. Diana was terribly pale, while Mary was clearly overcome with disappointment. After their mother, Mary said, Sarah was the bravest. Sarah's stiff upper lip quivered only slightly as she fought to summon her characteristic confidence in a better future. Rather than dwell on defeat, she began to dream of her father's bucolic paradise.

Though the results were devastating for her father, Sarah could not feel regret as she thought about the past five years. The war had been a shattering tragedy, but strangely, it had given her a certain contentment that she had never known as a child, especially in moments such as this one, as she sat beside her parents. 'The real happiness of these last years,' she had written to Clementine shortly after returning from Yalta, 'has been getting to know both you and Papa – I have always loved you, but not always known you, and this sudden discovery . . . is like stumbling on a gold mine!' For a little girl who always felt she was the 'loner', who was so nervous in front of her father that she could not speak in his presence and resorted to writing notes to him, it had been an invaluable and exhilarating discovery, not only of her father but also of herself.

The next morning, when she wrote Winston a letter, it was not because she was afraid to speak. What she wanted to say was too important to relegate to ephemeral spoken words. She wanted her father to see, to hold in his hands, what exactly these last years had meant to her.

'My darling darling darling Papa,' she began. 'You won't forget what you said last night – about the Chartwell Colony? Will you? No lovelier plot of land exists, and there would be plenty of space and we could till the land and milk the cows and feed the chickens and you could have an enormous bell you clanged when you wanted to see us. We would emerge from our little cottages . . . and we could all have an evening together – and when do we really have better ones?' Then she turned to the bitter disappointment of the election. Though the abandonment of the leadership that had brought the country through the war was shocking, Sarah still believed the people had not turned on her father. She repeated her belief that they were simply desperate for a better life, and thought the key to that better life was change. 'Whatever convulsion has taken place,' she reassured him, 'I know you are as high in their hearts as you ever were.' Being at his side these past years had given Sarah the greatest joy of her life, but at this moment, Sarah was not thinking of herself. She considered only her father. Above all others, he would always hold the highest place in her heart.

'You know your saying, "In war resolution – in peace goodwill – in victory magnanimity – in defeat defiance" – well, you taught me a great thing last night – in defeat – humour!' she wrote. 'The other thing that has been running through my head, has been a bit out of my favourite prayer – "To give and not to count the cost/To fight and not to heed the wounds/To toil and not to seek for rest/To labour and not to ask for any reward" – Well that is certainly your war record.'

These realisations were, for Sarah, the gift of the war years spent at her father's side. The war had taken her from the lowest point of her life to the summit of the world, but what mattered to Sarah more than the glamorous banquets, the travel to far-flung reaches of the earth, the privileged information, or the chance to meet the leaders whom history long would remember was the relationship she had built with her father.

Sarah closed her letter, the feelings she had so long wished to convey to her father now finally to be set in front of him, not with a shaking hand on a scrap of paper but written boldly, with confidence. 'God bless you darling. All my love to you . . . you're terrific . . . Wow wow and rewow forever.'

After Yalta

The Yalta Agreement has become something of a legend,' said the newscaster Chet Huntley on the Thursday evening ABC Radio broadcast of June 28, 1951. 'Sometimes the Yalta Agreement is defended. In most cases it's criticized and pointed to as a blunder in American diplomacy.' That statement could have applied just as easily to Britain. In its immediate aftermath, Yalta was seen as the high-water mark of wartime Allied unity. Just a few years later, Yalta seemed to tell a completely different story. It was not the pinnacle of cooperation, but rather the moment when the Allies teetered between World War and Cold War. Decades on, hindsight has allowed for new interpretations. Some see Yalta as a second Munich, a sellout to a deadly enemy; the joys of a short-term peace drowned by the fear, war and tragedy that followed. Others see it as fated, the inevitable outcome of a world stretched between two poles where the decisions of individuals could do little to mitigate geopolitical forces in play for centuries.

Yalta has also inspired a flurry of counterfactuals – questions asking 'What if?' What if Roosevelt had not been so ill? What if he had died in his third term and Henry Wallace had become president? What if the Allies had walked away with no deal? What if Churchill and Roosevelt had threatened Stalin with war? Though intriguing, such ponderings are unproductive. As Huntley affirmed in his broadcast, Yalta 'was not an isolated affair. To a great degree it was the product of what had gone before.' Because the Red Army had gained control across East-ern Europe, the western Allies could do little to force Stalin to coop-erate, short of threatening, or declaring, war. Europe had known five years of armed conflict; there was little appetite for more. Perhaps the only way the Red Army could have been kept from planting its boots across Europe, in places such as Poland, Romania and Hungary, was opening a second front in France, as much as two years earlier. But in 1942, American soldiers were not prepared for such an invasion, nor was American industry well enough mobilised to equip a joint British and American invasion force on the Western Front – while also fight-ing a war against Japan. That begs another question. What might have happened if both Britain and the United States had mobilised sooner? And thus the counterfactual spiral goes, an endless cycle of questions with no answers.

What might have happened is of little consequence in light of what did.

On August 6, 1945, the Americans dropped the atomic bomb on Hi-roshima. Two days later, the Soviet Union declared war on Japan. The next day, the Americans dropped a second atomic bomb, this time on Nagasaki. On August 15, the Japanese surrendered. As the final com-mon enemy was vanquished, any pretence of a continuing partnership between East and West quickly evaporated. While Stalin was alive, some hope remained that the Soviet Union could be persuaded to co-operate; after his death, in 1953, that illusion was gone.

Averell Harriman would comment, in retrospect, that he did not believe Stalin signed the Yalta agreements intending to flout them within a matter of months. Initially, said Harriman, Stalin 'mistakenly believed that there was little risk in promising free elections' in places like Poland 'because the Communists were popular enough to win'. After all, the Red Army was Poland's saviour and liberator. But Stalin gravely overestimated the Soviets' popularity. When Soviet will was re-sisted, he proceeded to break nearly every agreement in the Yalta ac-cords. In Poland, there were no elections until 1947, and those were anything but free. The Communists consolidated power, and Poland fell decisively into what George Kennan had predicted would be the Soviet sphere of influence. So too did eastern Germany, the zone the

Soviets had been tasked to administer in the period of postwar rehabilitation. Despite the guarantees of the Declaration on Liberated Europe, there was precious little the western Allies or Roosevelt's nascent
peace organisation, the United Nations, could do to secure the right to
self-determination for eastern European countries being swallowed
up by the Soviet Union one by one. Nor did the Soviets stop when confronted by Europe's borders. Soviet influence quickly spread across
China and parts of Vietnam and Korea.

In March 1946, barely a year after the Yalta Conference and at President Truman's encouragement, Winston Churchill addressed a crowd
at a little college in the town of Fulton in Truman's home state of Mis-
souri. There Churchill offered one of his most enduring statements:
'From Stettin in the Baltic to Trieste in the Adriatic an iron curtain has
descended across the Continent.' Fifteen years later, with the world
locked in the Cold War, that curtain became a physical wall dividing
East and West Berlin.

Though the Yalta agreements quickly crumbled, the good intentions behind them might have better endured in the public memory
had more of its chief architects lived to defend them. Less than five
years after Yalta, three principal American participants had died: FDR
in 1945, Harry Hopkins in 1946, and Edward Stettinius in 1949. Instead,
Yalta's legacy became tainted with charges of Soviet espionage when
Alger Hiss, Stettinius's assistant and secretary-general of the first gathering to organise the United Nations, was accused of being a Soviet
spy. In 1948, the long-suffering Whittaker Chambers denounced him
before the House Committee on Un-American Activities. But the stat-
ute of limitations for espionage had run out. At trial, the grand jury
could charge Hiss only with two counts of perjury – lying under oath.
He was sentenced to five years in jail. Though Hiss's supporters continued to insist he was innocent, documents later made public by the
CIA revealed conclusive evidence that Hiss had indeed been a Soviet
spy since the mid-1930s and through the Yalta period. Though it is unknown if Hiss undertook any espionage specifically at Yalta, the notion that the Soviets had agents embedded within the American delegation further discredited the conference.

In Britain, a large amount of the backlash against Yalta was driven by a decision not actually part of the protocol signed by the three Allied leaders: the repatriation of hundreds of thousands of Soviet and eastern European POWs and displaced persons – in some cases forcibly – who did not wish to return. Scores were sent to the gulags or killed. In 1980 Prime Minister Margaret Thatcher approved a memorial to their memory. In a testament to the divisiveness of Yalta's legacy, the original memorial was vandalised and damaged irreparably. In 1986, it was replaced. The new one stands in a small park across the street from London's Victoria and Albert Museum.

For many, the postwar period and the Cold War cemented Yalta as a turning point in the clash between nations, hemispheres and ideologies. Indeed, it is no coincidence that the area of the Crimea surrounding Yalta itself continues to be a geopolitical flashpoint in tensions between Russia and the West. Beginning in 2014, with Putin's annexation of the Crimea from Ukraine, hostilities flared once again. The United Nations quickly condemned this action and has adopted multiple resolutions, as recently as December 2019, calling for Russian armed forces to withdraw.

However, beneath geopolitics lie personal relationships. Entwined within the story of the end of one war and the beginning of another, there is also the story of three sets of fathers and daughters – fathers and daughters whose relationships were tested and strengthened by the history they experienced together.

Like many women, each of the three daughters found that the war allowed her a brief moment to engage talents that might have gone unrealised and to work in roles that would have otherwise been closed to her – Sarah in the WAAFs, Kathleen as a journalist, and Anna as a White House aide. The war allowed them to travel in countries with customs and traditions different from their own. Agents of diplomacy, they could sit at the table alongside world leaders at a time when female diplomats were few and far between. Though a handful of women had served in the American Foreign Service beginning in the 1920s, it was not until 1949, when President Truman appointed Helen Eugenie Moore Anderson as chief of mission in Denmark, that a woman would serve as an ambassador. In Britain, progress was even slower. Women were not allowed to join the diplomatic service until 1946, and not until 1976 would Britain have its first female ambassador – Anne Warburton, coincidentally also in Denmark.

For Sarah Churchill, Kathleen Harriman and Anna Roosevelt, Yalta allowed them to become indispensable to the fathers whose love, recognition and esteem they craved above all. It gave Sarah the chance to become the person who served as an extension of Winston's brain, to be the one who walked 'in silent step' with him, who left him secure in the knowledge that there was someone beside him who understood his every thought and emotion. Ever since the days Sarah had worked as Winston's bricklaying assistant, keeping the plumb line straight and true, that was all she had wanted. For Kathleen, it was the realisation of Averell's prediction that someday they would become 'the finest & best of friends'. The war gave both of them a chance at a partnership more meaningful than either could have predicted. For Anna, the war was her last, desperate chance to satisfy a lifelong dream of being close to and acknowledged by her father, from whom she had long been separated by a closed door. She had waited nearly a quarter of a century to capture the dream that had eluded her since childhood, and for a brief moment, she did.

Several months after the war, as Winston was reminiscing wistfully, he offered Sarah a word of wisdom. 'Out of a life of long and varied experience,' he said, 'the most valuable piece of experience I can hand on to you is to know how to command the moment to remain.' But for all his worldly experience, not even Winston Churchill, let alone his daughter, could make the moment last. As quickly as it had opened, the window of wartime opportunity closed. The world moved on, and the fathers and daughters had to move with it. Yet, as if bound by their wartime experience, the lives of these three daughters and their families would continue to intersect in the years to come. All three women would also come to know the pain of the invisible scars that the war had left behind, which touched each of them and the people they loved.

Upon returning home to New York in 1946, Kathleen Harriman conclusively decided that after living the life of a diplomat in Moscow, she had no interest in pursuing diplomacy as a career. She joked to her sister that the job 'involves too damned much tea and cookie pushing'. Instead, Kathy resumed work as a journalist for *Newsweek*. Meanwhile, Averell briefly returned to London to assume the role of ambassador to the Court of St James's when Gil Winant departed, in April 1946. This time, Kathy stayed behind. It was just as well. Averell remained in London only five months, returning that October to become Truman's secretary of commerce.

During that time in London, Averell did not renew his affair with Pamela Churchill. The unusual circumstances that had brought them together were now in the past, and Averell had reconciled with his wife, Marie. Coincidentally, Pamela spent much of that time in New York, where she promptly sought out her dear friend Kathy. Pamela confided in Kathy that she had run out of money. She and Randolph had officially divorced, and she was struggling to make ends meet while raising little Winston. Kathy, who felt sorry for her friend, had either forgotten about Averell's ongoing financial arrangement with Pamela or felt it was insufficient. Whatever the reason, she offered Pamela her *Newsweek* salary. Pamela was only too pleased to accept.

Pamela may have felt it an equitable arrangement, a sort of finder's fee, for it was Pamela who introduced Kathy to the man she would marry. One night while Pamela was in New York, she was out on a date with Henry Mortimer, the grandson of the founder of Standard Oil of California and a descendant of the founding father John Jay. They met up at the St. Regis Hotel. Pamela brought Kathy, and Henry brought his older brother, Stanley, who had also casually dated Pamela. Stanley was recently divorced from his wife, Babe Cushing, with whom he had two children, Stanley III and Amanda. Babe had left him to marry one of Pamela's many erstwhile suitors, the CBS chief, Bill Paley. Most men fell victim to Pamela's charms, but Stanley was instead taken with the slim American brunette. Stanley and Kathy were neighbours of a sort. He had grown up in fashionable Tuxedo Park, New York, not far from Arden House, but somehow the two had never met. Before long, Stanley was smitten. A year and a half later, wedding announcements were in the mail. Among the recipients were President Truman; former president Herbert Hoover; Generals Eisenhower, Marshall and MacArthur; the entire Supreme Court; J. Edgar Hoover; Frances

Perkins; the Canadian prime minister, Mackenzie King; numerous foreign ambassadors and Cabinet secretaries; the Yalta delegates Admiral Leahy, Chip Bohlen and Jimmy Byrnes; and a host of the Harrimans' British friends, including Anthony Eden, Peter Portal, Lord Beaverbrook and of course, the Right Honourable Winston S. Churchill. But not Joseph Stalin.

As Kathy and Stanley settled into married life, Averell continued in his career in government and public service. He became the coordinator of the Marshall Plan, a $12 billion aid package created in 1948 to spur western European postwar economic recovery, and special assistant to the president. In 1952, he ran in the primaries as a Democratic candidate for president of the United States. Though his bid to become his party's nominee was unsuccessful, he was elected governor of New York in 1954, beating out Kathy's one-time flame, Franklin D. Roosevelt Jr. In 1956 Averell once again failed in his bid to become the presidential nominee and never ran for elected office again, but he became one of the 'Wise Men' of the Cold War – an adviser, ambassador-at-large and elder statesman throughout the Kennedy and Johnson administrations. He served as the personal representative of President Johnson during peace talks with North Vietnam. In 1968, he was appointed chairman of the President's Commission of the Observance of the Human Rights Year. Anna Roosevelt was his vice chairman. After Yalta, they remained lifelong friends. In 1969 Averell Harriman received the Presidential Medal of Freedom.

True to her word, Kathy left politics and diplomacy to her father. After her marriage, she eschewed public attention. Instead, she dedicated herself to philanthropy (particularly to the board of her alma mater, Bennington College), to skiing, to her beloved horses and hunting dogs, and especially to her family – her husband, Stanley; her sons, David, Jay and Averell (nicknamed Avie); and her stepchildren, Stanley and Amanda. Avie maintained it was their mother, an avid sportswoman well into her eighties, who had taught their father to shoot.

As a philanthropist Kathy served as a board member of the Visiting Nurse Service of New York and the Foundation for Child Development. Aside from brief moments campaigning for Averell, Kathy never again served as her father's foremost partner in business or in politics, and she rarely addressed her experiences during the war. While many would have been tempted to share personal tales of adventures with Churchill, Roosevelt and Stalin, she, like so many in her generation, was humble and discreet about what she had witnessed. She simply never believed she was particularly important. There was also a practical side to her reticence. During a speech about Russia given at a dinner for Bennington College in New York in 1946, one of the rare occasions when she spoke publicly about the war, she described why she was so reluctant to discuss her time in Moscow. 'Everyone has preconceived ideas,' she explained. 'People one talks to invariably wish to have their particular notions backed up – whether they're true or false. To some, if I fail to portray Russia as a nation of blackguards I get damned as a would be commie. Other times if I don't create the image of a noble experiment – I find myself called a Russian baiter.'

Her feelings on the matter were vindicated in 1952, when she was called to give testimony before Congress during a House Select Committee investigation of the Katyn Forest Massacre. Despite extreme pressure from members of Congress to concede that she had purposely obscured the fact that the Soviets had murdered the Polish officers, Kathy remained steadfast. She affirmed that she had reported only what she had seen and could have known at the time. She did acknowledge the new, conclusive evidence, which demonstrated, without a doubt, that the Soviets had committed the atrocities. After the hearing she never discussed the matter again. Such restraint was consistent with Kathy's tendency to compartmentalise different parts of her life. She simply chose to look past whatever was irrelevant or uncomfortable in her present situation and move on. So tight-lipped was Kathy about her extraordinary time with her father and her own remarkable contributions that her sons knew little more than the fact that she had been in London and Moscow during the war. In certain moments, though, they would catch a glimpse of her earlier life, such as when she tucked her sons into bed and wished them '*Spokoynoy nochi*' – a Russian 'good night'. It was not until after she died in 2011, at the age of ninety-three, that David discovered a trove of letters shoved in the back of a closet. They were the ones that Kathy had written to her sister during the war. The discovery of these letters gave her sons the opportunity to appreciate, in an entirely new way, the fascinating woman who was their mother.

Though Kathy did not form close lifelong friendships with Anna Roosevelt or Sarah Churchill, it was only inevitable that the Harrimans and the Churchills would be bound to each other by a single significant person: Pamela. In 1971, thirty years after their first encounter, Averell and Pamela found themselves together again at a dinner party at the home of *Washington Post* publisher Kay Graham in Washington, D.C. They had not seen each other for many years. Averell was a widower; his wife, Marie, had died the year before. Pamela was a widow. After a number of affairs, she had married again. Her second husband, the American Broadway producer Leland Hayward, had just died. Though Pamela was fifty-one and Averell nearly eighty, it felt as if no time had passed since that fateful evening in London, with bombs dropping all around. The romance was rekindled, and they married later that year.

Kathy's one-time best friend was now her stepmother. Though it never became overtly inimical, the relationship between the two women changed in tone after Pamela's marriage to Kathy's father. Pamela had grown up in the English countryside, but she did not take well to the Harrimans' preference for simple country living and athletic pursuits at Arden. More important, with Pamela's constant presence, it became nearly impossible for Kathy to speak with her father alone. This new dynamic between the two women was perhaps best captured by an episode one Christmas, when Averell and Pamela arrived for lunch at Kathy and Stanley's Arden cottage. Kathy was arranging some hors d'oeuvres on the table. Just as she set down a plate of pâté, one of her many beloved dogs wandered in. Smelling something delicious, he jumped up to the table and snatched the pâté. In an instant, Kathy spun around, grabbed the dog by the ruff of its neck, and pried the food from its jaws. Then, in a single motion, she stood up, put the pâté back on the serving plate, turned to Pamela, and said, 'Wouldn't [you] like some of our delicious French pâté?' From then on, whenever she came to Kathy's house for lunch, Pamela remained suspicious of what she was being served.

All the while, Averell adored Pamela. She made him feel like a young man with many years ahead. They had fifteen happy years together, but when Averell eventually died in 1986 at the age of ninety-four, it was not without controversy. Noting that his daughters were well provided for, he decided to leave his fortune to his widow. By then, Pamela, having become an American citizen, was a force in the Democratic Party as a key fundraiser. In 1993, President Clinton named her ambassador to France. But Pamela had never lost her taste for the good life, and in the face of lavish spending and poor investments, Averell's once immense legacy quickly dwindled. As part of the Harriman family trust, Kathy and her sister Mary sued Pamela for financial mismanagement and eventually settled. In February 1997, Pamela was swimming in the pool at the Paris Ritz when she suffered a cerebral haemorrhage and died. In her will, she made two notable bequests: she had pledged Van Gogh's *Roses*, a still-life masterwork Averell had acquired during his honeymoon with Marie in 1930, to the National Gallery of Art in Washington, D.C. Her will completed the gift. And what remained of the Harriman fortune she left to her only child, Winston S. Churchill II, and his family.

The suddenness of FDR's death and the transition to the postwar world threw Anna into unfamiliar territory. For her entire adult life, her father's dominance on the state, national and global stage had defined her identity. What defined it now? After returning to Seattle, Anna and John hoped to resume work at the *Seattle Post-Intelligencer* but quickly discovered that the paper's owner, William Randolph Hearst, had little use for them. They had previously been the daughter and son-in-law of the president. Now they were just two ordinary people of reasonable but not extraordinary editorial talent and experience. The paper did not need them.

Anna and John decided to strike out on their own. It was prohibitively expensive to launch a newspaper from the ground up, so they looked to purchase one. They found a free weekly paper, the *Phoenix Shopping News*, in Arizona, and with the financial backing of wealthy and influential Democratic friends, they bought it and rechristened it the *Arizona Times.* Almost immediately, they ran into difficulties. First, they had launched a Democrat-leaning newspaper in a Republican-leaning city. The paper they had purchased also lacked printing equipment and other machinery, so they had to invest enormous amounts of capital to procure them. These problems were compounded by a shortage of paper products and newsprint in the United States. Months went by and circulation failed to grow at the rate they had hoped. Unable to repay their investors, the couple fell into debt.

Meanwhile, there was something the matter with John. He had not been right since he had deployed during the war. After FDR's death, he, even more than Anna, struggled to find a place for himself. Though he had been a successful journalist during the Great Depression, he was plagued with self-doubt. He feared that people valued him only for the access to the president that he could provide. Now he was no longer anyone's valuable son-in-law. Anna's heart broke as she watched her husband, the great love of her life, sink further and further into depression. He became a stranger to her. She begged him to seek help, but he refused. Psychiatrists were only for 'crazy people', he insisted. As John became increasingly unstable, Anna began to fear him. She told him to go away for a while to find some peace. While he was gone, Anna assumed the duties of editor and publisher of their paper and tried to keep the creditors at bay.

John's depression undoubtedly had something to do with what he had witnessed during his wartime service in North Africa and the Mediterranean, as well as with his sudden loss of identity after Roosevelt's death. But in her most honest moments, Anna recognised that John's problems had started long before. Anna had been repressing painful memories dating back to the early years of the war. These memories had to do with her daughter, Ellie, when they lived on Mercer Island, near Seattle. As Ellie would later recall, John Boettiger would come 'into my room once or twice a week when I was fifteen or sixteen when I was doing my homework', while Anna was downstairs preparing dinner. 'John would put his hands down the front of my blouse and start massaging my breasts,' she explained. Ellie 'knew it was wrong, but didn't know what [she] should do about it'. If she had screamed, the Secret Service guard outside would have heard her, and perhaps if her stepfather had gone further, she might have. Instead, Ellie would beg him, 'Please go, Popsey, I have lots of homework to do,' and eventually, after five or ten minutes, he would leave. All that time, Ellie feared her mother would be devastated if she knew, as Anna had such great love for John, so she did not tell her. A small part of her also worried that if she told Anna, 'maybe she wouldn't believe me'. Ellie also did not know how to reconcile her stepfather's acts with the love she and her brothers had for John, who was much more a father to her than her real father, Curtis Dall. 'Even if great love is supposed to exist,' Ellie would later say, after such an experience 'a place is set aside for fear.'

But all the while, Anna knew. She never told Ellie, but in private, Anna had confronted John about his actions. When she did, he simply told her he was 'trying to teach [Ellie] about sex'. Anna did not know what to do. Paralysed, she did nothing. Soon, Ellie went off to boarding school in San Francisco – where she was a student during her mother's time at Yalta – and then to Reed College. Anna hoped the problem had come to an end. But when Ellie came home to Arizona on school holidays, she was afraid. There was an intercom in their house, and at night, unbeknown to Ellie, Anna asked her older son, Curtis, to keep it switched on in his room and told him that if he heard a noise coming from the bedrooms, he was to come right away and knock on her door. Fortunately, John made no more 'passes' at Ellie, as she chose to call them, but she would bear the memories of that fear and abuse for the rest of her life.

In 1948, Ellie married her Reed College classmate Van Seagraves, and soon she had a home of her own. The night before Ellie gave birth to her first child, in August 1949, Anna confessed to Ellie that she knew what John had done. Ellie came to realize that Anna 'was afraid of John because she knew he was,' as Ellie called it, 'mentally quirky and sometimes unstable.' Throughout her life, Anna repeatedly found herself in the position of feeling forced to choose among the people closest to her. At Yalta, she felt she had to protect her father to the detriment of his relationships with his closest ally, Winston Churchill, and his closest adviser, Harry Hopkins. During the Lucy Mercer affair, she found herself keeping one parent's secret while betraying the other. And with John and Ellie, she made the decision to protect her husband and safeguard her marriage rather than face a second divorce and uproot her children. Perhaps seeing Ellie as she was about to become a mother made Anna ashamed that she had failed to protect her daughter when she had needed a mother most. That night, Ellie finally understood the burdens Anna had carried. Though Ellie could have dwelled on hurt and resentment, this newfound understanding of her mother and the profound experience of becoming a mother herself brought the two women closer. Five years earlier, when Anna returned from Yalta, she had given Ellie the little clay figurine of a mother holding a child, the one Averell Harriman had presented to her. She sent it to her daughter as a present for her eighteenth birthday. When Ellie first received it, she thought it a 'funny little doll'. After Anna's revelation to Ellie and the birth of her first child, perhaps it took on new significance. To this day, Ellie keeps it on the mantel above her fireplace, prominently displayed as a reminder of her mother.

In 1949, Anna and John divorced. The newspaper failed. Anna took Johnny away to Los Angeles. By that time, Anna and her mother had reconciled, and for a year the two collaborated on a joint radio show, the *Eleanor and Anna Roosevelt Program*. For a time, Anna also edited a magazine called *The Woman*. Anna soon learned that John had remarried and found work with a public relations firm in New York, but still he refused to seek psychiatric help. On Halloween 1950, John committed suicide by jumping from the window of a New York hotel. Anna's brother Elliott identified the body. Anna and John's son, Johnny, was eleven years old.

In 1952, Anna married James Halsted, a doctor working for the Veterans Administration. They moved back to New York, and Anna took up work in public relations for hospitals and medical centres. In 1958, they embarked on a new adventure and moved for two years to Iran, where, as a visiting professor on a Fulbright grant, Jim helped establish a hospital. When they returned to the United States, Anna immersed herself in humanitarian work, contributing to the legacy of both her father and her mother, who had become a force in her own right. After FDR's death, Eleanor served as a delegate to the United Nations General Assembly and as the U.S. representative to the United Nations Commission on Human Rights; she died in 1962. In 1963, President Kennedy appointed Anna to the Citizen's Advisory Council on the Status of Women, and, following in her mother's footsteps, she joined Averell Harriman on the President's Commission for the Observance of Human Rights. In these roles, Anna no longer had to choose between supporting her father or her mother. She could celebrate the lives and achievements of both. For the rest of her life, Anna remained a citizen of the world, an advocate for the betterment of humanity, and a passionate participant in discussions of global affairs both large and small.

Alongside the fulfilment Anna found professionally and in her marriage to Jim Halsted, those consequential weeks of 1945 were always with her. From time to time, she found herself in the midst of controversial debates surrounding FDR's final year. Anna was always quick to defend her father and his legacy, not least regarding Yalta. During the Cold War, the Yalta Conference became a political football, an easy target for criticism. Those wishing to distance themselves from any whiff of support for Communism accused the Roosevelt administration of having shown excessive sympathy for their adversary in the East. For example, in 1951, the Republican senator Robert Taft, son of President William Howard Taft and a presidential hopeful himself, began to spread such ideas about Yalta as he explored a run at the Republican nomination. Anna promptly wrote to him to correct the 'inaccuracies, innuendoes, and half truths concerning the Yalta Conference'. She defended not only her father but also Averell Harriman and Harry Hopkins.

There was also the matter of her father's health. Every few years, a supposed medical expert would publish 'scurrilous material' offering new explanations for Roosevelt's death. Though they stopped short of Stalinesque conspiracy theories about poison, they posthumously diagnosed him with everything from a series of strokes to a cancerous brain tumour. As FDR's medical records had mysteriously disappeared shortly after his death (some suspected at the hands of Dr Ross McIntire), there was no way to put the rumours to rest conclusively. Finally, Anna encouraged Dr Howard Bruenn to write a definitive account of FDR's health in the last year of his life, including his cause of death. In 1970, Bruenn published the article 'Clinical Notes on the Illness and Death of President Franklin D. Roosevelt', in *The Annals of Internal*

Medicine. After suffering from acute congestive heart failure, FDR had died of a massive cerebral haemorrhage. As Bruenn stated in the article, he did not feel that at any time Roosevelt's heart failure impeded his brain function or prevented him from doing his job to the best of his ability. Anna felt that Bruenn's article was 'proper and important', and she was grateful that Bruenn had finally put the matter to rest.

Even long after her father was gone, Anna enjoyed being in the midst of discussions central to FDR's world. When her children would come to visit in Hillsdale, New York, where Anna and Jim retired, she would cook a family meal. While the food was on the stove or in the oven, she would linger in the doorway, cigarette in hand, halfway between the kitchen and the living room as if a young girl again – eager to be part of the conversation about politics and global affairs and yet always somewhat on the fringe.

In 1975, thirty years after Yalta, Anna died of throat cancer at the age of sixty-nine. In yet another example of the perpetually intertwined nature of these families, after her death, her husband, Jim, married Harry Hopkins's daughter, Diana. Shortly before she died, Anna addressed an audience at Hunter College in New York City and shared some reflections on her life and her parents. She was unflinchingly honest about her adoration of FDR: 'For my father I had throughout his life the greatest of admiration and love, and wanted very much to please him and win his approval.' As her son Johnny maintained, each of Anna's husbands 'knew in some sense that there was one man above all who was expressive of her truest and strongest devotion'. For Anna, the time she spent with and the memories she cherished of her father would always be 'the gift of her life'.

After the shock of the election in July 1945, Winston struggled to cope with the landslide defeat. He knew he had to get away. Field Marshal Harold Alexander had a house in Italy on Lake Como. He offered it to Churchill as a quiet retreat for a month-long holiday in September; the former prime minister eagerly accepted. He would exchange his newspapers and daily red boxes full of government business for canvases, brushes, and several weeks of peace, quiet and painting. But he did not want to be alone for that month as he made his way in his new world. Clementine was too busy to accompany him; she was arranging for a new flat in London and opening Chartwell for their return. Once again, as Winston contemplated an uncertain future, he turned to Sarah. They had one last journey to make together.

When Sarah learned he had chosen her to go with him, she 'burst into pent up tears'. Though she was still actively serving as a WAAF and would not be demobilised until later that year, there was little for her to do, so her commanding officer granted her leave to accompany her father, 'not officially this time, simply as his daughter'. As Winston painted, Sarah sat beside him in the warm sun in quiet contemplation, relishing the happiness of being together. As they neared the end of their holiday, Winston wrote to Clementine, 'Sarah has been a joy. She is so thoughtful, tactful, amusing, and gay. The stay here would have been wrecked without her.' With Sarah at his side, Winston was beginning to settle into a new pace of life. One evening, as the crickets sang in the cool night air, he said to Sarah, 'I've had a happy day.' Sarah had lost track of how long it had been since she had last heard him say that.

When Sarah was finally demobilised from the WAAFs, in December 1945, she assumed she would return to the stage, but a telephone call changed everything. Acting in films had never held much appeal for her, but an Italian director, Mario Soldati, wanted to cast her as the star of his film *Daniele Cortis*. At first, Sarah felt uncomfortable about working in a former enemy nation so soon after the end of the war, but her father encouraged her to take the role. 'It is part of the victor's job to help the defeated,' he told her. Collaboration between Italian cinema and the prime minister's daughter would represent a sort of cross-cultural healing. But it also meant she would be away from the people she loved – her family, and also Gil Winant.

Sarah's marriage to Vic Oliver was officially dissolved in October 1945. When the papers came through, Sarah was at home with her parents. Her father beckoned her to come over to where he was sitting across the room and whispered in her ear, 'Free!' But Sarah had a sinking feeling that she was not really free. 'For the moment I am more or less free,' she later wrote to Winston from Italy, 'but then only at some-one else's expense.' She went on to tell her father, 'It seems I must always hurt the person who loves me.' Although Vic Oliver betrayed Sarah's feelings, both as an actor and a spouse, it seems that Sarah felt that the breakdown of their marriage was somehow her fault. She was also beginning to look at a postwar relationship with Gil Winant with apprehension. In the middle of 1944, Sarah had begun to develop an inkling of concern about Winant. At the time, his son was still a prisoner of the Germans, but perhaps Sarah sensed something more when she wrote to Harry Hopkins, 'Between you and me, I don't think he's too well . . . but don't say I said so.' When Sarah finished filming *Daniele Cortis*, Winant came to Italy to see her. He had stepped down as ambassador and had returned home to New Hampshire to write a memoir of his war years. But after the intensity of life during the war, Winant was struggling to adapt to the quiet of the peace. Estranged from his wife and in debt, Winant arrived in Italy deeply depressed and desperate to renew his relationship with Sarah. When her mother wrote, asking when she was coming home, Sarah responded, 'Gil needs me terribly – to help him with his proofs of his book – he has lost heart over it . . . He is so ill and despairing, and harassed about his book – that I must do something about that first.' Before she contemplated their relationship any further, his memoir, she resolved, 'must not be a failure'. Winant was not the only person struggling over his war memoirs. Her father was fighting with his editors concerning his own: 'Listen to a very few,' she urged Winston. 'Write this book from the heart of yourself.'

Sarah was eager to help Winant in hopes of reviving his spirits, but when it came to marrying him, something he had long desired, she could not say yes. She was out in the world on her own for the first time. She did love him, but she was not ready to remarry. Winant returned home disappointed.

On November 19, 1947, Sarah found herself in St Paul's Cathedral for a memorial service for the second time in two years. London was mourning the death of another beloved American: Winant. Two weeks earlier, on the very day his memoir was published, Winant had locked himself in his grown son's old bedroom, took out a pistol, and shot himself. As the Royal Air Force orchestra played the haunting strains of Elgar's 'Enigma Variations', Sarah felt Winant's death was her fault, that if she had agreed to marry him, she could have saved him from his depression. It reinforced her belief that she could not help but bring unhappiness to those who loved her.

In time Sarah found love again, this time with the British society photographer Antony Beauchamp. In 1951, they decided to elope while on holiday at the Cloister in Sea Island, Georgia. For a time, Sarah was swept up in the rush of new love and professional success. She and Antony moved to Los Angeles, where Sarah made a breakthrough – cast opposite her childhood idol, the Hollywood legend and master of dance Fred Astaire, in the film *Royal Wedding*. The only thing that could have made her happiness complete that year was if she could have been with her father to celebrate his return to No. 10 Downing Street, when he became prime minister for a second time. Whenever she returned home, he was the first person she wanted to see. She would fly up three flights of stairs and burst into his room, exclaiming, 'Wow, Papa!' and curl up at his feet. His face would light up, and they would talk and laugh, just as they had during the war.

But Sarah's happiness was only temporary. In 1957, after only six years of marriage, Beauchamp committed suicide with an overdose of sleeping pills. After his death, Sarah received a note of sympathy from someone who understood her pain: 'Life can be very tough on one (including the papers and its appendages), but, knowing you, I know you can meet it,' wrote Anna Roosevelt.

It was a grim twist of fate, a reminder that wartime sacrifices continued to take a toll. The impact of war on mental health, then so little understood, affected many, including the three daughters, who found themselves united by this tragic reality after the war. Depression and suicide touched the men they loved. John Boettiger and Antony Beauchamp were deeply affected by their experiences during the war: Boettiger as an officer in the army in North Africa and the Mediterranean, and Beauchamp as an official war artist in the Pacific. In 1969, Kathy's husband, Stanley Mortimer, would also attempt suicide by shotgun. Stanley struggled for years with bipolar disorder. His wartime experiences as a lieutenant commander and spotter in a navy reconnaissance plane in the South Pacific, especially after his best friend was killed, may have played a role in worsening this condition. Stanley also suffered from misdiagnosed early-onset Alzheimer's; the treatment for his depression may have exacerbated it. Remarkably, Kathy discovered Stanley before it was too late and saved his life. He recovered, and he and Kathy had another thirty years together, until his death in 1999.

After Antony's death, Sarah went into a downward spiral. She began to drink too much and was twice arrested for public drunkenness and disorderly conduct. She eventually sought treatment in Switzerland. Leaving acting behind, she settled down to a quiet life in Spain. There, when she least expected it, she found the love of her life, a fellow British expat, Henry Touchet-Jesson, 23rd Baron Audley. Like Sarah, Henry was a redhead, forty-nine, and previously married. Sadly, he had suffered a stroke, which had left him partially paralysed and unable to write more than his name in his own hand. Despite, or because of, each one's imperfections, they fell deeply in love. When Henry proposed to Sarah, he wrote to her father: 'I feel that I have so little to offer, Yet, Sir, I do love Sarah. I love her for her beauty, her sorrows, and her instinctive goodness. If I may be allowed to give her peace, excitement ... anything which may allow her happiness on her own terms then my own life will seem a full achievement for me.'

After a blissful fifteen months of marriage, full of love and happiness, Sarah's curse struck once again. Henry died of a cerebral haemorrhage. Three months later, her sister Diana committed suicide. After the crushing blow of double tragedies, Sarah again began to drink. She had a brief romance with Lobo Nocho, an African American jazz singer and artist, but it did not last. When, on January 24, 1965, her beloved father died at the age of ninety, her misery was complete.

When Winston died, it was as if a piece of his soul embedded itself in hers, for, as Sarah worked through her grief, she began to write. Like her father, Sarah was already an accomplished painter. Now she plunged headlong into the medium that had won Winston a Nobel Prize in 1953. Whereas Winston wrote of history, including his own place in it, Sarah's writing explored the heart. Her first book, *A Thread in the Tapestry,* an elegant, emotive reflection on her life with her father, was published in 1966. The next year, she published a book of fairy tales, followed by two volumes of poetry.

Sarah never had children of her own, but her nieces and nephews adored her. To her niece Celia Sandys, she was a 'fairy godmother' who swept in with fabulous presents. She dazzled the children when, starring in a London stage production of *Peter Pan*, she flew through the air, attached to the thinnest of wires. But over time they came to understand the depth of her struggle. Sarah had lost so many people in quick succession – Winant, Beauchamp, Audley, her sister and, finally, her father – that she never quite managed to recover from heartbreak. But still she tried to look to the future. In 1981, Sarah published one final volume, a memoir of her life titled *Keep on Dancing*, her personal mantra.

Sarah embodied so much of her father – his intelligence, his drive, his passion, and his exquisite facility with words and language – that it is not impossible to imagine her, in a different era, as his political successor. Indeed, she might have found happiness in such a career, where a greater sense of purpose, as she had discovered during the war, might have propelled her through tragedy. However, despite tragedies, personal struggles, and the heartbreaking belief that she brought unhappiness to those who loved her, Sarah was, as her niece Celia attested, a 'talented and brilliant' human being who was 'absolutely enchanting' to all who knew her. As one woman later told Sarah's sister Mary, 'While those of us who worked with Sarah and knew her will surely feel that her many talents were insufficiently recognized and perhaps not encouraged as they should have been, her gaiety and courage in often difficult times were an inspiration.' It was much like what Pamela had written to Kathy about Sarah many years earlier.

But even Sarah could not continue dancing forever. The alcohol eventually took its toll. Towards the end of her life, Sarah was at peace with the fact that she was dying. As she told a friend, 'I don't mind going because I know Papa is waiting.' Of all the extraordinary people who had touched her life, her father always was the brightest star. No doubt, for Winston, the feeling was mutual. As Sarah's niece Celia would later say, 'I am sure she was my grandfather's favorite child.' Sarah Churchill died in 1982 at the age of sixty-seven.

As years passed and the fraught legacy of the Yalta Conference continued to evolve as relations between East and West ebbed and flowed, few would remember that Kathleen Harriman, Anna Roosevelt and Sarah Churchill had been present at this turning point between World War and Cold War. Those who did recall them acknowledged the three daughters as little more than housekeepers or hostesses presiding over 'a country house party where the guests good-naturedly put up with overcrowding', as the spy Alger Hiss wrote in his self-serving memoir more than forty years after Yalta. When historians quoted the three daughters, it was only for 'fill-in material', as Anna called it – lighthearted observations about the lack of bathrooms or the prevalence of bed bugs – to bring levity to a complex and even tragic episode in the final days of World War II. When exploring the lives of these Great Men of history and their immense political influence, it is easy to forget that they, like many others, were also fathers. In spite of – or perhaps because of – the demands of a world at war, the relationships between these fathers and daughters were some of the most meaningful relationships in all of their lives.

Though Yalta was not the apex of Allied collaboration that many hoped it would be, for three women it was one of the highlights of their lives. In recent times, the presence on the world stage of elected leaders' children – especially their daughters – has become more commonplace, but in the era of Yalta, it was unprecedented. The postwar world would forget them, but they would never forget the chance to be their fathers' partners, protectors and confidantes, if only for a moment. As always, Sarah phrased it best, the eloquent words she wrote to her father after the Tehran Conference every bit as applicable to her feelings about Yalta – perhaps more so: 'Darling darling Papa,' she wrote, 'so long as I live I'll never forget our wonderful wonderful journey – over the years the pageantry and colour of those great events may dim or get confused – but I will never forget . . . All this, and more I have with me forever.'

Acknowledgments

The great joy of writing this book has been the wonderful people who have filled my life. This book began, fittingly, in a bookstore, Chartwell Booksellers in Manhattan, 'The World's only Winston Churchill Bookstore,' located in the lobby of my office in my previous life as a graduate history student turned financial analyst. The proprietor, Barry Singer, welcomed me as I enjoyed my afternoon tea among his treasures, and kindly introduced me to Lee Pollock, executive director of the International Churchill Society, the most thoughtful and generous friend and resource. Lee in turn introduced me to Dr David Freeman, editor of the ICS journal, *Finest Hour*. It was David who asked me to write an article about Sarah Churchill's papers, which the Churchill family was opening to researchers for the first time. 'If you are looking for a project for your own first book,' he said, 'this may be something for you to consider.' Thank you for the suggestion and encouragement that started me on this journey. I am eternally grateful.

I am so fortunate to have tremendous support on both sides of the Atlantic, especially from the families of the fathers and daughters at the heart of this story.

Thank you to the Churchill family, especially Randolph Churchill, who encouraged me from our earliest conversations; Emma Soames, who graciously allowed me access to her mother Mary's papers at the Churchill Archive Centre before they were publicly available; Jennie Churchill for her endless interest and support; and Celia Sandys for her lovely memories. An enormous thanks also to Lady Williams, whose beautiful recollections of Winston and Sarah from her tenure as Churchill's secretary brought them to life for me; to Hugo Vickers, who kindly introduced me to Lady Avon, Winston Churchill's niece and Anthony Eden's widow; and to the indomitable Laurence Geller, chairman of the International Churchill Society, for his boundless enthusiasm and incredible support for this project and so much more.

On the American side, two remarkable members of the Roosevelt family – Ellie Seagraves and John R. Boettiger, Anna Roosevelt's children – brought me to tears with their profoundly moving memories of their mother and grandfather. Thank you for your time, words, photographs, confidence, kindness and endless grace. Special thanks also to Ambassador William vanden Heuvel.

And to the Mortimer family, a million thanks, especially to David Mortimer and Shelley Wanger, Avie and Gigi Mortimer, Amanda Burden and Kitty Ames. David Mortimer went above and beyond to help me appreciate his extraordinary mother and grandfather, so that this project could come to fruition. Words cannot sufficiently express my gratitude for all that you have done to welcome me into your lives. I am forever grateful for your friendship. Thanks also to Kathleen's grandson, Nick Mortimer, for his research assistance at Georgetown, and to Peter Duchin for sharing his fond memories of Averell and Kathleen.

Historians would not be able to bring stories to life without the resources from archives and help from their superb archivists. I wish to thank the unparalleled Allen Packwood and his team at the Churchill Archives Centre at Churchill College, Cambridge; the archivists at the Library of Congress, especially Patrick Kerwin; Patrick Fahy and Dara Baker of the Franklin D. Roosevelt Library, as well as the National Parks Service, who gave me a behind-the-scenes tour of Springwood, so that I could fully understand Anna Roosevelt's childhood; and James Cross for his timely assistance with the James Byrnes Papers at Clemson. Thank you also to the Roosevelt Institute, whose grants make it possible for young historians to literally go the extra mile.

In addition to the wealth of resources of university libraries, I was lucky to have access to the fantastic library system on Chicago's north shore, especially the Glencoe, Winnetka and Wilmette public libraries. Thanks also to the University Club of Chicago and George William Price.

I have been fortunate to have the best mentors. Professor Sir David Cannadine provided tremendously insightful advice and direction at both the beginning and end of this process. The tutelage and guidance of my undergraduate and graduate advisers, Professors Niall Ferguson and David Reynolds, remain invaluable. Julian and Emma Fellowes, with whom I have enjoyed so many delightful and insightful conversations about history, narrative and life. And David Brooks, for his generous time and advice ever since I was an enthusiastic undergraduate, but most especially during this project's infancy.

Thanks to my friends who opened their homes to me on my numerous research trips: Marissa Yu, Hardik Gupta, Filip Vurdelja, Ian Mok, and especially Caroline Costin and Ted Wright. Thanks also to Phil Reed of the Cabinet War Rooms; Gioia Diliberto for the best writing advice; Dr Austin Culver for his cardiology expertise; Zach Uttich of BLVDier for his sartorial savvy; Adriana Jurado for her kindness; Candice Millard, Allison Pataki and Monique Brinson Demery for their early thoughts; Ned and Margaret Handy for their warm friendship and wonderful conversation; Julie Palmer for her photographs of the Crimea; Dr John Mather for his enthusiasm; my friends at Harvard Law School, especially my compatriots in Section One, who were there when I needed an extra hand and who made it great fun; Chris Vogt, a true fairy godmother who would put Cinderella's to shame; and my dearest friend Caroline Healy McLendon, who has been there for me since first grade.

A special thank-you to David and Rachel Waimon for their thoughtful feedback, brilliance and friendship – and specifically to Rachel for helping me untangle the intricacies of Russian language and culture.

And to Justice Anthony Kennedy, who encouraged me to read the Marquis de Custine's memoir of his nineteenth-century travels through imperial Russia. That memoir had a tremendous impact on this project.

I have the great fortune to have the best publishing team in the world: my editor, Deanne Urmy, one of the most thoughtful, elegant and insightful people I know. She understood these remarkable daughters from day one. Working with her on this book was meant to be. And a tremendous thank-you to everyone at Houghton Mifflin Harcourt, especially Jessica Vestuto and Leah Petrakis for their tireless efforts and assistance, and Bruce Nichols. I'd also like to thank my agent, Michael V. Carlisle, who unwaveringly and expertly shepherded me through this process. He is a sage who believed in me and in this story from the outset. Thanks also to Michael Mungiello of Inkwell Management, who was always there when I needed him. Thanks to Bruce Vinokour at CAA, who had a vision for this project from its earliest days and whose feedback has been invaluable. Thank you to my London editor, Arabella Pike, and agent Natasha Fairweather on this transatlantic endeavour.

Finally, and most important, thanks to my family, who lived every minute of *The Daughters of Yalta* alongside me. To my dad, who has supported and encouraged me. To my brother, Oliver, the most natural communicator I know, who helps me cut to the heart of the most complex matters. To my sister Anna (Bunny), who has wisdom and clarity of mind beyond her years, and whose extraordinary editorial eye helped me immeasurably. And to my mom, who instilled in me a love of reading, language and history by reading hundreds of books to us throughout our childhood. Conversations with you have prompted so many of my best ideas. You are always there to talk things through with me, no matter what time of day or night. Your instincts are always spot on, and you are the source of the kindest, best and most loving advice. I simply could not have written this book without you.

Abbreviations

People

Below are abbreviations for several of the main figures in the book and their primary correspondents, as used in the notes. For authorship of archival primary sources, I have abbreviated to the name that would be most recognisable to the reader. For example, Sarah Churchill and Anna Roosevelt were each married three times and their names changed between the time in which this story takes place and the dedication of their archival collections, so I use their birth-name initials as the abbreviation.

AER – Anna Eleanor Roosevelt
CSC – Clementine Spencer-Churchill
ER – Eleanor Roosevelt
FDR – Franklin Delano Roosevelt
JB – C. John Boettiger
KLH – Kathleen Lanier Harriman
MHF – Mary Harriman Fisk
PC – Pamela Churchill
SMHC – Sarah Millicent Hermione Churchill
WAH – W. Averell Harriman
WSC – Winston Spencer-Churchill

Archives and Archival Collections

AIR – Air Ministry Papers
ARHP – Anna Roosevelt Halsted Papers, Franklin D. Roosevelt Presidential Library and Museum, Hyde Park, NY
AHP – W. Averell Harriman Papers, Library of Congress, Washington, D.C.

CAB – Cabinet Papers

CAC – Churchill Archive Centre, Churchill College, Cambridge, UK

CHAR – Chartwell Papers, Churchill Archives Centre, Churchill College, Cambridge, UK

FDRL – Franklin D. Roosevelt Presidential Library and Museum, Hyde Park, NY

FO – Foreign Office Papers

FRUS – Foreign Relations of the United States

HLHP – Harry L. Hopkins Papers, Georgetown University, Booth Family Center for Special Collections, Washington, D.C.

IWM – Imperial War Museum, London, UK.

JBP – John Boettiger Papers, Franklin D. Roosevelt Presidential Library and Museum, Hyde Park, NY

LOC – Library of Congress, Washington, D.C.

MCHL – Papers of Lady Soames (Mary Churchill), Churchill Archives Centre, Churchill College, Cambridge, UK

NARA – National Archives and Records Administration, Chevy Chase, MD

PHP – Pamela Digby Churchill Hayward Harriman Papers, Library of Congress, Washington, D.C.

SCHL – Papers of Sarah Churchill, Churchill Archives Centre, Churchill College, Cambridge, UK

TNA – The National Archives at Kew, UK

Notes

Chapter One: February 1, 1945

page

3   *The furniture:* KLH to PC, January 30, 1945, LOC PHP B I-21; S. M. Plokhy, *Yalta: The Price of Peace* (New York: Viking, 2010), 44–45; David B. Woolner, *The Last 100 Days: FDR at War and at Peace* (New York: Basic Books, 2017), 67; Rick Atkinson, *The Guns at Last Light: The War in Western Europe, 1944–1945* (New York: Picador, 2013), 506. Eddie Page to Teresita Page, January 26, 1945.

new 116-room: Greg King, *The Court of the Last Tsar: Pomp, Power, and Pageantry in the Reign of Nicholas II* (Hoboken, NJ: John Wiley and Sons, 2006), 440.

sold her needlework: Robert K. Massie, *Nicholas and Alexandra: The Classic Account of the Fall of the Romanov Dynasty* (New York: Random House Trade Paperbacks, reprint ed., 2000), 177–78.

In the white ballroom: Ibid.

4   *Cots had been set up:* Plokhy, *Yalta,* 44–45. The Soviet bureaucrats did not tell the workers nor their families where they were going. They simply loaded them onto trains, no doubt striking fear into the hearts of many. Only after a day on the train was the official government photographer, Boris Kosarev, told they were bound for Yalta. He was allowed to send a telegram to his wife, saying, 'I will be in Yalta till February,' and that was all. Author's correspondence with Maria Kosareva, January 2, 2020.

They had intended to fly: KLH to MHF, February 4, 1945, Mortimer Papers, private collection, New York, NY.

5   *eight-hundred-mile journey:* KLH to PC, January 30, 1945, LOC PHP B-I 21.

Every train station: Ibid.

'The needless destruction': KLH to Elsie Marshall, February 1, 1945, Mortimer Papers.

'My God but this country': KLH to MHF, February 4, 1945, Mortimer Papers.

6   *On the advice:* FRUS, Conferences at Malta and Yalta, WAH to FDR, September 24, 1944, Document 6; Joseph Stalin to FDR, October 29, 1944, Document 16.

Roosevelt quietly directed: FRUS, Conferences at Malta and Yalta, WAH to FDR, December 27, 1944, Document 32. In his cable, Averell Harriman informed Roosevelt that he had told Molotov that 'the Prime Minister had agreed to go wherever you decided and therefore I suggested that the Marshal not communicate with Mr. Churchill until you had had a chance to do so after which I presumed Marshal Stalin would wish to extend him an invitation. I did this as I do not know how far you have kept the Prime

Minister informed of the recent developments. I would appreciate advice on this point.'

After assessing various: FRUS, Conferences at Malta and Yalta, WAH to FDR, December 14, 1944, Document 28; FDR to WSC, December 23, 1944, Document 30.

littered with mines: WSC to FDR, November 5, 1944, C-815, in Warren F. Kimball, ed., *Churchill and Roosevelt: The Complete Correspondence, Vol. III* (Princeton, NJ: Princeton University Press, 1984), 380.

By the New Year: FRUS, Conferences at Malta and Yalta, FDR to WSC, December 31, 1944, Document 36; WSC to FDR, January 1, 1945, Document 38.

7   *It had once belonged:* AER Yalta Notes, 'Notes on the Crimea', 5, FDRL ARHP, Box 84. Prince Felix Yusupov, who allegedly had engineered and helped carry out the murder of Rasputin, was forced to flee to France in exile after the Russian Revolution. Yusupov Palace continues to be a source of local intrigue. From 1991 to 2014, it belonged to the president of Ukraine. Notably, when hostilities between Russia and Ukraine broke out in the area, in the autumn of 2014, the Council of Ministers of Crimea transferred the property to the Russian president, Vladimir Putin.

    Lavrentiy Beria: Plokhy, *Yalta*, 44–45.

    including 835 supposed: Simon Sebag Montefiore, *Stalin: The Court of the Red Tsar* (New York: Alfred A. Knopf, 2004), 480.

8   *Three days after:* R. P. Meiklejohn Itinerary, Crimea Conference Trip, January 22–February 12, 1945, LOC AHP B 176 F 08.

    The small number: KLH to MHF, mid-October 1943, Mortimer Papers.

9   *her father's interpreter:* KLH to Elsie Marshall, March 10, 1944; KLH to Elsie Marshall, February 27, 1945; Mortimer Papers.

    'Gaspadeena Garriman': KLH to PC, November 16, 1943, LOC PHP B I-21.

    'seaside ranch in the mountains': 1941 Sun Valley Promotional Pamphlet, FDRL JBP, Box 28, 'Sun Valley'.

10   *he left Kathy:* Exchanges between WAH and KLH, January 19, 1939; January 29, 1939; February 5, 1939; January 10, 1940; December 17, 1940; LOC AHP B 05 F 03.

    Kathy had attended: 'Foxcroft, 1930s', courtesy of the Foxcroft School, Middleburg, VA.

    Before her father had chairlifts installed: Jeff Cordes, 'Skiing's the Life for Kathleen Harriman Mortimer', *Idaho Mountain Express*, February 1, 1989; photographs of KLH at Sun Valley, Mortimer Papers.

    calling her 'Puff': Author's conversation with David Mortimer, December 12, 2017.

    fifteen hundred railcars: Plokhy, *Yalta*, 44–45.

11   *Even the maids' uniforms:* Andrew Roberts, *Masters and Commanders: How Four Titans Won the War in the West, 1941–1945* (New York: Harper, 2009), 546.

    'just being "requisitioned"': KLH to Elsie Marshall, February 1, 1945, Mortimer Papers.

    They sprayed: 'Report of Medical Department Activities at Crimean Conference', February 18, 1945, FDRL, Ross T. McIntire Papers, Box 4, 'Crimean Conference'.

    On the train: KLH to MHF, February 4, 1945, Mortimer Papers.

    'As this is her': WAH to FDR, January 17, 1945, LOC AHP B 176 F 07.

    'I will leave her': WAH to FDR, January 19, 1945, LOC AHP B 176 F 07.

    Roosevelt did not: FDR to WAH, January 17, 1945, LOC AHP B 176 F 07.

    not, as she insisted: KLH to MHF, January 1, 1942; KLH to MHF, March 30, 1942, Mortimer Papers.

12   *'I only hope':* KLH to MHF, October 1943, Mortimer Papers.

'How do do!': KLH to MHF, December 16, 1941, Mortimer Papers.

as an 'amanuensis': Kathleen Harriman, 'Adele Astaire, Amanuensis', *Newsweek,* May 31, 1943.

'still [wore] silly bows': Ibid.

Newsweek had also printed: KLH to Marie Harriman, July 19, 1943, LOC AHP B 06 F 10.

13   *a friend of Kathy's stepmother:* WAH to Marie Harriman, April 17, 1941, LOC AHP B 03 F 01.

'bitch to end all': KLH to Marie Harriman, July 19, 1943, LOC AHP B 06 F 10.

Russian maître d'hôtel: AER Yalta Notes, 17, FDRL ARHP, Box 84.

'a little good': 'Report of Medical Department Activities at Crimean Conference', February 18, 1945, FDRL Ross T. McIntire Papers, Box 4, 'Crimea Conference'.

NKVD officers: Plokhy, *Yalta,* 45.

The room: Norris Houghton, 'That Was Yalta: Worm's Eye View', *The New Yorker,* May 23, 1953; photograph of FDR's suite at Livadia Palace, in Edward R. Stettinius Jr., *Roosevelt and the Russians: The Yalta Conference* (New York: Doubleday, 1949), insert facing page 129.

changed their minds: KLH to MHF, February 4, 1945, Mortimer Papers.

14   *Kathy pointed to:* Plokhy, *Yalta,* 45–46.

Nearby, a plumber: Ibid.

A mere nine: Atkinson, *The Guns at Last Light,* 509.

only Roosevelt's suite: Rudy Abramson, *Spanning the Century: The Life of W. Averell Harriman, 1891–1986* (New York: William Morrow, 1996), 371.

sixteen colonels: Roberts, *Masters and Commanders,* 546.

The bedrooms on: W. Averell Harriman and Elie Abel, *Special Envoy to Churchill and Stalin, 1941–1946* (New York: Random House, 1975), 384, 393; Abramson, *Spanning the Century,* 371.

15   *The scenery reminded:* KLH to PC, January 30, 1945, LOC PHP B I-21.

During the previous: KLH to MHF, June 19, 1944, Mortimer Papers.

Together with Eddie Page: AER Yalta Notes, 20, FDRL ARHP, Box 84.

In this letter: WAH to KLH, February 16, 1936, Mortimer Papers.

16   *'The Richest Woman':* 'Personalities', *Hampton's Magazine,* January 1910, 125.

'the finest & best': Ibid.

In 1899, when Averell: Harriman and Abel, *Special Envoy,* 39–41. At one point, the Harriman Expedition crossed into Siberia. As Averell's grandson, David Mortimer, explained, Averell enjoyed telling people this was his first visit to Russia – a visit made without a passport.

17   *a natural kinship:* Author's interview with Kitty Ames, October 21, 2019.

'Someone opens the door': KLH to Harry Hopkins, Georgetown University, Booth Family Center for Special Collections, HLHP3, Box 4, Folder 14.

But moving to: KLH to Elsie Marshall, January 14, 1943; February 18, 1943; July 5, 1943; Mortimer Papers.

'I am thrilled': WAH to KLH, undated, 1943, Mortimer Papers.

'paper doll cutting': KLH to MHF, January 14, 1944; February 9, 1944; Mortimer Papers. After a six-month bureaucratic ordeal, she finally received permission from the Soviets to publish a small magazine called *Amerika,* which she developed with the American Office of War Information to help everyday Russians better understand

American culture and life. KLH to MHF, December 24, 1943, and June 14, 1944, Mortimer Papers. See also Abramson, *Spanning the Century*, 360–61.

18   *'charming, full of life':* KLH to Elsie Marshall, February 1, 1945, Mortimer Papers.
'The natives who': Ibid.
When Kathy moved: KLH to MHF, October, no date, 1943, Mortimer Papers.
'I thought coming': Ibid.
She had expected: KLH to MHF, October 26, 1943, Mortimer Papers.
American Lend-Lease trucks: KLH to MHF, November 5, 1943, Mortimer Papers.
streetcars were so: KLH to MHF, October 27, 1943, Mortimer Papers.
All but the oldest: KLH to MHF, November 5, 1943, Mortimer Papers.

19   *'out and out':* KLH to MHF, December 24, 1943, Mortimer Papers.
It was not until: 'Samuel N. Harper', Red Press: Radical Print Culture from St. Petersburg to Chicago, Exhibition, University of Chicago Special Collections Research Center, 2017, https://www.lib.uchicago.edu/collex/exhibits/red-press/samuel-n-harper/.
she had to borrow: KLH, 'Do the crows still roost in the Spasopeckovskaya trees?' Mortimer Papers.
'friendly and frank': KLH to CSC, February 27, 1944, CAC MCHL 5/1/106.

20   *'they can no longer':* George Kennan to Edward Stettinius, February 2, 1945, LOC AHP B 176 F 10.
'sporting woman': Kitty Lanier Harriman Pool to Elsie Marshall, May 22, 1935, Mortimer Papers.
'state of spinsterhood': KLH to Marie Harriman, December 7, 1942, LOC AHP B 06 F 10.
calendar booked: KLH to MHF, mid-June 1941, Mortimer Papers.
'You are going': Ira Eaker to KLH, June 10, 1944, Mortimer Papers.

21   *Moscow shops beckoned:* KLH to MHF, October 27, 1943, Mortimer Papers.
There were luxuries: KLH to MHF, June 4, 1944, Mortimer Papers.
no glass: KLH to MHF, June 9, 1944; KLH, 'Do the crows still roost in the Spasopeckovskaya trees?' Mortimer Papers.

Chapter Two: *February 2, 1945*

23   *the cruisers anchored:* Newsreel footage, 'Official Pictorial Record of the Yalta Conference', January–February 1945, U.S. Army Signal Corps, http://www.criticalpast.com/video/65675033669_The-Yalta-Conference_Franklin-D-Roosevelt_Malta-Conference_Winston-Churchill.
As an aerial reconnaissance: SMHC to CSC, November 19, 1943, CAC SCHL 1/1/7.
It was not yet: SMHC to CSC, February 4, 1945, CAC SCHL 1/1/8; Anthony Eden, *The Memoirs of Anthony Eden, Earl of Avon: The Reckoning* (Boston: Houghton Mifflin, 1965), 592; Logs of the President's Trips: Crimea Conference and Great Bitter Lake, Egypt, January 22–February 28, 1945, 14, FDRL Grace Tully Papers, Box 7.

24   *Usually, crowds made:* SMHC to CSC, February 15, 1945, CAC SCHL 1/1/8.
Her father was pacing: Stettinius, *Roosevelt and the Russians*, 68.
The British delegation: Ibid.
Across the harbour: AER Yalta Notes, 10, FDRL ARHP, Box 84.
rude awakening: Eden, *The Reckoning*, 592.
Back in England: CSC to WSC, January 30, 1945, in Mary Soames, ed., *Winston and Clementine: The Personal Letters of the Churchills* (Boston: Houghton Mifflin, 1999), 511.

The average temperature that day was fifty-eight degrees. Trips, 16, FDRL Grace Tully Papers, Box 7.

leave her greatcoat: 'Photograph of Franklin D. Roosevelt with Anna Boettiger, Sarah Churchill and Winston Churchill aboard the USS *Quincy* at Malta before the Yalta Conference', February 2, 1945, FDRL Photographs.

25   *When Sarah had arrived:* Felicity Hill, IWM Oral History, December 6, 1985.

All she wanted: Sarah Churchill, *A Thread in the Tapestry* (New York: Dodd, Mead, 1967), 57.

Still, the recruiter: Felicity Hill, IWM Oral History, December 6, 1985.

4,883-mile journey: Logs of the Trips, 14, FDRL Grace Tully Papers, Box 7.

Then, in the early: Logs of the Trips, 19, FDRL Grace Tully Papers, Box 7.

Sarah had been granted: Sarah Churchill, *A Thread in the Tapestry*, 72.

26   *'walked on air':* Ibid., 57.

'Whatever follows': SMHC to CSC, December 4, 1943, CAC SCHL 1/1/7.

Once again her commanding: Sarah Churchill, *A Thread in the Tapestry*, 72.

Asking a trusted friend: SMHC to CSC, February 6, 1945, CAC MCHL 5/1/120.

They flew from RAF: Lord Charles Moran, *Churchill at War, 1940–45* (New York: Carroll and Graf, 2002), 264.

27   *'tomatoes screaming':* SMHC to CSC, January 31, 1945, CAC SCHL 1/1/8.

'in for something': Ibid.

Was it possible: Moran, *Churchill at War*, 265.

'You think there is': Ibid.

'My temperature': SMHC to CSC, February 1, 1945, CAC SCHL 1/1/8.

At eight that morning: Sarah Churchill, *A Thread in the Tapestry*, 76; Diary of Alan Brooke, 1st Viscount Alanbrooke of Brookeborough, Field Marshal, February 2, 1945, ALANBROOKE 5/1/10, Liddell Hart Military Archives, King's College London. Sir Charles (Peter) Portal also writes about learning about the tragedy that morning in his letter to Pamela Churchill, saying that the day was 'spoilt' by the news, Sir Charles Portal to PC, February 2, 1945 (continuous letter beginning January 29, 1945), LOC PHP B I-31.

28   *Averell Harriman had reported:* AER Yalta Notes, 6, FDRL ARHP, Box 84.

An RAF officer: WSC to FDR, January 26, 1945, C-896 in Kimball, ed., *Churchill and Roosevelt: The Complete Correspondence, Vol. III*, 519.

'running a conference': Joan Bright Astley, *The Inner Circle: A View of War at the Top* (Boston: Atlantic Monthly Press, 1971), 182.

29   *five functioning fighters:* James Holland, *Fortress Malta: An Island Under Siege, 1940–43* (New York: Miramax Books, 2003), 274.

The British aircraft carrier: Winston S. Churchill, *The Second World War, Volume IV: The Hinge of Fate* (Boston: Houghton Mifflin, 1950), 268–69, 273.

Throughout January: Churchill's persistence and Roosevelt's reluctance to meet can be seen in the communications between them in Kimball, ed., *Churchill and Roosevelt: The Complete Correspondence, Vol. III*, particularly messages C-874, C-875, R-692/1, C-880, C-881, R-696, C-884, R-699 and C-889.

'If only I could dine': Martin Gilbert, *Winston S. Churchill, Vol. VII: Road to Victory, 1941–1945* (Boston: Houghton Mifflin, 1986), 664.

30   *'informal' and saw:* FRUS, Conferences at Malta and Yalta, FDR to Joseph Stalin, November 18, 1944, Document 21.

Roosevelt wanted to: FRUS, Conferences at Malta and Yalta, FDR to WSC, January 9, 1945, Document 49.

'Even the Almighty': FRUS, Conferences at Malta and Yalta, WSC to FDR, January 10, 1945, Document 50. In the published version of his diaries, *The Fringes of Power: Downing Street Diaries, 1939–1955*, Sir John Colville, Churchill's then assistant private secretary, humorously notes that the prime minister's attention was quickly drawn to the slight inaccuracy of that statement, as Genesis states the seventh day was a day of rest, 551.

'follies of the victors': Winston S. Churchill, *The Second World War, Vol. I: The Gathering Storm* (Boston: Houghton Mifflin, 1948), 3.

'The end of this war': FRUS, Conferences at Malta and Yalta, WSC to FDR, January 8, 1945, Document 47.

'The only hope': Gilbert, *Winston S. Churchill, Vol. VII*, 1170.

31   *He had an aura:* Sarah Churchill, *A Thread in the Tapestry*, 17.

'Poor Puggy-Wug': Ibid., 28.

'second mate': Ibid., 26.

32   *Clementine was terrified:* Clementine did fly occasionally, for example, to Moscow in April 1945, when Stalin honoured her for work supporting the Soviet Red Cross. She was so afraid of flying that she wrote to Sarah, asking her to pray for her, and suggested to Mary that in the event her plane crashed and she died, could Mary please ask the ATS to release her from her duties in order to look after Winston. Sonia Purnell, *Clementine: The Life of Mrs. Winston Churchill* (New York: Viking, 2015), 338–39.

something of a 'loner': Sarah Churchill, *Keep on Dancing* (New York: Coward, McCann and Geoghegan, 1981), 27.

As a teenager: Purnell, *Clementine*, 200.

'tidy' her mind: Sarah Churchill, *A Thread in the Tapestry*, 31.

33   *'Sarah is an oyster':* Ibid., 32.

'with a trusted audience': Ibid., 33.

At 9.35 a.m.: Logs of the Trips, 14, FDRL Grace Tully Papers, Box 7.

34   *A squadron of six:* Stettinius, *Roosevelt and the Russians*, 68.

'God Save the King': SCHL to CSC, February 4, 1945, SCHL 1/1/8; AER Yalta Notes, 10, FDRL ARHP, Box 84.

With the aid: Newsreel footage, 'Official Pictorial Record of the Yalta Conference', January–February 1945, U.S. Army Signal Corps.

The two ships: SMHC to CSC, February 4, 1945, SCHL 1/1/8.

'very superior creatures': Ibid.

The prime minister: Newsreel footage, 'Official Pictorial Record of the Yalta Conference', January–February 1945, U.S. Army Signal Corps.

'waiting on the quay': FRUS, Conferences at Malta and Yalta, WSC to FDR, January 1, 1945, Document 38.

Churchill, standing: AER Yalta Notes, 10, FDRL ARHP, Box 84; Newsreel footage, 'Official Pictorial Record of the Yalta Conference', January–February 1945, U.S. Army Signal Corps.

'thrilling sight': Sarah Churchill, *A Thread in the Tapestry*, 75.

'seem[ed] to stand still': Eden, *The Reckoning*, 592.

Harriman, Stettinius: Logs of the Trips, 15, FDRL Grace Tully Papers, Box 7.

'piped aboard': AER Yalta Notes, 10, FDRL ARHP, Box 84.

Arriving on deck: 'Photograph of Franklin D. Roosevelt with Anna Boettiger, Sarah Churchill, and Winston Churchill aboard the USS *Quincy* at Malta before the Yalta Conference', February 2, 1945, FDRL.

35   *'If you are taking':* FDR to WSC, January 7, 1945, R-693, in Kimball, ed., *Complete Correspondence, Vol. III*, 500.

'How splendid': WSC to FDR, January 7, 1945, C-879, in Kimball, ed., *Complete Correspondence, Vol. III*, 500.

'Although,' Sarah noted: SMHC to CSC, February 14, 1945, CAC SCHL 1/1/8.

36   *He was so full:* SMHC to CSC, December 4, 1943, CAC SCHL 1/1/7.

a 'million years': SMHC to CSC, February 4, 1945, CAC MCHL 5/1/120.

primary 'buddy': Ibid.

'wooden headed': SMHC to CSC, February 1, 1945, CAC MCHL 5/1/120.

37   *When Winant:* SMHC to CSC, February 4, 1945, CAC MCHL 5/1/120.

'Is it health': Ibid.

Chapter Three: February 2, 1945

39   *He had a persistent:* Doris Kearns Goodwin, *No Ordinary Time: Franklin and Eleanor Roosevelt – The Home Front in World War II* (New York: Simon and Schuster, 1994), 491.

40   *Anna's mother:* Joe Lash, *Eleanor and Franklin: The Story of Their Relationship Based on Eleanor Roosevelt's Private Papers* (New York: W. W. Norton, 1971), 697.

Grace Tully, that he had: Howard Bruenn, Oral History, U.S. Naval Medical Department Oral History Program, January 31, 1990.

She summoned: Joseph Lelyveld, *His Final Battle: The Last Months of Franklin Roosevelt* (New York: Alfred A. Knopf, 2016), 93.

The president was: Howard Bruenn, 'Clinical Notes on the Illness and Death of President Franklin D. Roosevelt', *Annals of Internal Medicine*, Vol. 72, No. 4 (April 1970): 579–80. The American Heart Association classifies hypertensive crisis as a systolic reading over 180 mm Hg and/or a diastolic reading over 120 mm Hg.

Cardiology was: Philip Reichert, 'A History of the Development of Cardiology as a Medical Specialty', *Clinical Cardiology*, Vol. 1, No. 1 (1978): 15–5, https://www.acc.org/latest-in-cardiology/articles/2016/10/06/11/00/a-history-of-the-development-of-cardiology-as-a-medical-specialty.

acute congestive: Bruenn, 'Clinical Notes', 580–81.

Bruenn was not: Jim Bishop, *FDR's Last Year: April 1944–April 1945* (New York: William Morrow, 1974), 6.

41   *FDR never asked:* Howard Bruenn, Oral History, U.S. Naval Medical Department Oral History Program, January 31, 1990.

why his diet: FDR's diet was adjusted to include foods low in fat and high in carbohydrates. He was explicitly instructed not to eat pork, ham, salmon, mackerel, sardines, cheeses (except for cottage cheese), fatty desserts and 'gas forming foods', including cabbage, cauliflower, broccoli, Brussels sprouts, cucumbers, onions, turnips, rutabaga, peppers, radishes and dried beans. No more than one pat of butter was to be served per meal. 'Special Diet for the President', FDRL ARHP, Box 66, Folder 9.

than four hours: 'Treatment', FDRL ARHP, Box 66, Folder 16.

Bruenn broke: Goodwin, *No Ordinary Time*, 499, 502. By at least mid-April 1944, Anna was aware that her father had heart disease.

Then, Anna had: Ibid., 471–72.

42 *'stinker in his':* AER to JB, December 11, 1943, FDRL JBP, Box 6.

'Pa seems to': Copy of letter to ER, AER to JB, November 11, 1943, FDRL JBP, Box 6.

'Well, we'll just': Oral History interview with Anna Roosevelt Halsted, 1975, Columbia Center for Oral History Archives, Rare Book & Manuscript Library, Columbia University in the City of New York.

would be 'simpler': Eleanor Roosevelt, *This I Remember* (New York: Harper and Brothers, 1949), 339.

'What do you want': AER, 'What Does It Feel Like to Be an Offspring of Famous Parents?' 5, later draft. FDRL ARHP, Box 84, Undated Writings.

43 *'Mother, can't you':* Bernard Asbell, ed., *Mother and Daughter: The Letters of Eleanor and Anna Roosevelt* (New York: Coward, McCann & Geoghegan, 1982), 176.

'one of the gang': Anna Roosevelt Halsted interview by Bernard Asbell, 1972, FDRL ARHP, Box 63.

Anna knew: Ibid.

'no ax to grind': Ibid.

44 *Some of her fondest:* Oral History interview with Anna Roosevelt Halsted, 1975, Columbia Center for Oral History Archives, Rare Book and Manuscript Library, Columbia University in the City of New York; AER, 'What Does It Feel Like to Be an Offspring of Famous Parents?' FDRL ARHP, Box 84, Undated Writings.

Anna imagined: Asbell, ed., *Mother and Daughter*, 39.

'Hon. F.D. Roosevelt': AER to FDR, undated, FDRL ARHP, Box 62, Folder 10.

One evening: John R. Boettiger, *A Love in Shadow: The Story of Anna Roosevelt and John Boettiger* (New York: Norton, 1978), 59.

invited her into: Ibid., 94–95.

45 *He swore each:* Transcript of conversation with Anna Roosevelt Halsted for TV series, February 13, 1962, FDRL Robert D. Graff Papers, Box 3.

so often carried her: 'Franklin D. Roosevelt carrying daughter, Anna, on his shoulders at Campobello, New Brunswick, Canada', 1907, FDRL Photographs.

the infallible hero: Anna referred to FDR as her 'childhood hero – not politically or as a world leader – just as a man and *my* father'. Asbell, ed., *Mother and Daughter*, 19.

She and her father: Ibid., 175.

46 *his gatekeeper:* John Chamberlain, 'F.D.R.'s Daughter', *Life*, March 5, 1945, 102. Anna's son Curtis (Dall) Roosevelt also discusses Anna's role as gatekeeper in *Too Close to the Sun: Growing Up in the Shadow of My Grandparents, Franklin and Eleanor* (New York: PublicAffairs, 2008), 235.

Sometimes she took: Eleanor Roosevelt, *This I Remember*, 319.

After he went: Bishop, *FDR's Last Year*, 39.

'grafting on the taxpayers': Mary Jane G [Illegible] to Anna Roosevelt Boettiger, May 29, 1944, FDRL President's Personal File 7, Anna R. Boettiger, 1942–1945. Unlike James Roosevelt, who had received a $10,000 salary when he worked at the White House earlier in their father's presidency, Anna never took a salary. Chamberlain, 'FDR's Daughter', 96.

At 10 p.m.: Logs of the Trips, 28, FDRL Grace Tully Papers, Box 7.

47 *In November:* J. Currivan to FDR, November 11, 1944, FDRL William Rigdon Papers, Correspondence.

his birthday party: Michael Beschloss, *The Conquerors: Roosevelt, Truman, and the Destruction of Hitler's Germany, 1941–1945* (New York: Simon and Schuster, 2002), 177. *'Anna can do things':* Frances Perkins, Oral History, Part VIII, 287, Columbia University, http://www.columbia.edu/cu/lweb/digital/collections/nny/perkinsf/transcripts/perkinsf_8_1_293.html.

48   *'I HATE your':* JB to AER, January 25, 1945, FDRL JBP, Box 6.
      When she had moved: Asbell, ed., *Mother and Daughter*, 175.
      Jimmy Byrnes: James Byrnes, *Speaking Frankly* (New York: Harper & Brothers Publishers, 1947), 22. He repeats this observation in *All in One Lifetime* (New York: Harper & Brothers, 1958), 253.

49   *As the ship was travelling:* AER to JB, January 29, 1945, FDRL JBP, Box 6; Byrnes would later imply that FDR barely read the State Department briefings on the conference's topics of discussion, if at all. Byrnes claimed he found them nearly untouched in the quarters of FDR's naval aide, Lieutenant Rigdon. Byrnes, *Speaking Frankly*, 23. He further implies this in *All in One Lifetime*, 256. Anna, however, attested otherwise. She said that though he did not work long hours, per his doctors' advice, he did review the State Department papers in the privacy of his quarters. AER to John L. Snell, December 30, 1955, FDRL ARHP, Box 64, Roosevelt, Franklin D.: Correspondence with FDR, 1945–1955.
      During their journey: For the messages Churchill sent to FDR during the days FDR was at sea, see Kimball, ed., *Churchill and Roosevelt: The Complete Correspondence, Vol. III*, C-883 to C-889, 515–21.
      His generals projected: David Reynolds, *Summits: Six Meetings That Shaped the Twentieth Century* (New York: Basic Books, 2007), 123.

50   *As Wilson's assistant:* Michael Dobbs, *Six Months in 1945: From World War to Cold War* (New York: Alfred A. Knopf, 2012), 78.
      'practically rock': AER to JB, May 15, 1943, FDRL JBP, Box 5.

51   *'I like Mr. Churchill':* ER to AER, January 4, 1942, in Asbell, ed., *Mother and Daughter*, 141.

Chapter Four: February 2, 1945

53   *And yet, when lunch:* FRUS, Conferences at Malta and Yalta, 'Roosevelt-Churchill Luncheon meeting', February 2, 1945, Document 316.
      For days, Harriman: SMHC to CSC, February 1, 1945, CAC SCHL 1/1/8.
      'Well, it was there': Ibid.

54   *He had grown up:* Marjorie W. Brown, *Arden House: A Living Expression of the Harriman Family* (New York: The American Assembly, Columbia University, 1981), 109–10.
      $30 billion: This figure is roughly equivalent to $350 billion in 2020.
      'trading with the Russians': Harriman and Abel, *Special Envoy*, 412.

55   *Instead of sitting:* Logs of the President's Trips: Crimea Conference and Great Bitter Lake, Egypt, January 22–February 28, 1945, 16, FDRL Grace Tully Papers, Box 7.
      Anna invited Sarah: AER Yalta Notes, 10, FDRL ARHP, Box 84.
      'unwilling to lead': Harriman and Abel, *Special Envoy*, 19.

56   *'To put it bluntly':* Ibid., 108.
      in July 1941: Walter Isaacson and Evan Thomas, *The Wise Men: Six Friends and the World They Made* (New York: Simon and Schuster Paperbacks, 1986), 214.

'Girl's Cheery Song': Kathleen Harriman, 'Girl's Cheery Song Helped Londoners Forget Their Woes', *International News Service Fast Mail Service*, July 29, 1941, KLH scrapbook, newspaper clippings, Mortimer Papers.

'Girl Reporter Finds': Kathleen Harriman, 'War Has Little Change on Women Living in London', June 5, 1941, KLH scrapbook (name of newspaper not visible in clipping), Mortimer Papers.

Just three years: KLH Bennington College junior thesis papers, Mortimer Papers.

'Since I've been': KLH to MHF, January 13, 1942, Mortimer Papers.

57 *In October 1943:* FDR had offered Harriman the position once before, in late 1941, but at the time, London was the epicentre of wartime activity, while Moscow was but a lonely outpost. Harriman indicated he would rather stay in London. By the autumn of 1943, the situation had changed dramatically. This time, he accepted.

But Harriman did not: Isaacson and Thomas, *The Wise Men*, 223–24.

'storing up trouble': Harriman and Abel, *Special Envoy*, 206.

58 *Unable to comprehend:* Ibid., 337–42. 'When they depart from common decency we have got to make them realize it,' a furious Harriman wrote to his friend, General Ira Eaker. Ibid., 342.

59 *'very bloody time':* KLH to MHF, August 20, 1944, Mortimer Papers.

160 pounds: Ibid.

Kathy would sit: KLH, 'Do the crows still roost in the Spasopeckovskaya trees?' Mortimer Papers.

'The policy appears': Harriman and Abel, *Special Envoy*, 344.

One-quarter of the city's: Isaacson and Thomas, *The Wise Men*, 231. Stalin finally agreed to allow the Americans to aid the Home Army through a single airdrop of food and supplies on September 18, 1944.

60 *In the early 1900s:* In addition to trying to break up Union Pacific, Teddy Roosevelt also called E. H. Harriman 'An undesirable citizen and an enemy of the Republic', thus adding him to the roster of the 'Ananias Club', the name the Washington press gave to a growing list of people Teddy Roosevelt denounced as liars. Harriman and Abel, *Special Envoy*, 44.

'tame millionaires': Ibid., 14.

Before the Atlantic Charter: Isaacson and Thomas, *The Wise Men*, 210–11, 216. The British then delayed a military transport bound for Cairo so Harriman could catch up. The plane already had another passenger, who was quite irritated at having been delayed for the American envoy: Charles de Gaulle.

61 *It was nearly impossible:* 'Memorandum of Conversations with the President During Trip to Washington, D.C., October 21–November 19, 1944', LOC AHP B 175 F 07. Harriman was not the only person to encounter this issue. Secretary of War Henry Stimson had tried to deliver a report in November 1944 analysing army failures leading up to the failure to anticipate the attack on Pearl Harbor, but because he was not sure what could be said in front of Anna, he recorded that 'during the luncheon I sat quiet and listened to the chitchat that went on', despite having spent four weeks preparing a report. Lelyveld, *His Final Battle*, 260.

'The President consistently': 'Memorandum of Conversations with the President During Trip to Washington, D.C., October 21–November 19, 1944', LOC AHP B 175 F 07.

'I don't care': Reynolds, *Summits*, 110, 465–66, n20.

'didn't care whether': 'Memorandum of Conversations with the President During Trip to Washington, D.C., October 21–November 19, 1944', LOC AHP B 175 F 07.

62 *'Being brutally frank':* FDR to WSC, March 18, 1942, R-123/1, in Warren F. Kimball, ed., *Churchill and Roosevelt: The Complete Correspondence, Vol. I* (Princeton, NJ: Princeton University Press, 1984), 421.

'I do not believe': 'Memorandum of Conversations with the President During Trip to Washington, D.C., October 21–November 19, 1944', LOC AHP B 175 F 07.

'virtually a fait': WAH to Edward Stettinius, December 19, 1944, LOC AHP B 176 F 01.

63 *FDR had given her:* AER Yalta Notes, 11, FDRL ARHP, Box 84.

he had already: Ibid.

Chapter Five: February 2–3, 1945

65 *one lone spotlight:* Laurence Kuter, *Airman at Yalta* (New York: Duell, Sloan and Pearce), 13.

'The Russians had': SMHC to CSC, February 1, 1945, CAC SCHL 1/1/8.

Thousands of pieces: 'Arrangements for Conveyance of the British Air Party From "CRICKET" to "ARGONAUT",' Lord Moran Archive, PP/CMW/M8/2, Wellcome Library, London.

his customary Homburg: Photographs, LOC AHP B 882 F 18.

'a minor invasion': Stettinius, *Roosevelt and the Russians*, 75.

66 *They had to look:* Taylor Downing, *Spies in the Sky: The Secret Battle for Aerial Intelligence During World War II* (London: Little, Brown, 2011), 18, 85–89.

'At this very moment': Sarah Churchill, *Keep on Dancing*, 110–11.

67 *As Winston and Sarah:* Eden and Cadogan flew with the Foreign Office staff, while the Churchills flew on their own plane, accompanied by Churchill's private secretaries, naval aide, bodyguards, and doctor, Lord Moran. 'Arrangements for Conveyance of the British Air Party from "CRICKET" to "ARGONAUT",' Lord Moran Archive, PP/CMW/M8/2, Wellcome Library, London.

six thousand feet: Plokhy, *Yalta*, 35–36.

Turkish anti-aircraft: Kuter, *Airman at Yalta*, 11.

Roosevelt's and Churchill's: Plokhy, *Yalta*, 36; Kuter, *Airman at Yalta*, 10, 14.

heavy fog: Ibid., 10–11.

Soviet airfields lacked: Ibid.

68 *After the tour:* AER Yalta Notes, 10, FDRL ARHP, Box 84.

'frantically' raced: AER Yalta Notes, 11, FDRL ARHP, Box 84.

dental work: WSC to Field Marshal Sir Harold Alexander, January 29, 1945, CAC CHAR 20/211/62.

'annoy[ed] his father': AER Yalta Notes, 12, FDRL ARHP, Box 84.

'We had a visit': SMHC to CSC, February 4, 1945, CAC SCHL 1/1/8.

'pressing engagement': AER Yalta Notes, 12, FDRL ARHP, Box 84.

Dinner finally came: Ibid.

69 *At 11.30 p.m.:* Plokhy, *Yalta*, 35.

The noise: Roberts, *Masters and Commanders*, 545.

At 3.30 a.m.: Plokhy, *Yalta*, 35.

'It's lucky': Howard Bruenn, Oral History, U.S. Naval Medical Department Oral History Program, January 31, 1990.

The Soviets: Churchill's interpreter, Major Arthur Birse, had arrived at Saki a day earlier and described the extensive preparations underway. A. H. Birse, *Memoirs of an Interpreter* (New York: Coward-McCann, 1967), 181.

70   *He had brought:* Robert Hopkins wrote in his memoir that he used some of this colour film to take what would become his favourite picture of his father and Roosevelt. He noted that its setting was the arrival at Saki. Robert Hopkins, *Witness to History: Recollections of a WWII Photographer* (Seattle: Castle Pacific Publishing, 2002), 139–40 (image on page 140). However, this photograph must have been taken on a different day. Harry Hopkins departed immediately for Yalta upon arrival, and in the picture Robert Hopkins references, Molotov is wearing a trilby, which he wore to Saki on February 12. On February 3 he wore a traditional Russian *ushanka*, which has earflaps. Because of these details, it seems the photo was taken the day the delegation left Russia, February 12.

ALBATROSS: 'To Deane from the Joint Chiefs of Staff', January 13, 1945, LOC AHP B 176 F 06. Kuter notes that the plane on which he was travelling with Marshall landed within sixty seconds of the scheduled arrival time. *Airman at Yalta*, 14.

The landing strip: Astley, *The Inner Circle*, 181.

'tile floor': Stettinius, *Roosevelt and the Russians*, 79.

General Aleksi Antonov: Papers of George Catlett Marshall, Volume 5: The Finest Soldier, 5-031 Editorial Note on Combined Chiefs of Staff Meeting at Malta, January 29–February 2, 1945, George C. Marshall Foundation, https://marshallfoundation .org/library/digital-archive/editorial-note-on-combined-chiefs-of-staff-meeting-at -malta/.

feast-laden pavilion: Kuter, *Airman at Yalta*, 3.

'Let's get going': Roberts, *Masters and Commanders*, 545.

The others had to: Stettinius, *Roosevelt and the Russians*, 80; photographs, February 3, 1945, LOC AHP B 882 F 19.

71   *Anna hurried off:* AER Yalta Notes, 13, FDRL ARHP, Box 84.

Soon the door: Newsreel footage, 'Official Pictorial Record of the Yalta Conference', January–February 1945, U.S. Army Signal Corps, http://www.criticalpast.com/video/ 65675033669_The-Yalta-Conference_Franklin-D-Roosevelt_Malta-Conference _Winston-Churchill.

'cannon-ball head': Winston S. Churchill, *Great Battles and Leaders of the Second World War: An Illustrated History* (Boston: Houghton Mifflin, 1995), 296.

'smile of Siberian': Ibid.

Stalin had not yet arrived: Plokhy, *Yalta*, 53.

The Soviets had: Woolner, *The Last 100 Days*, 63.

72   *'tragic figure':* Gilbert, *Winston S. Churchill, Vol. VII*, 1171.

Kazak carpet: Woolner, *The Last 100 Days*, 63.

Churchill's doctor: Moran, *Churchill at War*, 267. Gilbert attributes this comparison to permanent undersecretary for foreign affairs Alexander Cadogan's diary. Following Gilbert's lead, subsequent historians have also attributed it to Cadogan; however, this appears to be a mistake, as this comment does not appear in Cadogan's diary at the Churchill Archive Centre.

As Roosevelt, Churchill and Molotov: Newsreel footage, 'Official Pictorial Record of the Yalta Conference', January–February 1945, U.S. Army Signal Corps.

Anna thought it: AER Yalta Notes, 13–14, FDRL ARHP, Box 84.

'a great wide': SMCH to CSC, February 15, 1945, CAC SCHL 1/1/8.

Any buildings: Astley, *The Inner Circle*, 181.

She noticed a group: AER Yalta Notes, 13, FDRL ARHP, Box 84.

Churchill seemed amused: Photographs, February 3, 1945, LOC AHP F 882 B 19.

73   *Anna knew that the long:* AER Yalta Notes, 13, FDRL ARHP, Box 84.

his cheekbones were: Photographs, February 3, 1945, LOC AHP F 882 B 19. Several observers wrote about Roosevelt's worrisome appearance that day. Lord Moran wrote, 'The President looked old and thin and drawn; he had a cape or shawl over his shoulders and appeared shrunken; he sat looking straight ahead with his mouth open, as if he were not taking things in. Everyone was shocked by his appearance and gabbled about it afterwards.' *Churchill at War*, 267. Major Birse wrote, 'I was surprised to see how Roosevelt's appearance had changed. A year ago at Teheran he had looked vigorous and buoyant; now, he seemed old, his cheeks were sunken and the colour of wax, and he looked desperately ill.' *Memoirs of an Interpreter*, 181.

'sticky start': SMCH to CSC, February 4, 1945, CAC SCHL 1/1/8.

slushy roads: Robert Hopkins, *Witness to History*, 139.

74   *The natural environment:* For additional information on the geography and natural features of the Crimea, visit NASA Earth Observatory: https://earthobservatory.nasa .gov/IOTD/view.php?id=47117.

'an eternity': SMCH to CSC, February 4, 1945, CAC SCHL 1/1/8.

'Really!': Ibid.

haunting moors: Lord Moran, *Churchill at War*, 267.

75   *'as bleak as':* SMCH to CSC, February 4, 1945, CAC SCHL 1/1/8.

Nowhere was: For further information about the famine in the Soviet Union and the Holodomor in Ukraine, see Anne Applebaum, *Red Famine: Stalin's War on Ukraine* (New York: Doubleday, 2017). The exile of the Tatars lasted forty-five years. See Mara Kozelsky, 'Casualties of Conflict: Crimean Tatars During the Crimean War', *Slavic Review*, Vol. 67, No. 4 (Winter 2008), 866–91, https://www.jstor.org/stable/27653028?seq =1#page_scan_tab_contents. For further reading about the deportation of Crimean Tatars, see Greta Lynn Uehling, *Beyond Memory: The Crimean Tatars' Deportation and Return* (New York: Palgrave Macmillan, 2004).

Nearly all the buildings: Description of the scenery comes from the letters, diaries and memoirs written by many of the conference participants, including Charles E. Bohlen, *Witness to History, 1929–1969* (New York: W. W. Norton, 1973), 173; AER Yalta Notes, 14–15, FDRL ARHP, Box 84; Oral History interview with Anna Roosevelt Halsted, 1975, Columbia Center for Oral History Archives, Rare Book and Manuscript Library, Columbia University in the City of New York; Birse, *Memoirs of an Interpreter*, 179, 181–82; SMCH to CSC, February 4, 1945, CAC SCHL 1/1/8; Winston S. Churchill, *The Second World War, Vol. VI: Triumph and Tragedy* (Boston: Houghton Mifflin, 1953), 345; Robert Hopkins, *Witness to History*, 139–40; Stettinius, *Roosevelt and the Russians*, 81; Moran, *Churchill at War*, 267; Ross T. McIntire, *White House Physician* (New York: G. P. Putnam's Sons, 1946), 213.

More striking than their: Oral History interview with Anna Roosevelt Halsted, 1975, Columbia Center for Oral History Archives, Rare Book and Manuscript Library, Columbia University in the City of New York.

76   *The few buildings:* AER Yalta Notes, 15, FDRL ARHP, Box 84.

'Neither gray nor': Ibid., 14–15.

Harriman had assured: Ibid., 16.

'*The rest house*': SMHC to CSC, February 4, 1945, CAC SCHL 1/1/8.

77 '*groaning with food*': Ibid.

They had even constructed: AER Yalta Notes, 16, FDRL ARHP, Box 84.

But when he arrived: Ibid.

'*to exact an eye*': Ibid., 16–17.

'*begged*' *her father:* Ibid., 16.

discovered with '*horror*': Ibid.

78 *FDR had never:* FDR to WAH, January 16, 1945, LOC AHP B 176 F 06; FRUS, Conferences at Malta and Yalta, WAH to FDR, January 17, 1945, Document 60.

Anna knew that: AER to JB, February 4, 1945, FDRL JBP, Box 6.

Anna spent the next: AER Yalta Notes, 16, FDRL ARHP, Box 84.

'*That tough old bird*': Ibid. Since their first meeting, Anna viewed Churchill as something of a caricature. The first time she met Churchill was at the Trident Conference in Washington, D.C., and Camp David in May 1943. She described her first impression to John in a letter on May 15, where she commented on both Churchill's storytelling abilities and sharp conversation, but also on some of his more eccentric behaviours and less appealing personal habits, such as his use of snuff and manner of sneezing. ARB to JB, May 15, 1943, FDRL JBP, Box 5.

Trying hard: SMHC to CSC, February 4, 1945, CAC SCHL 1/1/8.

But they would not: Both Winston and Sarah clearly described Roosevelt's hasty departure in their respective memoirs. Ever the diplomat, Winston generously wrote, 'The President's party had apparently slipped past unawares,' though he certainly knew this was not true. *The Second World War, Vol. VI: Triumph and Tragedy*, 345. Sarah reprinted her entire letter to her mother, including the part about Roosevelt driving on, in *Keep on Dancing*, 127.

Chapter Six: *February 3, 1945*

81 *At six o'clock:* FRUS, Conferences at Malta and Yalta, 1945, February 3, 1945, 'President's Log at Yalta', Document 319. In the president's official log, Kathleen Harriman is the only individual explicitly named as having welcomed Roosevelt and his party to Yalta.

Stalin she had first encountered: KLH to PC, October 16, 1944, LOC PHP B I-21.

Kathy had even: Kathleen met Queen Elizabeth (the Queen Mother) at a press conference with Lord Woolton, the wartime minister of food, who was making an appeal to American women. KLH to MHF, May 30, 1941, Mortimer Papers.

How ironic: KLH to MHF, February 4–10, 1945, Mortimer Papers.

82 '*Your Excellency*': AER Yalta Notes, 17, FDRL ARHP, Box 84.

Fires blazed: Ibid.

jockey to deliver: KLH to PC, February 13, 1945, LOC PHP B I-21.

83 *While out hunting:* JB to WAH, November 18, 1941; WAH to JB, December 5, 1941, LOC AHP B 161 F 03.

'*a "peach" to quote*': KLH to PC, January 30, 1945, LOC PHP B I-21.

'*set and unset*': AER Yalta Notes, 17, FDRL ARHP, Box 84.

Secret Service agents: Ibid.

'*supposed to be a Frigidaire*': Ibid.

Roosevelt seemed pleased: KLH to MHF, February 4–10, 1945, Mortimer Papers.

84   *'A bit thick':* KLH to PC, February 4, 1945, LOC PHP B I-21.

a 'cubicle:' AER Yalta Notes, 18, FDRL ARHP, Box 84.

'sent someone scampering': Ibid., 17.

Kathy and Averell made: Stettinius, *Roosevelt and the Russians*, 82.

The dinner: AER Yalta Notes, 18, FDRL ARHP, Box 84.

85   *With him he had brought:* Harriman had long respected Bohlen's abilities and had attempted to recruit him to the embassy in Moscow, albeit unsuccessfully. In Bohlen's stead, he managed to bring George Kennan, Bohlen's colleague, to Moscow as deputy chief. Harriman valued Kennan's astute analysis of the Soviet Union second only to Bohlen's.

The two men waited: Plokhy, *Yalta*, 69.

Ten minutes after: Ibid.

'a very tough man': Harriman and Abel, *Special Envoy*, 239–40. Molotov and his colleagues respected Harriman but would never understand why the millionaire liked to shovel snow or chop his own firewood for exercise. KLH to MHF, April 18, 1944, Mortimer Papers.

After a brief exchange: Charles Bohlen, 'Memorandum of conversation between Harriman, Bohlen, Molotov and Pavlov', February 4, 1945, LOC AHP B 176 F 10. Stettinius also reports on this exchange in *Roosevelt and the Russians*, 83–84.

86   *would be 'delighted':* Charles Bohlen, 'Memorandum of conversation between Harriman, Bohlen, Molotov and Pavlov', February 4, 1945, LOC AHP B 176 F 10.

'purely personal': Ibid.

'knew the Marshal's': Ibid.

Earlier that evening: John Martin to Charles Bohlen, February 3, 1945, LOC AHP B 176 F 10.

Bohlen had replied: Charles Bohlen to John Martin, February 3, 1945, LOC AHP B 176 F 10.

Molotov, Vyshinsky: SMHC to CSC, February 4, 1945, CAC SCHL 1/1/8.

87   *as if a mosque:* SMHC to CSC, February 6, 1945, CAC SCHL 1/1/8.

hung the portraits: Winston S. Churchill, *The Second World War, Vol. VI*, 347.

'But where is Sarah?': Astley, *The Inner Circle*, 193–94.

88   *Churchill told Harriman:* Averell Harriman's foreword to Gerald Pawle, *The War and Colonel Warden* (London: George G. Harrap, 1963), 4–5.

'because I am blunt': WAH to Marie Harriman, March 30, 1941, LOC AHP B 03 F01.

a full report: Diary of Alan Francis Brooke, 1st Viscount Alanbrooke of Brookeborough, February 2, 1945, Liddell Hart Military Archives, King's College London, ALANBROOKE 5/2/26. Documents from the complete investigation of the crash, including the testimony of the pilot, who survived, can be found in TNA AIR 8/841.

three Foreign Office experts: SMHC to CSC, February 4, 1945, CAC SCHL 1/1/8. Further details on those who died can be found at https://www.chch.ox.ac.uk/fallen-alumni/captain-albany-kennett-charlesworth.

89   *'We can't agree':* Moran, *Churchill at War*, 268.

'discouraged state': KLH to PC, February 4, 1945, LOC PHP B I-21.

'all set for the best': KLH to MHF, February 4–10, 1945, Mortimer Papers.

90   *Eden's beloved bodyguard:* Sir Alexander Cadogan to Lady Theodosia Cadogan, Febru-

ary 2, 1945, in David Dilks, ed., *The Diaries of Sir Alexander Cadogan, O.M., 1938–1945* (New York: G. P. Putnam's Sons, 1971), 701.

a stillborn child: CSC to WSC, February 3, 1945, in Soames, ed., *Winston and Clementine*, 514.

Brooke's aide-de-camp: Diary of Alan Francis Brooke, 1st Viscount Alanbrooke of Brookeborough, February 2, 1945, Liddell Hart Military Archives, King's College London, ALANBROOKE 5/2/26; see also 'Loss of York MW. 116', TNA AIR 8/841.

'We shall meet': Alex Danchev and Daniel Todman, eds., *War Diaries, 1939–1945: Field Marshal Lord Alanbrooke* (London: Weidenfeld and Nicolson, 2001), 661; see also Diary of Alan Brooke, February 10, 1945, ALANBROOKE 5/2/27.

'one of the wisest': KLH to MHF, May 30, 1941, Mortimer Papers.

especially pilots: Kathy wrote to her sister about their fighter pilot friends based near the cottage she shared with Pam on the weekends in the countryside. In one letter, she told about spending an evening with them at the local pub before they left to go on duty: 'Seeing them leave and wondering if they'd all come back gave me a funny feeling.' KLH to MHF, July 7, 1941, Mortimer Papers.

'At this point': KLH to PC, February 4, 1945, LOC PHP B I-21.

91   *'end of the beginning':* WSC remarks at Lord Mayor's luncheon, Mansion House, November 10, 1942.

Walt Disney's Fantasia: KLH to MHF, May 17, 1941, Mortimer Papers; Kathleen repeats this observation in her newspaper column 'War has brought many changes to London night life', *INS Fast Mail Service*, August 6, 1941, KLH scrapbook, Mortimer Papers.

'Just wait 'til': KLH to MHF, May 17, 1941, Mortimer Papers.

'If it weren't': WAH to Marie Harriman, May 20, 1941, LOC AHP B 03 F 01.

As Roosevelt had told: WAH to KLH and PC, August 1941, Mortimer Papers.

92   *'It's rather a shock':* KLH to MHF, June 2 or 3, 1941, Mortimer Papers.

'He showed me': KLH to MHF, July 7, 1941, Mortimer Papers.

'a very sweet lady': KLH to MHF, June 2 or 3, 1941, Mortimer Papers.

'a terribly nice girl': KLH to MHF, July 7, 1941, Mortimer Papers.

While she found: KLH to MHF, August 15, 1945, Mortimer Papers.

93   *'Going on stage':* KLH to MHF, July 7, 1941, Mortimer Papers.

When Kathy wrote to: Kathleen consistently wrote to Mouche with such requests, which appear numerous times throughout their correspondence. Mortimer Papers.

'loot suitcase': KLH to Marie Harriman, December 7, 1942, LOC AHP B 06 F 10. Marie specifically included hats for Sarah in this package.

'nicest, sanest girl': KLH to MHF, May 17, 1941, Mortimer Papers.

'Perhaps by now': KLH to MHF, August 8, 1941, Mortimer Papers.

Clementine mistakenly: Pamela Harriman, 'When Churchill Heard the News . . .', *Washington Post,* December 7, 1991. Harriman and Abel note that Churchill gave Kathy a signed copy of his book *The River War* as a birthday present. *Special Envoy*, 111.

94   *'danced a jig':* KLH to MHF, December 1941, Mortimer Papers.

her father stood: In his war memoirs, Churchill said of Harriman and Winant, 'One might almost have thought they had been delivered from a long pain.' Winston S. Churchill, *The Second World War, Vol. III: The Grand Alliance* (Boston: Houghton Mifflin, 1986), 538.

Averell had long: Harriman and Abel, *Special Envoy*, 112. Harriman was so staunchly against American isolationism and fearful that Americans underestimated the Nazi menace that two days later (December 9), during a dinner with Kathleen, Pamela and the American-born British Conservative MP Henry Channon, Harriman (according to Channon) had said he 'hopes that the American cities will be blitzed, so as to wake the people up'. James, ed., *Chips: The Diaries of Sir Henry Channon* (London: Weidenfeld and Nicolson, 1967), 314.

'I wonder': KLH to Elsie Marshall, January 5, 1942, Mortimer Papers.

'so excited about': KLH to MHF, June 2 or 3, 1941, Mortimer Papers.

'I have been': Randolph Churchill to WSC, July 5, 1941, CAC CHAR 20/33/37-44.

95   *Averell worried:* KLH to MHF, undated, retyped, 1941, Mortimer Papers.

'rather like a prize': Ibid.

Averell had first met: In Christopher Ogden's biography of Pamela, Ogden writes that Pamela said she met Harriman on March 19 at a dinner given by Emerald Cunard at the Dorchester Hotel. Christopher Ogden, *Life of the Party: The Biography of Pamela Digby Churchill Hayward Harriman* (Boston: Little, Brown and Company, 1994), 112. However, as Sally Bedell Smith illustrates in *Reflected Glory: The Life of Pamela Churchill Harriman* (New York: Simon & Schuster, 1996), 84, Pamela's statement was incorrect, as Cunard was then in the United States. Thus, the date of their first meeting is most likely March 29, at the Chequers luncheon.

She had a remarkable: Author's interview with Peter Duchin, July 19, 2018.

96   *his gleaming smile a rare gift:* John Colville, *Winston Churchill and His Inner Circle* (New York: Wyndham Books, 1981), 120.

games of croquet: One of Clementine Churchill's favorite croquet partners, Harriman was said to be the only one who could beat her. Abramson, *Spanning the Century*, 299–300.

the most 'beautiful': Elisabeth Bumiller, 'Pamela Harriman', *Washington Post*, June 12, 1983.

Shortly after: WAH to Marie Harriman, April 17, 1941, LOC AHP B 03 F 01.

'Needless to say': Ibid.

Churchill's friend: Smith, *Reflected Glory*, 91–92.

Sarah and Diana: Ibid., 104–5.

97   *'absolutely charming':* Winston S. Churchill II, *Memories and Adventures* (New York: Weidenfeld and Nicholson, 1989), 20.

'You know, they're': Lynne Olson, *Citizens of London* (New York: Random House Trade Paperbacks, 2010), 103–4.

'You know': Christopher Ogden interview with PC, 1991, LOC PHP B I-304.

Mark Hanna: Smith, *Reflected Glory*, 89.

Eddy Duchin: Author's conversation with David Mortimer, December 5, 2018.

off on an 'adventure': KLH to MHF, June 27, 1941, Mortimer Papers.

'no intention': KLH to Elise Marshall, spring 1942, Mortimer Papers.

'I had to decide': Christopher Ogden interview with PC, 1991, LOC PHP B I-304.

98   *In an effort to:* KLH to MHF, July 30, 1942, Mortimer Papers.

But rumours about: Smith, *Reflected Glory*, 104.

'Help Pam': WAH to KLH, undated, October 1943, Mortimer Papers.

deeds to his Ford: N. T. Bartlett to PC, August 9, 1943, LOC AHP B 04 F 07.

allowance of £3,000: Smith, *Reflected Glory*, 108–9. Three thousand pounds in 1943 is roughly equivalent to £135,000 in 2020.

Kathy was aware: KLH to PC, April 6, [1944], LOC PHP B I-21 Mar-Apr (no year). There was an issue of some kind, and Pamela was not receiving her payments, as Harriman had arranged, through Max Beaverbrook. Kathy assumed it was Beaverbrook's fault and told Pamela she hoped she had not 'run short.'

99   *Hundreds of pages:* Kathleen and Pamela's wartime correspondence, as well as letters between Pamela and Averell, are in LOC PHP B I-21 and I-22. Additional letters between Pamela and Averell are in LOC AHP B 04.

'One evening Ave': KLH to PC, January 30, 1945, LOC PHP B I-21. This is the only explicit reference to the affair that survives in Kathy's wartime correspondence. Whether others once existed is unknown. It is possible that Kathy later removed letters referring to the affair, but it is also conceivable that she did not reference the affair in her letters out of concern that someone who knew Marie might read them, as her letters were passed around and shown to friends in London and New York.

Chapter Seven: February 3, 1945

101   *her footsteps echoing:* Churchill's interpreter, Arthur Birse, described people's footsteps echoing in the practically empty palace. *Memoirs of an Interpreter*, 180.

Stettinius had taken: AER to JB, February 4, 1945, FDRL JBP, Box 6.

concerned about Hopkins: AER Yalta Notes, 12, 18, FDRL ARHP, Box 84.

102   *'old maids':* Lelyveld, *His Final Battle*, 26. Historically, the political leanings of the State Department tend to be more centrist than those of any given president, as the bulk of its workforce is made up of career civil servants with a broad array of political perspectives. They average out to give the agency a moderate tilt overall. The State Department had markedly less enthusiasm for Roosevelt's liberal politics than did the White House.

'I won't take Jimmy': Alger Hiss, IWM Oral History, 1972.

not properly slept: Anna had been too excited to sleep on the plane; she wanted to be awake to see the Greek islands and Turkey as the sun rose. AER Yalta Notes, 13, FDRL ARHP, Box 84.

a 'prima donna': Anna Roosevelt Halsted interview by Bernard Asbell, 1972, FDRL ARHP, Box 63.

103   *Stettinius sent him ahead:* AER Yalta Notes, 18, FDRL ARHP, Box 84.

'an ill-fed horse': Goodwin, *No Ordinary Time*, 31.

'Skinny': David L. Roll, *The Hopkins Touch: Harry Hopkins and the Forging of the Alliance to Defeat Hitler* (Oxford: Oxford University Press, 2013), 12.

His jowls were sagging: Photograph, February 11, 1945, LOC AHP B 882 F 19; photographs, February 1945, Georgetown University, Booth Family Center for Special Collections, Robert Hopkins Papers, Box 7B.

striped pyjamas: Photograph in Robert Hopkins, *Witness to History*, 156.

'got a good education': Harry Hopkins to Diana Hopkins, January 19, 1945, Georgetown University, Booth Family Center for Special Collections, HLHP1, Box 40, Folder 6.

'in a stew': AER Yalta Notes, 18, FDRL ARHP, Box 84.

In London: Robert Sherwood, *Roosevelt and Hopkins: An Intimate History* (New York: Harper and Brothers, 1948), 847.

104   *Many within the Washington:* Ibid., 1.

the two men: Goodwin, *No Ordinary Time*, 480.

Strains began to appear: Ibid., 349–50, 372; Roll, *The Hopkins Touch*, 284–85.

105 *By December 1943:* Ibid., 286.

He was so sick: Sherwood, *Roosevelt and Hopkins*, 804, 807. When Stephen Hopkins was killed, Sarah Churchill sent a touching note of condolence to Harry Hopkins, writing, 'No matter how often I hear that news – I don't know what to say – but know that your friends grieve for you.' SMHC to Harry Hopkins, May 12, 1944, Georgetown University, Booth Family Center for Special Collections, HLHP1, Box 4, Folder 4.

106 *On the ship:* AER Yalta Notes, 7, FDRL ARHP, Box 84; Jonathan Daniels to Steve Early, January 29, 1945, FDRL Steve Early Papers, Box 37.

'once was a firm': Press Wireless N.Y, WCX 1800Z SKED, FDRL ARHP, Box 84, Miscellaneous.

'spent ten years': FRUS, Conferences at Malta and Yalta, Harry Hopkins to FDR, January 24, 1945, Document 66.

'FDR must see': AER Yalta Notes, 18, FDRL ARHP, Box 84.

'Your mother only': Goodwin, *No Ordinary Time*, 179, from interview with James Roosevelt.

Sara would try: Oral History interview with Anna Roosevelt Halsted, 1975, Columbia Center for Oral History Archives, Rare Book and Manuscript Library, Columbia University in the City of New York.

107 *her grandmother's 'football':* Ibid.

'stir up some': AER Yalta Notes, 19, FDRL ARHP, Box 84.

convene with Ed Stettinius: Ibid.

While Hopkins was moving: Goodwin, *No Ordinary Time*, 480, 488–89; Sherwood, *Roosevelt and Hopkins*, 804.

108 *Louis Howe:* Asbell, ed., *Mother and Daughter*, 31.

To Hopkins, Anna seemed: Roll, *The Hopkins Touch*, 364.

Anna in turn: AER Yalta Notes, 7, FDRL ARHP, Box 84. In her diary Anna made particular note of FDR's irritated feelings towards Hopkins on the ship: 'FDR and his immediate entourage are laying for Harry because of all the interviews he's given out concerning the Conf. It appears that he had a firm agreement with Steve that he would be off the record during his recent visits to London, Paris and Rome and would give no interviews. Almost every day there have been stories from all three places giving his views as to what the Conf will cover!'

'deserting' FDR: Anna Roosevelt Halsted interview by Bernard Asbell, 1972, FDRL ARHP, Box 63.

'closest person to': Drew Pearson, 'Washington Merry-Go-Round', FDRL President's Personal File 7, Anna R. Boettiger, 1942–45.

109 *'FDR,' he told her:* AER Yalta Notes, 18–19, FDRL ARHP, Box 84.

thoroughly 'insulting': Ibid.

'Certainly it didn't': AER Yalta Notes, 19, FDRL ARHP, Box 84.

110 *'Mr. President':* FRUS, Conferences at Malta and Yalta, John Gilbert Winant to FDR, February 3, 1945, Document 471.

Chapter Eight: February 4, 1945

115 *It was as if two:* SMHC to CSC, February 6, 1945, CAC SCHL 1/1/8.

'There are views': Ibid.

116   *'conquests':* Anton Chekhov, *The Lady with the Dog and Other Stories* 1899, https://www
.gutenberg.org/files/13415/13415-h/13415-h.htm.
'Throughout your stay': 'General Information Bulletin', LOC AHP B 176 F 09. Norris
Houghton, one of the supplemental Russian-speaking officers the navy sent to Yalta,
claims authorship of this document. See Houghton, 'That Was Yalta', *The New Yorker*,
May 23, 1953, 95.

117   *FDR had finally:* Houghton, 'That Was Yalta', 96; Stettinius, *Roosevelt and the Russians*,
84; FRUS, Conferences at Malta and Yalta, 'Meeting of the President with his advisers', February 4, 1945, Document 322.
Armed sentries: AER Yalta Notes, 19–20, FDRL ARHP, Box 84.
green American: AER identity cards, FDRL ARHP, Box 84, Miscellaneous.
One claimed: AER Yalta Notes, 19–20, FDRL ARHP, Box 84.
The American delegation: Sir Charles Portal to PC, February 4, 1945, LOC PHP B I-31.
'snapping turtle': Kathleen Harriman Mortimer, IWM Oral History, September 10,
1996.
'come & stay': KLH to PC, January 30, 1945, LOC PHP B I-21.

118   *'absolutely charming':* KLH to MHF, February 4–10, 1945, Mortimer Papers.
story of Randolph: KLH to PC, February 4, 1945, LOC PHP B I-21.
'I like Kathleen': AER to JB, February 4, 1945, FDRL JBP, Box 6.
Moscow Slalom Championships: KLH to MHF, February 23, 1944, Mortimer Papers;
KLH to PC, February 27, 1944, LOC PHP B I-21.

119   *Anna felt she:* Curtis Roosevelt, *Too Close to the Sun*, 274–75. Eleanor's insecurity
showed in her strained relationships with women who, to her, seemed to be en-
croaching upon her domain. They included Louise Hopkins, her daughter-in-law
Betsey, and Franklin's close friend Princess Martha of Norway, who had fled to the
United States when the Nazis invaded. See Anna Roosevelt Halsted interview by
Bernard Asbell, 1972, FDRL ARHP, Box 63, and Goodwin, *No Ordinary Time*, 109, 439.
'save FDR too much': AER Yalta Notes, 19, FDRL ARHP, Box 84.
'responding nicely': Ibid.
'Harry tells me': AER to JB, February 4, 1945, FDRL JBP, Box 6.

120   *June 1942:* PC to Harry Hopkins, July 1, 1942, Georgetown University, Booth Family
Center for Special Collections HLHP1, Box 4 Folder 3.
'he used to have': AER to JB, February 4, 1945, FDRL JBP, Box 6. Harry Hopkins seemed
to take delight in facilitating other people's romantic affairs. A note to Pamela
Churchill from Averell Harriman, asking her to please call, was once mistakenly
slipped under the door of Hopkins's hotel suite during his visit to London. He sent the
note back with an amusing annotation: 'The door under which this was stuck was
the bedroom of Harry L. Hopkins who was damn proud of it.' LOC PHP B I-21.
'I suppose women': KLH to MHF, August 10, 1942, Mortimer Papers. Kathy documented
her ongoing conflict with Robb in her letters to her sister, Mary, on November 6,
1941; December 16, 1941; January 6, 1942; January 11, 1942; February 23, 1942; and August 10, 1942. In her January 6 letter, Kathy says, 'Inez Robb called me up and called
me every name imaginable . . . She was almost hysterical, told me she'd written . . . the
Foreign Editor about me and torn up some letters she was given to deliver to me . . .
The one thing I wanted to stay clear of was office politics. She also informed me that
last night she contemplated cabling INS that either she or I must leave. This is the

woman who I have met twice in my life, who each time has tried to make me feel like a complete fool.'

Chapter Nine: February 4, 1945

121   *armoured train:* Plokhy, *Yalta*, 53.

   Under Lavrentiy Beria's: Ibid., 54.

   He had also stationed: Arkady N. Shevchenko, *Breaking with Moscow* (New York: Alfred A. Knopf, 1985), 58. Shevchenko, one of the highest-ranking Soviet officials ever to defect to the United States during the Cold War, was a boy growing up in the Crimean coastal village of Yevpatoriya during World War II. His family was evacuated to the Altai Mountains in Siberia in the autumn of 1941. They returned to Yevpatoriya in 1944. His father was one of the doctors asked to observe Roosevelt at Saki.

   Thinking she had: Sir Charles Portal to PC, February 3, 1945, LOC PHP B I-31.

122   *'an agreeable discussion':* Winston S. Churchill, *The Second World War, Vol. VI*, 347–48.

   Stalin brought: FRUS, Conferences at Malta and Yalta, 'Roosevelt-Stalin meeting', Bohlen Minutes, February 4, 1945, Document 325.

123   *'propose a toast':* Ibid. Bohlen also references this exchange in his memoir, *Witness to History*, 180.

   'convinced that all': Winston S. Churchill, *The Second World War, Vol. V: Closing the Ring* (Boston: Houghton Mifflin, 1951), 374.

   'something indiscreet': FRUS, Conferences at Malta and Yalta, 'Roosevelt-Stalin Meeting', Bohlen Minutes, February 4, 1945, Document 325.

124   *Soviet soldiers armed:* Houghton, 'That Was Yalta', 96–97.

   Stalin arrived with Molotov: Newsreel footage, 'Allied delegates arrive for the international conference at Lavadia [*sic*] Palace in Yalta', February 4, 1945, https://www.criticalpast.com/video/65675033670_The-Yalta-Conference_Franklin-D-Roosevelt_Lavidia-Palace_conference-room.

   When Sarah arrived: Ibid.

   Churchill, by contrast: Houghton, 'That Was Yalta', 96–97; newsreel footage, 'Allied delegates arrive for the international conference at Lavadia [*sic*] Palace in Yalta', February 4, 1945, https://www.criticalpast.com/video/65675033670_The-Yalta-Conference_Franklin-D-Roosevelt_Lavidia-Palace_conference-room.

   Two British: Robert Hopkins, *Witness to History*, 144.

125   *Anna snapped:* AER Yalta Notes, 20, FDRL ARHP, Box 84.

   Nearby, Kathy: Photograph, 'Prime minister Churchill talks with his daughter Sarah, while Gen. Sir Harold R.L.G. Alexander looks on', U.S. Army Signal Corps, February 1945, Newberry Library, Chicago, Papers of Ralph Graham, B 01 F 05.

   He gave her arm: Ibid.

   interpreters rather than translators: In his book *Memoirs of an Interpreter*, Arthur Birse offers a thorough, thoughtful explanation of the role of the interpreter and why interpretation is much more complex than mere translation. See 113–15.

   FDR often kept: Bohlen, *Witness to History*, 165.

126   *While Bohlen arranged:* Newsreel footage, 'Allied delegates arrive for the international conference at Lavadia [*sic*] Palace in Yalta', February 4, 1945, https://www

.criticalpast.com/video/65675033670_The-Yalta-Conference_Franklin-D-Roosevelt_Lavidia-Palace_conference-room.

'Bad luck on A': Sir Charles Portal to PC, February 4, 1945, LOC PHP B I-31.

'talks be conducted': FRUS, Conferences at Malta and Yalta, 'First plenary meeting', Bohlen Minutes, February 4, 1945, Document 326.

'most cordial': Winston S. Churchill, *The Second World War: Vol. VI*, 349.

Admiral Cunningham: Roberts, *Masters and Commanders*, 552.

Over the next three: FRUS, Conferences at Malta and Yalta, 'First plenary meeting', Bohlen Minutes, February 4, 1945, Document 326.

127 *He spoke Russian:* Birse, *Memoirs of an Interpreter*, 101, 113.

'emphasize the spirit': FRUS, Conferences at Malta and Yalta, 'First plenary meeting', Bohlen Minutes, February 4, 1945, Document 326.

'The reason that': FRUS, Conferences at Malta and Yalta, 'First plenary meeting', Combined Chiefs of Staff Minutes, February 4, 1945, Document 327.

'an era of good feeling': Bohlen, *Witness to History*, 177.

128 *'I am aware':* Ibid., 175.

'simply an attempt': George Kennan, *Memoirs, 1925–1950* (Boston: Little, Brown, 1967), 215.

president optimistically: Bohlen, *Witness to History*, 210. In his memoir, Bohlen was very critical of FDR's approach to foreign policy, writing, 'In foreign affairs, Roosevelt did his job only moderately well. The methods and techniques that he usually used with consummate skill in domestic politics did not fit well in foreign affairs. He relied on his instinctive grasp of the subject, which was good, and his genius for improvisation to find solutions to problems . . . In foreign affairs, particularly when dealing with the Soviet leaders, this style meant a lack of precision, which . . . was a serious fault. A deeper knowledge of history and certainly a better understanding of reactions of foreign peoples would have been useful to the President. Helpful, too, would have been more study of the position papers prepared by American experts, more attention to detail, and less belief in the American conviction that the other fellow is a "good guy" who will respond properly and decently if you treat him right.'

But, Bohlen maintained: Ibid., 176.

From time to time: Houghton, 'That Was Yalta', 96.

129 *the 'children's party':* KLH to MHF, February 4, 1945, Mortimer Papers.

Someone from: AER Yalta Notes, 22, FDRL ARHP, Box 84.

'sitting on tacks': Ibid., 21.

Before the plenary: Ibid.

130 *'was having a tantrum':* Ibid.

'A tantrum was': Ibid.

FDR believed Stalin: Harriman and Abel, *Special Envoy*, 395.

'cooling his heels': AER Yalta Notes, 21, FDRL ARHP, Box 84.

He even threatened: Harriman and Abel, *Special Envoy*, 395.

131 *At lunch Anna had:* AER Yalta Notes, 20, FDRL ARHP, Box 84.

'have to watch certain': Ibid.

'a real prima donna': Anna Roosevelt Halsted interview by Bernard Asbell, 1972, FDRL ARHP, Box 63.

'free for all': ARB Yalta Notes, 21–22, FDRL ARHP, Box 84.

'corralled': AER Yalta Notes, 22, FDRL ARHP, Box 84.

including Anderson: KLH to PC, February 7, 1945, LOC PHP B I-21.
'a swell 2 starer': Ibid. Kuter was the youngest man promoted to general officer, a
record held until that point by the famed Civil War general William T. Sherman.

132   *His chefs had prepared:* Stettinius, *Roosevelt and the Russians*, 114.
and macaroni: Atkinson, *The Guns at Last Light*, 513.
a very 'fine toast!': AER Yalta Notes, 22, FDRL ARHP, Box 84.
Anna betrayed nothing: Ibid.

Chapter Ten: February 5, 1945

133   *'If you were':* SMHC to CSC, February 4, 1945, CAC SCHL 1/1/8.
a mere four: Astley, *The Inner Circle*, 183, 194–95.
Whenever he felt: Ibid.
picking the lock: Sir Charles Portal to PC, February 7, 1945, LOC PHP B I-31.
Kathy had mused: KLH to PC, January 30, 1945, LOC PHP B I-21.

134   *'Papa is very sweet':* SCHL to CSC, February 4, 1945, CAC SCHL 1/1/8.
Winston awoke: Moran, *Churchill at War*, 270.
At Livadia Palace: Houghton, 'That Was Yalta', 94; 'Report of Medical Department
Activities at Crimean Conference', February 18, 1945, FDRL Ross T. McIntire Papers,
Box 4, 'Crimea Conference'.
impromptu conferences: Kuter, *Airman at Yalta*, 122.
chambermaids wandered: Ibid., 121–22.
safe to drink: 'General Information Bulletin', LOC AHP B 176 F 09.
magnesium sulfate: Kuter, *Airman at Yalta*, 124.
First came the Russian: Ibid., 123.

135   *'speaking no known':* AER Yalta Notes, 22, FDRL ARHP, Box 84.
like 'brunch': SMHC to CSC, February 8, 1945, CAC SCHL 1/1/8.
'Comparing those meals': KLH to PC, February 7, 1945, LOC PHP B I-21.

136   *'A Russian imbues':* Mark Twain, *The Innocents Abroad* (New York: The Library of America, 1984), 311.
The next day: Christopher Andrew and Vasili Mitrokhin, *The Sword and the Shield: The
Mitrokhin Archive and the Secret History of the KGB* (New York: Basic Books, 1999), 133.
Peter Portal was admiring: Winston S. Churchill, *The Second World War, Vol. VI*, 347.
Sarah also notes Portal's affinity for the fish tank in the conservatory in SMHC to
CSC, February 6, 1945, CAC SCHL 1/1/8.
'bed warmers': Author's interview with Ellie Seagraves, January 26, 2018.

137   *'much telephoning':* Sir Charles Portal to PC, February 5, 1945, LOC PHP B I-31.
They arrived to the meeting: Diary of Alan Francis Brooke, 1st Viscount Alanbrooke
of Brookeborough, February 5, 1945, Liddell Hart Military Archives, King's College
London, ALANBROOKE 5/2/27.
Eventually, the chiefs: FRUS, Conferences at Malta and Yalta, 'First tripartite military
meeting', February 4, 1945, Document 330.
The cordiality continued: FRUS, Conferences at Malta and Yalta, 'Luncheon meeting of the Foreign Ministers', February 5, 1945, Document 331. On board the *Quincy*,
Roosevelt had placed bets as to whether the Americans would reach Manila before
the Soviets reached Berlin. He had mentioned this to Stalin in their private meeting
the day before; Stalin had replied with certainty that it would be the Americans at

Manila. FRUS, Conferences at Malta and Yalta, 'Roosevelt-Stalin meeting', February 4, 1945, Document 325. Though MacArthur thought they had dealt the decisive blow in Manila, the battle would continue until March.

The Soviets' negotiation: Sherwood, *Roosevelt and Hopkins*, 395.

138   *Winston and Sarah took:* SMHC to CSC, February 6, 1945, CAC SCHL 1/1/8.

perpetually shivering: SMHC to CSC, undated October 1941, CAC SCHL 1/1/6.

chilblains on her feet: SMHC to CSC, November 5, 1941, CAC SCHL 1/1/6.

On their walk: SMHC to CSC, February 6, 1945, CAC SCHL 1/1/8.

In the slick: Astley, *The Inner Circle*, 183.

A school of fish: SMHC to CSC, February 6, 1945, CAC SCHL 1/1/8.

Portal was daydreaming: Sir Charles Portal to PC, February 5, 1945, LOC PHP B-I31.

Brooke, who was: Diary of Alan Francis Brooke, 1st Viscount Alanbrooke of Brooke-borough, February 5, 1945, Liddell Hart Military Archives, King's College London, ALANBROOKE 5/2/27; David Fraser, *Alanbrooke* (New York: Athenaeum, 1982), 518.

'Surely,' she exclaimed: SMHC to CSC, February 6, 1945, CAC SCHL 1/1/8. In Plokhy, *Yalta*. S. M. Plokhy describes this scene on page 117 but misattributes Brooke's comments to Alexander. He mistakenly identifies Alexander, rather than Brooke, as the C.I.G.S., and also fails to note the reference Winston Churchill makes about Brooke's passion for birds, which doubly identifies Brooke, and not Alexander, as the speaker.

139   *'Not at all':* SMHC to CSC, February 6, 1945, CAC SCHL 1/1/8.

'usual cool dispassionate': Ibid.

Birch logs blazed: Alger Hiss, *Recollections of a Life* (New York: Seaver Books, 1988), 124.

looked markedly better: Bohlen, *Witness to History*, 174; Hiss, *Recollections of a Life*, 122.

140   *'confine themselves':* FRUS, Conferences at Malta and Yalta, 'Second plenary meeting', February 5, 1945, Bohlen Minutes, Document 333.

Stalin stopped him: Ibid.

He began to reminisce: Ibid.

As Roosevelt waxed: Bohlen, *Witness to History*, 183.

141   *'Dealing with the fate':* FRUS, Conferences at Malta and Yalta, 'Second plenary meeting', February 5, 1945, Bohlen Minutes, Document 333. This position was consistent with what Churchill had written to Anthony Eden on January 4, 1945: 'It is a mistake to try to write out on little pieces of paper what the vast emotions of an outraged and quivering world will be either immediately after the struggle is over or when the inevitable cold fit follows the hot.' Winston S. Churchill, *The Second World War: Vol. VI*, 351.

'fully understood': Ibid. It was a canny manoeuvre. The foreign ministers' study committee never met. Bohlen, *Witness to History*, 183.

142   *De Gaulle was furious:* For more on the meeting between Hopkins and de Gaulle, see Sherwood, *Roosevelt and Hopkins*, 847, and Jean Lacoutre, *De Gaulle: The Ruler, 1945–1970, Vol. 2* (New York: W. W. Norton, 1993), 55–59.

Stalin, however: FRUS, Conferences at Malta and Yalta, 'Second plenary meeting', February 5, 1945, Bohlen Minutes, Document 333.

and 'phlegmatic': Winston S. Churchill, *Great Battles and Leaders*, 254.

'not a British': Ibid., 260.

FDR's sudden announcement: FRUS, Conferences at Malta and Yalta, 'Second plenary meeting', February 5, 1945, Bohlen Minutes, Document 333.

143 *'Promise a zone':* FRUS, Conferences at Malta and Yalta, Harry Hopkins to FDR, February 5, 1945, Document 336.

Churchill and Stalin agreed: FRUS, Conferences at Malta and Yalta, 'Second plenary meeting', February 5, 1945, Bohlen Minutes, Document 333.

close professional: Perhaps due to his time in Britain, Maisky had a different opinion about postwar partnerships with the Allies than did others in the Soviet government. Maisky viewed the United States with much scepticism, particularly American 'dynamic imperialism'. He saw it as distinct from the traditional British form of imperialism, which he viewed as a force for global stability. He was a proponent of maintaining good relations with Britain. As Maisky stated, 'The logic of things must press Britain closer to the USSR, because its fundamental struggle in the postwar period will be against the USA . . . I am also . . . inclined to think that in this period it will be to the USSR's interest to keep Britain as a strong power: in particular, it will be interested in Britain's retention of a strong navy, for such a Britain can be needed by us to counter the USA's imperialist expansion.' Fraser J. Harbutt, *Yalta 1945: Europe and America at the Crossroads* (Cambridge: Cambridge University Press, 2010), 111. Just before Stalin's death in 1953, Maisky was arrested, accused of being a British spy and sentenced to six years in prison. In 1955, his sentencing was reversed and he was released.

As Maisky reminded: FRUS, Conferences at Malta and Yalta, 'Second plenary meeting', February 5, 1945, Bohlen Minutes, Document 333.

Harriman had long maintained: Harriman and Abel, *Special Envoy*, 404–5.

144 *amount of $6 billion:* Ibid., 384–85.

feeding eighty million: FRUS, Conferences at Malta and Yalta, 'Second plenary meeting'. February 5, 1945, Bohlen Minutes, Document 333.

'If you wished': Stettinius, *Roosevelt and the Russians*, 132.

'There would be': Ibid.

'spare no effort': Diary of Ivan Maisky, March 31, 1943, in Gabriel Gorodetsky, ed., *The Maisky Diaries: Red Ambassador to the Court of St. James's, 1932–1943* (New Haven, CT: Yale University Press, 2015), 502–4.

145 *Instead, he suggested:* FRUS, Conferences at Malta and Yalta, 'Second plenary meeting'. February 5, 1945, Bohlen Minutes, Document 333; Matthews Minutes, Document 334.

'came out at a run': KLH to PC, February 7, 1945, LOC PHP B I-21. Bohlen also describes this episode in *Witness to History*, 174.

146 *their respective 'lairs':* SMHC to CSC, February 8, 1945, CAC SCHL 1/1/8.

Chapter Eleven: February 5, 1945

147 *'built close to':* Gary Kern, 'How "Uncle Joe" Bugged FDR: The Lessons of History', *Studies in Intelligence*, Vol. 47, No. 1, https://www.cia.gov/library/center-for-the-study-of-intelligence/csi-publications/csi-studies/studies/vol47no1/article02.html#fn37. The quotation originally appearing in Harry Hopkins, 'The Inside Story of My Meeting with Stalin', *American Magazine*, December 1941.

'face was pockmarked': Kathleen Harriman Mortimer, IWM Oral History, September 10, 1996.

148 *'You said it':* Plokhy, *Yalta*, 318.

cowboy westerns: Montefiore, *Stalin,* 517.

'with a twinkle': Winston S. Churchill, *The Second World War, Vol. IV: The Hinge of Fate* (Boston: Houghton Mifflin, 1985), 446, 450. Svetlana found her father's behaviour during the meeting with Churchill very strange at the time, only later realising he was performing for Churchill and trying to seem like 'an ordinary human being'. Svetlana Alliluyeva, *Twenty Letters to a Friend* (New York: Harper and Row, 1967), 171.

sent Sarah a brooch: SMHC to CSC, January 31, 1945; SMHC to CSC, February 12, 1945, CAC SCHL 1/1/8.

149   *Nadezhda had committed:* Rosemary Sullivan, *Stalin's Daughter: The Extraordinary and Tumultuous Life of Svetlana Allilueyva* (New York: Harper, 2015), 42, 44, 103–4.

He refused to meet: Ibid., 130.

'bad daughter': Alliluyeva, *Twenty Letters to a Friend,* 9–10.

150   *'jealously cold':* KLH to MHF, June 9, 1944, Mortimer Papers.

The agency had: Plokhy, *Yalta,* 58.

151   *'He was a magnificent':* Alliluyeva, *Twenty Letters to a Friend,* 8.

One of Beria's underlings: Montefiore, *Stalin,* 76.

'class enemies': Andrew and Mitrokhin, *The Sword and the Shield,* 101–2; for more on Beria's actions as head of the NKVD, see Amy Knight, *Beria: Stalin's First Lieutenant* (Princeton, NJ: Princeton University Press, 1993), 113–14, 126–27, and Plokhy, *Yalta,* 58–59.

In his office: Montefiore, *Stalin,* 505–8.

Stalin had known: As a little boy, Sergo received paternal affection from Stalin of a kind that Stalin never gave Svetlana. As Montefiore writes, Stalin would wrap Sergo in his wolf-fur coat when Sergo was cold and tuck the boy into bed. *Stalin,* 127–28.

152   *personally asked him:* Plokhy, *Yalta,* 233.

Some daughters of: Sullivan, *Stalin's Daughter,* 136–37; Montefiore, *Stalin,* 509. Svetlana's best friend and Maxim Gorky's granddaughter Martha Peshkova married Sergo Beria.

directional microphones: Sergo Beria, *Beria, My Father: Inside Stalin's Kremlin* (London: Duckworth, 2001), 104.

From their listening centre: Sergo Beria, IWM Oral History, October 19, 1996.

many of them women: Andrew and Mitrokhin, *The Sword and the Shield,* 133.

on the scraps: Sergo Beria, *Beria, My Father,* 104.

Through powerful directional: Ibid.

153   *'poodle wagging':* Ibid.

breakup of the British Empire: Sergo Beria, IWM Oral History, October 19, 1996.

154   *If he asked permission:* 'Hearings Before the Select Committee to Conduct an Investigation of the Facts, Evidence, and Circumstances of the Katyn Forest Massacre', Eighty-Second Congress, 1952, 2147.

seventeen western journalists: 'Trip to Smolensk and the Katyn Forest, January 21–23, 1944', enclosures to 'Despatch of February 23, 1944 from the American Embassy, Moscow', Mortimer Papers.

155   *short-staffed embassy:* KLH to MHF, January 28, 1944, Mortimer Papers. Kathleen sent a copy of the same letter to Pamela Churchill, January 28, 1944. This copy can be found in LOC PHP B I-21.

eighteen hours: 'Trip to Smolensk and the Katyn Forest, January 21–23, 1944', enclosures to 'Despatch of February 23, 1944 from the American Embassy, Moscow', Mortimer Papers.

Of the eight thousand: KLH to MHF, January 28, 1944, Mortimer Papers.

'Compared to bombed': Ibid.

their guide: 'Trip to Smolensk and the Katyn Forest, January 21–23, 1944', Mortimer Papers.

recently planted: Report from Owen O'Malley to Anthony Eden, May 31, 1943, attached to WSC to FDR, August 13, 1943; NARA, President's Secretary's File, National Archives Identifier: 6851129.

main 'show': 'Trip to Smolensk and the Katyn Forest, January 21–23, 1944', Mortimer Papers.

156   *stench of decaying:* KLH to MHF, January 28, 1944, Mortimer Papers.

The Soviets had opened: 'Trip to Smolensk and the Katyn Forest, January 21–23, 1944', Mortimer Papers.

'Plastic Surgery Doing': Kathleen Harriman, 'Plastic Surgery Doing Wonders for R.A.F. Pilots Suffering Burns', syndicated column, KLH scrapbook, Mortimer Papers.

'It's not easy talking': KLH to MHF, July 29, 1941, Mortimer Papers.

While travelling with: WAH interview with Arthur Schlesinger Jr, Middleburg, VA, May 24, 1981, courtesy of David Mortimer and Peter Duchin.

157   *roughly twenty-five feet:* 'Trip to Smolensk and the Katyn Forest, January 21–23, 1944', Mortimer Papers.

in tidy rows: KLH to MHF, January 28, 1945, Mortimer Papers.

'varying stages of': Ibid.

and unquestionably: 'Trip to Smolensk and the Katyn Forest, January 21–23, 1944', Mortimer Papers.

Their guide then led: W. H. Lawrence, 'Soviet Blames Foe in Killing of Poles', *New York Times,* January 22, 1944, in KLH scrapbook, Mortimer Papers.

Each doctor wanted: 'Hearings Before the Select Committee', 2147.

'looked like a chef': KLH to MHF, January 28, 1944, Mortimer Papers.

The bluish-grey: 'Russia: Day in the Forest', *Time,* February 7, 1944, from KLH scrapbook, Mortimer Papers.

Even in the freezing: 'Trip to Smolensk and the Katyn Forest, January 21–23, 1944', Mortimer Papers.

158   *letters and receipts:* KLH handwritten notes from Katyn Forest, Mortimer Papers.

Finally, the westerners: 'Trip to Smolensk and the Katyn Forest, January 21–23, 1944', Mortimer Papers.

'The Poles are harmful': Ibid.

'glibly given, as though': Ibid.

She had no way: Ibid.

It was odd that: Ibid.

159   *smelled as if they:* 'Hearings Before the Select Committee', 2145.

'typically German': KLH to MHF, January 28, 1944, Mortimer Papers.

atrocities at Majdanek: Majdanek was the first concentration camp discovered by the Allies. The Soviets liberated it on July 22, 1944, during Operation Bagration. A group of western correspondents based in Moscow went to report on it in August 1944. Kathy was not among them, but she wrote about what the correspondents reported back to her, when they returned to Moscow, in her letter to her sister of August 30, 1944. Mortimer Papers.

Averell asked her: 'Hearings Before the Select Committee', 2149.

'It is apparent': 'Trip to Smolensk and the Katyn Forest, January 21–23, 1944', Mortimer Papers.

He transmitted: WAH to Cordell Hull, 'Investigation by Soviet authorities of the Massacre of Polish Soldiers in the Katyn Forest, Near Smolensk', February 23, 1944, Mortimer Papers.

160 *He ordered Beria:* Benjamin B. Fischer, 'The Katyn Controversy: Stalin's Killing Field', *Studies in Intelligence* (Winter 1999–2000), https://www.cia.gov/library/center-for-the-study-of-intelligence/csi-publications/csi-studies/studies/winter99-00/art6.html.

Three NKVD agents: Montefiore, *Stalin*, 333–34.

'engaged in construction': 'Memorandum: "Alleged Massacre of 10,000 Polish Army Officers"', April 17, 1943, NARA 760C.61 / 4-1743, National Archives Identifier: 6850459.

'investigation comedy': 'Material Regarding the Break of Polish-Soviet Diplomatic Relations', April 26, 1943, NARA 760C.61 / 4-2643, National Archives Identifier: 6850463.

161 *The western Allies:* See Fischer, 'The Katyn Controversy'; Geoffrey Roberts, *Stalin's Wars: From World War to Cold War, 1939–1953* (New Haven, CT: Yale University Press, 2006), 45, 169; and Alexandra Richie, *Warsaw 1944: Hitler, Himmler, and the Warsaw Uprising* (New York: Farrar, Straus and Giroux, 2013), 163–64.

'We have in fact': Report from Owen O'Malley to Anthony Eden, May 31, 1943, attached to WSC to FDR, August 13, 1943, NARA President's Secretary's File, National Archives Identifier: 6851129.

'What other hope': WSC to FDR, April 28, 1943, in Sumner Wells to FDR, 'Text of a telegram received from the Foreign Office on April 28th', May 1, 1943, NARA President's Secretary's File, National Archives Identifier: 6851130.

Chapter Twelve: February 6, 1945

163 *'every-other-day bath':* AER Yalta Notes, 22, FDRL ARHP, Box 84.

'separat[ing] the wheat': AER to JB, February 7, 1945, FDRL JBP, Box 6.

Anna was terrific: Interview with Eleanor Seagraves, June 21, 1978, interview by Dr Thomas F. Soapes, FDRL, Eleanor Roosevelt Oral History Project.

'any gossip': AER Yalta Notes, 22, FDRL ARHP, Box 84.

164 *'Little Three':* Sarah Churchill, *A Thread in the Tapestry*, 80.

'worked like mad': AER to JB, February 7, 1945, FDRL JPB, Box 6.

write him reminder notes: Lucy Mercer Rutherfurd to AER, May 9, 1945, in Boettiger, *A Love in Shadow*, 262.

Harriman was also: AER Yalta Notes, 22, FDRL ARHP, Box 84; FRUS, Conferences at Malta and Yalta, 'Roosevelt-Churchill Luncheon Meeting', February 6, 1945, Document 347.

WAAF standard issue: Photograph, KLH, scrapbook, Mortimer Papers.

'really very tortuous': SMHC to CSC, February 6, 1945, CAC SCHL 1/1/8.

165 *In that single image:* Photograph, 'The Road to Sevastopol', KLH scrapbook, Mortimer Papers.

hundreds of German tanks: Astley, *The Inner Circle*, 181.

'I presume': KLH to PC, February 7, 1945, Mortimer Papers.

167   *Winston Churchill had read:* Michael Richards, 'Churchill and Tennyson', The
       Churchill Project, Hillsdale College, July 17, 2015, https://winstonchurchill.hillsdale
       .edu/churchill-and-tennyson/.
       Bomb craters pitted: Diary of Alan Francis Brooke, 1st Viscount Alanbrooke of Brooke-
       borough, February 7, 1945, Liddell Hart Military Archives, King's College London,
       ALANBROOKE 5/2/27.
       German anti-tank guns: Hermione Ranfurly, *To War with Whitaker: The Wartime Diaries
       of the Countess of Ranfurly, 1939–1945* (London: William Heinemann, 1994), 328.
       A grave had been: Diary of Alan Brooke, February 7, 1945, ALANBROOKE 5/2/27.
168   *'to have undergone':* Leo Tolstoy, *The Sevastopol Sketches.* This series of short stories
       was one of Tolstoy's first major works. It has been translated numerous times, for
       example, the 1986 Penguin Classics edition, translated by David McDuff.
       'Would you see': The Marquis de Custine, *Empire of the Czar: A Journey Through Eternal
       Russia* (New York: Doubleday, 1989), 306. Custine continued, 'In this manner, they
       tyrannise over us in pretending to do us honour. Such is the fate of privileged travel-
       lers. As to those who are not privileged, they see nothing at all.'
       six still had roofs: KLH to PC, February 7, 1945, Mortimer Papers.
       'Statues had been': Ibid.
169   *'The Germans literally':* AER to JB, February 7, 1945, FDRL JBP, Box 6.
       'I suppose journalism': Sir Charles Portal to KLH, March 3, 1944, Mortimer Papers.
       Pamela had shown Portal the letter Kathy wrote about Katyn Forest. Portal had then
       written to Kathy, 'I can't think how you managed to get through it so calmly.'
       'showed us round': SMHC to CSC, February 6, 1945, CAC SCHL 1/1/8.
170   *'bedraggled queue':* Ibid.
       the Romanian Third: Micheal Clodfelter, *Warfare and Armed Conflicts: A Statistical En-
       cyclopedia of Casualty and Other Figures, 1494–2007,* 3rd ed. (Jefferson, NC: McFarland,
       2008), 497. The Red Army took seven thousand Romanian soldiers prisoner during
       the Crimean Offensive.
       to clear the gardens: AER Yalta Notes, 17, FDRL ARHP, Box 84.
       'stone by stone': KLH to PC, February 7, 1945, Mortimer Papers.
       'One has seen similar': SMHC to CSC, February 6, 1945, CAC SCHL 1/1/8.
       'The wise and right': Candice Millard, *Hero of the Empire: The Boer War, a Daring Escape,
       and the Making of Winston Churchill* (New York: Doubleday, 2016), 317.
171   *'I think Sarah was':* KLH to PC, February 7, 1945, Mortimer Papers.
       Sarah had given up: KLH to MHF, July 30, 1942, Mortimer Papers.
       struck her in the face: Robert Bruce Lockhart, *The Diaries of Sir Robert Bruce Lockhart,
       Vol. 2: 1938–65* (London: Macmillan, 1980), 352.
172   *'the debutante world':* Sarah Churchill, *Keep on Dancing,* 37.
       The girl's grandfather: Ibid., 38.
       When Sarah was: Ibid., 28–29.
       'Nijinsky leap': Ibid., 29.
173   *'high mental fatigue':* Clementine Churchill's biographer Sonia Purnell writes exten-
       sively about the mental and physical health struggles she faced, as well as the steps
       she took to overcome or hide her sometimes 'acute' depression. *Clementine,* 190–91.
       she left her husband: Ibid., 50.
       give his babies baths: Ibid.
       'Oh Mummie': SMHC to CSC, undated, CAC SCHL 1/1/2.

'I should simply': Ibid.

'talent or even': Mary Soames, *Clementine Churchill: The Biography of a Marriage* (Boston: Houghton Mifflin, 1979), 322.

174   *where he was killed:* The death of Dick Sheepshanks in Spain has given rise to conspiracy theories. Some say that Kim Philby actually killed him when Sheepshanks became suspicious that Philby was up to something. Reuters discusses this theory on its blog on company history, concluding that the theory has very little merit. John Entwisle, 'The Life and Mystery of Dick Sheepshanks', *Answers On*, May 8, 2012, https://blogs.thomsonreuters.com/answerson/life-mystery-dick-sheepshanks/. Judith Keene similarly explores this theme in *Fighting for Franco: International Volunteers in Nationalist Spain During the Spanish Civil War* (London: Bloomsbury Academic, 2007), 76–77.

'Here I am doing': CSC to WSC, February 27, 1936, in Soames, ed., *Winston and Clementine*, 413.

'married to the enemy': Sarah Churchill, *Keep on Dancing*, 67.

Vic criticised: Vic Oliver to SMHC, undated, 'Saturday 1 A.M.,' CAC SCHL 1/8/1.

Phyllis Luckett: Vic Oliver, *Mr. Showbusiness* (London: George G. Harrap, 1954), 131. In his memoir, Oliver writes that they never officially adopted Phyllis, but she did change her surname to Oliver in a deed poll.

175   *'The buzz and excitement':* SMHC to WSC, April 4, 1940, CAC CHAR 1/355/24.

People on the street: Ibid.

'They have allowed': SMHC to WSC, September 18, 1942, CAC CHAR 1/369/68-70.

176   *'Your sisters have':* WSC to Randolph Churchill, October 30, 1941, CAC CHAR 1/362/43-45.

'I must say': SMHC to CSC, undated October 1941, CAC SCHL 1/1/6.

'desperately unhappy': KLH to MHF, July 7, 1941, Mortimer Papers.

from time to time: Myra Nora Collier, IWM Oral History, October 24, 2002.

'Though I think': PC to WAH, February 15, 1944, LOC PHP B I-22 F 06.

177   *'if only he could':* KLH to MHF, October 14, 1941, Mortimer Papers.

The Nazis had imprisoned: In the final days of the war in Europe, Winant's son was removed from Colditz with a group of politically connected POWs whom the Nazis intended to use as bargaining chips with the Allies. He was ultimately released in May 1945. Wolfgang Saxon, 'John G. Winant, Jr., 71, Prisoner of Germans During WWII', *New York Times*, November 2, 1993.

'love affair which': Sarah Churchill, *Keep on Dancing*, 159.

gossiped unhelpfully: Coward writes about having a 'long gossip with Mrs. Churchill about Sarah and Vic' in his diary on October 24, 1943. Graham Payne and Sheridan Morley, eds., *The Noël Coward Diaries* (Boston: Da Capo Press, 2000), 22.

178   *'Are you flirting':* SMHC to CSC, February 1, 1945, CAC SCHL 1/1/8.

his 'private affairs': CSC to Mary Churchill, February 17, 1945, CAC MCHL 5/1/117.

'That will be all right': Ibid.

'Sarah does not know': Ibid.

179   *'We will build it':* SMHC to CSC, February 6, 1945, CAC SCHL 1/1/8.

'I do not suppose': Ibid.

Chapter Thirteen: February 6–7, 1945

181 *General Fred Anderson:* KLH to PC, February 7, 1945, LOC PHP B-I21.
   'I'm out in the garden': Ibid.
182 *'They've embarked on':* Ibid.
   'all the nations': FRUS, Conferences at Malta and Yalta, 'Third plenary meeting',
   February 6, 1945, Bohlen Minutes, Document 349.
183 *'eliminate disputes':* Ibid.
184 *'one of our first aims':* Ibid.
185 *chain-smoking, stone-faced:* Byrnes, *All in One Lifetime*, 265.
   to Stalin's right: Table diagram in FRUS, Conferences at Malta and Yalta, 'Third plenary meeting', February 6, 1945, Hiss Notes, Document 350.
   'gesture of magnanimity': FRUS, Conferences at Malta and Yalta, 'Third plenary meeting', February 6, 1945, Matthews Minutes, Document 351. Lviv once had a robust
   Polish-Jewish population, which was brutally targeted by the Nazis; by the war's end,
   the Jewish population was almost entirely eliminated. For more on the complex history of Lviv, see Plokhy, *Yalta*, 154–56, 168–75.
   The telegram still: February 6, 1945, note attached to FRUS, Conferences at Malta and
   Yalta, John Gilbert Winant to Edward Stettinius, February 3, 1945, Document 471.
186 *the Americans had:* FRUS, Conferences at Malta and Yalta, 'Third plenary meeting',
   February 6, 1945, Matthews Minutes, Document 351.
   'However,' Churchill stated: Ibid. Britain had declared war to protect this sovereignty,
   and Churchill had promised to support his exiled Polish allies in London; however,
   as noble as the exiled Polish leaders' cause was, Churchill felt they exhibited as much
   self-interest as anyone else. In the days after Germany annexed the Czech Sudeten-
   land, Poland had been quick to claim the Czech territory of Zaolzie. At the time,
   Churchill had been furious with the Polish government, but this territorial aggran-
   disement paled in comparison to the sins of the Nazis and the Soviets' subjugation of
   their own people. Winston S. Churchill, *The Second World War, Vol. 1*, 323.
   'be mistress in her own': FRUS, Conferences at Malta and Yalta, 'Third plenary meeting', February 6, 1945, Bohlen Minutes, Document 349.
187 *he quietly doodled:* Stettinius, *Roosevelt and the Russians*, 138.
   As Averell had: Kathleen Harriman Mortimer, IWM Oral History, September 10, 1996.
   doodling more vigorously: Stettinius, *Roosevelt and the Russians*, 138.
   'The Prime Minister': FRUS, Conferences at Malta and Yalta, 'Third plenary meeting',
   February 6, 1945, Matthews Minutes, Document 351.
   paced back and forth: Bohlen, *Witness to History*, 187.
   'They all say': FRUS, Conferences at Malta and Yalta, 'Third plenary meeting',
   February 6, 1945, Matthews Minutes, Document 351.
   'Mr. President': FRUS, Conferences at Malta and Yalta, Harry Hopkins to FDR,
   February 6, 1945, Document 355.
188 *'As a military':* FRUS, Conferences at Malta and Yalta, 'Third plenary meeting',
   February 6, 1945, Bohlen Minutes, Document 349.
   'I must put on': FRUS, Conferences at Malta and Yalta, 'Third plenary meeting',
   February 6, 1945, Matthews Minutes, Document 351.

drank, plundered: 'Reports from the Underground Army', January 30, 1945, TNA FO 371/47577.

'Perhaps we are mistaken': FRUS, Conferences at Malta and Yalta, 'Third plenary meeting', February 6, 1945, Matthews Minutes, Document 351.

'Poland,' Roosevelt commented: Winston S. Churchill, *The Second World War, Vol. VI,* 372.

189   *'All the more':* Ibid.

as Anna read: JB to AER, January 29, 1945; JB to AER, January 31, 1945; AER to JB, February 7, 1945, FDRL JBP, Box 6.

instructed Chip Bohlen: Bohlen, *Witness to History,* 188.

FDR then sent Harriman: Eden, *The Memoirs of Anthony Eden,* 597–98.

'not quite stiff': Ibid., 598.

suggested some modifications: Draft of FDR letter to Stalin with Eden's handwritten notes, TNA FO 371/47578.

'My Dear Marshal': FDR to Joseph Stalin, February 6, 1945, LOC AHP B 176 F 11.

190   *Harriman had long:* Harriman and Abel, *Special Envoy,* 94.

'[For a Soviet': George Kennan to Edward Stettinius, February 2, 1945, LOC AHP B 176 F 10.

'wanted to dominate': Harriman and Abel, *Special Envoy,* 405.

191   *On the terrace:* Sir Charles Portal to PC, February 7, 1945, LOC PHP B I-31.

The three delegations: FRUS, Conferences at Malta and Yalta, 'Agreed Text of Preliminary Yalta Press Release', February 7, 1945, Document 346.

'hold the fort: SMHC to CSC, February 6, 1945, CAC MCHL 5/1/120.

Sarah came upon: Sir Charles Portal to PC, February 7, 1945, LOC PHP B I-31.

zealous amateur historian: KLH to PC, February 7, 1945, LOC PHP B I-21.

'a man of granite': James, ed., *Chips: The Diaries of Henry Channon,* 277.

192   *she had once invited:* Sir Charles Portal to SMHC, November 28, 1942, CAC SCHL 1/8/1.

'very kind and': SMHC to CSC, February 6, 1945, CAC SCHL 1/1/8.

a 'buddy': SMHC to CSC, February 9, 1945, CAC SCHL 1/1/8.

newsreel crews: Sir Charles Portal to PC, February 7, 1945, LOC PHP B I-31.

'vivid angry blue': SMHC to CSC, February 8, 1945, CAC SCHL 1/1/8.

family chronicler: Sarah Churchill, *Keep on Dancing,* 113.

Offers from publishers: David Reynolds, *In Command of History: Churchill Fighting and Writing the Second World War* (New York: Random House, 2005), 8.

193   *'enchanting and entrancing':* CSC to WSC, February 3, 1945, in Soames, ed., *Winston and Clementine,* 515.

'Letters from My': CSC to Mary Churchill, February 8, 1945, CAC MCHL 5/1/117.

crisis of conscience: SMHC to CSC, February 6, 1945, CAC MCHL 5/1/120.

The British had never: Note attached to CSC to SMHC, February 8, 1945, CAC MCHL 5/1/120.

'Darling,' Sarah wrote: SMHC to CSC, February 6, 1945, CAC MCHL 5/1/120.

194   *She found Portal:* Sir Charles Portal to PC, February 7, 1945, LOC PHP B I-31.

A chilling breeze: Sir Alexander Cadogan to Lady Theodosia Cadogan, February 8, 1945, in Dilks, ed., *The Diaries of Sir Alexander Cadogan,* 707.

'best for the scene': SMHC to CSC, February 8, 1945, CAC SCHL 1/1/8.

'The Riviera of Hades!': Ibid.

'There was great': KLH to PC, February 8, 1945, LOC PHP B I-21.

195 *'it was only fair':* FRUS, Conferences at Malta and Yalta, 'Fourth plenary meeting', February 7, 1945, Bohlen Minutes, Document 370.

'boringly & at great': KLH to PC, February 8, 1945, LOC PHP B I-21.

canteen was now: 'General Information Bulletin', LOC AHP B 176 F 09.

'mob gathered': KLH to PC, February 8, 1945, LOC PHP B I-21.

'spy system': KLH to PC, February 7, 1945, LOC PHP B I-21.

196 *'I only arrived':* KLH to MHF, May 17, 1941, Mortimer Papers.

'I am sorry': Sir Charles Portal to PC, February 6, 1945, LOC PHP B I-31.

197 *passed thousands of documents:* Andrew and Mitrokhin, *The Sword and the Shield*, 126. In the first six months of 1945, Burgess alone smuggled 389 top-secret documents to the Soviets.

the British position: Plokhy, *Yalta*, 350.

total of zero spies: Ben Macintire, *A Spy Among Friends: Kim Philby and the Great Betrayal* (New York: Broadway Books, 2014), 58–59.

Almost six years: John Ehrman, 'A Half-Century of Controversy: The Alger Hiss Case', *Studies in Intelligence*, Vol. 44, No. 5, https://www.cia.gov/library/center-for-the-study-of-intelligence/kent-csi/vol44no5/html/v44i5a01p.htm.

198 *Harry Hopkins had made:* Christina Pazzanese, 'It's spy vs. spy vs. spy', *The Harvard Gazette*, February 20, 2019, https://news.harvard.edu/gazette/story/2019/02/harvard-expert-says-russian-spying-is-nothing-new-only-the-technology-is/.

own set of notes: Hiss's notes and attendance at meetings are recorded throughout FRUS, Conferences at Malta and Yalta.

When Hiss arrived: Hiss's contact at Yalta was possibly General Major Mikhail Milshtein, a plainclothes GRU officer attending the conference as a military adviser. Christina Shelton, *Alger Hiss: Why He Chose Treason* (New York: Threshold Editions, 2012), 139–40. For Hiss's activity at this time, see Andrew and Mitrokhin, *The Sword and the Shield*, 132–34; John Earl Haynes, Harvey Klehr and Alexander Vassiliev, *Spies: The Rise and Fall of the KGB in America* (New Haven, CT: Yale University Press, 2009), 18–21. Of course, in his own memoir, *Recollections of a Life*, Hiss does not admit to any of this. He is, however, highly complimentary of Stalin at Yalta on numerous occasions. See Alger Hiss, *Recollections of a Life* (New York: Seaver Books, 1988); Allen Weinstein, *Perjury: The Hiss-Chambers Case* (New York: Knopf, 1978); Allen Weinstein and Alexander Vassiliev, *The Haunted Wood: Soviet Espionage in America – The Stalin Era* (New York: Random House, 1998); and Sam Tanenhaus, *Whittaker Chambers: A Biography* (New York: Random House, 1997).

199 *At times:* Assorted photographs, Associated Press, November 7, 1944.

'The champ': Royal Brougham to AER and JB, November 8, 1944, FDRL President's Personal File 7, Anna R. Boettiger 1942–1945.

At other times: Edith Wilson, Woodrow Wilson's widow, saw FDR up close on the day of his inauguration and told Frances Perkins she thought he looked like her husband did when his health declined and he had a stroke. Goodwin, *No Ordinary Time*, 573.

The day before: Moran, *Churchill at War*, 276.

'very sick man': Ibid. Dr Roger Lee's source was possibly Dr James Paullin, who had been among those whom Admiral McIntire had consulted about FDR's health in March 1944. Paullin had succeeded Lee as president of the American College of Physicians.

'He has all the symptoms': Moran, *Churchill at War*, 276.

Chapter Fourteen: February 8, 1945

201 *'using all the ingenuity'*: AER to JB, February 7, 1945, FDRL JBP, Box 6.

  'especially arduous': 'Clinical Notes on the Illness and Death of President Roosevelt', FDRL Howard Bruenn Papers, Folder 2, 'Report of Cardiac Consultation'.

202 *'endeavored to reach'*: FRUS, Conferences at Malta and Yalta, 'Fourth plenary meeting', February 7, 1945, Bohlen Minutes, Document 370.

  'flimsiest possible': Harriman and Abel, *Special Envoy*, 408.

  'crucial point': FRUS, Conferences at Malta and Yalta, 'Fifth plenary meeting', February 8, 1945, Matthews Minutes, Document 393.

  He had already spent: FRUS, Conferences at Malta and Yalta, 'Roosevelt-Stalin Meeting', February 8, 1945, Bohlen Minutes, Document 390.

203 *eighteen months:* Harriman and Abel, *Special Envoy*, 397.

  Roosevelt agreed to: For more on this meeting, see FRUS, 'Roosevelt-Stalin Meeting', February 8, 1945, Bohlen Minutes, Document 390.

  'Since you and': FRUS, Conferences at Malta and Yalta, John Gilbert Winant to FDR, February 7, 1945, Document 481.

  Bruenn now listened: 'Clinical Notes on the Illness and Death of President Roosevelt', FDRL Bruenn Papers, Folder 2, 'Report of Cardiac Consultation'.

204 *'B.P. for the first'*: Ibid.

  While addressing: Howard Bruenn, Oral History, U.S. Naval Medical Department Oral History Program, January 31, 1990.

  'By God, that's not': Ibid.

205 *to 240/130:* Goodwin, *No Ordinary Time*, 545.

  'I have found out': AER to JB, February 7, 1945, FDRL JBP, Box 6.

  'He gets all wound': Ibid.

  Anna sometimes found: Oral History interview with Anna Roosevelt Halsted, 1975, Columbia Center for Oral History Archives, Rare Book and Manuscript Library, Columbia University in the City of New York.

206 *Some people:* Sir Alexander Cadogan to Lady Theodosia Cadogan, February 9, 1945, in Dilks, ed., *The Diaries of Sir Alexander Cadogan*, 707; Peter Portal was hoping to make a similar escape, but to no avail. Sir Charles Portal to PC, February 8, 1945, LOC PHP B I-31.

  The dinner table: There were exactly thirty people at the dinner, according to FRUS, Conferences at Malta and Yalta, 'Tripartite dinner meeting', February 8, 1945.

  At half past eight: Logs of the President's Trips: Crimea Conference and Great Bitter Lake, Egypt, January 22–February 28, 1945, 29, FDRL Grace Tully Papers, Box 7.

  close the road: Houghton, 'That Was Yalta', 96.

  Ed Stettinius, Admiral Leahy: See list of dinner attendees, FRUS, Conferences at Malta and Yalta, 'Tripartite dinner meeting', February 8, 1945.

  twenty-course meal: Stettinius, *Roosevelt and the Russians*, 218.

207 *true personal feelings:* In her oral history with Columbia University Center for Oral History Archives in 1975, Anna reasserted this, saying, 'He never discussed his real personal life with anyone.'

  'He doesn't know': John Morton Blum, ed., *The Price of Vision: The Diary of Henry Wallace, 1942–1946* (Boston: Houghton Mifflin, 1973), 380.

  'sat at a desk': AER, untitled, FDRL ARHP, Box 84, Undated Writings.

Eleanor felt insecure: AER, 'What Does It Feel Like to Be an Offspring of Famous Parents?' FDRL ARHP, Box 84, Undated Writings.

'addicted to': Ibid.

once locked James: Ibid.

208   *They dropped paper:* Ibid.

warmth and friendliness: AER, untitled, FDRL ARHP, Box 84, Undated Writings.

Anna had one: Ibid.

Tennis Week: Anna Roosevelt Halsted interview by Bernard Asbell, 1972, FDRL ARHP, Box 63.

'forced' to make: Ibid.

'this horrible thing': Ibid.

209   *'another woman':* AER, untitled, FDRL ARHP, Box 84, Undated Writings.

'very much gossiped': Anna Roosevelt Halsted interview by Bernard Asbell, 1972, FDRL ARHP, Box 63.

Franklin began spending: Blanche Weisen Cook, *Eleanor Roosevelt, Vol. 1: 1884–1933* (New York: Viking Adult, 1992), 216.

seemed cold: Asbell, ed., *Mother and Daughter*, 40.

As Eleanor explained: AER, untitled, FDRL ARHP, Box 84, Undated Writings. FDR's political adviser Louis Howe was closely involved in the decision as to whether the couple should seek a divorce. He warned FDR that divorce would end his career and persuaded Eleanor that FDR needed her talents and intellect in order to succeed. Cook, *Eleanor Roosevelt, Vol. I*, 231.

'mad – mad at Father': Asbell, ed., *Mother and Daughter*, 40.

choose a side: Anna Roosevelt Halsted, Oral History, Columbia University Center for Oral History Archives, 1975.

210   *'could easily happen':* Anna Roosevelt Halsted interview by Bernard Asbell, 1972, FDRL ARHP, Box 63.

Eleanor was spending: According to the White House daily logs, Eleanor was in Hyde Park from June 16 to July 13, 1944. Franklin D. Roosevelt: Day by Day, http://www .fdrlibrary.marist.edu/daybyday/.

'invited a very': Anna Roosevelt Halsted, Columbia University Center for Oral History Archives, 1975.

'a terrible decision': Ibid.

211   *a kitchen knife:* Author's interview with Ellie Seagraves, January 26, 2018.

for their marriage: Author's interview with Ellie Seagraves, September 30, 2018; Eleanor Roosevelt Oral History Project, interview with Eleanor Seagraves, February 2, and June 21, 1978, interview by Dr Thomas F. Soapes, FDRL.

'You shouldn't do': Anna Roosevelt Halsted, Columbia University Center for Oral History Archives, 1975.

'Here was a man': Ibid.

212   *The dinner was set:* Goodwin, *No Ordinary Time*, 518–20.

Anna convinced herself: Anna Roosevelt Halsted, Columbia University Center for Oral History Archives, 1975.

At 6.30: Goodwin, *No Ordinary Time*, 519.

'Anna is a dear': Asbell, ed., *Mother and Daughter*, 188.

'friendly' yet 'stately': AER, untitled, FDRL ARHP, Box 84, Undated Writings.

'grateful' to Lucy: Ibid.

213 *'not capable of giving':* Anna Roosevelt Halsted interview by Bernard Asbell, 1972, FDRL ARHP, Box 63.

would 'wolf' down: Ibid.

'Mrs. Johnson': Ibid.

213 *'clandestine':* AER, untitled, FDRL ARHP, Box 84, Undated Writings.

'Over there': Ibid.

special surprise: AER to JB, January 30, 1945, FDRL JBP, Box 6.

cloth napkins: Diary of Daisy Suckley, January 17, 1945, in Ward, ed., *Closest Companion,* 385.

pocket-sized combs: AER to JB, January 30, 1945, FDRL JBP, Box 6.

'until this package': Ibid.

From Eleanor: AER Yalta Notes, 8, FDRL ARHP, Box 84.

'I haven't had': AER to JB, February 7, 1945, FDRL JBP, Box 6. As Anna writes in her next letter to John, FDR received his first letter from Eleanor only on February 9.

letters from John: JB to AER, January 29, 1945; JB to AER, January 31, 1945; AER to JB, February 7, 1945, FDRL JBP, Box 6.

215 *'with funny pictures':* JB to AER, January 31, 1945, FDRL JBP, Box 6.

'a very sad': AER to JB, February 7, 1945, FDRL JBP, Box 6.

Chapter Fifteen: February 8, 1945

217 *'horribly embarrassed':* KLH to PC, February 13, 1945, LOC PHP B-I 21.

room he shared: Howard Bruenn, Oral History, U.S. Naval Medical Department Oral History Program, January 31, 1990.

217 *drinking tea:* Hiss, *Recollections of a Life,* 122.

and sitting on: Ed Flynn to Helen Flynn, postmarked February 8, 1945, FDRL Papers of Edward Flynn, Box 25, Folder 5.

With both Flynn: KLH to PC, February 13, 1945, LOC PHP B I-21.

situation would look: Stettinius, *Roosevelt and the Russians,* 219.

'damned well': KLH to PC, February 13, 1945, LOC PHP B I-21.

'price' of her 'meal': KLH to MHF, February 4–10, 1945, Mortimer Papers.

'stomach sink': Kathleen Harriman Mortimer, IWM Oral History, September 10, 1996.

'in English': KLH to PC, February 13, 1945, LOC PHP B I-21.

long rectangular: KLH to MHF, February 4–10, 1945, Mortimer Papers.

Kathy was curious: Ibid.

219 *were confused as to why:* Sir Charles Portal to PC, February 9, 1945, LOC PHP B I-31.

he told the best: KLH to PC, February 7, 1945, LOC PHP B I-21.

'My God he hates': Ibid.

Portal, who was leaving: Sir Charles Portal to PC, February 9, 1945, LOC PHP B I-31.

220 *'the life of Stalin':* Sergei Khrushchev, ed., *Memoirs of Nikita Khrushchev, Vol. I: Commissar, 1918–1945* (University Park: Pennsylvania State University Press, 2004), 287–88.

'Occasionally on Sundays': KLH to CSC, February 27, 1944, CAC MCHL 5/1/106.

Ave's 'angels': Kathleen Harriman Mortimer, IWM Oral History, September 10, 1996.

'I can't figure': KLH to CSC, February 27, 1944, CAC MCHL 5/1/106. Averell had also written to his wife, Marie, about the NKVD's presence on the slopes. On their first foray to the Lenin Hills, Averell had raced down the hill, top to bottom. The NKVD man tried to stay with him, but, 'unfortunately for him,' Averell wrote to Marie, 'he

is not too skillful.' He had crashed into a pile of snow midway down the slope. The Soviets then wisely added a former member of the Russian national ski team to the Harrimans' ski detail. Isaacson and Thomas, *The Wise Men*, 221.

'little and fat': KLH to MHF, February 4–10, 1945, Mortimer Papers.

221 *Pavel Sudoplatov:* Pavel Sudoplatov and Anatoli Sudoplatov, *Special Tasks* (Boston: Back Bay Books, 1995), 223–26.

'look closer at': Ibid., 225–26.

222 *'very friendly':* Ibid., 226.

pinned . . . the brooch: SMHC to CSC, February 12, 1945, CAC SCHL 1/1/8. Sarah told her mother she wore 'the brooch on my uniform the whole time' she was at the conference.

'very friendly' Ivan: SMHC to CSC, February 9, 1945, CAC SCHL 1/1/8.

yellow teeth: Sergo Beria, *Beria, My Father*, 337.

223 *'State-maintained':* Pawle, *The War and Colonel Warden*, 357.

Russian phrasebooks: Sir Charles Portal to PC, February 7, 1945, LOC PHP B I-31.

224 *'yes', 'no':* Ibid.

'Can I have a hot': SMHC to CSC, February 9, 1945, CAC SCHL 1/1/8.

'I cannot believe': Ibid.

'twinkly-eyed' Andrey: Ibid.

'a serious mistake': Byrnes, *All in One Lifetime*, 261. Byrnes's strong feelings on the matter are reflected in the transcript he made of the shorthand notes he took at the conference, available in the James Francis Byrnes Papers, Mss 90/Series 4: War Mobilization, Box 19, Folder 9, Clemson University Libraries' Special Collections and Archives, Clemson, SC. No one, however, has been able to make an independently confirmed transcription of these notes, as Byrnes used a unique and so far indecipherable system of shorthand.

225 *'raised no objection':* Ibid.

red caviar, herring: Menu, February 8, 1945, FDRL ARHP, Box 84, Miscellaneous.

Stalin sat in the middle: The seating arrangements are taken from descriptions in several individuals' accounts, including KLH to MHF, February 4–10, 1945, Mortimer Papers, and from the Diary of Alan Brooke, 1st Viscount Alanbrooke of Brookeborough, Field Marshal, February 8, 1945, Liddell Hart Military Archives, King's College London, ALANBROOKE 5/1/10.

Molotov, serving: KLH to MHF, February 4–10, 1945, Mortimer Papers.

'I propose a toast': Winston S. Churchill, *The Second World War, Vol. VI*, 361.

226 *never made eye contact:* Sir Charles Portal to PC, February 9, 1945, LOC PHP B I-31.

'a frightening figure': Sarah Churchill, *A Thread in the Tapestry*, 65.

'great sense of humor': SMHC to CSC, December 4, 1943, CAC SCHL 1/1/7.

'in terrific form': SMHC to CSC, February 9, 1945, CAC SCHL 1/1/8.

'It is no exaggeration': Winston S. Churchill, *The Second World War, Vol. VI*, 361.

shabbily dressed waiter: Sir Charles Portal to PC, February 9, 1945, LOC PHP B I-31.

'There have been': Winston S. Churchill, *The Second World War, Vol. VI*, 361.

walked around the table: Sir Charles Portal to PC, February 9, 1945, LOC PHP B I-31.

recovering alcoholic: Interview with John F. Melby, June 16, 1989, LOC.

the banquet's numerous toasts: KLH to PC, February 13, 1945, LOC PHP B I-21.

'fighting for their very': FRUS, Conferences at Malta and Yalta, 'Tripartite dinner meeting', February 8, 1945, Bohlen Minutes, Document 400.

227 *There was a time:* Samuel I. Rosenman, *Working with Roosevelt* (New York: Harper and Brothers, 1952), 478.

'The atmosphere at this': FRUS, Conferences at Malta and Yalta, 'Tripartite dinner meeting', February 8, 1945, Bohlen Minutes, Document 400.

'a little bit far': Kathleen Harriman Mortimer, IWM Oral History, September 10, 1996.

'even greater changes': FRUS, Conferences at Malta and Yalta, 'Tripartite dinner meeting', February 8, 1945, Bohlen Minutes, Document 400.

'sentimental twaddle': Sir Charles Portal to PC, February 9, 1945, LOC PHP B I-31.

228 *Molotov toasted:* Winston S. Churchill, *The Second World War, Vol. VI*, 363–64.

'a gloomy man': KLH to MHF, February 4–10, 1945, Mortimer Papers.

'more and more bored': Danchev and Todman, eds.,*War Diaries, 1939–1945: Alanbrooke*, 660; see also Diary of Alan Brooke, February 8, 1945, Liddell Hart Military Archives, King's College London, ALANBROOKE 5/1/10.

being eaten alive: Diary of William Leahy, February 8, 1945, LOC William D. Leahy Papers, Box 6.

Doctors McIntire and Bruenn: AER to JB, February 4, 1945, FDRL JBP, Box 6.

'a most sinister': AER to JB, February 9, 1945, FDRL JPB, Box 6.

Admiral Leahy was growing: Eleanor Roosevelt, *This I Remember*, 342.

229 *'Who's that in the':* Montefiore, *Stalin*, 483, from V. F. Nekrasov, *Beria: Konets karey* (Moscow: Moskva Izdatelistvo politicheskoi literaturi, 1991), 221–22.

gleeful malevolence: Sergo Beria describes Stalin's tone when he introduces Lavrentiy Beria as laced with a 'drop of venom'. See *Beria, My Father*, 113.

rimless eyeglasses: Nekrasov, *Beria*, 221–22.

sex life of fish: Montefiore, *Stalin*, 483.

'always seem[ed] to get': KLH to MHF, February 4–10, 1945, Mortimer Papers.

230 *'Be careful, be careful':* Ibid.

'I must say': Winston S. Churchill, *The Second World War, Vol. VI*, 362.

'smil[ing] like a benign': KLH to MHF, February 4–10, 1945, Mortimer Papers.

'could be so expansive': Winston S. Churchill, *The Second World War, Vol. VI*, 362.

'a garrulous old man': KLH to MHF, February 4–10, 1945, Mortimer Papers.

'That . . . is why': Winston S. Churchill, *The Second World War, Vol. VI*, 362–63.

231 *'common man':* FRUS, Conferences at Malta and Yalta, 'Tripartite dinner meeting', February 8, 1945, Bohlen Minutes, Document 400.

232 *dumping their vodka:* Dobbs, *Six Months in 1945*, 75.

By the time the suckling pig: SMHC to CSC, February 9, 1945, CAC SCHL 1/1/8.

third meat course: KLH to MHF, February 4–10, 1945, Mortimer Papers.

to the 'ladies': KLH to PC, February 13, 1945, LOC PHP B I-21.

Now Stalin walked: KLH to MHF, February 4–10, 1945, Mortimer Papers.

to 'get up': Kathleen Harriman Mortimer, IWM Oral History, September 10, 1996.

233 *'great interest':* Ibid.

'Jesus,' she thought: KLH to MHF, February 4–10, 1945, Mortimer Papers.

'both sides working': Kathleen Harriman Mortimer, IWM Oral History, London, September 10, 1996.

'Replying for the three': FRUS, Conferences at Malta and Yalta, 'Tripartite dinner meeting'. February 8, 1945, Bohlen Minutes, Document 400.

'surpassed herself': SMHC to CSC, February 9, 1945, CAC SCHL 1/1/8.

Of the forty-five: KLH to PC, February 13, 1945, LOC PHP B I-21.

Chip Bohlen: For the recorded toasts, see FRUS, Conferences at Malta and Yalta, 'Tripartite dinner meeting', February 8, 1945, Bohlen Minutes, Document 400.

234   *the twentieth course:* KLH to PC, February 13, 1945, LOC PHP B I-21.

'worked while we': Bohlen, *Witness to History*, 182.

'Interpreters of the world': Ibid.

'Interpreters of the world': Sir Charles Portal to PC, February 9, 1945, LOC PHP B I-31.

'"big business" men': AER to JB, February 9, 1945, FDRL JBP, Box 6.

to look with hope: In his memoir, Ed Stettinius recalls the change in Churchill that night, writing, 'At Malta he had been extremely discouraged and distressed, but in his toasts this evening at Yalta he manifested real hope that there could be a world of happiness, peace, and security. *Roosevelt and the Russians*, 221.

'The Glory Song': Gilbert, *Winston S. Churchill, Vol. VII*, 1195, observation from the diary of secretary Marian Holmes.

Chapter Sixteen: February 9–10, 1945

235   *'How do you want':* Robert Hopkins, *Witness to History*, 153.

'First, Mr. President': Ibid.

Three large oriental: 'Allied delegates arrive for the international conference at Livadia Palace in Yalta', February 1945, https://www.criticalpast.com/video/65675033670 _The-Yalta-Conference_Franklin-D-Roosevelt_Lavidia-Palace_conference-room.

236   *After much jostling:* Photographs, February 9, 1945, LOC AHP B 882 F 19; photographs, February 9, 1945, Georgetown University, Booth Family Center for Special Collections, Robert Hopkins Papers, Box 7C; author's correspondence with Maria Kosareva, January 2, 2020.

The senior military: 'Allied delegates arrive', February 1945, https://www.criticalpast .com/video/65675033670_The-Yalta-Conference_Franklin-D-Roosevelt_Lavidia -Palace_conference-room.

'a most disorganized': Danchev and Todman, eds., *War Diaries, 1939–1945: Alanbrooke*, 660; see also Diary of Alan Brooke, 1st Viscount Alanbrooke of Brookeborough, Field Marshal, February 9, 1945, Liddell Hart Military Archives, King's College London, ALANBROOKE 5/1/10.

more than half an hour: Sir Charles Portal to PC, February 9, 1945, LOC PHP B-I 31.

Then, Roosevelt, Churchill: FRUS, Conferences at Malta and Yalta, 1945, 'Roosevelt-Churchill luncheon meeting', February 9, 1945, Document 417.

agreement from Churchill: James Byrnes Notes, 'Memorandum as to the membership of the Ukraine and White Russia in the Assembly', James Francis Byrnes Papers, Mss 90/Series 4: War Mobilization, Box 19, Folder 9, Clemson University Libraries' Special Collections and Archives, Clemson, SC.

237   *Peter Portal was surprised:* Sir Charles Portal to PC, February 8 and 9, 1945, LOC PHP B I-31.

One of the crews: Photograph, February 9, 1945, Georgetown University, Booth Family Center for Special Collections, Robert Hopkins Papers, 7C; 'Soviet Premier Joseph Stalin and Soviet Foreign Minister Vyacheslav Molotov in Livadia Palace during Yalta Conference', February 9, 1945, https://www.criticalpast.com/video/65675075143 _Joseph-Stalin_Sarah-Churchill_Anna-Boettiger_Kathy-Harriman.

'Steve is a poor': AER to JB, February 9, 1945, FDRL JBP, Box 6.

238   *'I hear lots':* Ibid.

just learned from John: JB to AER, February 2, 1945; AER to JB, February 9, 1945, FDRL JBP, Box 6.

At least FDR had: Ibid.,

239   *'[hanging] by a':* Plokhy, *Yalta*, 242–43. Guary's photo ended up on the cover of *Pravda* and became one of the most iconic photos of the Big Three ever taken. Another notable Soviet photographer at Yalta was Boris Kosarev, one of the official government photographers.

Sarah departed: SMHC to CSC, February 9, 1945, CAC SCHL 1/1/8.

240   *'I mean more':* FRUS, Conferences at Malta and Yalta, 'Sixth plenary meeting', February 9, 1945, Matthews Minutes, Document 421.

'better to take': FRUS, Conferences at Malta and Yalta, 'Sixth plenary meeting', February 9, 1945, Bohlen Minutes, Document 420.

'Of course you could': FRUS, Conferences at Malta and Yalta, 'Sixth plenary meeting', February 9, 1945, Matthews Minutes, Document 421.

'We should not': FRUS, Conferences at Malta and Yalta, 'Sixth plenary meeting', February 9, 1945, Bohlen Minutes, Document 420.

'These are among': FRUS, Conferences at Malta and Yalta, 'Sixth plenary meeting', February 9, 1945, Matthews Minutes, Document 421.

'I find that it is': Ibid.

'They said that': Ibid.

After a break: According to FRUS, H. Freeman Matthews from the State Department and Gladwyn Jebb and Denis Allen of the British Foreign Office also participated in this meeting.

241   *'Found the Russians':* Eden, *The Memoirs of Anthony Eden*, 599.

constant amendments: Stettinius, *Roosevelt and the Russians*, 251–52; Chiefs of Staff Minutes, 'Argonaut': Record of Proceedings at Malta and in the Crimea between 29th January and 11th February, 1945; Record of a conversation between the Prime Minister and Marshal Stalin, February 10, 1945, TNA CAB 99/31; Gilbert, *Winston S. Churchill, Vol. VII*, 1203.

242   *'highly unpleasant matter':* Plokhy, *Yalta*, 248.

Red Army soldier: Robert Hopkins, *Witness to History*, 151.

'protective custody': Sir Charles Portal to PC, February 9, 1945, LOC PHP B-I31.

Anna was back: Photograph, February 10, 1945, Georgetown University, Booth Family Center for Special Collections, Robert Hopkins Papers, 7B.

He had his film: 'Joseph Stalin and Winston Churchill arrive for the Yalta Conference in Crimea, Soviet Union during World War II', February 1945, https://www .criticalpast.com/video/65675065771_Joseph-Stalin_Winston-Churchill_Yalta -Conference_Sarah-Churchill.

243   *Robert pointed:* Photograph, February 10, 1945, Georgetown University, Booth Family Center for Special Collections, Robert Hopkins Papers, 7B.

twenty paces behind: Robert Hopkins, *Witness to History*, 151–52.

With elegant seafront: Ibid., 152.

Orthodox crosses: AER to JB, February 13, 1945, FDRL JPB, Box 6.

Robert took a picture: Photograph, February 10, 1945, Georgetown University, Booth Family Center for Special Collections, Robert Hopkins Papers, 7B.

entirely hand-painted: Robert Hopkins, *Witness to History*, 152. For a brief history of billboards, see Out of Home Advertising Association of America, 'History of OOH', https://oaaa.org/AboutOOH/OOHBasics/HistoryofOOH.aspx.

The left side: Photograph, February 10, 1945, Georgetown University, Booth Family Center for Special Collections, Robert Hopkins Papers, 7B.

244   *'Gentlemen, we are':* Ibid.

'*I wouldn't dream':* SMHC to CSC, February 10, 1945, CAC SCHL 1/1/8.

crowd of children: SMHC to CSC, February 12, 1945, CAC SCHL 1/1/8; Robert Hopkins, *Witness to History,* 151–52; AER to JB, February 13, 1945, FRUS JBP, Box 6.

245   *'There is no need':* SMHC to CSC, February 12, 1945, CAC SCHL 1/1/8.

Kathy knew well: KLH to MHF, March 4, 1944, Mortimer Papers.

The group made a brief: AER to JB, February 10, 1945, FDRL JBP, Box 6.

propaganda sheets: Propaganda sheets, FDRL ARHP, Box 84, News Clippings. The propaganda sheet featuring the soldier shooting the frog is based on Aesop's fable titled 'The Frog and the Ox'. In it, a jealous frog tries to puff up to the size of an ox to the point that it explodes and dies. This story had been translated by the Russian fabulist Ivan Krylov and was well known in the Soviet Union. The propaganda sheet depicting Hitler in the vice includes a caption that translates to this: 'The trick will be to hold off Germany in the vice between the two fronts.' Finally, the sheet with the grotesque beast, pierced by bayonets marked with each of the Allies' flags, includes a caption that translates to this: 'What remains now for the Red Army is its last, final mission to execute, together with the armies of its partners, in the matter of the German, fascist Army, the killing of the fascist animal in its own den, and jointly raise the victory flag on top of Berlin.'

FDR had told her: AER to JB, February 10, 1945, FDRL JBP, Box 6.

There was a service: SMHC to CSC, February 12, 1945, CAC SCHL 1/1/8.

'religion was stifled': Robert Hopkins, *Witness to History,* 153.

246   *Kathy had written:* KLH to MHF, April 18, 1944, Mortimer Papers.

'*lit only by myriads':* SMHC to CSC, February 12, 1945, CAC SCHL 1/1/8.

men's voices: Robert Hopkins, *Witness to History,* 152.

The entire congregation: SMHC to CSC, February 12, 1945, CAC SCHL 1/1/8.

'*prostrated themselves':* Robert Hopkins, *Witness to History,* 152.

247   *'These trips':* SMHC to CSC, February 10, 1945, CAC SCHL 1/1/18.

'*I wish I could':* SMHC to CSC, February 12, 1945, CAC SCHL 1/1/8.

248   *'The Russians have':* FRUS, Conferences at Malta and Yalta, Harry Hopkins to FDR, February 10, 1945, Document 452.

Churchill most certainly: FRUS, Conferences at Malta and Yalta, 'Seventh plenary meeting', February 10, 1945, Bohlen Minutes, Document 448.

'The Provisional Government': FRUS, Conferences at Malta and Yalta, 'Report of the Crimea Conference,' Document 497.

249   '*In Russia toleration':* The Marquis de Custine, *Empire of the Czar,* 112.

Chapter Seventeen: February 10–11, 1945

251   '*If we meet':* FRUS, Conferences at Malta and Yalta, 'Seventh plenary meeting', February 10, 1945, Matthews Minutes, Document 449.

252   *The nuances:* Ibid.

He proposed: Ibid.

As they sat down: Menu, February 10, 1945, FDRL ARHP, Box 84, Miscellaneous.

'there had been': Memorandum, 'Dinner Given by the Prime Minister', February 10, 1945, LOC AHP B 177 F 01.

253   *'this was very':* Ibid.

Later in the meal: Menu, February 10, 1945, FDRL ARHP, Box 84, Miscellaneous.

'intended to make': Memorandum, 'Dinner Given by the Prime Minister', February 10, 1945, LOC AHP B 177 F 01.

'one concession': Ibid.

Finally, Roosevelt relented: Ibid.

254   *'The President':* Moran, *Churchill at War*, 282.

'As if,' Sarah shot back: Ibid.

lost eighteen pounds: Lelyveld, *His Final Battle*, 288.

'shown that they': Moran, *Churchill at War*, 283.

255   *'For what we have':* Reynolds, *Summits*, 127.

Anna had just returned: Logs of the President's Trips: Crimea Conference and Great Bitter Lake, Egypt, January 22–February 28, 1945, 32, FDRL Grace Tully Papers, Box 7.

two documents: The text of both documents can be found online at the U.S. Department of State, Office of the Historian website. While the public communiqué was released on February 12, 1945, the Protocol of the Proceedings of the Yalta Conference was not released by the Department of State until March 24, 1947. https://history .state.gov/historicaldocuments/frus1945Berlinv02/ch27.

256   *the word 'joint':* Stettinius, *Roosevelt and the Russians*, 279.

sixty thousand western: Reynolds, *Summits*, 141.

'embarrassment': 'Record of a Conversation Between the Prime Minister and Marshal Stalin', February 10, 1945, 3 P.M., TNA CAB 99/31.

Some . . . tried to: S. M. Plokhy cites the example of 154 Soviet POWs at a camp in Fort Dix, NJ, who tried to commit mass suicide rather than be repatriated. Plokhy, *Yalta*, 304.

Beria would oversee: Harriman and Abel, *Special Envoy*, 416.

The State Department: Plokhy, *Yalta*, 303. See also Bohlen, *Witness to History*, 199.

257   *sent Yakov's wife:* Montefiore, *Stalin*, 379–80. Under Order No. 270, which demanded all soldiers fight to the last, all POWs were classified as traitors, and even their families were subject to arrest and stripped of their rights.

'for a lifetime': SMHC to CSC, February 12, 1945, CAC SCHL 1/1/8.

looked genuinely cheerful: Photograph, February 11, 1945, Plokhy, *Yalta*, insert between 228 and 229.

Despite FDR's insistence: Harriman and Abel, *Special Envoy*, 417.

258   *'I don't see how':* AER to JB, February 10, 1945, FDRL JBP, Box 6.

diplomatic gift exchange: Memorandum, Admiral C. E. Olsen, February 9, 1945, LOC AHP B 176 F 11; Atkinson, *The Guns at Last Light*, 520; Logs of the Trips, 32–33, FDRL Grace Tully Papers, Box 7; Moran, *Churchill at War*, 286.

Harriman had managed: Author's interview with Ellie Seagraves, January 26, 2018, Bethesda, MD. When I interviewed Ellie Seagraves at her home, she showed me the figurine, which Anna did give to her after Yalta. It sits prominently on her mantelpiece.

259   *Ed Stettinius and his:* Stettinius, *Roosevelt and the Russians*, 286–87; Thomas M. Campbell and George C. Herring, eds., *The Diaries of Edward R. Stettinius, Jr., 1943–1945* (New York: New Viewpoints, 1975), 257–58.

'*to make the Russians*': KLH to MHF, February 4–10, 1945, Mortimer Papers.

'*All are going home*': Ibid.

'*You can imagine*': KLH to PC, February 13, 1945, LOC PHP B I-21.

As he said: Bohlen, *Witness to History*, 199–200.

260 '*trouble ahead*': Harriman and Abel, *Special Envoy*, 412.

'*much care what*': Ibid., 399.

'*established nothing more*': Ibid., 412.

'*Mr. President, this*': William D. Leahy, *I Was There: The Personal Story of the Chief of Staff to Presidents Roosevelt and Truman Based on His Notes and Diaries Made at the Time* (New York: Whittlesey House, 1950), 315–16.

'*There is no doubt*': WAH to FDR, December 15, 1944, LOC AHP B 176 F 01.

261 *The ambassador had spent:* FRUS, Conferences at Malta and Yalta, 'Harriman Memorandum of Conversations', February 10, 1945, Document 447.

'*makes the trip*': Harriman and Abel, *Special Envoy*, 399.

And as Kathy overheard: Jon Meacham, *Franklin and Winston* (New York: Random House Trade Paperbacks, 2003), 317. Anthony Eden was similarly concerned about the concessions to the Soviets in the Pacific and urged Churchill not to sign the document, especially as Britain had no part in negotiating it. However, Churchill felt if he did not sign, it would signal that the British were ceding Pacific-related interests to the Soviets and the Americans, who would then have reason not to include the British in Pacific-related discussions. Safeguarding British influence in the Pacific was of considerable importance to Churchill, given the British Empire's presence in Hong Kong; FDR would have been glad to see this presence disappear entirely. Eden believed that the Soviets would enter the war against Japan of their own accord – for the sake of their national interest and the desire to recover territory lost in the Russo-Japanese War. There was no need to tempt them with territorial promises, and if the western Allies were to accept their territorial demands in exchange for entry, it should be only with significant Soviet concessions on other matters. Furthermore, he felt the agreement was 'discreditable', as it had been negotiated entirely without consulting the Chinese, who would be directly impacted. When it came time to sign the document, Churchill and Eden broke into an argument in the presence of Roosevelt and Stalin. Their disagreement was so fierce that Alexander Cadogan, who had previously served as the British ambassador to China, was summoned to mediate. Cadogan agreed with Eden. But Churchill would not budge. Whether they liked it or not, failure to sign would dramatically weaken British authority in the Pacific. He signed. Eden, *The Memoirs of Anthony Eden*, 591, 594.

'*My dear Mr. Ambassador*': FDR to WAH, February 11, 1945, LOC AHP B 177 F 01.

262 *The full complement:* 'Joseph Stalin and Winston Churchill arrive for the Yalta Conference in Crimea, Soviet Union during World War II', February 1945, https://www.criticalpast.com/video/65675065771_Joseph-Stalin_Winston-Churchill_Yalta-Conference_Sarah-Churchill.

On the trip back: SMHC to CSC, February 12, 1945, CAC SCHL 1/1/8.

'*Why do we stay*': Ibid.

263 '*Where's Tommy?*': Moran, *Churchill at War*, 282.

'*trunks and large*': SMHC to CSC, February 12, 1945, CAC SCHL 1/1/8.

'*Naturally,*' *Sarah told:* Ibid.

'*They can't do this*': Ibid.

'genial and sprightly': Ibid.

264 *'a cavalcade of cars'*: Ibid.

the prime minister's extra: Astley, *The Inner Circle*, 198.

The car carrying: Diary of Admiral William D. Leahy, February 11, 1945, LOC William D. Leahy Papers, Box 6.

'Stalin, like some genie': SMHC to CSC, February 12, 1945, CAC SCHL 1/1/8.

'Mr. Secretary': Stettinius, *Roosevelt and the Russians*, 284.

the lemon trees: Plokhy, *Yalta*, 322.

265 *'grey and indestructible'*: SMHC to CSC, February 12, 1945, CAC SCHL 1/1/8.

'I'm so relieved': Moran, *Churchill at War*, 282–83.

'so straight, it seemed': SMHC to CSC, February 12, 1945, CAC SCHL 1/1/8.

Though it was dark: Ibid.

266 *On board, Roosevelt*: Logs of the Trips, 36, FDRL Grace Tully Papers, Box 7.

some of his party: AER Yalta Notes, loose notes, February 11, 1945, FDRL ARHP, Box 84.

The programme featured: Programme, February 11, 1945, FDRL ARHP, Box 84, Miscellaneous.

short of 'astonishing': SMHC to CSC, February 12, 1945, CAC SCHL 1/1/8.

Winston had lingered: In his account of looking out at the lights of Sevastopol from the deck of the *Franconia*, Churchill says that Alan Brooke and the chiefs of staff were there too. This reminiscence is incorrect; Brooke and the chiefs of staff had left on the tenth and landed in England on the eleventh. Winston S. Churchill, *The Second World War, Vol. VI*, 394.

'a revelation': SMHC to CSC, February 12, 1945, CAC SCHL 1/1/8.

267 *'Strangely enough'*: Sarah Churchill, *A Thread in the Tapestry*, 83.

268 *'It's no use saying'*: SMHC to CSC, February 12, 1945, CAC SCHL 1/1/8.

Chapter Eighteen: April 12–July 27, 1945

271 *'You really have been'*: JB to AER, February 15, 1945, FDRL JBP, Box 6.

save for the grumblings: AER to JB, February 18, 1945, FDRL JBP, Box 6.

'You may be assured': FDR to Tomasz Arciszewski, February 15, 1945, in note attached to FRUS, Conferences at Malta and Yalta, John Gilbert Winant to Edward Stettinius, February 3, 1945, Document 471.

272 *'Arabs would choose'*: Lelyveld, *His Final Battle*, 291–92.

Sarah was undoubtedly: AER Yalta Notes, loose notes, FDRL ARHP, Box 84. Not realising she would see him in Alexandria, Sarah had written a rather cryptic letter to Gil Winant the day before, perhaps concerned that someone else might open it: 'I have had occasion to think of you often. It has been a wonderful trip and everyone seems pleased with the results . . . You have been greatly missed – but I have unerring faith that things happen for the best!' SMHC to John Gilbert Winant, February 13, 1945, FDRL John G. Winant Papers, Box 190, Folder 13.

273 *Roosevelt accused*: Sherwood, *Roosevelt and Hopkins*, 874.

'Truly, Anna': Bishop, *FDR's Last Year*, 450–53.

'I'm pretty well convinced': AER to JB, February 18, 1945, FDRL JBP, Box 6.

'Good-bye': Bishop, *FDR's Last Year*, 453.

274 *He had not seen*: Rosenman, *Working with Roosevelt*, 522–23.

Anna worked with Rosenman: Draft of address to Congress, FDRL ARHP, Box 84, FDR Speech. Her pencil notations are visible on the drafts she saved.

'I hope that you': FDR address to Congress, March 1, 1945, Presidential Speeches, Miller Center, University of Virginia, https://millercenter.org/the-presidency/presidential-speeches/march-1-1945-address-congress-yalta.

In the three decades: Frances Perkins, *The Roosevelt I Knew* (New York: Viking, 1946), 395; Goodwin, *No Ordinary Time*, 586.

'justify and surpass': Logs of the President's Trips: Crimea Conference and Great Bitter Lake, Egypt, January 22–February 28, 1945, 39, FDRL Grace Tully Papers, Box 7.

275   *'political fairy tale':* Whittaker Chambers, 'The Ghosts on the Roof', *Time*, March 5, 1945.

'We are not in': WSC to Peter Fraser, February 24, 1945, TNA FO 371/47850.

276   *'have as little publicity':* JB to AER, February 15, 1945, FDRL JBP. John also mentions the *Life* request in his February 11 letter to Anna.

'For purposes of': Chamberlain, 'F.D.R's Daughter', 96–108. Anna would later say that she felt this article offered the best description of her duties in her father's White House. Anna Roosevelt Halsted interview by Bernard Asbell, 1972, FDRL ARHP, Box 63. Alongside the negative press, Anna found that her increasing fame had also earned her a few fans. A letter arrived for the president from a young woman in Chicago named Anna Conroy. The woman wrote, 'Dear Mr. President . . . I read an article in the newspaper about your daughter Anna. I never liked my name until then . . . But since reading that your dear lovely daughter's name is Anna also, I would not want to ever change my name. I am proud that my Mummy christened me Anna. May our patron St. Anna keep watch over you.' Anna Conroy to FDR, January 29, 1945, FDRL President's Personal File 7, Anna R. Boettiger 1942–1945.

her son Johnny: Looking back, Anna's son believes his illness was exacerbated by the fear that his mother had abandoned him. Author's interview with John Roosevelt Boettiger, February 20, 2018.

Every night FDR: Interview with Anna Roosevelt Halsted, 'The Roosevelt Story', February 13, 1962, FDRL Graff Papers, Box 3.

'Hello, girl': Lucy Mercer Rutherfurd to AER, May 9, 1945, in Boettiger, *A Love in Shadow*, 262.

277   *'thoroughly enjoy it!':* Interview with Anna Roosevelt Halsted, 'The Roosevelt Story', February 13, 1962, FDRL Graff Papers, Box 3.

She had summoned: Goodwin, *No Ordinary Time*, 598.

'Mrs. Boettiger': Anna Roosevelt Halsted interview by Bernard Asbell, 1972, FDRL ARHP, Box 63.

As she rode: Lelyveld, *His Final Battle*, 324, originally from AER interview with Joe Lash.

Eleanor was wearing: Goodwin, *No Ordinary Time*, 604.

entertaining Clementine Churchill: KLH to MHF, April 9, 1945, Mortimer Papers.

Josip Broz Tito: Ibid., KLH to MHF, April 12, 1945, Mortimer Papers.

The Harrimans were now: KLH to PC, April 12, 1945, LOC PHP B I-21; John Melby interview, June 16, 1989, LOC; Harriman and Abel, *Special Envoy*, 440.

278   *'The honeymoon':* KLH to PC, March 26, 1945, LOC PHP B I-21.

'gallant' Soviet allies: Harriman and Abel, *Special Envoy*, 419.

'Lord knows I fell': KLH to PC, March 26, 1945, LOC PHP B I-21.

boiler exploded: KLH, 'Do the crows still roost in the Spasopeckovskaya trees?' Mortimer Papers.

on February 17: Stephen Dando-Collins, *The Big Break: The Greatest American WWII POW Escape Story Never Told* (New York: St. Martin's Press, 2017), 140.

Two days later: 'Memorandum to: Miss Harriman', February 19, 1945, LOC AHP B 177 F 03.

'the rate of several': KLH to Elsie Marshall, February 27, 1945, Mortimer Papers. By February 27, they had all been sent home. Few American POWs appeared in Moscow after this, as the NKVD began to corral them and send them to repatriation points. Dando-Collins, *The Big Break*, 142.

279   *of wandering through:* Harriman and Abel, *Special Envoy*, 421–22.

'The Government': FRUS Vol. V: Diplomatic Papers, 1945, Europe, WAH to Edward Stettinius, March 7, 1945, 145.

By the end of March: In May, Stalin finally acknowledged the missing Poles, saying they had not been invited to Moscow. Rather they were 'diversionists' who had come to sow trouble and had been arrested for their subversive, espionage, or terrorist-related activity. They were brought to trial in June. Thirteen were sentenced to prison for periods ranging from four months to ten years. Three were acquitted. Winston S. Churchill, *The Second World War, Vol. VI*, 498; Eden, *The Memoirs of Anthony Eden*, 608.

the Soviet employees: KLH, 'Do the crows still roost in the Spasopeckovskaya trees?' Mortimer Papers.

'We are in [the] presence': FRUS Vol. V: Diplomatic Papers, 1945, Europe, WSC to FDR, March 13, 1945, 159–60.

280   *'So far there has been':* FRUS Vol. V: Diplomatic Papers, 1945, Europe, FDR to Joseph Stalin, April 1, 1945, 194.

'Unless we do take': Harriman and Abel, *Special Envoy*, 423.

281   *'There must not, in any':* FRUS Vol. III: Diplomatic Papers, 1945, European Advisory Commission, Austria, Germany, FDR to Joseph Stalin, April 12, 1945, 756.

'I confess': FRUS Vol. III: Diplomatic Papers, 1945, European Advisory Commission, Austria, Germany, WAH to FDR, April 12, 1945, 756.

'I do not wish to': FRUS Vol. III: Diplomatic Papers, 1945, European Advisory Commission, Austria, Germany, FDR to WAH, April 12, 1945, 757.

Rather, the operator: KLH to PC, April 12, 1945, LOC PHP B I-21.

282   *'Jesus,' she thought:* Ibid.

She knew that Averell: Ibid.

'that name no longer': Ibid.

'Somehow I never': Ibid.

283   *Stalin made it known:* Bruenn, 'Clinical Notes', 591; Goodwin, *No Ordinary Time*, 605.

'as stern as': Notes attached to AER to Joseph Lash, January 28, 1972, LOC ARHP, Box 36.

Anna had been issued: FDR Funeral Card, FDRL ARHP, Box 65a, Folder 3, Funeral 1945.

James was racing: James Roosevelt, *My Parents: A Differing View* (Chicago: Playboy Press, 1976), 280, 286–88. James would arrive an hour and a half too late for the funeral. Woolner, *The Last 100 Days*, 285.

284   *Its armoured doors:* Edward G. Lengel, 'Franklin D. Roosevelt's Train Ferdinand Magellan', The White House Historical Association, https://www.whitehousehistory.org/franklin-d-roosevelt-rsquo-s-train-ferdinand-magellan.

But when Anna looked: Boettiger, *A Love in Shadow*, 261.

'an important friendship': Asbell, ed., *Mother and Daughter*, 187–88.

'Anna dear': Lucy Mercer Rutherfurd to AER, May 9, 1945. The full text of the letter is quoted in Boettiger, *A Love in Shadow*, 262–63.

286   *The afternoon following:* Harriman and Abel, *Special Envoy*, 441.

Red flags with black: KLH to PC, April 12, 1945, LOC PHP B I-21.

Jimmy Byrnes: Harriman and Abel, *Special Envoy*, 508–10.

'When I return': KLH to MHF, August 14, 1945, Mortimer Papers.

287   *Stalin had sent:* KLH to MHF, June 4, 1945, Mortimer Papers. Kathy told Mary that after a dinner with Stalin in Moscow, Averell had been admiring an English-bred horse that General Antonov could be seen riding in newsreel footage of a parade. It was this horse that Stalin gifted to Averell. How the horses acquired their names Kathy does not say. See also 'Stalin's Gift Horses to Harrimans Arrive', *New York Sun*, April 30, 1945, KLH scrapbook, Mortimer Papers.

'For me Stalin': Harriman and Abel, *Special Envoy*, 536.

home to Arden House: Author's interview with Kitty Ames, October 21, 2019.

288   *He sat slumped:* Elizabeth Nel, *Mr. Churchill's Secretary* (New York: Coward-McCann, 1958), 170.

He wanted to travel: Dilks, ed., *The Diaries of Sir Alexander Cadogan*, 727.

Like her father: Bob Landry, photograph, 'The King and Queen, and Princess Elizabeth, leaving St. Paul's', April 17, 1945, *Life*, Getty Images, https://www.gettyimages .ca/detail/news-photo/the-king-and-queen-and-princess-elizabeth-leaving-st-pauls -news-photo/50496864?adppopup=true.

'a bitter loss': Robert Rhodes James, ed., *Churchill Speaks, 1897–1963: Collected Speeches in Peace and War* (New York: Barnes and Noble Books, 1980), 857–59.

When the memorial: James, ed., *Chips: The Diaries of Sir Henry Channon*, 402; photograph, 'British Prime Minister, Winston Churchill with his daughter Sarah, leaving the memorial service at St Paul's Cathedral for the American President Franklin D Roosevelt', April 17, 1945, Alamy, https://www.alamy.com/stock-photo-british-prime -minister-winston-churchill-with-his-daughter-sarah-leaving-176257351.html.

289   *Sarah sensed these:* SMHC to WSC, c. July 1945, undated, CAC SCHL 1/8/1.

290   *'fall back on':* Rhodes James, ed., *Churchill Speaks*, 864.

When the speech: SMHC to WSC, June 5, 1945, CAC MCHL 5/1/120.

'You asked me if': Ibid.

291   *'Your Father showed':* CSC to SMHC, June 12, 1945, CAC MCHL 5/1/120.

'angry and bewildered': SMHC to WSC, July 27, 1945, CAC SCHL 1/1/8.

292   *'I hope the meeting':* SMHC to WSC, c. July 1945, undated, CAC SCHL 1/8/1.

amusingly 'trivial': Sarah Churchill, *A Thread in the Tapestry*, 85.

instead of war maps: Ibid., 86.

293   *a Labour 'tidal wave':* Ibid.

As Winston tried: Ibid.

'Winston, this may be': Ibid.

'Chartwell Colony': SMHC to WSC, July 27, 1945, CAC SCHL 1/1/8.

Sarah and Mary: Pawle, *The War and Colonel Warden*, 409.

As ever, Clementine: Mary Soames, *A Daughter's Tale: The Memoir of Winston Churchill's Youngest Child* (New York: Random House, 2011), 327.

294   *'The real happiness':* SMHC to CSC, April 7, 1945, CAC SCHL 1/1/8.

'My darling darling': SMHC to WSC, July 27, 1945, CAC SCHL 1/1/8.

295   *'God bless you':* Ibid.

After Yalta

297   *'The Yalta Agreement':* Chet Huntley, ABC News transcript, June 28, 1951, FDRL ARHP, Box 85, Yalta 1951.

    'was not an isolated': Ibid.

298   *'mistakenly believed':* Harriman and Abel, *Special Envoy*, 414.

299   *'From Stettin':* Winston S. Churchill, 'The Sinews of Peace', March 5, 1946, Westminster College, Fulton, MO.

300   *The United Nations:* See https://www.un.org/press/en/2019/ga12223.doc.htm; https://www.un.org/press/en/2018/ga12108.doc.htm.

301   *first female ambassador:* In 1962, Dame Barbara Salt was appointed British ambassador to Israel, but due to serious illness, she was unable to serve in the post.

    'in silent step': Sarah Churchill, *A Thread in the Tapestry* (New York: Dodd, 1967), 33.

    'the finest': WAH to KLH, February 16, 1936, Mortimer Papers.

    'Out of a life': SMHC to CSC, September 15, 1945, CAC SCHL 1/1/9.

302   *'involves too damned':* KLH to MHF, February 16, 1944, Mortimer Papers.

    Newsweek *salary:* Smith, *Reflected Glory*, 131.

    One night while Pamela: Ibid., 130.

    and Amanda: Amanda Burden recalled the first time she met Kathy. Amanda was three years old and was so nervous, she hid under the bed for hours and refused to come out. Kathy sat beside the bed the whole time, waiting and reassuring her with the greatest patience until Amanda was ready. Author's interview with Amanda Burden, December 30, 2019.

    A year and a half: 'List of people to whom wedding announcements were sent', LOC AHP B 11 F 03. This list runs thirty-four pages in length, with a separate addendum for British friends.

303   *Avie maintained:* Averell Mortimer, remarks at KLH memorial service.

    As a philanthropist: Margalit Fox, 'Kathleen Mortimer, Rich and Adventurous, Dies at 93', *New York Times*, February 19, 2011.

304   *She simply never:* Author's interview with Kitty Ames, October 21, 2019.

    'Everyone has preconceived': KLH notes for Bennington College speech, Mortimer Papers. See also Gledhill Cameron, 'Hard Practicality Rule in Russian Education', *World-Telegram*, October 21, 1946, in LOC AHP B 11 F 03.

    Despite extreme pressure: Hearings before the Select Committee to Conduct an Investigation of the Facts, Evidence, and Circumstances of the Katyn Forest Massacre, Eighty-Second Congress, 1952, copy in Mortimer Papers. The only other time Kathy went on the record about Russia was in an article called 'Opera in Russia Today', *Opera News*, March 25, 1946, KLH scrapbook, Mortimer Papers.

    'Spokoynoy nochi': Author's interview with Averell Mortimer, October 24, 2019.

    trove of letters: Author's interview with David Mortimer, December 12, 2017.

305   *with Pamela's constant:* Author's interview with David Mortimer, December 5, 2018.

    'Wouldn't [you] like': Averell Mortimer, remarks at KLH memorial service; author's conversation with Averell Mortimer, October 24, 2019.

306   *After returning to Seattle:* Boettiger, *A Love in Shadow*, 267, 269–70.

307   *shortage of paper products:* The U.S. House of Representatives launched a Select Committee investigation into the shortage after complaints from publishers, February 26,

1947, https://www.archives.gov/legislative/guide/house/chapter-22-select-newsprint
.html.

plagued with self-doubt: Boettiger, *A Love in Shadow*, 267–68.

'crazy people': Author's interview with Eleanor Seagraves, January 26, 2018.

She told him to go: Boettiger, *A Love in Shadow*, 273–74.

'into my room': Author's interview with Eleanor Seagraves, September 30, 2018. In
1978, during an oral history interview with Dr Thomas Soapes at the FDR Library,
Ellie would allude to these traumatic experiences, saying John Boettiger 'used to
sneak down to my room and try to make passes and that sort of thing'. But she did
not directly address what he had done until this 2018 interview. Incidentally, Ellie
and John had the same birthday, March 25. This was evidently special for Ellie, as she
wrote lovingly to John about 'our birthday'. Eleanor Dall to John Boettiger, 'Tuesday',
undated, c. March 1945, FDRL ARHP, Box 71, Folder 6. This further complicated their
relationship.

308   *'trying to teach':* Author's interview with Eleanor Seagraves, September 30, 2018.

There was an intercom: Ibid.

'was afraid of John': Ibid.

309   *Though Ellie could have:* Author's interview with Eleanor Seagraves, September 30,
2018.

'funny little doll': Eleanor (Dall) Seagraves to AER and JB, March 1945, FDRL Halsted
Papers, Box 71, Folder 6.

To this day: Author's interview with Eleanor Seagraves, January 26, 2018.

Anna's brother Elliott: Asbell, ed., *Mother and Daughter*, 278.

310   *'inaccuracies, innuendoes':* AER to Robert Taft, January 29, 1951, FDRL ARHP, Box 85,
Yalta 1951.

Averell Harriman and Harry Hopkins: AER to Robert Taft, March 8, 1951, FDRL ARHP,
Box 85, Yalta 1951.

'scurrilous material': AER to James, Franklin Jr, and John Roosevelt, November 5, 1969,
FDRL Howard Bruenn Papers, Folder 6.

311   *'proper and important':* Ibid.

When her children: Author's interview with John Roosevelt Boettiger, February 20,
2018.

'For my father': Albin Krebs, 'Anna Roosevelt Halsted, President's Daughter, Dies', *New
York Times*, December 2, 1975, https://www.nytimes.com/1975/12/02/archives/anna
-roosevelt-halsted-presidents-daughter-dies-white-house.html?url=http%3A%2F
%2Ftimesmachine.nytimes.com%2Ftimesmachine%2F1975%2F12%2F02%2F78270832
.html%3FpageNumber%3D42.

'knew in some sense': Author's interview with John Roosevelt Boettiger, February 20,
2018.

312   *'burst into pent':* Sarah Churchill, *A Thread in the Tapestry*, 89.

'Sarah has been': WSC to CSC, September 18, 1945, in Soames, ed., *Winston and Clementine*, 539.

'I've had a happy': SMHC to CSC, September 3, 1945, CAC SCHL 1/1/9.

'It is part of': Sarah Churchill, *Keep on Dancing*, 142.

'Free!': Ibid., 158–59.

313   *'Between you and':* SMHC to Harry Hopkins, May 12, 1944, Georgetown University,
Booth Family Center for Special Collections, HLHP1, Box 4, Folder 4.

'Gil needs me terribly': SMHC to CSC, March 18, 1947, CAC MCHL 5/1/139.

'Listen to a very few': Reynolds, *In Command of History*, 84.

Two weeks earlier: Lynne Olson, *Citizens of London: The Americans Who Stood with Britain in Its Darkest, Finest Hour* (New York: Random House Trade Paperbacks, 2011), 384.

314   *As the Royal Air Force:* Programme of John Gilbert Winant memorial service, St Paul's Cathedral, London, November 19, 1947.

was her fault: Olson, *Citizens of London*, 385.

'Wow, Papa!': Author's interviews with Lady Williams of Elvel, July 24, 2017; April 12, 2019.

'Life can be <u>very</u>': AER to SMHC, January 14, 1958, CAC SCHL 1/8/2.

official war artist: Soames, *Clementine Churchill*, 457.

Stanley struggled: Author's interview with David Mortimer, December 5, 2018; author's interview with Amanda Burden, December 30, 2019; 'Harriman Son-in-Law Recovering After Shooting', *New York Times*, June 21, 1969.

315   *'I feel that I have':* Henry Audley to WSC, April 3, 1962, CAC SCHL 1/1/17. Henry's physical limitations caused by his stroke are evident in his letters to Winston and Clementine Churchill. They are all typewritten, save for his large, shaky signature.

316   *'fairy godmother':* Author's interview with Celia Sandys, July 20, 2017. Sarah's niece Emma Soames shared a similar memory of watching Sarah play Peter Pan. Author's interview with Emma Soames, April 6, 2018.

'talented and brilliant': Author's interview with Celia Sandys, July 20, 2017.

'While those of us': Deirdre Burns to Mary Churchill Soames, September 27, 1982, CAC MCHL 10/20.

'I don't mind going': John Pearson, *The Private Lives of Winston Churchill* (New York: Simon and Schuster, 1991), 422.

'I am sure she was': Author's interview with Celia Sandys, July 20, 2017.

317   *'a country house party':* Hiss, *Recollections of a Life*, 121.

'fill-in material': AER to JB, February 18, 1945, FDRL JBP, Box 6.

'Darling darling Papa': SMHC to WSC, March 28, 1944, CAC CHAR 1/381/59-91.

Selected Bibliography

Archival Collections

Franklin D. Roosevelt Presidential Library

John Boettiger Papers
Howard Bruenn Papers
Stephen T. Early Papers
Edward J. Flynn Papers
Robert D. Graff Papers
Anna Roosevelt Halsted Papers
Ross T. McIntire Papers
William Ridgon Papers
Anna Eleanor Roosevelt Papers
Franklin D. Roosevelt Papers, President's Personal File 7
Grace Tully Papers
John G. Winant Papers

Library of Congress

Charles E. Bohlen Papers
Pamela Digby Churchill Hayward Harriman Papers
W. Averell Harriman Papers
William D. Leahy Papers

Churchill Archive Centre

The Papers of Sarah Churchill
The Papers of Sir Winston Churchill, Chartwell Papers
The Papers of Sir Winston Churchill, Churchill Papers
The Papers of Lady Soames

Mortimer Papers

Kathleen Harriman Mortimer Papers

National Archives and Records Administration (US)

President's Secretary's File
General Records of the Department of State

National Archives at Kew (UK)

Air Ministry Papers
Foreign Office Papers
War Cabinet Papers

Georgetown University Archives

Harry Hopkins Papers
Robert Hopkins Papers

Liddell Hart Military Archives

ALANBROOKE, FM Alan Francis, 1st Viscount Alanbrooke of Brookeborough

Wellcome Library

Lord Moran (Charles McMoran Wilson) Papers (PP/CMW)

Newberry Library (Chicago)

Ralph L. Graham Papers

Clemson University Libraries' Special Collections and Archives

James Francis Byrnes Papers

Other Select Primary-Source Records

Imperial War Museum, Sound Archive
Columbia Center for Oral History Archives, Rare Book and Manuscript Library,
        Columbia University in the City of New York
Foreign Relations of the United States
Hansard, House of Commons Debate Minutes
George Marshall Papers

Tuxedo Park Historical Society, Tuxedo Park, NY
Foxcroft School, Middleburg, VA
Dorchester Hotel
Life magazine
Time magazine
Newsweek magazine
New York Times
The New Yorker
Washington Post

Author's Interviews and Conversations

Kitty Ames
John Roosevelt Boettiger
Amanda Burden
Jennie Churchill
Randolph Churchill
Peter Duchin
Clarissa Eden, Countess of Avon (née Clarissa Spencer-Churchill)
Maria Kosareva
Averell Mortimer
David Mortimer
Celia Sandys
Eleanor Dall Seagraves
Emma Soames
William vanden Heuvel
Lady Williams of Elvel (née Jane Portal)

Oral Histories

Sergo Beria (IWM), 19 October 1996
Howard Bruenn, U.S. Navy Medical Department Oral History Program, 31 January 1990
Myra Collyer (IWM), 24 October 2002
Anna Roosevelt Halsted interview, 11 May 1973, Columbia Center for Oral History
Anna Roosevelt Halsted interview, 1972, Halsted Papers, FDRL
W. Averell Harriman interview, 8 December 1960, Columbia Center for Oral History
W. Averell Harriman interview, May–July 1969, Columbia Center for Oral History
W. Averell Harriman (IWM), 1972
Averell Harriman interview by Arthur Schlesinger Jr, 24 May 1981
Kathleen Harriman Mortimer (IWM), 10 September 1996
Felicity Hill (IWM), 6 December 1985
Alger Hiss (IWM), 1972

John Melby interview, 16 June 1989, Association for Diplomatic Studies and Training Foreign Affairs Oral History Project, Library of Congress

Frances Perkins interview, 1951–1955, Columbia University Center for Oral History

Hazel Scott (IWM), 17 August 2001

Eleanor Seagraves interview, 2 February 1978 and 21 June 1978, FDRL

Published Primary Sources and Memoirs

Alliluyeva, Svetlana. *Twenty Letters to a Friend.* New York: Harper and Row, 1967.

Asbell, Bernard, ed. *Mother and Daughter: The Letters of Eleanor and Anna Roosevelt.* New York: Coward, McCann and Geoghegan, 1982.

Astley, Joan Bright. *The Inner Circle: A View of War at the Top.* Boston: Atlantic Monthly Press, 1971.

Berezhkov, Valentin M. *At Stalin's Side: His Interpreter's Memoirs from the October Revolution to the Fall of the Dictator's Empire.* New York: Birch Lane Press, 1994.

Beria, Sergo. *Beria, My Father: Inside Stalin's Kremlin.* London: Duckworth, 2001.

Birse, A. H. *Memoirs of an Interpreter.* New York: Coward-McCann, 1967.

Bohlen, Charles E. *Witness to History 1929–1969.* New York: W. W. Norton, 1973.

Bruenn, Howard G. 'Clinical Notes on the Illness and Death of President Franklin D. Roosevelt', *Annals of Internal Medicine*, Vol. 72, No. 4 (April 1970).

Byrnes, James. *All in One Lifetime.* New York: Harper and Brothers, 1958.

———. *Speaking Frankly.* New York: Harper and Brothers, 1947.

Campbell, Thomas M., and George C. Herring, eds. *The Diaries of Edward R. Stettinius, Jr., 1943–1946.* New York: New Viewpoints, 1975.

Chamberlain, John. 'F.D.R's Daughter', *Life*, March 5, 1945.

Churchill, Sarah. *Keep on Dancing.* New York: Coward, McCann and Geoghegan, 1981.

———. *A Thread in the Tapestry.* New York: Dodd, Mead, 1967.

Churchill, Winston S. *Great Battles and Leaders of the Second World War: An Illustrated History.* Boston: Houghton Mifflin, 1995.

———. *My Early Life, 1874–1904.* New York: Simon and Schuster, 1996.

———. *The Second World War, Volumes 1–6.* Boston: Houghton Mifflin, 1948–1953.

Churchill, Winston S. (II), *Memories and Adventures.* New York: Weidenfeld and Nicholson, 1989.

Colville, John. *The Fringes of Power: 10 Downing Street Diaries, 1939–1955.* New York: W. W. Norton, 1985.

———. *Winston Churchill and His Inner Circle.* New York: Wyndham Books, 1981.

Custine, Astolphe, Marquis de. *Empire of the Czar: A Journey Through Eternal Russia.* New York: Doubleday, 1989.

Davies, Joseph E. *Mission to Moscow.* New York: Simon and Schuster, 1941.

Deane, John R. *The Strange Alliance: The Story of our Efforts at Wartime Co-Operation with Russia.* New York: Viking, 1947.

Dilks, David, ed. *The Diaries of Sir Alexander Cadogan, O.M., 1938–1945.* New York: G. P. Putnam's Sons, 1972.

Eden, Anthony. *The Memoirs of Anthony Eden, Earl of Avon: The Reckoning.* Boston: Houghton Mifflin, 1965.

Gorodetsky, Gabriel, ed. *The Maisky Diaries: Red Ambassador to the Court of St. James's, 1932–1943.* New Haven, CT: Yale University Press, 2015.

Gromyko, Andrei Andreevich. *Memoirs.* New York: Doubleday, 1989.

Harriman, W. Averell, and Elie Abel. *Special Envoy to Churchill and Stalin, 1941–1946.* New York: Random House, 1975.

Hiss, Alger. *Recollections of a Life.* New York: Seaver Books, 1988.

Hopkins, Robert. *Witness to History: Recollections of a WWII Photographer.* Seattle: Castle Pacific Publishing, 2002.

Houghton, Norris. 'That Was Yalta: Worm's Eye View,' *The New Yorker*, May 23, 1953.

Kennan, George. *Memoirs, 1925–1950.* Boston: Little, Brown, 1967.

Khrushchev, Nikita. *Memoirs of Nikita Khrushchev, Vol. 1: Commissar, 1918–1945.* University Park, PA: Pennsylvania State University Press, 2004.

Kimball, Warren F., ed. *Churchill and Roosevelt: The Complete Correspondence, Vol. III.* Princeton, NJ: Princeton University Press, 1984.

Kuter, Laurence S. *Airman at Yalta.* New York: Duell, Sloan and Pearce, 1955.

Leahy, William D. *I Was There.* New York: Whittlesey House, 1950.

Lockhart, Robert Bruce. *The Diaries of Sir Robert Bruce Lockhart, Vol. 2: 1938–65.* London: Macmillan, 1980.

McIntire, Ross T. *White House Physician.* New York: G. P. Putnam's Sons, 1946.

Moran, Lord Charles. *Churchill at War, 1940–45.* New York: Carroll and Graf, 2002.

Nel, Elizabeth. *Mr. Churchill's Secretary.* New York: Coward-McCann, 1958.

Oliver, Vic. *Mr. Showbusiness.* London: George G. Harrap, 1954.

Pawle, Gerald. *The War and Colonel Warden.* New York: Alfred A. Knopf, 1963.

Payne, Graham, and Sheridan Morley, ed. *The Noël Coward Diaries.* Boston: Da Capo Press, 2000.

Perkins, Frances. *The Roosevelt I Knew.* New York: Viking, 1946.

Ranfurly, Hermione. *To War with Whitaker: The Wartime Diaries of the Countess of Ranfurly, 1939–1945.* London: Heinemann, 1994.

Reilly, Michael. *Reilly of the White House.* New York: Simon and Schuster, 1947.

Reynolds, David, and Vladimir Pchatnov, eds. *The Kremlin Letters: Stalin's Wartime Correspondence with Churchill and Roosevelt.* New Haven, CT: Yale University Press, 2018.

Rhodes James, Robert, ed. *Chips: The Diaries of Sir Henry Channon.* London: Weidenfeld and Nicolson, 1967.

———. *Churchill Speaks, 1897–1963: Collected Speeches in Peace and War.* New York: Barnes and Noble Books, 1980.

Roosevelt, Curtis. *Too Close to the Sun: Growing Up in the Shadow of My Grandparents, Franklin and Eleanor.* New York: PublicAffairs, 2008.

Roosevelt, Eleanor. *This I Remember.* New York: Harper and Brothers, 1949.

Roosevelt, Elliott, ed. *F.D.R.: His Personal Letters, 1928–1945.* New York: Duell, Sloan and Pearce, 1950.

Roosevelt, James. *My Parents: A Differing View.* Chicago: Playboy Press, 1976.

Rosenman, Samuel I. *Working with Roosevelt.* New York: Harper and Brothers, 1952.

Shevchenko, Arkady N. *Breaking with Moscow.* New York: Alfred A. Knopf, 1985.

Smith, A. Merriman. *Thank You, Mr. President: A White House Notebook.* New York: Harper and Brothers, 1946.

Soames, Mary. *A Daughter's Tale: The Memoir of Winston Churchill's Youngest Child.* New York: Random House, 2011.

Soames, Mary, ed. *Winston and Clementine: The Personal Letters of the Churchills.* Boston: Houghton Mifflin, 1999.

Standley, William H., and Arthur A. Ageton. *Admiral Ambassador to Russia.* Chicago: Henry Regnery, 1955.

Stettinius, Edward R. *Roosevelt and the Russians: The Yalta Conference.* New York: Doubleday, 1949.

Sudoplatov, Pavel, and Anatoli Sudoplatov. *Special Tasks.* Boston: Back Bay Books, 1995.

Tully, Grace. *F.D.R., My Boss.* New York: Charles Scribner's Sons, 1949.

Wallace, Henry A. *The Price of Vision: The Diary of Henry A. Wallace, 1942–1946.* Boston: Houghton Mifflin, 1973.

Ward, Geoffrey, ed. *Closest Companion: The Unknown Story of the Intimate Friendship Between Franklin Roosevelt and Margaret Suckley.* Boston: Houghton Mifflin, 1995.

Winant, John Gilbert. *Letter from Grosvenor Square: An Account of a Stewardship.* Boston: Houghton Mifflin, 1947.

Index